I.H.C.C. LIBRARY

American Taboo

The Forbidden Words, Unspoken Rules, and
Secret Morality of Popular Culture

LAUREN ROSEWARNE

PRAEGER

AN IMPRINT OF ABC-CLIO, LLC
Santa Barbara, California • Denver, Colorado • Oxford, England

Copyright 2013 by Lauren Rosewarne

All rights reserved. No part of this publication may be reproduced, stored in a retrieval system, or transmitted, in any form or by any means, electronic, mechanical, photocopying, recording, or otherwise, except for the inclusion of brief quotations in a review, without prior permission in writing from the publisher.

Library of Congress Cataloging-in-Publication Data

Rosewarne, Lauren.
  American taboo : the forbidden words, unspoken rules, and secret morality of popular culture / Lauren Rosewarne.
      pages cm
  Includes bibliographical references and index.
    ISBN 978–0–313–39933–6 (cloth : alk. paper) — ISBN 978–0–313–39934–3 (ebook) 1. Sex in popular culture—United States. 2. Sex—Social aspects—United States. 3. Popular culture—Moral and ethical aspects—United States. I. Title.
  HQ16.R667   2013
  306.70973—dc23   2013011452

ISBN: 978–0–313–39933–6
EISBN: 978–0–313–39934–3

17 16 15 14 13   1 2 3 4 5

This book is also available on the World Wide Web as an eBook.
Visit www.abc-clio.com for details.

Praeger
An Imprint of ABC-CLIO, LLC

ABC-CLIO, LLC
130 Cremona Drive, P.O. Box 1911
Santa Barbara, California 93116-1911

This book is printed on acid-free paper ∞

Manufactured in the United States of America

Contents

Acknowledgments   v

Introduction: The Where and Why of Pop Culture's Hottest Buttons   vii

The Gay Chapter: Sketching the Animated Homosexual   1

The Oral Sex Chapter: Cunnilingus and the Politics of the Lick   17

The Flatulence Chapter: Exploring Matters of the Fart   35

The Rude Gestures Chapter: Flicking the Channel and Flipping the Bird   51

The Euphemisms Chapter: Sex and Bodily Euphemisms on Screen and in Song   67

The Vegetarian Chapter: Introducing the Hippies, Sad Sacks, and Fundamentalists   87

The Alcohol Chapter: The Drunk in Film and Television   115

The Drugs Chapter: Advertising Mother's Little Helper   131

The Abortion Chapter: Back Alleys and Back Stories on Screen   153

The Penis Chapter: Undressing Male Nudity   175

The Circumcision Chapter: Capturing Cuts in Popular Culture   195

The Vibrator Chapter: That Buzzing Sound in Film and Television   217

Conclusion: The Rarely Simple Taboo Presentation	237
Media References	239
Notes	259
Bibliography	291
Index	309

Acknowledgments

With thanks to Daniel Harmon and James Sherman at ABC-CLIO. Thanks to my dear friends Bec Jackson and Melissa Donchi for many good conversations on the topics inside... And Simon...

Introduction: The Where and Why of Pop Culture's Hottest Buttons

Sex, politics, and religion. Three topics routinely considered off-limits in polite company—in mixed company; in *refined* company. Three subjects deemed personal, inflammatory, and best avoided out of respect, consideration, and diplomacy.

Historically, when popular culture dared present sex, politics, or religion explicitly—or even just *frankly*—it was met with the wrath of censors, if not also rejection by audiences and advertisers. It is sex, politics, and religion that remain the perpetual hot button—the proverbial *lightning rod*—topics that even today in a post-Hays Code, tech-savvy, cable television mediascape consistently attract controversy and condemnation, bans and boycotts.

As a political scientist, as a feminist, *without* discussing sex or politics I'd have very little to publish and certainly much less to talk about. Equally, while religion is generally not at the forefront of my work, there are some topics inextricably bound to all three lightning rods: abortion, homosexuality, masturbation, and circumcision are four discussed in this volume.

While sex, politics, and religion might be conversation topics that make first dates awkward, dinner parties uncomfortable, and classroom, staffroom, and locker-room discussions *fiery*, the very fact that they summon such strong—such *visceral*—reactions highlights that these are also the very topics that we have the most passion for and certainly harbor the most curiosity about.

In this book, I've chosen to focus on some of my favorite taboos. From vibrators to cunnilingus, homosexuality to prescription drugs, naughty hand gestures to farting, these topics are all gloriously—and variously—divisive.

Time and time again, these topics have been shown to titillate, offend, arouse, and create angst—if not outrage. Likewise, each has a history of controversy and scandal, be it related to censorship, restricted classification, protest, or just accusations of poor taste.

While I've titled this book *American Taboo*, the taboo topics analyzed in this volume aren't actually taboo *enough* to remain completely unspoken. In fact, while these topics consistently attract controversy, such depictions—be they flagrant displays or subtle allusions—are readily detected. Culturally, we might not *like* talking about vibrator use, but as explored in my Vibrator Chapter, screen scenes involving them are easily detected. Similarly, full frontal male nudity might be much less common than strategically concealed genitals, and yet my Penis Chapter includes more than 50 examples of penis displays from mainstream film and television. This trend occurs in every chapter whereby in real life discomfort haunts the discussion of a taboo, yet each has a distinct place in popular culture.

That presentations of taboos are easily detected highlights an interesting paradox. Evidently there are many subjects that remain difficult to talk about—if not thoroughly polarizing—in real life, yet each has a noticeable presence in popular culture. What does this strange situation reveal? Why are we so drawn to consuming *portrayals* of these controversial topics? Why do these subjects so heatedly divide in real life and yet are so fervently consumed through entertainment media?

As discussed in this Introduction and expanded upon throughout this volume, the manner in which controversial subjects are portrayed is not homogenous, nor is it easily understood. Off screen, anxieties are intimately entangled with these taboo topics and as many representations testify, anxieties often influence depictions. This, however, is not always the case: screen presentations are every bit as diverse as our opinions. While real-life portrayals often reflect cultural anxieties, they also function in a variety of other ways. Popular culture provides an opportunity for taboos to be tested and *challenged*, and for boundaries to be crossed and fears assuaged. While my Abortion Chapter, for example, explores narratives such as *If These Walls Could Talk* (1996) and *Revolutionary Road* (2008)—where women were, ostensibly, *executed* following their abortions—in other films, such as *Fast Times at Ridgemont High* (1982) and *Coach Carter* (2005), women—daringly—aborted their pregnancies without any obvious punishment or guilt. Such diverse presentations are analyzed to explore what they reveal about society as well as the sexual and cultural politics inherent.

Worth noting, popular culture also provides audiences with a unique opportunity to simply *experience* taboos: to be involved with them vicariously, to hear about them, to be aroused by them, and to have our curiosity about them quenched.

American Taboo focuses on taboos primarily associated with the body: how we use our bodies (see the Farting Chapter and the Rude Gestures Chapter), expose our bodies (see the Penis Chapter), what we put into them (see the Drugs Chapter, the Vegetarian Chapter, and the Alcohol Chapter), do to them (see the Abortion Chapter and the Circumcision Chapter), and how we give and draw pleasure from them (see the Vibrator Chapter, the Oral Sex Chapter, and the Gay Chapter). Each of these chapters explores those many occasions when popular culture dares to tempt the wrath of audiences, advertisers, and censors by grappling with society's most challenging topics.

The hundreds of popular culture examples discussed in this volume are analyzed to explore the *how* and *why* of their depiction as well as the *what* that they reveal about society, about media production, and notably about our continually complicated relationship with our bodies. This volume draws on a very wide range of disciplines to do this, including cultural studies and queer theory, psychology, political science, feminist theory, and sociology. Identifiable in each chapter are some important findings. Rarely, for example, are taboo topics presented as *uncontroversial*. When abortion is portrayed on screen, rarely is it presented as ordinary or commonplace: it is nearly always treated as the serious and divisive topic it is *off-screen*.

Gender is a topic particularly relevant to all the topics explored. Sexual double standards, for example, abound. In the Oral Sex Chapter, the difference in the way cunnilingus is presented compared to fellatio is spotlighted: scenes are noticeably shorter and rarely is cunnilingus performed to orgasm. In the Penis Chapter, the issue of the double standard related to nudity is examined: full frontal male nudity is substantially less common than full frontal female nudity. This issue highlights that audiences are very willing to accept—and *expect*—that the female body is presented as an object of desirability, but are much more reluctant to think about the male body similarly. As discussed in the Vibrator Chapter, not only are women more likely to be presented naked than men, but depictions of them engaged in behavior such as masturbation are common and routinely framed as voyeuristic rather than as centered on women's own pleasure. Such issues highlight the well-established burden women have of constantly appearing attractive on screen—a burden disproportionately inflicted on them. This same issue is also addressed extensively in the Farting Chapter: while a man who farts might be considered uncouth, for a female to do so summons the far more damaging indictment of her being deemed *unattractive*. The all-importance of female beauty—and the devastation of its loss—is also addressed in the Alcohol Chapter, where the faded beauty archetype is examined.

Euphemisms—gifted a chapter of their own—are a very common way that popular culture presents taboo. Euphemisms, along with circumlocutions, innuendo, and allusions, allow taboo topics to enter narratives by being coded, concealed, and thus visible only to a knowing audience and, in turn, being less likely to outrage. The Rude Gestures Chapter, for example, provides a discussion of this same idea as related to the image of a person using a middle finger to scratch their nose: this serves as a perfectly innocuous gesture to one person and functions as an obfuscated bird-flip to another.

Comedy frequently acts as the proverbial *spoonful of sugar*, enabling a controversial topic to slide into popular culture under the guise of humor or satire. While comedy can serve as a kind of lubricant, it would be erroneous to assume this always aids in lifting the taboo. On many occasions the controversy—be it vibrator use or alcoholism or vegetarianism—actually gets *mocked* in comedy. While comedy can be a way to facilitate a discussion of difficult topics, it can also actually reinforce prejudices and stereotypes. This issue highlights a very important topic in communications research as related to the role of the media in helping lift taboos or, alternatively, reinforce them.

On the one hand, in this post-Hays Code period, popular culture appears to have had a substantial role in changing attitudes as related to topics once considered as unmentionable: while stigmas and controversy obviously still exist, popular culture has increased the visibility of these issues, encouraging discussion and debate. The role of cable television, for example, has been instrumental in creating both an appetite as well as a market for cutting-edge material. More representations of topics that were previously closeted or marginalized create increased exposure. In turn, our familiarity is improved, which can lead to normalization if not increased tolerance and a heightened appetite for things once demonized and marginalized.

While increased visibility *can* increase acceptance, such a situation is not guaranteed. Representations of taboos can also *inflame* audiences and remind them why they should feel revolted or outraged. Similarly, some of the ways that these taboos continue to be portrayed highlight that even with greater visibility, the manner in which subjects are presented can, in fact, *inhibit* dialogue. Noted earlier, was the fact that taboos are frequently presented using euphemism, circumlocution, and innuendo. The fact that on many occasions taboos are presented in tentative and coded ways works to perpetuate the idea that such topics still shouldn't be spoken about openly or frankly—that there is something *wrong* with homosexuality, with masturbation—thereby potentially reinforcing marginalization. When comedy is the vehicle by which these issues often enter narratives—when, for example, gay characters and vibrator users are presented as worth laughing *at*—instead of dismantling taboos, these representations can be construed as upholding them and reinforcing an audience's worst preconceptions. The Euphemisms Chapter spotlights the many examples—and notably the many downsides—of avoiding explicit descriptions: meanings get muddled and impact gets modulated. Demonization can also occur when depictions are cast in ways that function to perpetuate the negative connotations of certain topics, working to not only maintain taboos but also cast participants as fringe, if not as deviant, characters.

In each chapter in *American Taboo*, regardless of how very common involvement in the taboo might be in real life, such everydayness is rarely mirrored on screen. For example, while most men would have moments of nudity daily, full frontal male nudity is still a very *unusual* screen inclusion. Thus, while examples of each taboo are explored in each chapter, and while these presentations are interrogated for what they reveal about culture, also questioned are the continued *absences*: why—given that there are so many masturbators and vegetarians and homosexuals and cunnilinguists in real life—are these topics routinely avoided in popular culture? Proposed in this volume—using a wide variety of theoretical frameworks—are answers ranging from production and marketing decisions, audience considerations, and politics.

American Taboo is an exploration of a wide range of topics that are still haunted by politics, stigma, and controversy, yet each of which has a distinct, complicated, and ultimately *fascinating* presence in our popular culture.

The Gay Chapter: Sketching the Animated Homosexual

Media representations of homosexuality have long been a concern for communications and cultural studies scholars—and more recently queer theorists—who have identified an underrepresentation of gay and lesbians on screen[1] along with a routine mocking, othering, and demonization when they do appear.[2] This chapter focuses on the presentation of homosexuality in television cartoons. As a relatively recent inclusion, homosexuality in cartoons raises a number of interesting topics for discussion. Animation has traditionally been considered as a *children's* medium. The incorporation of controversial topics such as homosexuality, therefore, can be interpreted as a substantial taboo breach as related to both topic *and* medium. While animation might appear constrained given its connection to children, the fact that it is animation—that it involves *drawings* rather than live action—means that cartoons are, in fact, uniquely placed to breach taboos under the guise of comedy, (presumed) innocence, and illustration (i.e., by not using any humans). This chapter examines the representation of homosexuality in *The Simpsons* (1989–), *South Park* (1997–), and *Family Guy* (1999–), exploring the gay and lesbian depictions and analyzing the very specific appeal of cartoons breaking a sexual taboo.

CARTOONS AND ANIMATED INNOCENCE

When cartoons attract controversy, it is something most frequently associated with print media: scandals such as the 2005 depictions of Mohammed printed in the Danish newspaper *Jyllands-Posten*, for example, are indicative of the kind of controversies that normally plague cartoons. In contrast, *television* cartoons have traditionally had a much more innocent reputation, invariably associated with children's entertainment. Two of the most famous early primetime television cartoons—*The Flintstones* (1960–1966) and *The Jetsons* (1962–1963; 1985–1987)—were never overtly controversial. Both were animated domesticoms[3]—animated sitcoms centered on the domestic life of a family—and in both cases the humor was gentle, the behavior comically outlandish, and the social mores left unchallenged; in fact, some theorists have argued that both *The Flintstones* and *The Jetsons* actually *promoted* the American cultural values of the 1960s.[4]

With the introduction of *The Simpsons* in 1989, the television cartoon genre was overhauled. Suddenly, the target audience, the narrative content, and the propensity for the medium to challenge social values expanded exponentially. While *The Simpsons* was similar to *The Flintstones* and *The Jetsons* in that it was also a primetime domesticom, it distinguished itself through overt inclusion of controversial subjects that had been absent or heavily disguised in earlier cartoons. Suddenly politics, religion, and sexuality were all fair game in a medium that was once solely associated with children, slapstick, and puns.

The Simpsons paved the way for a slew of other boundary-crossing cartoons, such as *South Park* and *Family Guy*—and later *Drawn Together* (2004–2007), *American Dad!* (2005–), *The Venture Bros.* (2003–2012) and *Archer* (2009–). Collectively, these cartoons thoroughly altered the genre from being children's entertainment that *accidentally* amused adults,[5] to actively doing double duty and courting both adult *and* youth audiences.[6]

CARTOONS AND TARGET AUDIENCE

Cartoons have traditionally been considered as a children's medium and have long been relegated to after-school and Saturday morning timeslots. The first televised cartoon—*Crusader Rabbit* (1949–1951; 1957–1958)—centered on the adventures of a gung-ho rabbit and his animal sidekicks. While *Crusader Rabbit* was watched by a wide audience, the animation, storylines, and humor were youth oriented; if adults were entertained, it was merely a bonus.

Hanna-Barbera changed the landscape of television animation with the introduction of *The Flintstones* and *The Jetsons*. Both cartoons aired during primetime in an overt attempt to court both children and adults. The style of humor distinguished these cartoons from earlier animation, something that explained their broad appeal and which Bob Smith—star of *Howdy-Doody* (1947–1960)—identified in 1961: "Hanna and Barbera are creating children's visual shows and adult audio shows. Turn off the sound and children will enjoy what they see. Turn off the picture, and adults will enjoy what they hear."[7] Most interesting in Smith's comment is the idea of adults enjoying what they *heard*—an idea elaborated on in a modern context by media theorist Jason Mittell: "The puns, malapropisms, and old jokes that may seem stale today, made Hanna-Barbera cartoons appear groundbreaking ..."[8]

While many contemporary cartoons *still* use puns and malapropisms and oftentimes may appear relatively uncontroversial,[9] contemporary cartoons *also* solicit laughter from less traditional sources; it is these less traditional sources—most notably the inclusion of homosexuality—that is the focus of this chapter. While puns and malapropisms might once have been sufficient to entertain, by the late 1980s television cartoons needed more than slapstick to retain audiences. Television was a relatively new medium in the Hanna-Barbera heyday and program choice was minimal. By the 1980s, however, the number of channels and the variety of content had expanded enormously. In turn, audiences had become more selective, more discerning, and—most relevant to this chapter—"more sophisticated."[10] More sophisticated by 1989 meant an appetite for irony, satire, and intertextuality—cravings that *The Simpsons* helped satisfy. Suddenly, the jokes of *The Flintstones* and *The Jetsons* seemed far too timid—if not *old-fashioned*—for the comparatively worldly palates of the modern television audience who had been exposed to decades of different genres and who had much familiarity with sitcom humor that regularly employed sophistication *beyond* puns and physical hilarity.

In his discussion of the history of American television, media researcher James Roman noted that cartoons such as *The Simpsons*, *South Park*, *The Ren and Stimpy Show* (1991–1998), and *Beavis and Butt-Head* (1993–1997; 2011–) had "entered the realm of cutting-edge entertainment that is driven by attitude and chic."[11] While these contemporary cartoons still appealed to children via their use of well-established cartoon staples such as "silly images and lurid colours,"[12] an adult audience was also targeted through the more modern inclusions of *attitude and chic* which can be illustrated through the incorporation of more adult—more taboo—topics. Whereas *attitude* can be defined variously, for the purposes of this chapter I consider it to be cartoon's exhibition of bravado through daring to include subjects such as homosexuality that have long been underrepresented on television and often considered divisive and inflammatory.

THE ANIMATED GAY IN *THE SIMPSONS*

The taboo of homosexuality in popular culture has been well established by other theorists. Suffice it to say that a number of themes related to homosexuality are detectable, including invisibility, marginality, and demonization. This chapter begins with an exploration of the portrayal of homosexuality in contemporary cartoons—something that distinguishes *The Simpsons*, *Family Guy*, and *South Park* from earlier animation.

In *The Flintstones*, the closest the series got to broaching homosexuality was the "gay ol' time" promised in the theme song: in the 1960s, however, gay meant *happy*. Nowadays, it is standard fare to see homosexual characters on television, including in animation; *The Simpsons* played a pivotal role in normalizing such a presentation. While it would be premature to consider homosexuality as *common* in television cartoons today, gay characters nevertheless have an identifiable presence.

The Simpsons was the first cartoon to have *recurring* gay characters. Allusions to homosexuality were made in the earliest episodes through the presentation of the presumably homosexual characters of Wayland Smithers and Patty Bouvier. Subtle hints to both characters' sexuality were made early on and as the series progressed, the characters were presented as ever more obviously gay—that is, *identifying* as homosexual rather than merely being speculated as so. In early episodes, the allusions were to things open to interpretation, such as Wayland's Barbie doll collection and Patty being spotted leaving a burlesque house. By 2002, however, the two characters had seemingly come out of the closet and were both shown dancing on a gay pride float in the "Jaws Wired Shut" episode. In a 2011 episode, Wayland even went into business with Moe to turn the tavern into a gay bar.

While Patty and Wayland are Springfield's only *recurring* gay characters, there have certainly been other gay guests. John, for example, was a collectibles store owner who befriended the Simpson family. Roscoe was the manager of the Ajax steel mill, which seemingly only employed gay steel workers. In one episode, Homer moved into an apartment with two gay men—Grady and Julio—and embraced the gay lifestyle.

While homosexuality in animation can be explored through an analysis of the portrayals of openly gay characters, in cultural theorist Jo Johnson's research on queer characters in animation, she suggested the analysis be broadened, noting that "[t]he queer character lives not only in the few 'outed' residents of animated suburbia."[13] Here, Johnson highlights that homosexuality—or at least, non-heterosexuality—in animation is a concept much bigger than the out-of-the-closet gay characters. While Johnson's discussion focused on queer readings of anthropomorphism, transvestism, and "passing" as straight in animation, as related to this discussion her ideas can be applied to the presentation of sexuality as fluid and the subtle acknowledgment that it is now passé to think in a gay/straight binary manner. This view is well illustrated in *The Simpsons* as related to the sexuality of the family patriarch, Homer. According to communications theorists Karma Waltonen and Denise Du Vernay, heterosexual Homer has repeatedly "moved along the sexuality spectrum."[14] In one episode, for example, upon seeing his neighbor, Ned Flanders, flexing in his tight ski suit, Homer thought aloud to himself, "Stupid, sexy Flanders!" In another episode, Homer misinterpreted an invitation from his boss and said, "Sorry, Mr. Burns, but I don't go in for these backdoor shenanigans. Sure, I'm flattered, maybe even a little curious, but the answer is no." While Homer *isn't* gay, he is indicative of how *The Simpsons* has chosen to present sexuality as being, at the very least, something *complicated*.

While the simple inclusion of nondemonized homosexual characters might be considered progressive compared to earlier cartoons,[15] *The Simpsons* has gone substantially further than this. More than just including nondemonized gay characters, the series has also included a number of gay-themed episodes where—in varying degrees—gay issues were at the forefront. In 1997, for example, an episode titled "Homer's Phobia" focused on Homer's burgeoning friendship with the aforementioned collectibles seller, John. Reflected well by the title, the episode spotlighted two of Homer's fears: (1) that if his friendship with John were to become public, he would be ostracized, and (2) that if his son, Bart, spent too much time with John, he might get "contaminated."

The 2003 episode titled "Three Gays of the Condo," focused on Homer moving out of the family home after a fight with his wife Marge and into a condominium with Grady and Julio. By this episode, Homer had clearly moved far beyond his fears of *contracting* homosexuality and instead chose to embrace the social opportunities. At one point, he was actually kissed by one of his housemates. Later, when reunited with Marge, after he kissed her he remarked, "That was the best kiss I've had tonight," and then paused for thought: "or was it?" While raising less overtly political issues than "Homer's Phobia," the "Three Gays" episode nonetheless alluded to the queer notion of sexuality not being stagnant; the suggestion that Homer—a presumably heterosexual father—could have gained pleasure from a same-sex kiss is a controversial assertion and indicative of a postmodern approach to sexuality where attraction is no longer deemed fixed.[16]

In the anthology *Leaving Springfield*, cultural theorist Matthew Henry contended that *The Simpsons* has progressively become more political in regard to homosexuality: "whereas in the past Smithers's sexual orientation was private and apolitical, it has now become public and overtly political."[17] The episode "There's Something about Marry" (2005), for example, is very much indicative of this progression: in it, Marge's sister Patty outed herself as a lesbian, and Springfield legalized gay marriage (as a ploy for tourist dollars). Reflecting the continued real-life controversy about gay marriage—as well as political progress being inextricably linked to economics[18]—this episode is certainly open to interpretation as reflecting a growing politicization: it suggests that homosexuality is more than a matter of individual sexual preference—it is a political and notably a *human rights* issue.

A number of possible explanations exist for this growing politicization. On the one hand, arguably the audience of *The Simpsons* is simply more ready for such taboo breaches: research indicates that the public today is more tolerant of homosexuality than at any other time in history.[19] Arguably *The Simpsons* itself has had an integral role in this transformation, through its subtle hints and allusions dropped over the years; its audience has long been primed for ever more sexual taboos to be breached. On the other hand, the series is in a relatively safe position to conspicuously test boundaries; it has been airing for several decades and is now part of the established television landscape. Audiences are thus unlikely to perceive homosexual presentations on *The Simpsons* as merely emblematic of the attention-seeking antics that some upstart television programs might be accused of.

While *The Simpsons* might be credited with helping increase the number of presentations of homosexual characters on screen, and in turn helping to normalize such portrayals, for cartoons such as *Family Guy* or *South Park*—both comparatively cruder and edgier—the presentation of homosexuality is substantially more complicated, in line with both series' attempts to dare to go where *The Simpsons* never has.

THE ANIMATED GAY IN *FAMILY GUY* AND *SOUTH PARK*

The animated domesticom *Family Guy* has been described as "much riskier in its humor than its network mate of *The Simpsons*" and as boasting a "concerted appeal to a much narrower scope of comedy that is edgier, more vulgar and more sexual (or sexist)."[20] *Family Guy*'s reputation as being riskier and edgier has meant that taboos such as homosexuality have often been broached in ways far more complicated—and controversial—than in *The Simpsons*.

Most obviously, like *The Simpsons*, *Family Guy* has included some presumably gay characters: central character baby Stewie for example—known for his procession of queer barbs—was described by series creator Seth MacFarlane as "almost certainly gay"[21] and by *Out* magazine as a "a gay icon."[22] Also like *The Simpsons*, the series has explored homosexual issues such as gay marriage (for example in the episode "You May Now Kiss the ... Uh ... Guy Who Receives," 2006).

Unlike *The Simpsons*, however, *Family Guy* has—more controversially—presented homosexuality in a far less positive light: homosexuality in *Family Guy* is routinely portrayed as something to laugh *at*. Philosopher Jeremy Wisnewski, in his discussion of the series, identified this concern: "Consider the way Jews and African Americans are stereotyped, how Mexicans and philosophers are typecast as lazy, and gays are all flamboyant in *Family Guy*. The writers of *Family Guy* play on people's hasty generalizations to make their points in episode after episode."[23]

More than simply *flamboyant*, however, is the show's troubling convergence of homosexuality and pedophilia. The recurring elderly character Herbert, for example, is presented as having an obsession with his teenage neighbor Chris and is described by communications researchers John Kundert-Gibbs and Kristin Kundert-Gibbs in their book on animation as "the consummate old man lech."[24] The muddling of homosexuality and pedophilia has long been viewed as problematic by homosexual activists, who rightfully resent their legal sexual preferences being construed as predatory or akin to criminal activity. While it could be contended that Herbert is just one character—and thus shouldn't be perceived as speaking on behalf of *all* homosexuals—the reality is that Herbert is one of a very small number of recurring gay characters and is presented as embodying not merely a stereotype, but a *hateful character indictment* that continues to be made against homosexuals in real life.

The idea of homosexuality being something suitable to mock is more obvious in *South Park*, a cartoon consciously and consistently more risqué than *The Simpsons* or even *Family Guy*. One of *South Park*'s lead characters, Mr. Garrison, while not always presented as homosexual, is certainly presented as *queer* throughout. Dubbed by media theorist Ted Gournelos as both "the show's resident freak"[25] and the most "deviant authority figure in town,"[26] Mr. Garrison is permanently portrayed as sexually ambiguous with his sexual interests vacillating widely: he has, for example, been speculated as having had sex with a pig, a pigeon, and musician Kenny G; attempted a threesome with Chef and Liana Cartman; offered to let soldiers "have their way" with him; lamented not having been molested by his father; joined NAMBLA (North American Man/Boy Love Association); and in one episode provided a lesson to schoolchildren on how to put on condoms with their mouths. Like Herbert in *Family Guy*, Mr. Garrison is illustrative of some of the more problematic ways homosexuality is presented in popular culture: as not merely something different or nonmainstream, but rather as freakish, if not potentially *criminal*. Gournelos discussed this issue, identifying two main problems as related to the presentation of Mr. Garrison's sexuality: he "is always considered as both a sexual deviant as well as being possibly gay" and he "retains his status as a deviant in addition to his homosexuality."[27]

As with Herbert in *Family Guy*, the portrayal of homosexuality in *South Park* is more complicated than just being presented as "other," but rather involves criminality that includes pedophilia. The nasty edge to the treatment of homosexuality is further reinforced by homosexual characters frequently using the word *gay* to condemn things or people. The issue of *gay* being used as a negative adjective has been thought to both reflect and contribute to homophobia. Queer activist Pabitra Benjamin, for example, described that in her high school experience, "It was extremely commonplace to hear 'That's so gay' or 'He's such a gay.' "[28] Gay activist and scholar Eric Rofes similarly identified that teenagers frequently use the word as a slur: "they are using the word to brand an individual as odd, nontraditional, or 'girlish.' "[29] *Gay* used as a negative adjective offers an ongoing *background noise* presentation of homosexuality as something bad—an unsubtle form of homophobia that is readily identifiable in both *Family Guy* and *South Park*.

Another aspect of *Family Guy*'s negative portrayal of homosexuality is the preoccupation with outing characters suspected of being in the closet, a cultural pastime that I have written about previously: "Just what underpins this fixation with uncovering sexual truths? Perhaps the most obvious explanation is our fervour for a good ol' fashioned witch-hunt. Such an idea reminds us that homosexuality is still too frequently deemed an abnormality and as such, anyone daring to live such a renegade lifestyle must be exposed for the deviant that they are."[30] One episode of *Family Guy*, for example, centered on patriarch Peter's attempts to out actor Luke Perry. Forced outing also occurred in *South Park*: an episode titled "Trapped in the Closet" (2005), for example, centered on the long-standing rumors regarding the sexuality of actors Tom Cruise and John Travolta. Again, such presentations reiterate the idea of homosexuality not being merely something shameful, but also something best kept hidden: that it is a sufficiently embarrassing— if not heinous—quality that should remain marginalized.

Worth spotlighting is that, of course, *Family Guy* and *South Park* are *comedies*: first and foremost, their objective is to entertain as opposed to deliver political messages. While in practice they certainly might be construed as delivering political messages, it would be erroneous to imply that they are political above all else or that they have any agenda as related to social engineering.

Also worth noting is that just because the portrayals of gay characters are not always positive—in fact, in *South Park* and *Family Guide* they can often be construed as quite *negative*—it doesn't mean that they necessarily are construed by audiences this way or interpreted as proscriptive or speaking for all queer people. In fact, it could be argued that contemporary audiences—particularly given that they have likely been primed by watching shows such as *The Simpsons*—are more savvy and are able to read characters as *just characters* rather than as reflections or demonizations of entire cultural groups. A media-literate audience, for example, may be able to discern that sometimes negative characters are deliberately designed to malign stereotypes and caricatures—that they are *intended* to be satirical. A cautionary note to this interpretation, however, is that it assumes a mature and media-literate audience: given that stylistically cartoons appeal to young people, obviously concerns are raised about the messages that they are receiving and their limited ability to process nuance.

Earlier in this chapter I suggested that a maturing of the palate of the television audience is an obvious explanation for the evolution of animation. As noted previously, a central way that the genre has been modernized is through the incorporation of taboos such as homosexuality. Evidently for audiences of contemporary cartoons, there is appeal in watching topics widely considered *risky*. In the next section, a number of other explanations for audience enjoyment of controversial inclusions in cartoons are proposed.

THE APPEAL OF NAUGHTY TELEVISION

A central rationale for the appeal of taboo portrayals is that their inclusion reflects audience interest in material that we "shouldn't" consume. *Reactance theory* is a phenomenon that describes this response well. First discussed by psychologist Jack Brehm in 1966,[31] reactance theory describes the link between liberties being curtailed and the forbidden suddenly becoming enticing, if not *irresistible*. Psychologists Roy Baumeister and Brad Bushman explained this idea in very simple terms: "If you weren't sure you wanted to see the concert, being told that you can't see it may increase your desire to see it and make you think it is likely to be a really good one."[32]

At its most basic level, reactance theory underpins the *wanting what you can't have* idea. As related to the media, this theory helps to analyze audience behavior and has much applicability in explaining popular interest in controversial media presentations. Research undertaken by psychologists Bushman and Joanne Cantor for example, indicated that labels designed to warn about the taboo material contained in TV programs, films, video games, and music often make consumers *more* interested in the product, not less.[33] In their consideration of Internet censorship, psychologists James Olson and Victoria Esses discussed reactance theory as relevant to public policy and Internet filters: "[W]hen people first learn that they are being denied access to information (or the ability to disseminate information), the external constraints on them will be salient. Under these conditions, the restricted information will become more attractive and people may actively resist the attempted control."[34]

While homosexuality is presented in *The Simpsons*, *South Park*, and *Family Guy*, gay characters are not so common in these shows, nor elsewhere in popular culture, that their presence is trivial. Not only does the comparatively small number of gay characters mean that negative portrayals have more impact, but it also means that some audiences will be drawn to these cartoons because by viewing them they get access to material that is not effortlessly sourced elsewhere. It might even be contended that in an increasingly politically correct world, shows such as *South Park* and *Family Guy* are actively sought out by audiences because they offer politically *incorrect* presentations of homosexuality that are unlikely to be found elsewhere. (This issue of political correctness and popular culture is discussed further in the Euphemisms Chapter.) Of course, cartoons are not the only genre that presents homosexuality; they are however, one that does, and thus the ability to exploit audience interest in the "naughty" undoubtedly influences—and enhances—program appeal.

CARTOONS AND THE CUTTING EDGE

Mindful of Bushman and Cantor's research about warning labels, I propose that there is evidently something particularly captivating about material that is controversial and that this, in part, explains the appeal of taboos experienced in cartoons: something desirable from both production *and* consumption perspectives.

From a production side, the attraction of using controversial material is simple: it often leads to increased attention and, in turn, greater sales. In research on news, for example, sociologist Diana Kendall explained why the media routinely sideline social issues such as poverty in favor of more political and likely polarizing stories: "controversy sells more newspapers and draws larger TV and website audiences."[35] The same point has been made in the context of music: Ed Christman, writing for *Billboard* magazine, discussed metal band Deicide's album *Once Upon The Cross* (1995) and identified the deliberate use of controversy as part of the marketing strategy: "The marketing of this record comes under the category "controversy sells" ... for those of you who haven't seen this drama before, it goes something like this: Act 1, release album, with controversial artwork prominently displayed; Act 2, when no one notices, issue press release claiming controversy; Act 3, make sure press release implies that music retailers ... are refusing to carry the controversial album cover."[36] This issue was similarly addressed by novelist David Guterson, whose book *Snow Falling on Cedars* (1994) was banned in some U.S. school districts. Guterson, in discussing the ban, explained that rather than controversy being a problem, it is actually something *encouraged* at a production level: "No publisher has ever asked me to alter something to avoid controversy and I can't imagine that happening for a couple of reasons ... The first is that publishers like controversy because it sells books... Isn't it true that censoring a book often means more curiosity about its contents? ... So it's more censorship and controversy, *please*, as far as publishers are concerned."[37]

While reactance theory explains why controversy sells—people want what they are told that they can't have—the other explanation is simply publicity: as Christman explained, an album may have gone unnoticed, so "controversy" is sometimes *manufactured* to conjure attention: controversial products get more attention, often leading to increased sales.

For consumers, while of course there is appeal in purchasing controversial goods because doing so sates a yen for the forbidden, another explanation is that the desire for such goods exists primarily *because* debate and controversy exists around the item. In other words, some people are *drawn* to certain films and books not because the topic particularly interests them, but rather because (1) they want to exert their rights not to have their media restricted, and (2) they want to feel a part of a controversy. In my book *Part-Time Perverts: Sex, Pop Culture, and Kink Management*, I briefly discussed that for "some perverts it is essential that they feel like the most perverted person in the room/city/world."[38] This idea could be used to analyze consumer behavior as related to controversial animation: there will always be some people who want to be on the cutting-edge of culture and to consume the most taboo and renegade materials available because close association with controversy—feeling like a participant *in* a controversy—provides pleasure, if not also greater esteem.

In cultural theorist Rebecca Arnold's book on fashion, she discussed "the desire for the unattainable ... and the thrill of owning something unique."[39]

While the appeal of the unattainable can, again, be explained through reactance theory, the concept of the unique—of consuming things that few other people have, i.e., a kind of positional good[40]—can be construed as another explanation for audience interest in taboos in cartoons. In his book about Madonna, for example, Mark Bego wrote that during the early 1990s *the* cocktail party question was "Have you read Madonna's *Sex* book?"[41] Be it Nazi memorabilia or Madonna's limited-edition book, cultural cachet is frequently attached to objects that are both hard to procure and highly controversial. Being someone "in the know"—being someone, for example, who has seen *South Park* when it was in its pre-television, film school production state—can gift a person social kudos. While broadcast episodes of *South Park* and *Family Guy* are now easily procured, for some people, the appeal of such shows may derive from the prospect of being part of an audience for material that generates continued controversy.

ANIMATION AND PLEASURES VICARIOUS

Part-Time Perverts focused on nonmainstream sexuality and extensively examined the manner in which such topics are portrayed in—and experienced through—popular culture. In that book, I proposed that that a central explanation for audience interest in representations of sexual taboos such as pedophilia, incest, and bestiality was *sexual stimulation*; that watching representations of such forbidden topics can give an audience vicarious access to taboo activity that would be difficult to participate in during real life and, in turn, that *stimulation* can be experienced by watching a portrayal. Watching a *depiction* of a taboo can give a person access to a non-vanilla sexuality without them having to suffer the mess or difficulty or expense of organizing to act it out in real life.[42] This concept of *vicarious participation* explains that through the process of *watching*, a viewer can experience something at arm's length—for example, can experience a sex life that they have not experienced simply by watching a cartoon character do so. Certainly for young people who may not yet have come out as gay, *representations* of homosexuality—notably those presented in socially accepted media such as cartoons—enables them to feel part of a culture that they might not otherwise experience. The idea of vicarious pleasures as related to cartoons was explored by film critic Leonard Maltin in his discussion of *The Simpsons* and *Ren and Stimpy*: "We get a vicarious kick out of watching them speak the unsayable, do the unthinkable—because they're 'only' cartoons characters, we can cheer them without seeming antisocial ourselves … Cartoons allow us to indulge our youthful dreams, act out the thoughts society teaches us to inhibit and have a good time in the bargain."[43]

Perhaps even more so than live-action television, cartoon consumption enables audiences to watch cartoon characters engage in all kinds of taboos, many which might be too controversial or potentially too politically incorrect to depict in live-action television. Media researcher Peter Orlik discussed this issue in the context of cartoons including *South Park*: "[E]ven as an adult-oriented, late-evening cable show, *South Park* would not long survive if its scurrilous language was seen and heard to come out of the mouths of flesh-and-blood child actors. But voiced by animated characters—graphically rendered with anything but Disney/kid-friendly finesse—*South Park*'s graffiti-like guerilla warfare can be enjoyed by grown-ups as deceptively unthreatening satire."[44]

While of course a person can download pornography and purchase explicit DVDs, doing so would demonstrate a level of conscious *acceptance* of one's own perversion. Experiencing such perversions through the "innocent" medium of cartoons, however, offers a comparatively innocuous taste of the taboo without it being attached to a more overtly perverted purchase, in turn facilitating a person to avoid the deviant label and the associated negativity.

ANIMATION AND INNOCENCE PERVERTED

Another explanation for the appeal of experiencing taboo through television cartoons relates to the nature of the medium: that there is something *specifically* appealing about taboo experienced through a traditionally innocent medium such as animation.

In 2009, *Playboy* magazine included a spread of cartoon character Marge Simpson. Reflective of the MILF phenomena, part of the appeal of the spread lay in Marge Simpson—a mother and a character not primarily defined as sexual—being photographed in provocative positions and in an *adult* magazine. Even stronger than her newfound MILF status was that Marge is a cartoon character and that there is something so wrong—so *perverted*—about a cartoon character being conceived of as sexy: as discussed earlier, cartoons are synonymous with *children's* entertainment, so seeing characters presented as erotic is considered as something particularly troubling. In recent years, much feminist commentary has been predicated on growing concerns with the supposed sexualization of culture, notably of *childhood*.[45] The appearance of a children's cartoon character in an adult sex-themed magazine might be construed as evidence of this trend.

The Marge Simpson *Playboy* spread, of course, is substantially less salacious than the burgeoning genre of cartoon pornography, in which unauthorized animators have recreated characters from shows including *The Simpsons* and *Family Guy* and drawn them in explicit sexual situations. Such images do not merely involve the central husband-and-wife couplings, but include siblings having sex with one another as well as parents with children. Homosexual couplings are also notably prominent. While such cartoons have been accused of luring unsuspecting children into the world of adult imagery,[46] another interpretation is that such pornographic cartoons are indicative of the arousal that can come from the fusion of children's entertainment and sex. Perhaps such depictions are arousing because familiar characters who would never otherwise be shown having sex at all—let alone *together*—are presented explicitly for titillation: they are arousing because they are so naughty.[47]

By inserting taboo themes into a genre that is traditionally associated with children—if not also innocence—a specific appeal associated with transgression is created. Put simply, a greater sense of taboo and boundary crossing and an enhanced feeling of audience pleasure are achieved.

CARTOONS AND CREATIVE LIBERTY

In the previous section I suggested that taboos breached in animation hold specific appeal because the medium is so frequently associated with innocence. The medium, of course, also explains the unique capacity cartoons have to cross boundaries and to present taboos in comparison with other kinds of popular culture.

In Mittel's research, he offered an explanation for why cartoon characters can often get away with more—more violence or more calamity, for example. Mittel focused on the nature of the genre: "since they are 'only cartoons,' the writers can heap indignities and trauma upon them without making audiences feel too bad for the characters."[48]

The *it's only television* idea has long been used as a way to downplay the supposed effects of television, notably television violence. The assumption is that because it is *only television*, audiences will know that the violence or danger is *not real*. Such an idea is theoretically even more applicable to television cartoons, whereby animated figures are involved rather than live-action people. While existing as avatars to facilitate vicarious pleasures for the audience, cartoon characters also function as safe, nonhuman outlets for real human fears, penchants, and perversions. It could also be contended that risqué animation provides an insight into the darker aspects of human nature, *South Park* for example, acknowledges this very idea—and the appeal underpinning it—through the character of Mr. Garrison. Mr. Garrison often carries a puppet named Mr. Hat that he considers to be his "assistant." In one episode, a psychiatrist diagnosed that Mr. Hat is Mr. Garrison's "gay side." This idea of a puppet existing as an outlet for sentiments not socially sanctioned can be construed as a metaphor for the function of television cartoons more broadly in providing audiences access to taboo topics: cartoon characters—easily able to be dismissed as *only cartoons*—are able to be more daring, more controversial, and more offensive, so that viewing them provides audiences with an opportunity to experience taboos via a kind of avatar.

SPECULATING ON IMPACT

The impact of media consumption has been heatedly debated ever since the first work on media effects was conducted in the early 1920s.[49] In this section I speculate on some of the possible ramifications related to the presence of homosexuality in television animation.

The Moderating Effect of Humor

In my book on sex in advertising—*Sex in Public: Women, Outdoor Advertising and Public Policy*—I discussed the use of humor in advertisements that objectified women: "Rather than 'humour' exonerating demeaning portrayals, arguably its use actually worsens advertisements by trivialising and making inappropriate imagery palatable and thus contributes to the perceived insignificance of audience complaints."[50] One way to interpret *South Park* and *Family Guy*'s homosexual stereotypes, then, is to say that by presenting negative imagery as *entertainment*, the good feeling that comes with laughing comes to be associated with bigotry; in other words, it becomes funny to mock people who are "different." This, however, is not the only interpretation. Earlier I mentioned satire and irony, which represent another way that seemingly homophobic presentations have been justified: such presentations are said to be sardonic attempts to actually *mock* homophobia; they are examples of *satire*. This, most definitely, is how controversial and potentially offensive elements of *South Park* and *Family Guy* have been rationalized and even excused. In Matt Sienkiewicz and Nick Marx's work on *South Park*, for example, they summarized the irony argument by contending that "such texts are often assumed not to be truly racist by virtue of the fact that they so effortlessly engage in the offensive."[51]

While I have no interest in making a finite argument about whether contemporary cartoons are homophobic, their presentation of homosexuality certainly raises concerns related to their role in attitude change. Social scientist Simon Weaver has discussed the impact of racist humor on audiences, noting that it "has a communicative impact, is persuasive, and can affect impressions of truth and ambivalence."[52] Applied to seemingly homophobic comedy, these cartoons are open to interpretation as—even if only in a small way—contributing to the ostracizing and stereotyping of homosexuals. Thus, while it is not the only reading, this interpretation certainly needs to be considered.

Bearing little semblance to the Warner Bros. and Hanna-Barbera incarnations of yesteryear, cartoons such as *The Simpsons*, *South Park*, and *Family Guy* have completely transformed the cartoon genre as well as the audience. This chapter has explored the presence of homosexuality in cartoons, highlighting ways of perceiving the animated gay and interpreting representations as one of a number of ways cartoons test—and *traverse*—the boundaries of taste, decency, and acceptability.

The Oral Sex Chapter: Cunnilingus and the Politics of the Lick

Two of the best picture nominees at the 83rd Academy Awards—*Black Swan* (2010) and *The Kids Are Alright* (2010)—featured scenes of cunnilingus. Three of the best leading female performance nominees that same year—Michelle Williams for *Blue Valentine* (2010), Natalie Portman for *Black Swan*, and Annette Bening for *The Kids Are All Right*—each participated in cunnilingus scenes. The Greek film *Dogtooth* (2010)—nominated for Best Foreign Language Film—also showed cunnilingus. In fact, the repeated presentation of oral sex that year cajoled Hadley Freeman, writing for the U.K. newspaper *The Guardian*, to wryly suggest that cunnilingus was 2010's "disabled/abused/gay/mental illness/foreign accent!": "How best to win an Oscar? If you've played gay, done the learning disability, tried the foreign accent, well here's a new trick—female oral sex."[1]

Even on the small screen, 2010 was a watershed year for cunnilingus: *The Good Wife* (2009–), for example, became the first network television series to break the taboo in a scene between Alicia (Julianna Margulies) and her husband Peter (Chris Noth).[2] In 2012, the series broke this taboo again in a scene between two women.

While detecting such scenes may indeed be possible, to presume that cunnilingus is now *common* or uncontroversial or that the taboo has now evaporated would be premature. While cunnilingus may no longer create the controversy it did in the 1970s—with memorable oral sex scenes in *Play Misty for Me* (1971), *Don't Look Now* (1973), and *Coming Home* (1978)—cunnilingus is not yet a mainstream staple in the way that intercourse is, nor is it portrayed with as much frequency as fellatio.[3] Despite *Blue Valentine* eventually receiving an Academy Award nomination, the Motion Picture Association of America (MPAA) initially gave it an NC-17 rating based on the cunnilingus scene between the central characters Cindy (Michelle Williams) and Dean (Ryan Gosling). Even without extensive nudity, even without violence, the *Blue Valentine* controversy demonstrated that (1) a man having oral contact with a woman's genitals is still apparently "troubling" and (2) a woman's sexual pleasure presented as disconnected from a penis still stirs debate.

In sociologist Edward Laumann et al.'s research on cunnilingus, the authors described the act as being "fraught with symbolic ambiguity."[4] Sociologists John Gagnon and William Simon made an equally interesting observation: "We must keep in mind the multiple *meanings* of oral sex which are less well measured or often may only be inferred on the basis of inadequate evidence. At different times in the same relationship or in differing relationships the same physical movements may be performed as an avoidance of coitus, an expression of intimacy, a sign of erotic competence, a measure of degradation of the self or the partner."[5] While Laumann et al. and Gagnon and Simon were discussing oral sex in real-life relationships, their ideas are highly relevant to interpreting portrayals of cunnilingus *on screen*: as explored throughout this chapter, a single scene of oral sex can provide a multitude of social and political insights. In this chapter I explore depictions of cunnilingus, offering some ways of interpreting such scenes and examining the rationales for both their inclusion and frequent *exclusion*.

CUNNILINGUS: A NUMBERS GAME

While cunnilingus, of course, is not a new sex act, depictions of it have historically been rare. In her discussions of ancient Greek art, for example, classics scholar Leslie Kurke noted that "while scenes of women fellating men are fairly common, depictions of cunnilingus are almost nonexistent."[6] Classics scholar Ray Laurence made the exact same point in the context of ancient Roman art, noting that "[i]mages of *cunnilingus* are extremely rare."[7] Numerous writers have similarly spotlighted that the Kama Sutra only mentions cunnilingus in the context of it being something that women do *to each other*.[8] Explanations for this absence are varied, referencing sexual politics related to bodies, pleasure, and positions. Theologians Todd Penner and Caroline Vander Stichele discussed the works of the poet Martial, who lived and wrote in Ancient Rome and who described that to accuse a man of enjoying cunnilingus was the ultimate insult: "cunnilingus made a man's mouth a 'cunt' and the man so passive that, in effect, he was 'fucked by a woman.' "[9] Other explanations for the absence centered on it being viewed as disgraceful for a man to sexually service a woman[10] as well as fears related to pollution, contamination, and disgust associated with female genitals.[11]

In more modern presentations of sexuality—pornography being the obvious example—cunnilingus is much easier to detect. Most contemporary porn will include at least *some* mouth-vulva contact. While cunnilingus may be easier to detect today, it nevertheless continues to be portrayed in a fundamentally different manner than the equivalent oral sex practice of fellatio, which is presented more often and in longer scenes. Richard Michael, in his 1972 book *The ABZ of Pornography*, noted that "[s]ince pornography is male-orientated, fellatio is more commonly featured than cunnilingus."[12] Contemporary research repeats this argument: journalist and screenwriter Jonathan Light, for example, contended that "the preponderance of fellatio over straight cunnilingus is strikingly evident."[13] Cultural historian Joseph Slade similarly noted that "[p]erformed properly, cunnilingus remains invisible to the film audience, whereas fellatio results in the arcing ejaculation."[14] Social researchers Alan McKee et al. in *The Porn Report* also identified that porn "still has more fellatio than cunnilingus."[15]

While cunnilingus is common in contemporary pornography, to suggest that the same is true in mainstream cinema is hyperbolic. While Freeman in *The Guardian* spotlighted an apparent *surge* in presentations in 2010, interestingly the same point was made in the same newspaper in 2003 when Rebecca Traister alluded to "Hollywood experienc[ing] early tremors of a graphic (oral) sexual revolution."[16] Traister drew attention to cunnilingus scenes in *In the Cut* (2003) and *The Cooler* (2003) to signify what she suggested was growing comfort in depicting oral sex. While 2003 and 2010 may exist as landmark years where cunnilingus appeared to have greater visibility in popular culture, it would be erroneous to exaggerate the impact of a still relatively small number of depictions. First, while presentations of cunnilingus may be more common today than in the past, this is most likely simply indicative of a general trend toward showing more sex— notably more *non-vanilla* sex[17]—in mainstream popular culture rather than any specific championing of cunnilingus. Second, the controversy surrounding the cunnilingus scene in *Blue Valentine* reminds us that—at least from a film classification perspective—such a sex act is still considered problematic for general audiences and, notably, is deemed something that some audiences need to be restricted from. Of course, perhaps the most pressing reason to be skeptical of a lifted taboo relates to how cunnilingus is presented: just as in porn, not only is fellatio still more common in mainstream cinema, but the duration and objectives of cunnilingus scenes are often substantially different from fellatio scenes.

Quoted earlier, Slade noted that cunnilingus "performed properly... remains invisible."[18] If we define *properly* in this context to mean performed until orgasm—or at least cunnilingus for the purposes of bringing *the woman* pleasure (as opposed to voyeuristic pleasure for the audience)[19]—highlighted is the issue of the differences in its portrayal compared to fellatio: while cunnilingus might appear more often than it once did, rarely does it involve the *arcing* orgasm as in fellatio depictions, and rarely is it portrayed as a sex act sufficient to constitute a complete sex scene. In popular culture writer Dave Thompson's research on pornography, he detected a shift toward more cunnilingus but also spotlighted that the act is presented more flippantly and for shorter durations than fellatio: "maybe three-quarters of the movies that depict fellatio also include at least a few moments of oral-labial contact."[20] Other researchers have similarly noted the brevity issue: social researchers Robert Jensen and Gail Dines in their content analysis of modern porn noted, "[T]he scenes of men performing cunnilingus, if they appeared at all, were shorter in duration than those of women performing fellatio."[21] These authors highlight a reality that underpins not only cunnilingus portrayals but also screen depictions of *any* traditionally underrepresented act: *more* presentations on their own are insufficient to imply the dissolving of stigma, tokenism, or controversy. While cunnilingus may be more readily identifiable on screen today, (1) to consider it as a sex act of the same worth, legitimacy, and entertainment value as intercourse; (2) to consider it enough to constitute a *complete* sex scene; or (3) to treat it as a sex act worth performing for more than "a few moments" would each be premature.

In a scene from *The Getaway* (1994), "Doc" McCoy (Alex Baldwin) spent a few seconds performing oral sex on Carol (Kim Basinger) before the characters moved into an intercourse position. In *Margaret* (2011), Paul (Kieran Culkin) began to perform oral sex on Lisa (Anna Paquin) before she stopped him and they moved onto fellatio and then to intercourse. In *Greenberg* (2010), Roger (Ben Stiller) performed cunnilingus on Florence (Greta Gerwig) during one of their early dates: she was distracted and quickly stopped him. Such presentations are the typical cunnilingus portrayal: if it is included, the oral-genital contact is brief, functioning more as foreplay and largely serving as a progression to a "main event." While there are, of course, rare exceptions where oral sex between men and women does serve as the centerpiece of the sexual action—*Coming Home, Monster's Ball*

(2001), *9 Songs* (2004), and *Lie with Me* (2005) all include longer-than-standard cunnilingus scenes with a specific intent of bringing the woman pleasure, and lesbian-themed films do this much more readily as apparent in *Go Fish* (1994) and *Better Than Chocolate* (1999)—more common is cunnilingus presented as a precursor to intercourse.[22] As related to duration, it is worthwhile highlighting that just as in porn, in real life cunnilingus is also often performed briefly and only because women increasingly expect it (as opposed to men *wanting* to perform it),[23] thus spotlighting a possible screen mirror. In sex researcher Shere Hite's *The Hite Report*, she discussed this issue, writing that "although most women loved cunnilingus ... all too often cunnilingus was offered by the partner for very short intervals ... as 'foreplay.'"[24] Hite reported, for example, that only 32 percent of the men in her study who claimed to perform cunnilingus did so until the woman reached orgasm.[25]

The idea of not only shorter episodes of cunnilingus but not *much* cunnilingus is also identifiable on screen. In *The Girl with the Dragon Tattoo* (2011), for example, Lisbeth (Rooney Mara) made an observation about Mikael's (Daniel Craig) sex life: "He's had a longstanding sexual relationship with his co-editor of the magazine. Sometimes he performs cunnilingus on her. Not often enough in my opinion." In an episode of *The Sopranos* (1999–2007), a similar reference to infrequency was made when Tony (James Gandolfini) and his wife Carmela (Edie Falco) discussed Uncle Junior's (Dominic Chianese) talent for cunnilingus. Carmela told Tony that men are hypocrites for condemning Junior and the following exchange transpired:

Tony: Hey, what goes on in this bedroom stays here and you know that.
Carmela: Once a year? I can resist the urge to gossip.

Like Lisbeth, Carmela alluded to the frequency issue, implying that cunnilingus is something she rarely experienced.

While we don't know enough about Mikael's or Tony's motivations for performing oral sex, one interpretation—and something strongly tied to the infrequency issue—is that cunnilingus is performed only on special occasions. In my book *Part-Time Perverts: Sex, Pop Culture, and Kink Management*, I made the observation that special occasions can provide people the opportunity to engage in sexual practices that would otherwise be unusual for them: "A special occasion like a birthday may provide an opportunity for the reluctant/uninterested partner to give a perverse gift, to appear generous, but nonetheless to restrict participation to an infrequent occurrence. (It may also be interpreted as an act of martyrdom by a partner wanting to appear generous or self-sacrificing.)"[26] Perhaps Mikael and Tony perceived cunnilingus as something done only on very special occasions; thus cunnilingus is not a standard part of their sexual repertoire and is engaged in only occasionally, *generously*, as a gift. Certainly, if cunnilingus is considered this way in real life—as a rare exception to standard intercourse rather than a norm—such a perception may explain its absence from the screen. Worth noting, often things that are perceived as complicated or time-consuming may also be done only on special occasions: cunnilingus, often construed as an "advanced technique," may fit into this category.

CUNNILINGUS AND THE CHANGING MALE

Mentioned earlier were three films from the 1970s—*Play Misty for Me*, *Don't Look Now*, and *Coming Home*—each of which featured cunnilingus scenes. The presentation of this sex act—one that prioritizes *female* sexual pleasure—marked a watershed moment in cinema history where not only were the sexual desires of women granted attention, but most importantly where men were shown to cater to them. This section explores cunnilingus being used as a tool on screen to signify the *new* man—the sensitive New Age guy—an identity shaped by exposure to second-wave feminism and sexual liberation. In this section I propose that through participation in cunnilingus, a male character is presented as sensitive to the needs and wants of his partner and is cast as someone who is willing to sideline—or at least *postpone*—his own gratification. Such characters are also presented as men who know what it takes to sexually arouse—and notably *satisfy*—women.

In sociologist Raewyn Connell's book *Masculinities*, the author discussed the impact that exposure to feminism has had on men, contending that a softening has occurred whereby men are nowadays more supportive of women and more critical of the behavior of other men.[27] In Susan Crain Bakos's sex manual *The Orgasm Bible*, she linked the impact of the 1970s Zeitgeist to changes in bedroom scripts: "In the 1970s, young baby boomer women gave their men a message: cunnilingus. Many got the message."[28] Other research similarly identifies the increased frequency of oral sex as one of the biggest changes to sex lives in recent decades.[29] One explanation, therefore, for the inclusion of cunnilingus on screen is to portray male characters as being a product of the Zeitgeist and to present a *modern* narrative. For David (Clint Eastwood) in *Play Misty for Me*, John (Donald Sutherland) in *Don't Look Now*, and Luke (Jon Voigt) in *Coming Home*, while each character's reasons for participating in cunnilingus likely varied, one explanation is that these men were presented as being influenced by the times that they lived in—that they were new, 1970s-style men.

In media theorist Adam Knee's discussion of cunnilingus in *Play Misty for Me*, he addressed the issue of the changing male on screen: "This is, of course, structured as another indicator of 1970s male sensitivity, of David's move into new age; indeed, the very act of representing this form of sexual activity foregrounds its *historical* importance."[30] A similar point was made in a *Vanity Fair* article where *Coming Home* producer Jerome Hellman discussed the cunnilingus that Sally (Jane Fonda) had with her affair-partner Luke, a paralyzed war veteran: "She's had a traditional guy who jumps on and pumps away until he comes and gets off. But manliness wasn't necessarily related to a big stiff dick. This big macho guy with his medals was a total wipeout as a husband and lover. And the vet who had only half a body, he was a real man."[31]

Cultural theorist Linda Williams took this idea further by discussing the same scene and noting that Sally's orgasm "ultimately operates to restore a semblance of masculinity to an initially emasculated veteran."[32] In these 1970s films, cunnilingus was a way to convey that a male character had been influenced by the Zeitgeist. Something similar occurs in more contemporary films, where cunnilingus scenes also serve as a way to convey a man's evolved masculinity. In my book on menstruation—*Periods in Pop Culture: Menstruation in Film and Television*—I discussed the idea of menstrual sex being often presented as something engaged in by *avant garde* and unconventional lovers: that generally only sensitive, evolved, and progressive men participate.[33] Oral sex can be construed similarly: that men who participate are likely aware of the heinous mythology surrounding female genitals but are presented as being too progressive to allow such ideas to limit their sex lives.[34] This point was made in cultural theorist Mark Allinson's discussion of the cunnilingus scene in the Spanish film *Carne trémula* (*Live Flesh*) (1997): "The young men in *Live Flesh*, however, are reconstructed, 'new men.' We see David [Javier Bardem] perform cunnilingus on Elena [Francesca Neri]—a selfless and sophisticated technique in contrast to the thrusting selfishness of men in earlier films."[35] In *Californication* (2007–), Marcy's (Pamela Adlon) new lover Stu (Stephen Tobolowsky) is presented in a similar way: while her ex-husband Charlie (Evan Handler) was highly sexed, he was also highly *insensitive* to Marcy's needs. Stu, in contrast, is a new man: a man who—in one episode—was shown performing cunnilingus on Marcy, and rhapsodizing about menstruation in another.

As porn testifies, cunnilingus can, of course, be performed roughly and without much concern for the women's pleasure—with a focus instead on providing voyeuristic titillation for an audience rather than the female character (a topic explored further in the Vibrator Chapter). Nevertheless, in mainstream narrative cinema, because portrayals are less explicit, the act is more likely to serve narrative purposes as opposed to exclusively voyeuristic ones; the act is designed to say things about the male character, about his relationship with women, and about a couple's relationship more broadly.

Cunnilingus prioritizes female pleasure and doesn't involve the penis. Thus when enacted it can soften the male character on screen: he cares about her, accepts her genitals, and is willing to prioritize her sexual needs; he's not selfish. This act demonstrates a man's acknowledgment of a woman's sexual needs, of her anatomy. Notably, it presents a recognition (1) that cunnilingus ranks high among women's favored heterosexual activities[36] and (2) that the female orgasm is more likely to come from nonpenetrative sex acts. Such a presentation can endear a male character to the audience and cast him as a man who *knows* women. In the film *Dr. T and the Women* (2000), for example, the title character (Richard Gere) was a gynecologist who was enormously popular with his female patients: in a very simple metaphor, Dr. T's *knowing* female genitals was portrayed as proof that he *knew* women. As applied to cunnilingus depictions, a male character who performs cunnilingus is presented as a man who *knows* women—who is, as Gagnon and Simon term, "erotically competent."[37] This is certainly an idea apparent in *Coming Home*. Following her orgasm, Sally says, "It never happened before." Sally is, of course, further drawn to Luke on the basis of his knowledge of her body and his awareness of what is needed to bring her sexual pleasure. Luke's knowledge in this regard is presented as a sharp contrast to the pleasureless sex Sally has experienced with her husband, and is portrayed as more than compensatory for his paralysis.

While the successes of second-wave feminism may have changed sexual relationships between men and women, they also created the capacity for women to *expect* that men be concerned with more than just their own pleasure. While cunnilingus, of course, may not actually transpire in every male-female bedroom scenario, second-wave feminism and sexual liberation have created a situation where cunnilingus is permanently on the agenda—whether actually participated in or not—and exists as a sexual option that the nice guy/generous lover is expected to engage in. A man quoted in psychologist Patrick Suraci's work on men and sex claimed, "I always perform oral sex because I feel it is one of my duties to please her."[38] Another man remarked similarly, "I perform oral sex even when I don't want to because I'm a gentleman and she doesn't have to worry that I'll say no."[39] Such quotes are demonstrative of men's internalization that cunnilingus is nowadays expected. With the internalization narrative in mind, cunnilingus scenes can also be used to convey women's sexual agency—if not their *dominance* in a scene—and, in turn, can demonstrate a male character's possible "pussy whipping."

While men catering to the sexual needs of their partners can be read as emasculating, this behavior can equally be interpreted as *empowering* for men: that more than just casting him as a sensitive New Age guy, a man's ability to sexually satisfy his partner makes him *more* masculine; that feminism and the sexual revolution have changed definitions of masculinity for the better; and that a man who is a good lover can be rewarded in modern society. In communications theorist Jody Pennington's discussion of the *Coming Home* cunnilingus scene, he made the point that in the film, "The ability to satisfy a lover sexually becomes metonymic for satisfying a lover in all ways."[40] Hellman (quoted earlier) also commented on the sharp contrast Luke provides with Sally's brutish husband. These ideas help demonstrate how the male has changed on screen and how, more broadly, definitions of masculinity have evolved: rather than assuming that feminism and the sexual revolution have emasculated men, instead they can be construed as having helped expand the definition. In short, being a good lover and wanting a partner satisfied can now be construed as virtuous pursuits.

While in this section I have contended that representations of a man performing cunnilingus can present him as a nice guy, it is important to acknowledge that niceness isn't always without an agenda: cunnilingus may, in fact, be performed for the specific intent of *reciprocity*.

QUID PRO QUO CUNNILINGUS

In a scene from the comedy *The Sweetest Thing* (2002), Christina (Cameron Diaz) has a fantasy about her dream boyfriend (Thomas Jane), who, after orally pleasuring her to orgasm, says, "If you don't mind I'd like to do that every hour on the hour for the rest of our lives. And don't worry about returning the favor. Men don't really like oral sex." This scene is humorous because the idea of a man purporting *not* to want anything in return for cunnilingus seems thoroughly farcical. Indeed, a more expected narrative is that a man performs oral sex because he wants reciprocation.

In research on cunnilingus undertaken by sociologist Laura Backstrom et al., the authors unearthed two particularly interesting findings: (1) that men assumed women like and want cunnilingus and (2) that both men and women "took for granted" that cunnilingus would occur in committed relationships.[41] While men may expect to perform cunnilingus purely on the basis of it being deemed important to women's sexual pleasure, the act may also be performed as a way for men to ensure that they are similarly attended to; in other words, they lick and suck so that a dynamic is created where they are licked and sucked in return. In sex researchers Laina Bay-Cheng and Nicole Fava's work on cunnilingus, the authors noted that when cunnilingus is portrayed in the mainstream media, it is frequently done to pave the way for the man's own pleasure, often via coitus or fellatio, in a quid pro quo sexual script.[42] This idea was alluded to in an episode of the sitcom *Scrubs* (2001–2010). In a conversation between J. D. (Zach Braff) and his colleague Jordan (Christa Miller), J. D. commented, "He's just mad because I didn't help him move," to which Jordan replied, "Well, you should have done it. Helping someone move is like oral sex; you do it once and they owe you for life." Here, the idea—while hyperbolic—is that cunnilingus is worth doing because it ensures future credit. Such a notion was presented much more explicitly in *The Sitter* (2011). In the opening scene, Noah (Jonah Hill) performed cunnilingus on Marisa (Ari Graynor) to orgasm, after which he hinted that she should return the favor. While Marisa blatantly refused, Noah's objective nonetheless was clear: his agenda was reciprocity. Marisa's refusal interestingly highlights another way cunnilingus can be portrayed on screen: to connote a power imbalance between two parties.

While appearing less formal than a quid pro quo exchange, more common on screen is cunnilingus presented as a precursor to intercourse; cunnilingus is what men do to get women in the mood for the sex they supposedly prefer—intercourse. This idea was alluded to in the same-sex cunnilingus scene in *The Good Wife* mentioned earlier: after Lana (Jill Flint) had performed oral sex on married Kalinda (Archie Panjabi), Kalinda claimed that she had to go home. Lana remarked, "You come here, and I feel like I'm warming you up for someone else." This idea of cunnilingus functioning as a *warm-up* is well illustrated on screen.

CUNNILINGUS AS FOREPLAY

As noted earlier, cunnilingus is very rarely presented as the main event of a sex scene; instead, it is generally relegated to a brief, preliminary role. Interestingly, his idea is documented in research on real-life sexual scripts: Hite, for example, noted that most men think of cunnilingus primarily as *foreplay*.[43] Considering the act this way raises a number of interesting topics for discussion.

The first is that the significance of the event is downplayed. Discussed throughout this chapter is the fact that cunnilingus is very infrequently presented on screen as a sex act in its own right. One explanation for this depiction is that it is widely considered as insufficient to constitute sex. When Bill Clinton claimed not to have had sexual relations with Monica Lewinsky, he raised the issue of whether oral sex is popularly construed as *real* sex. Whether Clinton actually believed in a distinction or merely seized on a possible technicality, the idea conveyed was that sex is generally assumed to involve a penis in a vagina and that other kinds of intimate contact aren't quite as serious. In Backstrom et al.'s research, the authors identified that women frequently *exclude* oral sex partners from their total number of sexual partners, only counting those with whom they had intercourse.[44] In a similar vein, a 14-year-old girl in theologian Jim Burns's research claimed, "Oral sex is not real sex. I would do it to preserve my virginity."[45] These ideas again allude to the possibility of screen presentations of cunnilingus mirroring real life: if oral sex is not considered to be real sex, then it stands to reason that it alone is not enough to constitute a completed sex act on screen.

Visitors to the Museum of New and Old Art in Tasmania, Australia, are supplied with a modified iPhone that contains information about the artworks as well as short pieces of commentary from authors, including the collector who established the museum, David Walsh. In one piece, Walsh told the story of compiling a list of his sexual partners: he noted that he only included the partners with whom he ejaculated. This same idea played out in an episode of *Californication* when Charlie—who was on a mission to have sex with 100 women—shouted out "100!" only *after* he ejaculated with the hundredth woman.

Walsh's and Charlie's penis-centric interpretation of sex is certainly relevant to this discussion: *of course* cunnilingus is rarely shown in sex scenes because it doesn't involve the ejaculation that apparently constitutes *completion*. In Bakos's work, she discussed this issue, noting that "Some men perform cunnilingus and delight in the sensations of a woman's vagina. Others do it because it gets the job done. They just want her to come so they can move on to what they really like, intercourse."[46] A woman quoted by Hite illustrated this same idea: "I still feel my partner is doing something that for him is a mere technical obstacle to deal with before going on to the 'main event.' "[47] Cunnilingus in such circumstances can be construed as nothing more than a means to an end.

In Light's discussion of pornography, he observed, "Often what cunnilingus we see has an obligatory feel, as if the actor were simply getting some unpleasant foreplay over with quickly."[48] Light's comments also have relevance to mainstream screen narratives as well as real life: as alluded by the woman who described cunnilingus as a "technical obstacle," cunnilingus can be read as simply what men endure on the road to "proper" sex. In an episode of the sitcom *Curb Your Enthusiasm* (2000–), Larry (Larry David) was asked whether he likes cunnilingus; his stilted response was, "You know, it's ... I'm a little ... I like it ... I like it ... But I'm a little too lazy to do it. It's a whole to-do. It hurts my neck." In another episode, he remarked that "there are only two ways to injure your neck: a car accident and cunnilingus." While hyperbolic, of course, these scenes allude to a popular idea that cunnilingus requires effort and perhaps even danger. In one episode, the "to-do" of cunnilingus was demonstrated when one of Larry's wife's pubic hairs became lodged in his throat after the previous night's cunnilingus: he coughed and made choking sounds throughout the episode.

The supposed difficulty factor is also identifiable in numerous other screen examples. In the opening scene of *Laurel Canyon* (2002), for example, Sam (Christian Bale) was shown performing cunnilingus on his partner Alex (Kate Beckinsale). Sam's efforts were not viewed by Alex as particularly successful. He checked with her to see if she wanted him to continue, she said she did, and she provided him with instructions. She then asked him to just fuck her. In a scene from the comedy *American Pie* (1999), Kevin (Thomas Ian Nicholas) had to read from instructions scrawled on a notepad to know how to perform oral sex on his girlfriend Vicky (Tara Reid). In a scene from *Ken Park* (2002), Rhonda (Maeve Quinlan) provided instruction to Shawn (James Bullard)—slower, keep licking, and so on—until she reached an orgasm. In a scene from *Somewhere* (2010), the protagonist Johnny (Stephen Dorff) actually *fell asleep* while performing cunnilingus. These scenes all portray cunnilingus as not only something difficult but often as grueling work with a pay-off that is not guaranteed. Worth noting in each of these scenes is that, rather than cunnilingus being presented as natural—as a sex act that both parties instinctively know how to do, the way intercourse is generally portrayed—it is presented as some kind of advanced technique.

Mentioned earlier was cunnilingus often performed with an agenda. While the agenda may be reciprocity, another compensation is the ego-boosting objective of a man being perceived as the consummate lover.

CUNNILINGUS AND THE DEMONSTRATION OF PROWESS

Cunnilingus exists on screen as a way for a man to demonstrate sexual prowess and to convey his willingness to do whatever it takes to please a woman: as noted by Gagnon and Simon earlier, cunnilingus can convey erotic competence. There are many interpretations as to why being perceived this way is important to a man. Being the consummate lover may, for example, enable him to reap further sexual encounters as well as bolster his esteem as a lover. As a man in Suraci's work claimed, "[S]exual prowess is unfortunately still linked to my self-concept."[49]

Discussed earlier were the scenes from *American Pie* and *Ken Park* where Vicky and Rhonda reached their orgasms based on the hard work of Kevin and Shawn. Both men were shown to be making substantial efforts; cunnilingus wasn't easy, but there was a pay-off for the boys in getting it right and being considered as good lovers. While such efforts link to the previous section—whereby cunnilingus can be connected to a man being portrayed as a nice guy—another interpretation is that such an act is part of a man's attempts at being construed as erotically competent. In Bay-Cheng and Fava's research, the authors noted that on the rare occasions when cunnilingus is presented in the mainstream media, it is often framed within the context of a man's attempt "to show off his own sexual prowess."[50] Women's real-life accounts of cunnilingus certainly allude to this idea. A woman in Hite's research for example, commented: "Men think they are really being hip and up front in the vanguard if they do it without your asking."[51] Men, interestingly, also allude to their own experience of an ego boost from participation. In anthropologist Sarah Chase's research, she quoted one boy, who, on discussing cunnilingus, commented, "I think it's amazing. A good time. A good time. Have a girl squirm all over the place because of you. Oh yeah!"[52] In this example, a boy's esteem was tied to the credit he felt in delivering her pleasure.

While cunnilingus virtuosity can denote erotic competency, it can also be used as a substitution or compensation for other areas where a man might be less skilled. *The Sitter*, for example, opened with Noah performing oral sex on Marisa. Noah was an overweight, nerdy-looking man: one interpretation of this scene is that oral sex was what Noah *had* to do to ingratiate himself with a woman positioned "out of his league."

While in *The Sitter*, cunnilingus substituted for aesthetic shortcomings, another way it can be presented is as compensation for a small penis. Sex researcher Bob Berkowitz claimed that "cunnilingus is the best thing you can do for a woman. It makes her feel sexy and loved. You may have the smallest penis on the planet, but if you do this well, you are a fabulous lover to her."[53] Small penis compensation is rarely portrayed explicitly on screen, but the idea does allude to a much more prevalent idea: that being a good lover has nothing to do with penis size and everything to do with oral sex prowess. This issue was explored in an episode of *Sex and the City*

(1998–2004) when Charlotte (Kristin Davis) was dating a renowned cunnilingus aficionado, Mitchell (Charlie Schroeder), whom Samantha (Kim Cattrall) dubbed "a legend. He's just amazing at eating pussy." Charlotte found Samantha's observations distasteful and alluded to perhaps "wanting more" than cunnilingus from a relationship. Samantha confidently asserted, "If a man is good at that, there is nothing more." A similar idea was apparent in *Coming Home*: paralyzed Luke's cunnilingus prowess was presented as more than compensatory for his physical shortcomings: Sally's husband Bob (Bruce Dern) had a fully functional penis, but sex with him was unpleasurable; Luke's penis was not functioning, yet he was able to satisfy Sally and notably give her her first orgasm.

In Gagnon and Simon's analysis of the varying meanings of cunnilingus in real life, the authors noted that sometimes it may be performed as "an avoidance of coitus."[54] This is something identifiable in the film *Boys Don't Cry* (1999): Brandon (Hilary Swank)—a biological woman posing as a man—performed very successful oral sex on Lana (Chloë Sevigny). Brandon was able to successfully satisfy Lana without his gender performance being exposed: the oral sex was so pleasurable that Lana had no reason to want his "penis." Just as Brandon couldn't perform intercourse without a penis, Luke in *Coming Home* and David in *Carne trémula* (*Live Flesh*) similarly couldn't perform because of disability: cunnilingus in these films was a way to compensate for, substitute, and deflect their inability to engage in penile penetration while adequately satisfying their lovers.

Discussed throughout this chapter has been the lack of frequency of oral sex and duration. Such ideas allude to male reluctance to participate, a narrative idea evident extensively on screen.

CUNNILINGUS AND MALE RELUCTANCE

Discussed earlier was the scene from *The Sweetest Thing* when Christina's dream boyfriend wanted to perform cunnilingus on her every hour for the rest of her life. The presentation was funny because it was so ridiculous; screen narratives are far more inclined to present cunnilingus as something men are *reluctant* to do.

In the comedy *Hall Pass* (2011), the concept of "fake chow" was defined by Fred (Jason Sudeikis): "when you're going south on them and you don't want to use your tongue, so you just use your fingers and smack your lips real loud." In this scene, Fred mentioned a time when his wife realized he was giving her fake chow; in a later scene Fred fake chowed Aunt Meg (Kristin Carey). The concept of fake chow presents a number of interesting themes. That a man might feel a need to *fake* cunnilingus presents an acknowledgment that a significant number of women expect oral sex; men, for their part, now know this but are sometimes reluctant to corroborate. This idea certainly correlates with existing research: perhaps unsurprisingly, apparently most men would prefer to *receive* oral sex rather than give it.[55] Certainly comments made by men and boys about cunnilingus in real life demonstrate this reluctance. Discussed earlier was a man quoted in Suraci's work who claimed that he performs oral sex even when he doesn't want to. In Chase's research, one boy commented, "I hate it. I don't like that shit."[56] The absence of cunnilingus on screen could therefore be interpreted as referencing men's real-life reluctance to participate.

Such reluctance may explain why cunnilingus is infrequently portrayed on screen. Understanding the *why* of this reluctance however, highlights some of the politics. Something I discussed throughout *Periods in Pop Culture*—and something often at the root of many misogynist jokes—is the negativity surrounding the smell, look, and taste of women's genitals, negative sentiments internalized by both men *and* women. In Hite's research, she quoted a number of women who mentioned their own perceptions of genital odor: "I haven't gotten away from the feeling I'm 'dirty' down there"; "I never had orgasm during cunnilingus. I hope to soon but I still feel my cunt is dirty and this preoccupies me if anyone attempts it with me"; and "I am *always* self-conscious that I might smell or look disgusting."[57] Men in Hite's research make similar references to the supposed smell: "I haven't done cunnilingus much, but it tastes kind of bitter, smells like bad breath, and looks red, wrinkly, and wet"[58] and "What I dislike is that some women have an offensive—well, not really offensive but strange—smell, I'm still trying to get used to it."[59]

Just as some women have internalized negative thoughts about their genitals, men also seemingly sometimes harbor—or at least purport to harbor—negative views about women's genitals: oral contact with something considered so repellent is unappealing. While I extensively addressed men's negativity around women's bleeding genitals—in real life and on screen—in my research on menstruation,[60] a good example of general negativity premised on women's genitals was apparent in the comedy *Superbad* (2007). In one scene, teenager Seth (Jonah Hill) asked his friend Evan (Michael Cera), "Have you ever seen a vagina by itself?" Seth then made a disgusted face, shook his head, and said, "Not for me."

While there are, of course, examples of men finding cunnilingus abhorrent, conversely—but admittedly rare—there are also male characters who in fact *champion* it. In an episode of *Curb Your Enthusiasm*, for example,

Krazee-Eyez Killa (Chris Williams) commented, "I have to eat the pussy ... You have to have all different flavors of pussy." Krazee-Eyez Killa *loves* cunnilingus. So much in fact, that eventually he was exposed for cheating on his fiancée (Wanda Sykes) by performing cunnilingus on other women.

While cunnilingus is not a common inclusion on screen, as Krazee-Eyez demonstrated, some men do enjoy it, a situation reflecting reality. Noted earlier was the boy quoted in Chase's study who enjoyed making women squirm.[61] Hite similarly identified that most men in her research identified *enjoying* cunnilingus.[62] If this is the truth, the absence of this behavior from screen may be connected to the perception of what a love of oral sex might say about a man.

CUNNILINGUS AND EMASCULATION

In Laumann et al.'s research on cunnilingus, the authors wrote: "Oral sex is fraught with symbolic ambiguity. Should 'good' women do it? What kind of man would do it?"[63] For this section I am interested in the second question and whether there is a certain *type* of man who performs cunnilingus. In Chase's research, she explored boys' views on cunnilingus and one provided an interesting possible answer to Laumann's question: "If you give oral sex, you're fuckin' queer."[64] This notion of cunnilingus being associated with homosexuality—or at the very least with the loss of *masculinity*—is a very popular idea. Discussed at the beginning of this chapter was the poet Martial's observations that cunnilingus made men passive and turned them into cunts. In Gagnon and Simon's comments, the authors noted that one interpretation of cunnilingus is that it serves as "a measure of degradation of self or other."[65] This idea certainly has traction both on screen and in academic research.

In the episode of *The Sopranos* mentioned earlier, Junior's talent for performing oral sex was discovered. The topic was later discussed between Junior's nephew Tony and Tony's wife Carmela:

Carmela: Let's just say your uncle has acquired quite a *taste* for her.
Tony: Uncle Jun gives head?
Carmela: World class.
Tony: The old man's whistling through the wheat field?
Carmela: Don't be disgusting!
Tony: Oh, he's a Bushman of the Kalahari! [Laughs]

Carmela: [Laughs] That's why I don't tell you anything 'cause you don't know when to stop!

Tony: Oh my God, if this ever gets out.

Tony, of course, couldn't resist mentioning his knowledge to his uncle. When Junior said he didn't "go down enough" (meaning to Florida), Tony jeered, "That's not what I heard." Junior was appalled when he discovered that his girlfriend had divulged his "real instinct" for oral sex. In their social circle, a man who performed cunnilingus was perceived as weak; doing so was considered subordinating, humiliating, and degrading. The same theme was also apparent in a scene from the polygamy-themed series *Big Love* (2006–2011): after Nicolette (Chloë Sevigny) eyed her sister-wife Margene (Ginnifer Goodwin) receiving oral sex from their husband, Nicolette accused Margene of "emasculating" him.

There are many elements to Junior's and Nicolette's concern, the first being that cunnilingus renders a penis as unnecessary to a woman's sexual pleasure. This, in essence, means that maleness—in the anatomical sense—is unnecessary. For a man who attaches a strong sense of self to his penis and his perceived ability to pleasure a woman with it, removing the penis from the equation and showing a woman able to experience pleasure without it is potentially confronting, if not threatening (this idea is expanded on in the Vibrator Chapter). A woman in Hite's research, in fact, used this idea to explain why cunnilingus was something that she and her husband only rarely participated in: "If I have an orgasm by cunnilingus it negates the power of his penis. He feels like a pseudo woman, a crippled man perhaps."[66]

Another aspect of the emasculating connotations of cunnilingus is the idea that being concerned with a woman's pleasure is emasculating, that sexually *serving* a woman is somehow belittling. Discussed earlier was the idea that men who participate in cunnilingus are often construed as nice guys—*nice* being a quality open to interpretation as potentially euphemistic for being a pushover or weak-willed. In *Periods in Pop Culture*, I discussed the absence of menstruation on screen, suggesting that its omission may be explained by the possibility that its presence would introduce too much politics into a scene.[67] A similar interpretation may be applied to the absence of cunnilingus: if cunnilingus is portrayed, a man may accidentally be construed as a nice guy or a sensitive lover; niceness and sensitivity may not be attributes that a filmmaker wants associated with a particular character; the filmmaker might not want the man to appear too fond of women or too interested in pleasuring them. Connected to this issue is the possible avoidance of intimacy on screen. In sex therapist Ian Kerner's book on sexuality, he contended, "[C]unnilingus, with its elimination of distance and its unavoidable intimacy, is often a lightning rod for unleashing anxiety."[68] On screen, cunnilingus invariably connotes intimacy—after all, it is not the kind of sex act that strangers would generally engage in[69]—and thus may be avoided except in those circumstances where filmmakers actually *want* to convey intimacy. Also addressed in *Periods in Pop Culture* was the idea that our culture seems to reward men who demonstrate little knowledge about women's bodies; knowing too much about women potentially casts them as creepy. Avoiding such perceptions may explain why cunnilingus is eschewed—to avoid a male character appearing too aligned to femaleness.

Another way that emasculation is conveyed is through the presumption that in cunnilingus a man is taking on a *woman's role*: that it is the woman who should get down on her knees and service her man. For a man to do so, therefore, casts him as a cunt and as *woman-like*. Discussed earlier was the opening scene of *Laurel Canyon* where Sam performed cunnilingus on his partner Alex: she issued directions and then instructed him to fuck her; as soon as she orgasmed, he stopped, foregoing his climax. This sex scene was used to illustrate an obvious power disparity between the characters; opening the film in this way cast Alex as the dominant character in the relationship and presented Sam as functioning primarily to tend to her needs. Something similar transpired in *Two Girls and a Guy* (1997): in one scene Carla (Heather Graham) was shown in an intimate scene with Blake (Robert Downey, Jr.). While there was much kissing—and Carla was shown to manually stimulate Blake—the main focus was on him performing oral sex on her to orgasm. As soon as she orgasmed, Carla adjusted her clothes and left the room, leaving Blake unsatisfied. In *The Sitter*, after Noah performed cunnilingus on Marisa to orgasm, he tried to convince her to return the favor; she refused. Clearly Marisa was calling the shots; her pleasure was not only prioritized, but left no room for his. The behavior of the women in *Laurel Canyon*, *Two Girls and a Guy*, and *The Sitter* seems so strange—and casts the female character as so very brazen—because the idea of a woman receiving pleasure disconnected from any quid pro quo sexual script is unusual,[70] reminding us of the extent to which male pleasure is prioritized on screen.

The inclusion of cunnilingus in a narrative can convey a multitude of meanings, ranging from intimacy, to male sensitivity, to female empowerment, to male subordination. Equally, its absence is highly revealing about the state of contemporary sexual politics and still-fervent sexual and bodily anxieties.

The Flatulence Chapter: Exploring Matters of the Fart

In a scene from *Blazing Saddles* (1974), following a cookout meal of beans, the cowboys sat around the fire farting. This scene was one of American cinema's first flatulence scenes: farting was presented as something funny, in turn establishing a tone for future flatulence portrayals. This chapter explores the how and the why of the humor of farts, as well as some of their less funny and more surprising appearances in popular culture where the gesture is less about humor and more so about intimacy if not also *sexiness*.

THE FART: A STAPLE TABOO

When a fart is smelt or heard, it exists as a reminder of the most intimate functions of a body, functions that are routinely considered disgusting. Just as all bodily excretions—urine, blood, saliva, and semen—have degrees of taboo attached, farts are widely considered as a bodily process that should remain private. Farts are considered to smell bad and to function as an allusion to perhaps *the* most taboo excretion: feces. Jim Dawson discussed this in his book *Who Cut the Cheese?*: "Our taboo against farting is part of our taboo against shit. Everything we eat turns to shit or internal gas, yet we act as if turds and farts don't exist."[1]

While farts might be considered a taboo, like many of the not-in-polite-company bodily topics examined in this book, they are easily detected in popular culture. In the blurb of Stephen Bryant's book *Art of the Fart*, it was noted that the fart "is taboo in polite society, but has a wide appreciation nonetheless."[2] This appreciation is grounded in the fact that despite their inappropriateness, farts *can* be funny: they disrupt silence, sound strange, smell bad, and frequently unsettle, perturb, and even offend. Placing characters in unusual circumstances or having them do—or witness—unusual things is often at the heart of comedy. In an episode of the sitcom *Veronica's Closet* (1997–2000), for example, Veronica (Kirstie Alley) dated a man with a flatulence problem. His persistent farting created an unusual situation that Veronica and her colleagues were forced to respond to; comedy thus ensued. For certain genres of comedy—the sophomoric humor discussed in the next section is a good example—the humor stems from circumstances being not merely unusual but also grotesque; the humor comes from the madcap, exaggerated, and frequently disgusting scenarios that are effortlessly detected in mass-market comedy.

At the beginning of the film *Tropic Thunder* (2008), for example, there were a number of fake film trailers; one was for *The Fatties: Fart 2*. Drawing heavily from the dinner-table farting scene from *The Nutty Professor* (1996), the *Fatties: Fart 2* trailer showed an obese family sitting around the dinner table, each taking turns to fart. The trailer mocked a type of comedy that is incredibly well established in American popular culture: grotesque humor centered on bodily foibles. The trailer mocked the easy laughs solicited from the taboo while spotlighting that very few elements are needed in mainstream American comedy to prompt laughter; farts apparently can be sufficiently humorous on their own.

While *Blazing Saddles* is an early example of farting on screen, farting in popular culture has a much longer lineage. Dawson, for example, noted, "To the ancient Greeks, our Western cultural ancestors, farting was low comedy, but comedy nonetheless."[3] While fart jokes are present in the works of literary luminaries such as Aristophanes, Dante, Chaucer, and Shakespeare, then, just as today, such jokes were considered crass—funny, perhaps, but crass. The idea of the fart joke being low humor is identified in much existing academic work on farting. Dawson noted, "Flatulence remained a highly regarded source of humor throughout most of European history, *especially among the lower classes*."[4] Literature scholar Valerie Allen similarly wrote, "Medieval farts bear the same burden of anxiety, *low humor*, and indifferent necessity that they do today."[5] The strong association between fart jokes and low humor continues in contemporary examples.

FARTING AND THE CRASS

Farting is a taboo because it is considered both disgusting and impolite. Our culture dictates that it is rude to subject others to your gastric gases;

to do so positions a person as uncouth. In this section two ideas are discussed as related to the concept of the uncouth: (1) that fart jokes tend to feature in a certain *kind* of low humor genre, notably sophomoric comedies, and (2) that on screen, farting can be a shorthand way to present a character as repellant.

The Fart Joke Canon

In Judd Apatow's comedy *Funny People* (2009), after watching Ira's (Seth Rogen) stand-up act, his friend George (Adam Sandler) approached him:

> Can I ask you something? Is your act just designed to make sure no girl will ever sleep with you again? All you fucking talk about is jacking off and farting. You think a girl's gonna come up to you after the show, "Oh, oh would you just jack off for me and then fart in my face?" That's fucking insane! Do you want to get laid, ever?

George's comment—much like the aforementioned *The Fatties: Fart 2* trailer—mocks the preoccupation with fart jokes in American comedy. Routinely mocked perhaps, but Ira performs fart jokes because *he* finds them funny and because he is aware that there is an audience for them. In a scene from *Chasing Amy* (1997), comic book artist Holden (Ben Affleck) commented, "It all goes back to something my grandmother told me when I was a kid. 'Holden,' she said, 'the big bucks are in dick and fart jokes.'" *Chasing Amy* was directed by Kevin Smith—who also directed *Jay and Silent Bob Strike Back* (2001), discussed later in this chapter—and whose work has been described as primarily consisting of "dick and fart jokes."[6] That the *big bucks* lie in this type of humor—regardless of how crass such jokes may seem—is a truism; sophomoric comedies are frequently box-office successes. This is something Apatow appears to understand well. In his *Knocked Up* (2007), for example, it was discovered that three of the characters—Jonah (Jonah Hill), Jason (Jason Segel), and Jay (Jay Baruchel)—had contracted pink-eye through farting pranks:

Jay: Um, I farted on Jason's pillow as a practical joke. He farted on Jonah's, thinking it was mine, and then eventually pink-eyed my pillow. I'm not proud of any of this, but I think we've all forgiven each other. Um, but we can't go anywhere.

Film theorist Robert Kolker has described Apatow's films as "self-conscious, ironic, and in poor taste."[7] In *Weed: 420 Things You Didn't*

Know (or Remember) about Cannabis, it was claimed that Apatow's work "appeals deeply to the stoner sensibility."[8] *Sophomoric* is a useful way to describe films of the Smith and Apatow ilk: they are defined by immaturity and, most relevant for this chapter, create an environment where fart jokes sit comfortably amongst other grotesquery staples such as burps, dick jokes, and hijinks-plagued attempts at seduction. In a restaurant scene in *Caddyshack* (1980)—an early example of this genre and one described repeatedly by commentators as sophomoric[9]—Al (Rodney Dangerfield) made funnily derogatory comments about the food. He then leaned to his side, farted, and asked, "Did somebody step on a duck?" In the more recent example *Scary Movie 3* (2003), Cindy (Anna Farris) visited psychic Aunt ShaNeequa (Queen Latifah). When Cindy sat down in a chair, a fart noise was heard; she attributed the noise to the chair. Aunt ShaNeequa then sat down and a number of longer, noisier farts were heard; Aunt ShaNeequa responded, "Yes, the chair." Such comedies rely on noncomplicated slapstick of which farts are well suited.

Communications scholar Stephen Bloom contended that "[f]or a host of complex cultural reasons, farts render 10-year-old boys silly."[10] While it might be assumed that boys find the grotesquery of farts funnier than girls do, farts actually have a broad audience. In his discussion of the conversations of eight-year-old girls, psychologist Timothy Jay noted: "Many of the [girls'] stories and jokes contained taboo words. In fact some of the humor relied mainly on the use of a particular word such as *turd* or *fart*, as if, no matter what the storyline was, the word once pronounced was enough to evoke a laugh."[11]

Given the commercial success of fart-themed films such as *Thunderpants* (2002), as well as Jo Nesbø's books about Doctor Proctor's Fart Powder and the William Kotzwinkle, Glenn Murray, and Elizabeth Gundy books about Walter the farting dog, evidently children of *both sexes* find farts funny.

Part of the funniness of toilet humor is that it transgresses social boundaries: when the fart taboo is breached, strong and entertaining reactions can ensue. While often the intention of the fart is to solicit laughter, sometimes the fart can function in other guises—for example, as an act of aggression. Two other explanations I propose for the appeal of toilet humor lie in nostalgia and the vicarious. The word *sophomoric* refers to humor associated with young people; often, for example, it is synonymous with immaturity. It should, therefore, come as no surprise that the material is found funny by the youth audience that it is intended for; it is sophomoric because it is *intended* to be so. For older audiences, the humor might be amusing because it facilitates a kind of sophomoric nostalgia: it reminds audiences of the good and funny times of their youth, of a past when being socially appropriate was less important.

Another explanation for the appeal of such humor is the vicarious access provided to transgressive behavior. Through such comedy, audiences get to experience what it would be like to be inappropriate and socially disruptive without actually having to incur any of the ramifications. During a dream sequence from comedy *Dumb and Dumber* (1994), for example, Lloyd (Jim Carrey) set fire to his fart and received riotous applause. During a talent show scene in *Wet Hot American Summer* (2001), Bert's (Jacob Shoesmith-Fox) act consisted of him rolling onto his back and lighting up one of this farts. While the lighting of a fart might be something that adults are curious about—and something that science-themed television programs such as *Mythbusters* (2003–) have explored—the danger that can result means that pleasure for audiences is more easily experienced *vicariously*. By watching sophomoric presentations such as fart fires, audiences can vicariously experience fart-centered hijinks without incurring injury or being branded as immature.

Farting is also frequently used on screen as a shorthand way to frame a character as unrefined. If a character is farting openly, the act often casts a character as being without human decency.

Farting and the Uncouth

In sociologists Gale Largey and Rod Watson's research on odor, they contended that "anyone who "lets go a fart" in public is usually considered somewhat crass and undisciplined."[12] In Don Nibbelink's book *Fearsome Folklore of Farting*, he similarly identified that "Throughout classic literature, the farting role has been traditionally assigned to the villain, the rogue, the criminal, the old crony, the bully, and the Devil himself."[13]

While farting might be more common in popular culture today than it was in classic literature—and thus is no longer exclusively associated with villainous characters—Largey and Watson's and Nibbelink's connection of farts with crass characters is a trend that continues. In an episode of sitcom *30 Rock* (2006–2013), Jack (Alec Baldwin) remarked to his employee Liz (Tina Fey): "Lemon, isn't there a Slanket somewhere you should be filling with your farts?" The humor in this scene stems from Liz being presented as a somewhat slovenly character; that Jack would assume that she would (1) own a Slanket and, even worse, (2) fart into one helps to convey his views on her lack of refinement. In a recurring sketch from the comedy show *In Living Color* (1990–1994), Damon Wayans played Anton Jackson, a homeless man who regularly found himself in unusual, fish-out-of-water situations. Anton's uncouthness was bolstered by his flatulence—something showcased when he was shown farting while attending a society dinner as the guest of honor. Anton's farts were a way to demonstrate his difference from other people and to convey his complete lack of social grace. In a scene from *Ghost World* (2001), Seymour (Steve Buscemi) recounted his romantic woes to his slobby housemate Joe (Tom McGowan). Joe listened and then dispassionately offered, "Maybe she got another boyfriend?" and then let out a fart. As in the *In Living Color* scene, Joe's fart was shorthand for presenting himself as comparatively unkempt and undesirable. The same thing transpired in *Dances with Wolves* (1990): Lieutenant Dunbar (Kevin Costner) was quietly sketching in his notebook by the campfire when the evening silence was broken when his companion, Timmons (Robert Pastorelli), bent over and farted and suggested, "Put that in your book!" In Lieutenant Dunbar's narration, he described Timmons as "quite possibly the foulest man I have ever met."

While farts in each of these examples rendered men uncouth, the idea of the fart serving as a character indictment is made even more apparent when *women* fart. In such cases, women are not merely rendered unrefined but are presented as dramatically less attractive.

SCHADENFREUDE AND THE HUMAN CONDITION

In an April Fool's Day-themed episode of cartoon *Hey Arnold* (1996–2004), Helga asked her schoolmate Arnold to pick up her pencil. As he did, Helga pushed a button and a loud farting noise was heard. Everyone laughed and pointed at Arnold. In an episode of sitcom *Ned's Declassified School Survival Guide* (2004–2007), Ned (Devon Werkheiser) accidentally farted in class; he was laughed at and got the nickname "Farticus." In an episode of the sitcom *Roseanne* (1988–1997), oldest daughter Becky (Alicia Goranson) accidentally farted while giving a report to her student council. While youngest daughter Darlene (Sara Gilbert) and their parents found this all very funny, Becky considered the incident as social suicide, explaining: "I'm quitting pep squad, I'm quitting school, I'm never going back again, and if anyone calls me, tell them I'm dead." Being situated in sitcoms, of course, Arnold's faux fart and Ned's and Becky's real farts were supposed to be funny. While the noise and smell obviously made such farts amusing, two other reasons explain audience entertainment: (1) the humor found in human foibles and (2) schadenfreude.

In his book on Italian comedy, literature scholar Rudolph Altrocchi asked, "What is more entertaining than stories of human foibles?"[14] Humor, in fact, frequently revolves around such foibles, notably those that, while less than desirable, are nevertheless universally experienced. Just as audiences find humor in unappealing attributes, humor can also be found in undesirable situations: characters tripping down stairs or slipping on banana peels, for example. Arnold's, Ned's, and Becky's farts were funny primarily because audiences understood the characters' humiliation—could empathize with it—but also felt relief that it was them and not us.

Taking this idea a step further is funniness found in characters' misfortunes. *Schadenfreude* is a German word coming from the union of *schaden*, meaning "damage," and *freude*, meaning "joy"; it is defined as taking pleasure in the misfortunes of others.[15] One explanation for the humor of Becky farting in front of her school council is the amusement audiences found in her humiliation. While Arnold, Ned, and Becky were not characters whose comeuppance audiences necessarily craved, nevertheless the schadenfreude within the narrative can serve to entertain.[16] This was something well illustrated in the *Roseanne* episode: Becky's youngest sister Darlene was thoroughly *delighted* by her sister's downfall, so much so that her parents had to confine her to the bathroom so that she stopped vocally reveling. (Schadenfreude is a topic discussed further in the Vibrator Chapter.)

FARTS AS AGGRESSION

In my book *Part-Time Perverts: Sex, Pop Culture, and Kink Management*, I discussed a variety of scenes from television whereby urination was presented as an act of aggression:

> In an episode of series two of *Top Chef* [2006], the contestant Ilan [Hall] comments, "I would have loved to pee on Marcel." In one episode of *House* (2004–2012), Dr. House [Hugh Laurie] threatens, "I have a full bladder and I'm not afraid to use it" and in another, one of House's subordinates, Dr. Kutner (Kal Penn), urinates on House's chair. In an episode of *Big Love* [2006–2011], Rhonda (Daveigh Chase) urinates over a toilet seat in anger. Ilan and House's angry comments and Kutner and Rhonda's angry actions aptly demonstrate not only popular disgust about urine but show how it can be used as a tool of warfare.[17]

Urine in these scenes functioned as a *tool of warfare* because it is a taboo bodily waste product; placing it near someone else against their will is disgusting and can be construed as an act of aggression. Farts can be deployed in a similar manner: as historian Geoffrey Hughes noted, farts have long been a "symbolic and idiomatic form of insult."[18] Psychologists George Bach and Herb Goldberg made a similar claim: "While the fart may simply be a symptom of internal gas, it may at other times also be an indicator of a repressed aggressive feeling."[19]

In a scene from *Donnie Darko* (2001), Donnie (Jake Gyllenhaal) threatened his sister (Daveigh Chase), "When you fall asleep tonight, I'm gonna fart in your face." In *Monty Python and the Holy Grail* (1975), John Cleese, as a French soldier, shouted at a group of knights: "I fart in your general direction." In a scene from *The Simpsons* (1989–), Homer was paralyzed after being bitten by a spider. Homer's daughter, Lisa, decided to "entertain" him by reading to him from Fyodor Dostoyevsky's *The Brothers Karamazov*. As Lisa read, the audience could hear Homer's internal dialogue: "Oh my God she's still on the first sentence. Must make her stop. How to express my—" Homer then farted. Lisa continued to read and Homer farted again. In *Jay and Silent Bob Strike Back*, after Jay (Jason Mewes) was apprehended by a police officer, he farted in the officer's face. In *Click* (2006), Michael (Adam Sandler)—after using his magical remote control to pause time—farted repeatedly in the face of his overbearing boss Ammer (David Hasselhoff). In *Find Me Guilty* (2006), Jackie (Vin Diesel) was handcuffed in the back of a police car. When Jackie asked for the window to be opened, he was told it was too hot. He farted and the windows were opened. Taken a step further, in *Mystery Men* (1999) the character Spleen's (Paul Reubens) superpower was his toxic farts. The same idea was used in *Zoom* (2006), with one superhero, Jupiter (Rashad Richards), describing himself as "the Gas Giant."

In each of these examples, farts were used to assault. One of the reasons that farts are so readily deployed in comedy is because while they may be taboo, they are also ultimately harmless. Had Homer used a *real* weapon to quiet his daughter, it would have been considered egregious; had Jay or Jackie attempted to hurt police with anything *other* than a fart—or had Michael done anything more violent to his frozen boss—these scenes wouldn't have been funny. Because of the harmlessness of the fart, the true offense is the disgust, the grotesqueness, and notably the impropriety, which in comedy is easily excusable, if not hilarious.

FARTING AND IMPROPRIETY

In his discussion of the farting scene from *Blazing Saddles*, literature scholar Maurice Charney claimed that the humor "stems from its taboo-busting vulgarity rather than from making fun of the convention itself."[20] While farts—as already noted in this chapter—can be funny of their own accord because they smell bad and involve strange noises, they are notably entertaining because they convey impropriety; their taboo nature means that when inserted into a scene, they are disruptive, rude, out of place, and thus often hilarious. In *Step Brothers* (2008), step-brothers Brennan (Will Ferrell) and Dale (John C. Reilly) attended a job interview together. Both wore tuxedos—already demonstrating a lack of respect for the process—and after they were both offered the job, each farted repeatedly. Their job offers were promptly retracted. While the sound and impropriety of the farts were funny, humor was also derived from something private being relocated into the public sphere and disrupting a serious situation.

While the taboo nature of farts can be used as a way to demonstrate impropriety, their silence-breaking properties can also be used as a way to diffuse tension. Discussed earlier was the scene from *Dances with Wolves*: Timmons's fart was his attempt to lighten the scene and to get a rise out of Lieutenant Dunbar. In *The Master* (2012), the technique was similarly used in a scene when Freddie (Joaquin Phoenix) was being "processed" by cult leader Lancaster (Philip Seymour Hoffman): Freddie farted both out of immaturity and to convey his character's inability to show self-restraint. This same idea was apparent in a scene from the sitcom *Two and a Half Men* (2003–): Jake (Angus T. Jones) and his father Alan (Jon Cryer) were in the car; Jake clearly didn't want to be there and his father was trying to coax him into conversation:

Alan: We're two men on the open road. Free and unencumbered.
Jake: Oh. What's unencumbered?
Alan: No restraints. We can do whatever we want.
Jake: Okay. I want to drive.
Alan: Later. Pick something else.
Jake: (Farts)

Jake and Alan then had a farting competition; tension was replaced with comic relief.

As discussed in all of the scenes thus far, on-screen farting is something *men* do. In the next section the issue of farting and gender is explored.

GENDER AND FARTING

The premise of *White Chicks* (2004) involved two black male FBI agents—Kevin (Shawn Wayans) and Marcus (Marlon Wayans)—working undercover as white women. In one scene, quiche had a bad effect on Marcus-as-Tiffany, so the character went into the toilet, accompanied by a group of new female acquaintances. In the cubicle, much farting was heard. The inference was that the toilet noises were an essential aspect of his *masculinity*—that female attire and make-up failed to conceal Marcus's true gender. While Marcus's identity was not actually exposed in this scene, the reactions of the women listening implied that the behavior was considered as highly unusual for a woman. This scene helps to introduce the idea that farting is generally presented on screen as a *male* activity; for a woman to fart is strange and uncouth and certainly *unfeminine*. This idea is identifiable in a number of examples. In an episode of the cartoon *Rugrats: All Grown Up* (2003–2008), for example, the following exchange occurred between twins Lil and Phil:

Lil: Eew! Phil farted!
Phil: I did not! *You* did!
Lil: Did not! It's biologically impossible for girls to fart.

In *Carpool* (1996), the following conversation transpired between carpoolers Franklin (Tom Arnold), Daniel (David Paymer), and Kayla (Rachael Leigh Cook):

Franklin: Hey who farted? Did you cut the cheese, Dan?
Daniel: For God's sake, no, I did not.
Franklin: How about you, Kayla?
Kayla: Girls don't fart.

These two examples highlight a popular culture truism: women don't fart. While of course *everybody* farts, on-screen farting is invariably something associated with men. In this section I examine the issue of farting and gender, notably through the exploration of (1) what happens when women do fart on screen and (2) the stereotype of the straight woman pitted against the farting man.

Femininity and Attractiveness

In a scene from *Sex and the City* (1998–2004), Carrie (Sarah Jessica Parker) was in bed with Mr. Big (Chris Noth) when she let out a small fart. She was mortified, and quickly rushed out of his apartment claiming that she was "late for a thing." While Carrie felt humiliated, Mr. Big appeared

The Flatulence Chapter

unperturbed. This was actually a highly unusual scene: more often than not, if a woman's fart is heard, a man's attraction to her diminishes. In *The Heartbreak Kid* (2007), for example, Eddie (Ben Stiller) was in bed with his new wife Lila (Malin Ackerman) on their honeymoon. At one point, Lila left the bed and Eddie asked her where she was going; she said to "pee pee." From the bed, Eddie could hear farting noises from the en suite bathroom:

Lila: That wasn't what you think it was!
Eddie: What? I didn't hear anything.
Lila: Oh, good. 'Cause I just queefed, big-time.

While Lila's bathroom noises seemingly served as an early sign to Eddie that he perhaps *didn't* marry the right woman, Eddie didn't actually appear quite as revolted as men are in similar scenes. In *Harold & Kumar Go to White Castle* (2004), for example, Harold (John Cho) and Kumar (Kal Penn) snuck into a women's restroom. The boys hid in a stall and two attractive twins entered. Sisters Christy (Kate Kelton) and Clarissa (Brooke D'Orsay) discussed their breasts in front of the mirror—the boys watched in rapture, clearly pleased to have been granted access to the women's inner sanctum—and then one sister mentioned that she had the "taco shits." The two women entered stalls on either side of the boys; farting noises were heard, followed by diarrhea. Harold and Kumar were *horrified*.

In a scene from *Not Another Teen Movie* (2001), Mitch (Cody McMains), Ox (Sam Huntington), and Bruce (Samm Levine) were hiding in a ceiling vent. At one point they were above the female toilets when an attractive young woman entered a toilet cubicle and sat down. As the girl pulled down her underwear, the sounds of her urination were heard. The boys looked on and Bruce commented, "This make me kind of happy in pants." The girl then started farting; Bruce looked mortified and said, "That make me kind of sad in pants."

In *Extreme Movie* (2008), in one scene, Lindsey (Shasa Dabner) and David (Byron Cotton) were kissing and she let out a small fart. Like Carrie in *Sex and the City*, she appeared instantly embarrassed:

David: Lindsey, relax. Everybody farts. This is huge. We've crossed the Fart Barrier.
Lindsey: Really?
David: (Farts) See? It's nothin'!
Lindsey: I do feel comfortable with you.

Lindsey then proceeded to fart continuously, to which David progressively looked more and more revolted, eventually responding, "Now, that's just nasty."

In these three examples, once they farted, attractive women were suddenly deemed dramatically less so. As discussed throughout this chapter, farting is something often considered rude and uncouth—attributes that women generally don't want to be associated with and that, men generally find unattractive.

While Nibbelink, quoted earlier, noted that the farting role is often assigned to characters including the old *crony*, in fact, it is also sometimes presented as a trait associated with the old *crone*. In *The Second Sex*, feminist philosopher Simone de Beauvoir wrote about how the older woman—once revered in society—is nowadays held in much lower esteem: "From the day a woman consents to growing old, her situation changes. Up to that time she was still a young woman...now she becomes a different being, unsexed but complete: an old woman."[21] Farting can be a way to contribute to this unsexing. The film *10* (1979) provides a good example of this: the very advanced age, as well as the feebleness, of a housekeeper (Nedra Volz) was demonstrated well with her shaking, clumsiness and, notably, her farting.

In my book on infidelity, *Cheating on the Sisterhood: Infidelity and Feminism*, I summarized the attributes of "good women" as identified in research on gendered traits: "she must be stable, emotionally secure, kind, forbearing, supportive, contented, giving, feminine, beautiful, pure, chaste, noble, self-sacrificing, self-abnegating, self-restraining, and self-denying."[22] While feminine, beautiful, pure, and self-denying are all traits that could underpin why women generally *don't* fart in most screen narratives, forbearance is a notable explanation for the way women are generally depicted in the context of on-screen farts: women are frequently shown to *forbear* the farts of their menfolk.

Women and Farting Forbearance

In a scene from the cartoon *Family Guy* (1999–), Meg and her father Peter were in the car. Meg asked her father why they were just sitting there and Peter asked her to give him a minute. There was silence, Peter then sighed in relief, and Meg exclaimed, "Oh my God, Dad, you farted. That is so nasty!" Meg tried to escape from the car but Peter held onto her and explained, "The sexiest thing a woman can do for a man is learn to love his gas. Love the gas, Meg, *love it*!" While women, of course, likely don't ever grow to *love* the farts of their menfolk, evidently they do learn to put up with them, as evidenced in a number of screen examples.

The film *Year One* (2009) was about two prehistoric hunter-gatherers. In one scene a caveman, Seth (Gabriel Sunday), was shown lying next to a woman. He was farting and finding it hilarious, saying "Little surprise on the end of that one, right?" The woman next to him lay still, appearing thoroughly unimpressed. This scene also emphasizes the supposed very long history of women forbearing such behavior. In *Over Her Body* (2008), Paul Rudd (Henry) checked into a hotel with his new partner Ashley (Lake Bell). Ashley headed to the bathroom and Paul, seemingly, started to fart. Ashley watched him do this from the doorway, horrified. She then asked him if he was aware that she was still in the room; he said he was. In *This Is 40* (2012), Debbie (Leslie Mann) was in bed with her husband Pete (Paul Rudd). Pete farted, Debbie cringed and forbore. In these two scenes, women were shown to put up with men's farts: they were not shown as finding them funny, but rather as *tolerating* them because, apparently, they are synonymous with masculinity and the men they love.[23]

While women on screen generally do not find men's farts amusing—let alone attractive—*Austin Powers: International Man of Mystery* (1997) subverted this and included a scene of a woman appearing to enjoy male flatulence. Austin Powers (Mike Myers) was in a hot tub with Alotta Fagina (Fabiana Udenio). He farted and Alotta teasingly reprimanded, "How dare you break wind before me?" but then suggested, "Let's make love." This scene was funny because it was so ridiculous to think a woman *would* be aroused by a fart. Of course, Alotta didn't actually find Austin's farts sexy at all; rather, she seduced him merely to find out his real identity. This is much like the *Dumb and Dumber* dream sequence discussed earlier: among those laughing at Lloyd's flaming fart was his love interest Mary (Lauren Holly); only in Lloyd's *dreams* would Mary find such a display attractive.

While farts are normally not something considered attractive, there are examples on screen—but more so in other media, such as viral videos—where the sexualized fart has a noticeable presence.

SEXY FARTS

In the scene from *Extreme Movie* discussed earlier, Lindsey and David were kissing and she let out a small fart and appeared embarrassed. David reassured her—"Lindsey, relax. Everybody farts. This is huge. We've crossed the Fart Barrier." While Lindsey took things too far in the scene by letting out a stream of exaggerated farts, initially at least, her fart seemed to bring the couple closer.

This is certainly something that happened in an episode of the sitcom *3rd Rock from the Sun* (1996–2001), where farts were used to demonstrate Mary (Jane Curtin) and Dick's (John Lithgow) growing marital comfort; their new level of intimacy was demonstrated when they were comfortable enough to fart in front of each other. While farting wasn't necessarily presented as *sexy* in either scene, it did denote comfort; a theme also identifiable in *This is 40* scene

Taking this idea a step further was a scene from the comedy *Good Luck Chuck* (2007), when Stu (Dan Fogler) commented, "I'd suck a fart out her asshole and hold it like a bong hit." For Stu, his remark was a description about just how attractive he found a particular woman—a comment that can also provide insight into how farts can be construed as attractive. In my book *Periods in Pop Culture*, I discussed scenes from Scott Spencer's novel *Endless Love* (1979), Erica Jong's *Parachutes and Kisses* (1984), and Philip Roth's novel *The Dying Animal* (2001) where the taboo substance of menstrual blood was consumed by men: "While these scenes are each open to a potential feminist reading—as examples of men being truly comfortable with women's bodies and of men being avant garde lovers ... such scenes are particularly good illustrations of menstrual sex being a demonstration of true devotion. Such a reading does not necessarily eliminate the horror of menstrual blood—although this could be contended—but presents love, passion and obsession as far stronger emotions than squeamishness."[24]

Just as Stu likely doesn't have a *fart fetish* and just as the characters in the aforementioned novels weren't *actually* menstrual blood fetishists, in each case the substances that emerged from the bodies of their lovers—be it their farts or their blood—were considered as merely extensions of someone they found attractive. Certainly, as demonstrated in writer James Joyce's love letters to his wife Nora—where he wrote of "quick little merry cracks and a lot of tiny little naughty farties ending in a long gush from your hole"[25]—farts can become sexy simply by virtue of them being the bodily output of a lover.

While Stu in *Good Luck Chuck* wasn't a fart fetishist, the idea of farts being fetishized—of some people having a particular sexual attraction to them—is nonetheless a reality. *Eproctophilia* describes a fart fetish. While not a topic that has received extensive academic attention, fart fetish-themed material is relatively easy to locate online. In media researcher Susanna Paasonen's work on pornography, she briefly referred to "Brazilian fart fetish porn" as an example of the "extremity and disgust" evident in viral videos.[26] One YouTube channel called "Hot Sexy Girls," for example, has more than 50 videos tagged with "Sexy girls farting."[27] The Internet, in fact, is filled with such fringe material. In *Part-Time Perverts*, in a discussion of another kind of fringe material—fat-themed pornography—I offered one explanation for the appeal: "like many humiliation-related fantasies, the popularity of fat porn is about attraction to that which we should not find arousing; an attraction to porn that is humiliating to masturbate to."[28] As discussed throughout this chapter, the taboo of farts is grounded in disgust. While some of the fart-fetish material is likely to be found funny—much like the comedies discussed throughout this chapter—part of the appeal may also lie in the "wrong" of the material: that an attractive woman doing something so *disgusting* simply *shouldn't* be found attractive; the appeal, therefore, comes from the naughtiness and the voyeurism offered by audiences being allowed to stickybeak into a scene that is normally kept private.[29]

While flatulence might be a taboo akin to other body-waste unpleasantness, as explored in this chapter, it does have an identifiable presence in popular culture. While farts may often be a quick and crass way to solicit humor from a scene, they can also serve other functions such as diffusing tension, conveying intimacy, and exploiting gender stereotypes.

The Rude Gestures Chapter: Flicking the Channel and Flipping the Bird

While words are often considered the most obvious way to insult, hand gestures can cross language and cultural barriers to shock, outrage, and offend without even a single word. Predominantly focused on The Finger—but also incorporating a discussion of The Shocker and the V-lick—this chapter examines the social, sexual, and political underpinnings of these often offensive gestures, with examples drawn from popular culture.

The Finger, a gesture thought to date back some 2,000 years, is understood across all ethnic groups, classes, sexes, and social groups and is likely the most common offensive hand gesture. Described using a variety of names—including *digitus impudicus* (impudent finger), the one finger salute, flipping the bird, or flicking someone off—the erect middle finger translates as *up yours* at the innocent end of the spectrum, and *fuck you* or *fuck off* at the more aggressive extreme. This chapter begins with an exploration of the sexual connotations of the gesture, thought to be the earliest—and also most literal—interpretation, and extends to explorations of meanings related to gender, aggression, and antiestablishmentism.

THE FINGER: THE SEXUAL ORIGINS

While in contemporary practice The Finger has taken on a variety of meanings, scholars repeatedly draw attention to its sexual origins. Nancy Armstrong and Melissa Wagner, in their book *Field Guide to Gestures*, identified the gesture's resemblance to a phallus: "the middle finger as the erect penis and the tucked-under fingers as testicles."[1] Classics scholar Craig

Williams, in his the work on the poet Martial, similarly dubbed the gesture a "symbolic display of the erect phallus ... [and] also a reminder of masculine potency."[2] Art historian Angus Trumble elaborated on the potency idea and spotlighted the sexual connotations: "[it] seems to have taken as its cue the fact that the normal middle finger is almost invariably the longest of the five, and therefore either (a) the most satisfactory stimulator; or (b) the proudest as regards any implied declaration of the size of the gesturer's own penis."[3] Folklorist Simon Bronner similarly linked the gesture to a show of virility in his book *Explaining Traditions*: "In aggressive taunts such as 'giving the finger' or 'flipping the bird,' with the middle finger outstretched in imitation of an erect penis ... boys are investing emotional capital in the mature ability to hold an erection."[4]

Identified here are a number of themes related to the sexual nature of the gesture: (1) it *looks* phallic; (2) the finger itself has a sexual stimulation function (i.e., it can be used to stimulate and penetrate); and (2) the gesture can both reference the gesturer's own phallus—thus functioning as a visual substitute for the phrase *fuck you*—and showcase a mode to do so. A 2011 photo showed singer Kanye West giving The Finger to paparazzi and simultaneously squeezing his crotch. While The Finger alone may have conveyed West's sentiments—indeed, an infinite number of photos exist showing celebrities giving the same *fuck you* Finger to paparazzi—in the photo, West left no room for his gesture to be read as *go away*; his crotch-grab made his meaning explicit: *fuck off*.

While The Finger can be a suggestive gesture—whereby the inference is that the gesturer is giving a metaphoric fucking—it can also reference unwanted sexual penetration—that is, the recipient is being emasculated through a symbolic fucking or rape. When The Finger was given in *My Science Project* (1985), for example, Vince (Fisher Stevens) accompanied the gesture with the phrase: "Sit on this, butt plug!" In this scene, the gesture functioned as a gestural and verbal attack on a fellow motorist accompanied by a prop that would make the threatened penetration possible.

Anthropologists Alan Dundes and Carl Pagter note that historically the gesture was "used primarily by males to other males."[5] The gendered nature of the gesture—of men giving The Finger to other men—spotlights the emasculating possibilities: the gesture both references the male gesturer's own phallus—notably its size and ability to maintain an erection—and conveys the capacity for the symbolic fuck and, in turn, the ability to feminize a recipient. This was an issue Dundas highlighted: "the basic gesture signifies that the addressee is a passive homosexual. To be the recipient of the phallic finger is to assume the 'female' position or role."[6] Throughout this chapter I discuss a variety of scenes from film and television whereby characters give The Finger: while the gesture can be read as variously hostile and defiant, it can also be interpreted as a sexual flaunt and an attempt to emasculate.

Given the masculine connotations of the gesture, when women give The Finger, a number of interesting topics for analysis are raised, including disrupted gender expectations.

WOMEN AND MIDDLE FINGERS

When women give The Finger, the gesture can equally be an attempt to emasculate; it, too, can connote a digital fucking. In an episode of *Californication* (2007–), for example, Marcy (Pamela Adlon) stuck her middle finger up at her ex-husband Charlie (Evan Handler) and said, "Die young and suffer, Dickless!"

There are, of course, a range of other ways that the gesture can be read. During her performance at the 2012 Superbowl, for example, British singer M.I.A. gave The Finger to the camera. One explanation for the controversy that followed was simply that it wasn't a very *feminine* thing for her to do: that M.I.A. was being *vulgar*, and that vulgarity is much more controversial when women engage in it. Taking the analysis further, if the position of M.I.A.'s body during her performance is examined, it was only when she lifted one leg onto a platform—thus parting her legs—that she gave The Finger. Thus, like West's crotch grab, her performance had a sexually aggressive edge; it worked to bolster M.I.A.'s sexual presence and also potentially functioned as a metaphoric fucking, or emasculation, of her audience.

A similar analysis can be extended to the photograph on the front of Elizabeth Wurtzel's book *Bitch* (1998), something discussed by writer Catherine Orenstein in her book on sex and morality: "Elizabeth Wurtzel appears topless and flipping the bird to her readers—an image that combined the sensibilities of so-called 'pro-sex' or 'do-me' feminists with good old-fashioned objectification."[7] In the photo, Wurtzel—an attractive woman with long blonde hair and a slender physique—rested her palm on her forehead, her middle finger was used to form the "I" in the book's title. When this attractive woman posed in such a way—compounded with the controversial title of her book—expectations of women, of femininity, and of desirability were disrupted: despite Wurtzel's appearance, she clearly had no yen to portray herself as sweet, demure, or stereotypically *feminine*. To the contrary, she seemingly wanted to present herself as anything but.

When women give The Finger on screen, frequently it functions—as it did during M.I.A.'s performance and on the *Bitch* cover—to unsettle expectations about gender. In *Titanic* (1997), in a scene where Rose (Kate Winslet) and her new love interest Jack (Leonardo DiCaprio) were in an elevator, Rose—immaculately dressed as a first-class passenger—gave her fiancé's bodyguard The Finger. Rose's gesture disrupted expectations of how a beautiful, elegantly dressed, and presumably *refined* woman would act. In the comedy *The Hangover* (2009), when Alan (Zach Galifianakis) attempted—from the convertible that he was traveling in—to get the attention of a little girl in another car, he thumped down on the side of the car and frantically waved. The girl eventually gave him The Finger: the humor of the scene was based on the unexpected, *ungirlish* reaction from a blonde, almost angelic-looking child. Something similar occurred in *Don't Tell Mom the Babysitter's Dead* (1991): the babysitter, Mrs. Sturak (Eda Reiss Merin) told Melissa (Danielle Harris) that "little girls should dress like little girls ... sugar and spice." As soon as Mrs. Sturak left the room, Melissa gave her The Finger.

Women giving The Finger can also function to portray a character as resisting expectations related to heterosexuality; in such a case, The Finger serves as just another accessory to cast a woman as rough, promiscuous, or even just *different*. In a scene from *Bring It On* (2000), for example, Missy (Eliza Dushku) auditioned for the cheerleading squad. Standing in front of the judges, Missy looked aggressive—she was tattooed and keys and a chain hung from her belt—and one of the cheerleaders, Whitney (Nicole Bilderback), jeered, "Excuse me. Where'd you park your Harley?" Another cheerleader, Courtney (Clare Kramer), described Missy as an "über dyke." Before her performance, Missy was told, "Tattoos are strictly verboten"; in response, Missy gave The Finger in an unsubtle display of running her middle finger over her tongue and then moving it to her arm to smudge her fake tattoo. In *Wild Things* (1998), Suzie (Neve Campbell)—dressed much like Missy—was similarly mocked for her appearance; Kelly (Denise Richards), for example, remarked, "Jesus. Where'd she get those shoes? Whores for Less?" Like Missy, Suzie's response was to give Kelly The Finger and lasciviously wiggle her tongue. Just as their physical appearances worked to present Missy and Suzie as not confirming to the heterosexual archetype of feminine desirability, their use of The Finger bolstered this impression.

Celebrities such as Courtney Love, Avril Lavigne, and Pink—all of whom dress and have public reputations as ballsy, brazen women, much like Missy and Suzie—have been repeatedly photographed giving The Finger both to paparazzi and in staged publicity shots. In Stuart Jeffries's *Guardian* article about M.I.A.'s Finger, he proposed a number of interpretations for her gesture, one being that she was "Sticking it to the man, old school."[8] While Jeffries was seemingly being facetious, his suggestion nonetheless provides an interesting interpretation. In Sarah Sawyer's book on Avril Lavigne, she noted that "punk rock always was about flipping the bird to the world."[9] It could be argued that part of the rationale for Courtney Love, Avril Lavigne, Pink, and Wurtzel giving The Finger in photographs is to present themselves as punk, as renegade. Because women are culturally expected to be the fairer sex and to be sweeter, softer, gentler, and generally "good," tactics such as giving The Finger can help women prove themselves otherwise—can help shatter expectations—as well as help in branding.

Another way to interpret a woman giving The Finger is as an attempt to convey that she is somebody who won't take any shit; that she refuses to be restricted by societal expectations related to her gender; that she can handle herself, make her own decisions, and assert independence from men (thus providing another reading of Jeffries's "sticking it to the man" comment). Certainly this was body language researcher Robert Phipps's interpretation of The Finger given by singer Adele at the 2012 Brit Awards: "She calls a spade a spade and her fans like that. She wasn't behaving provocatively to plug the brand, she was impulsively rebuking the organisers, not her fans ... It's her consciously saying: 'I don't like this. I want it to show.'"[10]

In a similar act of defiance, in 1981—after being insulted about her sexual identity—tennis player Billie Jean King gave The Finger to a heckler. Such no-nonsense presentations are certainly in line with the impressions that Missy and Suzie conveyed. Another good screen example of this usage occurred in the film *Office Space* (1999) when Joanna (Jennifer Aniston)—in response to being once again hassled by her boss about her appearance—gave him The Finger and quit. Similarly, in *10* (1979), feminist Samantha (Julie Andrews)—while in bed with her lover George (Dudley Moore)—gave The Finger to a peeping tom neighbor. Taking this behavior a few steps further is a scene from *True Romance* (1993), when Alabama (Patricia Arquette)—after being beaten within an inch of her life by Virgil (James Gandolfini)—baited him by giving him The Finger in defiance. In each of these examples, the gesture served as a demonstration of a woman refusing to have her identity and values compromised.

While each of these examples references sex and gender, it is the *fuck you* and *fuck off* connotations of The Finger that are the most common interpretations. In such a display, the directive is less about *fucking* in the sexual sense, and more a gesture of impudence where *fuck* is a word of aggression and rage rather than a reference to intercourse.

THE FINGER, THE FUCK YOU, AND THE FUCK OFF

Communications scholar Russell Frank discussed an altered photograph of the World Trade Center that he was emailed shortly after the September 11, 2001, attacks: instead of two towers, there were five, positioned to look like a hand with the middle finger erect. In discussing possible interpretations of this photo, Frank wrote that "the *digitus impudicus* is simply a gesture of impotent rage: it's about all a driver can do to express his displeasure with another motorist who has cut him off."[11] On screen, the gesture's function as an impotent *fuck you* was explained well by Dave (Arj Barker) in an episode of the sitcom *Flight of the Conchords* (2007–2009):

> Well look, if you just want to let this guy know that you're not going to take his shit any more, just flip him the bird. Yeah? If you need a comeback but you can't think of something, flip him the bird ... It's your way of saying hey, you better not disrespect me, man. Even though I'm gonna disrespect you.

Often termed the *highway salute*, The Finger is routinely presented on screen as a humorous way for motorists to convey displeasure with the actions of other drivers: Vince's use of the gesture on *My Science Project* illustrated this usage well. Clark (Chevy Chase) in *National Lampoon's Christmas Vacation* (1989) similarly gave another driver The Finger, as did a chimp in *Cannonball Run 2* (1984). In *Naked Gun* (1988), Stephie (Winifred Freedman) was encouraged by her driving instructor (John Houseman) to give The Finger to a truck driver. Interestingly, all of these examples come from comedies—notably those of the *sophomoric* genre. The gesture, therefore, functions primarily as a way to shock; The Finger is used because degrees of taboo remain attached to it, so the gesture can appear salacious, but it is one with no lasting consequences—hence the implied impotency.

While functioning as the *highway salute* is an obvious way that The Finger appears on screen, the gesture also functions to convey impudence in a variety of other examples. Certainly it is degrees of impudence—from mild annoyance to full-blown rage—that motivate celebrities to give The Finger to paparazzi: they are responding to unwanted attention with a nonverbal *fuck you* or *fuck off*. Particularly given that much paparazzi material ends up as still photography, when The Finger is given to the camera it is immortalized in a way that the phrase *fuck you* never can be.

In narratives, the gesture functions as a similar, nonverbal *fuck off*. In a scene from *The Breakfast Club* (1985), for example, Bender (Judd Nelson) told Claire (Molly Ringwald) that she would get fat when she got older.

In response, Claire gave him The Finger, complete with a sneer. A similar scene occurred in *Glengarry Glen Ross* (1992), when Shelley (Jack Lemmon) gave his manager John (Kevin Spacey) a dressing down and then The Finger. In *The Matrix* (1999), Neo (Keanu Reeves) was being interrogated by Agent Smith (Hugo Weaving). Smith presented him with an offer, to which Neo responded, "Yeah, well that sounds like a really good deal. But I think I've got a better one. How about I give you The Finger and you give me my phone call," and then gave him The Finger. After escaping the police in *Ghost Rider* (2007), the title character (Nicolas Cage) similarly responded with The Finger. As mentioned earlier, during her acceptance speech at the 2012 Brit Awards, Adele gave The Finger to ceremony organizers who were trying to truncate her acceptance speech. In each of these examples, the gesture functioned as an explicit rebuttal.

While in these cases the rebuttal existed as a response to comments or unwanted attention, in other examples the gesture is read as less motivated by any single instigator and is more so indicative of general arrogance. In Dave Urbanski's book on singer Johnny Cash, he discussed an advertisement that ran in *Billboard* magazine in 1998 after Cash won a Grammy for his album *Unchained*:

> The ad was the famous photo of an incensed Cash flipping the bird to a photographer during his concert at San Quentin prison. The copy read, "American Recordings and Johnny Cash would like to acknowledge the Nashville music establishment and country radio for your support."
>
> The crux of the issue was that Cash, a country music legend, wasn't getting airplay on music stations ...[12]

While the Cash image could be read as a publicity stunt, an obvious interpretation of the gesture was it simply serving as a general *fuck you* and a brag about success *in spite* of the industry. In 2010, singer Iggy Pop was inducted into the Rock and Rock Hall of Fame. During his acceptance speech, he directed two middle fingers to the audience. While it might be speculated that Iggy Pop shared similar sentiments about the music industry as Cash, another interpretation might be akin to those associated with the female rockers discussed earlier: Iggy Pop was in his early 60s when he was honored; perhaps The Finger was his way for him to convey that he was *still punk* even well past middle age. More so than being punk, however, is the idea of Iggy Pop presenting himself as a bastard: he wanted to be portrayed as arrogant; it doesn't serve the punk image for him to be portrayed as a nice guy; he wanted to be the badass and flaunt a still-taboo gesture.

This interpretation of orchestrated arrogance is certainly applicable to situations when artists give The Finger to their audience. Madonna during a concert in 2008, talk show host David Letterman during a show in 2011, and talk show host Bill Maher during a 2012 episode each directed the gesture at their audience. While there may be a shock value element involved, an obvious interpretation is simply sheer arrogance; The Finger helps add to the performer's *don't give a shit*, egotistical persona. Such a gesture can toughen a public image and also be read as antiestablishment, in line with Johnny Cash's attempt to appear dark and renegade or Iggy Pop's efforts to appear punk.

In this section I have largely focused on the *fuck you* inferences of the gesture. Also worth discussing are the *fuck off* meanings, whereby the gesture is used to dismiss.

Kanye West's song "So Appalled" (2010) included the lyrics: "Middle finger in the air if you really don't care." Examples of The Finger conveying *not caring* and general disregard are easily detected. Discussed above was Bill Maher giving the finger to his studio audience on *Real Time with Bill Maher* (2003–). Maher had just told a politically incorrect joke but audience laughter was patchy, so he responded by giving The Finger and saying, "Oh, fuck you." He was dismissing his audience for apparently being politically correct and uptight. The same *fuck you* disregard motivated Letterman's dual fingers in retaliation to his audience's sarcastic "Awww" to a sentimental comment he made about his son on *The Late Show with David Letterman* (1993–). While perhaps Maher and Letterman were trying to be funny—and perhaps even conveying their comfort and rapport with their audience—more simply, the gesture can be read as their response to a situation that they found disagreeable.

Just as celebrities who give The Finger may want to exhibit disregard for paparazzi, politicians have also been known to use the gesture to dismiss those whom they consider as ratbags or recalcitrants. In 1966, for example, then California Governor Ronald Reagan flipped the bird at protestors at Berkeley. In 1976, Vice President Norman Rockefeller gave The Finger to a group of hecklers. In 2010, Senator Jim Bunning raised his middle finger at an *ABC News* producer. In each case, the gesture functioned as a *fuck off* as much as it demonstrated contempt; the gesture was a way to denote that the recipient was considered lowly and easily dismissed.

While all of these examples highlight the gesture used to connote a *fuck off*, it should be noted that there are examples of more subtle attempts to convey the same message—notably when the gesture is obfuscated. Armstrong and Wagner discussed occasions when The Finger is "flashed in a seemingly innocent way, as when one scratches one's head or points to something using the middle finger."[13] Many examples of disguised fingers exist. *Men in Black* (1997), for example, included a scene where Agent K (Tommy Lee Jones) responded to Agent J's (Will Smith) questions about privileges by saying, "When you grow up." J responded, "Oh ... okay," while scratching his head with his middle finger. In *Scott Pilgrim vs. the World* (2010), Kim (Alison Pill) gave The Finger to Gideon (Jason Schwartzman) by using her middle finger to rub under her eye.

The gesture is also often used in real life. A photo exists of union leader James "Jimmy" Hoffa at a 1957 Senate inquiry, rubbing his eye with his middle finger. President Barack Obama has repeatedly been accused of making the same gesture. In his 2008 primary campaign, while he was discussing his opponent Hillary Clinton, he scratched his cheek with his middle finger and the audience applauded. In his presidential victory speech, Obama mentioned opponent John McCain—congratulated him on his campaign—and then again scratched his face; his audience again applauded. Footage from 2009 similarly shows Obama introducing Pennsylvania mayor John Callahan, and scratching his face with his middle finger.

The beauty of this gesture is that it can be easily denied: technically a person *could* simply be scratching his or her face and the impudence could simply be a projection. The obfuscated Finger also gives the gesture an air of gentle impropriety, if not brattiness and youthful rebellion. Singer Madonna, for example—who had, as noted, given the gesture to her audience in 2008—criticized M.I.A.'s gesture by claiming that "it's such a teenager, irrelevant thing to do."[14] The obfuscated gesture most certainly has a silly, underhanded air to it, allowing it to convey youth, if not also immaturity.

In the next section I propose that one interpretation of The Finger is to help achieve shock.

THE FINGER AND SHOCK VALUE

Shock value can describe the power and appeal of a stunt used to solicit a reaction from an audience, be it disgust, anger, or fear. Given that The Finger is frequently construed as an offensive gesture, when a celebrity demonstrates this behavior, the gesture can be a way to solidify a reputation as a renegade, antiestablishment figure. Jeffries, for example, referred to speculation that M.I.A.'s Finger at the Superbowl was a publicity stunt—not dissimilar to Janet Jackson's "wardrobe malfunction" in 2004—and orchestrated purely to solicit controversy.[15] Whether or not M.I.A.'s gesture was simply manufactured outrage, the reality is that she did give The Finger in a very public forum. The gesture appeared choreographed—rather than spontaneous—and it seems highly unlikely that a gesture that was posed and given directly to the camera would not have caused controversy. As noted earlier, Madonna criticized M.I.A.'s gesture as "a teenager, irrelevant thing to do."[16] M.I.A.—36 years old at the time of her performance—was obviously not a teenager, but nevertheless she was dabbling in the kind of youthful rebellion akin to that evidenced by the young David Cassidy and Danny Bonaduce—actors in the family-oriented *The Partridge Family* (1970–1974)—who posed as teenagers in photos during the 1970s where they gave The Finger to the camera. In such examples, the gesture could be read as being shocking purely for the purposes of *being* shocking and as disconnected from malice, rage, or impudence.

Earlier I discussed the advertisement that ran in *Billboard* magazine in 1998 in which Johnny Cash gave The Finger. The image was a decades-old one, but was used because even if the gesture might be increasingly commonplace decades on, it still has impact and shock value. In their book on professional wrestling, R. D. Reynolds and Randy Baer discussed the wrestler "Stone Cold" Steve Austin, whose use of The Finger was part of his routine: "Austin began to ratchet up the character several notches, using four-letter words and flipping the bird to fans and opponents alike. Such a thing had never been done in wrestling, so the shock value along was tremendous."[17]

While it could be argued that use of The Finger was simply part of a broader marketing strategy for Cash, M.I.A., or Austin—where the gesture was used to manipulate a performer's image—there are other examples in which The Finger, in fact, became the central selling point. The 1974 cover of Issue #166 of *Mad* magazine, for example, showed an illustration of a hand giving The Finger: the edition turned out to be *Mad*'s most controversial issue as well as its most remembered. *The Economist* similarly used a cactus in the shape of The Finger on its cover in 2003. In 2010, an issue of the German magazine *Focus* used a manipulated image of the statue of Venus de Milo giving The Finger; the same doctored de Milo statue was used on a 2012 issue of the Greek magazine *Crash*. In 2010, the *New York Post* newspaper used an image of NFL coach Rex Ryan giving The Finger. Wurtzel's book *Bitch*—discussed earlier—also used the image. Album covers such as Serius Jones's *Serius Bizness 2* (2011) showed a seated man giving The Finger. In publicity shots for her book *Official Book Club Selection: A Memoir According to Kathy Griffin* (2009), Griffin was posed holding her book and giving The Finger. In each of these examples, the gesture delivered added attention to a product by using a shocking image to encourage audiences to take notice. The gesture was used because in a crowded marketplace the rude gesture can still cut through the clutter and stir up controversy.

FUNNY FINGERS AND FINGERS OF ENDEARMENT

Armstrong and Wagner noted that The Finger "has lost much of its sexual meaning. It can even be a playful or humorous insult, especially when it is flashed in a seemingly innocent way."[18] In his discussion of M.I.A.'s Superbowl Finger, Jeffries similarly discussed the possibility for the gesture being read as something *other* than impudence: "Perhaps the London-born rapper didn't realise that in the US, flipping the bird is offensive, coming as she does from Hounslow, where extending the middle finger is a mild, sometimes even jaunty, rebuke."[19] While Jeffries was being sarcastic—and, when examining M.I.A.'s posturing, it seems highly *unlikely* that she was being funny—nonetheless, the capacity most certainly does exist for some Fingers to be construed as humorous—more akin to a laughing *go away*—if not also, as discussed in the next section, as endearment.

Humorous Middle Fingers

In the silent film *Speedy* (1928)—during a visit to Coney Island—the title character (Harold Lloyd) gave himself The Finger in a funhouse mirror. While the gesture could be read as self-deprecating, it is more likely that the gesture was simply intended to be funny. When Letterman gave the dual fingers to his audience while he was feigning offense, ultimately the gesture was designed to entertain: his show is intended to be funny. On screen, there are also examples where—while still connected to a *fuck off* intent—the gesture is more about being funny than being truly offensive. In *Bruce Almighty* (2003) and *High Fidelity* (2000), for example, two silly and over-the-top finger gestures highlighted this intention. In *Bruce Almighty*, Bruce (Jim Nolan) remarked, "You like jazz, Evan? Let me play something for you?" and, with his fingers configured to resemble a trumpet—proceeded to blow a fake Finger note to his rival colleague Evan (Steve Carrell). In *High Fidelity*, an ostentatious Finger display involved Barry (Jack Black) theatrically blowing out each of his fingers until only the middle one was left erect and directed at his boss Rob (John Cusack). In an episode of sitcom *Community* (2009–), Britta (Gillian Jacobs) attempted to perform a similar gesture. While these gestures can be read as rude, their theatricality was also designed to make them appear funny. Ultimately, their funniness may mitigate the sting and the offense (certainly so for the audience).

Middle Fingers of Endearment

Armstrong and Wagner noted that The Finger can be a "playful or humorous insult."[20] Certainly the capacity for the gesture to be less about offense and more as a jaunty rebuke can be detected both in real life and on screen. In 2009 at the Golden Globe awards, actor Mickey Rourke received a Best Actor accolade for his performance in the film *The Wrestler* (2008). In his acceptance speech, Rourke spoke fondly of his director, Darren Aronofsky, by describing him as "one tough son of a bitch." In reply, Aronofsky—smiling broadly—gave The Finger to Rourke. While Tim Winter, president of the Parents Television Council, contended that the gesture was "yet another example of arrogant behavior by someone who seems intoxicated by being controversial,"[21] arrogance in fact *didn't* appear to be Aronofsky's intent at all. To the contrary, the two men just seemed comfortable enough with each other to engage in a gentle kind of gentle sparring. In her discussion of swearing, Natalie Angier noted that meanings are not always clear-cut: "In some settings, the free flow of foul language may signal not hostility or social pathology, but harmony and tranquility and function as a way for close friends to 'let off steam' with one another."[22]

While a broader audience might find the gesture offensive—as apparently did Winter—the dynamics between the gesturer and the recipient may simply allow for, if not embrace, The Finger. On screen, this dynamic transpired in *8 Mile* (2002): Alex (Brittany Murphy) and B-Rabbit (Eminem) gave each other the Finger when they parted at a subway station. Similarly, in *Remember the Daze* (2007), Julia (Amber Heard) said goodbye to her sister Angie (Brie Larson) by giving her The Finger. This may also be a way to interpret the Letterman and Maher Fingers discussed earlier that were directed to their audiences. In a similar way to dirty talk, the gesture—while appearing rude, if not offensive, to onlookers—can, in fact, connote intimacy.

Thus far this chapter has focused on The Finger as a hand gesture with a wide variety of interpretations. In the next sections, two other gestures—the V-lick and The Shocker—are briefly discussed.

THE V-LICK

Not to be mistaken for the peace symbol or the victory sign—where the palm faces outward—the V is often considered as the British take on The Finger—the two-fingered *up yours*. While the gesture can be interpreted much the same as The Finger, in recent years it has come to incorporate other features and be used to convey different meanings. The V gesture held over the mouth and with a tongue positioned between is widely thought to connote cunnilingus, whereby the fingers can represent parted legs or parted labia. Done this way, the gesture is often termed the *V-lick*. A notable example of this occurred on screen in the comedy *Kingpin* (1996): a lecherous landlady (Prudence Wright Holmes) gave the sign to her recalcitrant tenant (Woody Harrelson) as a reminder of the cunnilingus duties he would need to keep doing if he couldn't pay his rent.

The V-lick appears commonly in Facebook photos—Facebook photos of the Australian Olympic swimmer Stephanie Rice giving the V-lick received extensive media attention in 2008—but has also been seen in other realms. Professional wrestler Mickie James, for example, gave the gesture in the ring after grabbing the crotch of an opponent. In publicity shots of the band Steel Panther, the members have posed many times doing the V-lick. In the film *Rock of Ages* (2012), the rocker Stacee Jaxx (Tom Cruise) similarly performed the V-lick gesture on stage and in publicity photos.

Like The Finger, the V-lick is open to a number of interpretations. In my book *Part-Time Perverts: Sex, Pop Culture, and Kink Management*, I discussed that perversion can be participated in in very noncommitting ways such as via the selection of items of apparel or piercings that have fetish connotations, "whereby in their display the wearer conveys the illusion of perversion: perversions which may or may not be of actual interest to the wearer."[23] The V-lick gesture can be interpreted as functioning similarly. It can *reference* the still-taboo sexual practice of cunnilingus without any commitment to involvement; the gesturer may have no interest in actually performing cunnilingus, but the gesture nonetheless hints at the possibility. Also worth noting is the possibility for the gesture—when performed by a man—to ingratiate himself to a female audience. In 2011, actor Ryan Gosling made some remarks about female sexual pleasure and how aggrieved he was about the controversy stirred by the cunnilingus scene in his film *Blue Valentine* (2010).[24] Gosling now has a strong female—and notably *feminist*—following[25]: his connection to, and supposed comfort with, cunnilingus likely plays a significant part in developing such support. For a man to do this gesture, it can similarly be construed as casting him as pro-female.

When a woman does the V-lick gesture—particularly a putatively heterosexual woman such as Rice—the gesture gives the hint of not just nonmainstream sexual practice, but perhaps even dabbling in same-sex sexual practice. Such a gesture can work to cast the gesturer as sexual, as sexy, and as potentially liberated. The nature of cunnilingus remaining taboo can also help cast the gesturer as somewhat antiestablishment. While he may not have done the V-lick, singer Jimi Hendrix frequently gave lascivious tongue licks during his stage performances, something discussed by Hendrix biographer Charles Murray: "He would lean over to women in the audience, rapidly lapping his tongue in an explicit mime of cunnilingus (at a time when it was still considered as exotic sexual activity that only wicked, depraved men would perform, and even wickeder and more depraved women would want)."[26] For Hendrix, part of his reputation was about being antiestablishment; simulating cunnilingus was one way to demonstrate this stance. The V-lick can function similarly—as a renegade, potentially sexually aggressive gesture.

THE SHOCKER

The Shocker is a genital manipulation done to a woman: two fingers in the vagina and the "shocker" being the little finger in the anus. As sex writers Dorian Solot and Marshall Miller note, it is "one of only a handful of sexual acts with the honor of having its own hand gesture."[27] In her song "Rock the Shocker" (2006), Canadian artist Peaches promised to "show you what, what a girl wants" by explaining how to do The Shocker: "thumbs up, fingers out, pull back." Steel Panther similarly had a song titled "The Shocker" (2009) and also explained the gesture: "two in the pink and one in the sink / that's called the shocker." In 2011, Jarryd Blair, a player in the Australian Football League, was thought to be doing the gesture in a team photo after the team's Grand Final win.[28] Like the V-lick, the gesture also appears in many photographs posted on Facebook.

On the one hand, like the V-lick, The Shocker can convey sexual impropriety and non-vanilla sexual interests. Given the continuing taboo nature of heterosexual anal sex,[29] for someone to be gesturing this way highlights an interest—real or feigned—in nonmainstream sexual behavior. Also like the V-lick, The Shocker is something designed to give pleasure to the woman; it is a gesture that the man receives no obvious physical benefit from—much like cunnilingus (see the Oral Sex Chapter)—so the gesture can be interpreted as conveying a man's generosity as a lover. Peaches sings of the gesture winding women up like a "hurdy gurdy," and Steel Panther dubs it the "the movement that rocks all girls." For a man to purport that he just might do it can cast him as being a quality lover.

On the other hand, another interpretation of The Shocker is contained in its name. The gesture can *be* shocking only when it is unexpected; the shock is the surprise finger to the anus. While the gesture may convey an interest in kinky sex, there is also the capacity for the gesture to be interpreted as sexually aggressive. The idea of unwanted penetration was discussed earlier in the context of The Finger; certainly one interpretation of The Shocker is men "surprising" women with sexual acts that they have not consented to.

This chapter has examined hand gestures often construed as offensive. While rudeness and impudence are obvious interpretations, gestures such as The Finger, the V-lick, and The Shocker have a variety of other social and sexual meanings as well as interpretations referencing gender, power, intimacy, and politics.

The Euphemisms Chapter: Sex and Bodily Euphemisms on Screen and in Song

Expressions like *go down on* and *blow job* are much more familiar to audiences than cunnilingus or fellatio. *Sleep together*, *go to bed with*, and *make love to* sound so much less serious—and certainly less clinical—than *copulation*. To *wank* or *jerk off* is linguistically much more common than to *masturbate*, and *menstruation* is invariably substituted by expressions such as *period* or *that time of the month*. Genital names are commonly replaced with euphemisms ranging from the childish to the crude; likewise, *gay* and *queer* are heard much more frequently than *homosexual*. As psychologist Timothy Jay noted in his book *Why We Curse*, "the sheer abundance of euphemisms for sex is a good indication of how important it is for speakers to talk around the topic."[1]

Euphemism comes from the Greek *euphemia*, meaning "words of good omen" and, more commonly, "to speak well." While in contemporary parlance the use of euphemism is often about sugar-coating, in practice this is not always the case: euphemism can also be used to neutralize politics or negativity, to confuse, to conceal meaning, and to outright deceive. Euphemism is often considered a form of spin, used notably by politicians, bureaucrats, and advertisers to package something—an idea, a policy, a product—as attractive through disingenuous or manipulative means. Such linguistic trickery is, of course, nothing new; its systematic and highly politicized use is thought to have its origins in George Orwell's novel *Nineteen Eighty-Four* (1949), where "newspeak" was the new language imposed by the state to restrict the lexicon, eliminate gradations of meaning, and, ultimately, control thought.

According to linguists Keith Allan and Kate Burridge, the English language offers more than 1,000 euphemisms for *penis*, 1,200 euphemisms for *vulva/vagina*, and 800 euphemisms for *intercourse*.[2] As Jay contended, clearly sex is a topic we find complicated to discuss. This complexity is borne out of reasons including embarrassment, conservatism, and fear of offense, and resultantly euphemisms are used to temper subjects perceived as difficult. This chapter explores examples of, and rationales for, sex-themed euphemisms. Such euphemisms are often deployed for predictable reasons such as avoiding offense and tentatively broaching taboo topics, but there are also other rationales whereby the intent is to shock, to titillate, to dissociate, and to be humorous.

THE SUGAR-COATING OF LANGUAGE

Sugar-coating is the most obvious explanation for euphemism: to make something sound nicer or less offensive than a franker, more clinical description—something that Burridge refers to as a "linguistic deodorizer."[3] Numerous rationales can be cited for such sugar-coating. This section examines two of them: (1) consideration of one's audience and (2) personal prudishness.

All about the Audience

The most obvious rationale for euphemism use is being mindful of one's audience. That *there are children present* or *ladies present* is often used as shorthand for the assumption that some audiences need shielding from certain language; some audiences are viewed as less worldly, less mature, and less able to cope with more explicit descriptions. The toning down of language for children is a very obvious justification for euphemism: *urine*, for example, often becomes *wee wee* or *tinkle*, *potty* replaces *toilet*, and *penis* becomes *pee pee*. This issue was discussed in a 1969 *Time* article on euphemism: "Housewives on television may chat about their sex lives in terms that a decade ago would have made gynecologists blush; more often than not, these emancipated women still speak about their children's 'going to the potty.' "[4]

Out of fear of embarrassing, offending, or ostracizing an audience, dialogue may be tempered: as Dr. House (Hugh Laurie) explained—after using a barrage of euphemisms for masturbation on *House* (2004–2012)—"I was trying to be discreet. There's a child in the room!" Tempering language because of children is similarly well illustrated in an episode of the sitcom

Full House (1987–1995). Youngest daughter Michelle (Mary-Kate Olsen/ Ashley Olsen) complained that her uncle Jesse (John Stamos) and aunt Becky (Lori Loughlin) weren't playing with her as much as usual. Michelle's other uncle, Joey (Dave Coulier), explained their absence, alleging that Jesse and Becky "were doing their taxes":

Michelle: Are they going to be doing their taxes *every night*?
  Joey: For the first few months, yes.

Joey assumed that his niece was too young to be told that her newlywed aunt and uncle were busy having sex, so instead he used *doing their taxes* as a child-friendly—and, given the target audience for the show, *audience-*friendly—euphemism for sex. In the Gay Chapter, I discussed the humor in animation often doing double duty and courting both adult and children audiences; the *Full House* scene is an example of this practice where the euphemism is funny for the knowing adult viewer and harmless for children.

Being mindful of an audience is particularly well illustrated in advertising, whereby the most everyday objects get sugar-coated to avoid offense: *bath tissue*, for example, often substitutes for *toilet paper*; *feminine protection* and *feminine hygiene* substitute for *sanitary napkins* and *tampons*. In 2010, Kotex actually tried to desist with euphemisms and used terms including *vagina* in a commercial. Three networks refused to air the commercial, so it had to be reshot using the euphemism *down there*.[5] The decision by these networks highlights that *vagina* is a word that is assumed to conjure offense and, therefore, needs to be spoken about cryptically. Predictably, euphemisms for *vagina* abound on screen. The word *vajayjay*, for example, stemmed from pressure imposed by media watchdog groups who complained that *vagina* was used too often in *Grey's Anatomy* (2005–); a euphemism was concocted to counter this demurral, which then quickly entered the popular lexicon.

While on screen women's anatomy and associated products are often spoken about euphemistically,[6] this trend actually extends to all sex-themed words and ideas. Television commercials for the erectile dysfunction drug Enzyte, for example, predictably eschewed the words *penis* and *erection* and instead offered a variety of euphemisms, including *big boost of confidence*, *natural male enhancement*, *living large*, and *a generous swelling of pride*. Such euphemisms are suggestive to a knowing audience but avoid offense by being (comparatively) subtle.

While euphemisms for genitals are offered for a number of reasons, as identified in this section, the sugar-coated euphemism is considered appropriate for a general audience.

Being Prudish

While the hypothetical mother in the *Time* article discussed earlier might have moderated her language for her children, another explanation is that she did so because she was loath to use language that she considered dirty or uncouth. When "rude" words or subject matters are found embarrassing—particularly by women—euphemisms may be deployed as part of a self-preservation strategy. In an episode of *Sex and the City* (1998–2004), for example, the following dialogue was exchanged between friends Charlotte (Kristin Davis), Samantha (Kim Cattrall), and Carrie (Sarah Jessica Parker):

Charlotte: Is it so much to ask that you not wear your dress up around your See You Next Tuesday?
Samantha: My what?
Charlotte: See ... you ... next ...
Carrie: Tuesday? Oh my god, was that a *Schoolhouse Rock* I missed?

Charlotte, a character portrayed throughout the series as prudish, often did use the word *vagina*, but the fact that she eschewed it in this scene demonstrates that *see you next Tuesday* served not as a euphemism for *vagina* but rather as a euphemism for *cunt*. Charlotte evidently could not bring herself to say that word, but the euphemism allowed her to say something more biting than *vagina*.[7]

While Charlotte's choice of language was likely attributable to her being comparatively conservative, a connected explanation is that her usage of this euphemism was part of her efforts at impression management; in other words, her language choice was used to manipulate how she was perceived by others. This idea is something discussed by communications theorists Nancy McCallum and Matthew McGlone: "Euphemism provides a method for discussing sensitive topics, as it allows users to representationally displace topics that evoke negative affect by avoiding direct reference to them."[8] Euphemism allows Charlotte the opportunity to use a word with vulgar connotations without actually *being* vulgar. Charlotte's efforts to use language to manage her façade highlight another rationale for sex-themed euphemism: psychology.

EUPHEMISM AND PSYCHOLOGY

A central motivation for euphemism use is to put space between oneself and an idea. There are numerous psychological reasons why this might be done; two that I propose in this section relate to (1) putting distance between the self and something considered too horrible to speak about explicitly and (2) self-esteem rationales. Both of these reasons have notable applicability to a discussion of sex.

Euphemism and Dissociation

While news reports readily use euphemisms to discuss rape—*indecent assault*, *carnal knowledge*, *attack*, and *abuse*, for example—the use of euphemism by victims is particularly relevant for this section, highlighting some of the psychological underpinnings of euphemism use. When linguistic anthropologist Shonna Trinch undertook research with women who had experienced domestic violence, she noted that 80 percent who had experienced marital rape had used euphemisms in their descriptions.[9] Psychologists Judith Parker and Deborah Mahlstedt, in their work on rape, similarly noted that victims "use a variety of linguistic resources to manage their (un)willingness to acknowledge their sexual assault."[10] By using euphemisms, a distance can be established between the victim and the word *rape* and all of its taboo, inflammatory, and emotional connotations and judgments.

One reason why a victim might eschew the word is to avoid becoming a *rape victim*; in essence, by not explicitly naming the rape, a person is able to avoid the label of *victim* and, therefore, avoid the identity, possible blame, and stigma.[11] This idea is highlighted well by a rape victim quoted in legal theorist Patricia Easteal and Louise McOrmond-Plummer's book *Real Rape, Real Pain*: "Saying 'I was raped' felt equal to proclaiming 'I have no dignity.' If I did not say the word, I could retain at least the pretence of dignity."[12] By using a euphemism, a rape victim can conjure an identity that is separate from her attack; language, therefore, becomes part of a coping mechanism. Examples of such dissociation are readily detected in music. *Rape* is explicitly mentioned in a number of songs: 2Pac's "Baby Don't Cry (Keep Ya Head Up II)" (1999), Belle and Sebastian's "The Chalet Lines" (2000), Korn's "Thoughtless" (2002), and Amanda Palmer's "Oasis" (2008), for example, each refer to rape by using the actual word. More common, however, is rape discussed via euphemism. There is a long history of creative works skirting *around* difficult topics; rape is one example where euphemisms invariably substitute for frank, clinical, and frequently upsetting descriptions.

The Stone Temple Pilots song "Sex Type Thing" (1992) is a first-person narrative song seemingly about date rape ("I am a man, a man / I'll give ya somethin' that ya won't forget / I said ya shouldn't have worn that dress"). Rape is not mentioned explicitly in the song; instead, the title exists as a typical example of an equivocating euphemism used by rape victims. Ann, a woman quoted in psychologist Nicola Gavey's research, reflected on unwanted sex; in doing so, she used an example of an equivocating euphemism:

> I was saying to my friend, Kelly, the other day, it was amazing how ... we weren't raped as teenagers, you know, like the things we used to do. And then I thought, well we were sort of raped, really, when you think we were driven off in cars and we would end up in the park somewhere and we would have sort of boys having sexual experiences with us that we didn't—We often—like it was quite disgusting ...[13]

In this quote, Ann is *hedging* through euphemism. Parker and Mahlstedt define such hedging, identifying that it occurs when a speaker "modulates the impact of her own utterances by using a word or phrase ... By using such terms as *kind of*, *sort of*, *maybe*, *I think* and others, a speaker can moderate the strength or weakness of an utterance."[14] The woman in Gavey's research—much like the title of the Stone Temple Pilot's song—used euphemism to hedge and equivocate, reflecting the difficulty victims have in labeling their crime. *Sex type thing* facilitates dissociation but also muddles the events, thereby highlighting one of the central problems with using euphemism in the context of crime.

In the song "Summer Nights" from the film *Grease* (1978), the boys sing about Danny's (John Travolta) interactions with Sandy (Olivia Newton John), asking, "Did she put up a fight?" *Putting up a fight* is a common euphemism used to reference sex refusal and can be identified in women's real-life recollections of rape. In Jim Wood's book *The Rape of Inez Garcia*, he recounted the story of Garcia who was tried for killing her rapist in 1974. In her recollections, Garcia told the court: "I was scared that if I might put up a fight that I might have been killed or stabbed ... I let them use me."[15] The very same euphemism was apparent in a rapist's discussion of his crime quoted in psychoanalyst Sylvia Levine and Joseph Koenig's work on rape: "So she was naturally, crying, and putting up a fight and we carried her out to the cornfield."[16] In such examples, *rape* doesn't need to be spoken; *put up a fight* is a euphemism used frequently to imply rape.

Tori Amos's "Me and a Gun" (1992)—a song drawing heavily on Amos's own rape—uses phrases such as "a man on my back" and "spread[ing]" but eschews mention of the actual word. Motörhead's "Don't Let Daddy Kiss Me" (1993) takes the rape euphemism a few steps further by dubbing it the "world's worst crime" and "his seed is sown where it should not be." Similar theatrical rape euphemisms are used in Emilie Autumn's "Gothic Lolita" (2006), where the rape is described as "The kind of murder where nobody dies," and in The Offspring's "Kristy, Are You Doing Okay?" (2008), where "innocence left behind" and "what was taken away" are the chosen euphemisms. These examples are particularly interesting because they use emotive, heartstring-tugging language to highlight the seriousness and devastation of the rape, but simultaneously avoid the explicit, close contact that actually using the word would bring; the rape is dramatized without being discussed frankly.

In Ludacris's song "Runaway Love" (2007), "tryin' to have his way" is the chosen euphemism for rape. This phrase is similarly deployed in The Dresden Dolls' song "Delilah" (2006): "The stupid bastard's gonna have his way with you." *Have his way* also appears in real-life descriptions: in one woman's testimony she explained: "He lay on top of me and started physically abusing me ... he threatened to kill me if I wouldn't let me have his way."[17] A similar euphemism—*done his thing*—appears in women's real-life stories. A victim quoted by Parker and Mahlstedt, for example, offered this description: "He grabbed me, then started taking my pants off, and then he done his thing."[18] *Have his way* and *done his thing* are substantially softened ways to speak of rape: they offer a watered-down description of a heinous crime, facilitating dissociation but also, problematically, presenting a possibly less harsh judgment of the perpetrator (an idea returned to at the end of this chapter).

While it could be contended that euphemisms are used in these songs for censorship or creative reasons,[19] they also demonstrate situations where a rape victim attempts to avoid having identity shaped by her victimhood and where a rapist attempts to dissociate from a crime. These applications are indicative of how euphemisms are often instrumental in manipulating identity.

Euphemism and Identity

In the aforementioned *Time* article, it was contended that "certain kinds of everyday euphemisms have proved their psychological necessity": "A girl may tolerate herself more readily if she thinks of herself as a 'swinger' rather than as promiscuous. Voyeurs can salve their guilt feelings when they buy tickets for certain 'adult entertainments' on the grounds that they are implicitly supporting 'freedom of artistic expression.' "[20] Highlighted in this quote is the idea of a psychological necessity for a person—in the first case, for a girl—to shape her identity through her language choices; thus, by using a (now outdated) word such as *swinger*, she is able to conceive of herself as something other than promiscuous. Promiscuity, of course, is a highly political, value-laden, and ultimately sexist concept—ideas that likely motivate the use of euphemisms in lieu of *promiscuous* in popular culture. Promiscuity can be defined in many different ways, but for the purposes of this section my definition centers on casual sex and female sexual liberation.

Theologian John Elliott, in his discussion of biblical euphemisms, wrote: "Euphemisms also serve as markers of social identity (specific social and cultural sensibilities, values, norms) and demarcations of in-group from out-groups."[21] While language can, of course, be very revealing about our education, class, and ethnicity, as related to a discussion of sex, it can also be demonstrative of how a sexual identity can be shaped and understood. In the aforementioned *Time* article, a woman having a lot of sex was demonized; hence the application of the word *promiscuous*. Allan and Burridge, for example, noted that there are more than 2,000 euphemisms for "wanton woman."[22] In song, euphemisms for the wanton woman in lieu of *promiscuous* abound.

Ani DiFranco has a song called "Promiscuity" (2012) that explicitly uses the word to celebrate a sexually liberal lifestyle, asking how one would know one's sexual preferences "til' you been around the block / a few times on that bike." While DiFranco proposes that promiscuity can be positive and advantageous, of specific note, the lyrics present the singer's identity as one associated with sexual liberation: DiFranco is embracing the word and using it to proclaim that sex is an important part of her identity—that she wants to project an identity associated with sexual emancipation and feminism. Unlike DiFranco's song, however, most other song's lyrics eschew use of *promiscuity*—perhaps due to its formality, multiple syllables and judgmental connotations—but convey the same idea through euphemism.

Bessie Smith's "Empty Bed Blues" (1928) is an early example of the use of euphemism to describe sex and the longing for it. Smith recounts her sexual experiences with terms such as "coffee grinder" and "deep sea diver" and muses on her yearnings: "My springs are getting rusty, sleeping single like I do." The same idea was presented in her "I Want a Little Sugar in My Bowl" (1931): "I need a little hot dog, on my roll / I could stand some lovin', oh so bad." A much more recent example using the same techniques is The Veronicas' song "Untouched" (2007) ("I feel so untouched / And I want you so much"). Euphemisms such as *empty bed*, *rusty springs*, *stand some lovin'* and *untouched* are much more genteel than *promiscuous or horny*; instead of prompting judgment, these songs offer metaphors that are open to interpretation. The subjective nature of these lyrics facilitates a kind of *hedging*; while an audience can infer that sex is being described, the explicit meaning is concealed. This idea was discussed in linguist Paul Baker's

The Euphemisms Chapter 75

research on euphemisms and homosexuality: "The use of the 'double meaning,' or saying one thing that can be interpreted in two ways, usually one innocent and one subversive, is a way of being controversial and funny at the same time, obviating the potential amount of offense caused and obscuring the meaning from those too young or innocent to understand."[23]

Like the Smith songs, Donna Summer's "Hot Stuff" (1979) was about a horny woman phoning various men to coerce one to visit: "gotta have some hot stuff / gotta have some lovin' tonight." Like Smith, rather than dubbing herself promiscuous, Summer sings about "waitin' for some lover to call"; she is painting the picture of a sexually liberated woman without using inflammatory language. As often repeated in discussions of gender and sexuality, a woman who has many sexual partners is called a *slut*; conversely; highlighting the well-established double standard, a man who does the same is called a *stud*. For Smith and Summer—particularly considering the periods in which they were singing—through euphemism, they were able to discuss sexual appetite while simultaneously eschewing judgment.

Some far more explicit examples of euphemisms for *promiscuous* occur in Khia's song "My Neck, My Back (Lick It)" (2002) ("my neck, my back / lick my pussy and my crack") and Peaches' "Fuck the Pain Away" (2000). In these two examples, the euphemisms are actually *more* explicit than the clinical terms. In the Smith, Summer and The Veronicas examples, casual sex was romanticized and euphemisms were used for modulation; for Khia and Peaches, the euphemisms are less about presenting oneself as demure, but rather are used to shock and to project a sexually aggressive identity. As mentioned earlier, Elliott noted that euphemisms can be used as "markers of social identity (specific social and cultural sensibilities, values, norms)."[24] Khia and Peaches rely on their language choices to help establish their public identities—to manage the impressions they convey—as sexually liberated. Just as performers such as Courtney Love and Pink have used The Finger to portray themselves as edgy, the deliberate use of controversial language can function similarly. Interestingly, the Khia and Peaches examples illustrate another rationale for sex-themed euphemisms: to be *offensive*. Whereas euphemisms are often assumed to sugar-coat to *avoid* offense, as these examples highlight, sometimes a more explicit, *dirtier* euphemism is chosen to shock, to outrage, and to solidify a nonconservative audience.

THE INTENTION OF OFFENSE

As discussed in the context of the Khia and Peaches lyrics, sometimes euphemisms eschew the assumed sugar-coating intentions and instead are deployed to be offensive. In this section I examine the abundance of euphemisms for *homosexual* to illustrate this point. While in popular parlance *homosexual* is often substituted by *gay* or *queer*, such euphemisms hold very similar connotations, just with fewer syllables. On screen, however, euphemisms with much more baggage and vitriol attached are frequently deployed. In the film *Clueless* (1995), for example, Murray (Donald Faison) tried to convince his friend Cher (Alicia Silverstone) that her boyfriend was gay:

> Your man Christian is a cakeboy! He's a disco-dancing, Oscar Wilde-reading, Streisand ticket-holding friend of Dorothy. Know what I'm saying?

In *Philadelphia* (1993), during a courtroom scene, the lawyer, Joe Miller (Denzel Washington), asked his client whether he was homosexual:

> Are you a homosexual? Answer the question! Are you a homo? A faggot? A punk? A queen? Pillow biter? Fairy? Booty snatcher? Rump roaster? *Are you gay?*

In an episode of the British television series *Life on Mars* (2006–2007), Gene (Philip Glenister) discussed the suspected homosexuality of another character with his colleague Sam (John Simm):

Gene: Because Stephen Warren is a bum bandit. D'you understand? A poof. A fairy. A queer. A queen. Fudge packer. Uphill gardener. Fruit-picking sodomite.
Sam: He's gay?

In the British series *Queer as Folk* (1999–2000), Stuart (Aidan Gillen) came out to his family using a thorough *barrage* of euphemisms:

> Because I'm queer. I'm gay. I'm homosexual. I'm a poof, I'm a poofter, I'm a ponce. I'm a bumboy, baddieboy, backside artist, bugger. I'm bent. I am that arsebandit. I lift those shirts. I'm a faggot-ass, fudge-packing, shit-stabbing uphill gardener. I dine at the downstairs restaurant, I dance at the other end of the ballroom. I'm Moses and the parting of the red cheeks. I fuck and I am fucked. I suck and I am sucked. I rim them and wank them, and every single man's had the fucking time of his life. And I am *not* a pervert.

Just as in real-life dialogue, the euphemisms in these examples are deployed for a variety of reasons. Homosexuals themselves, in fact, have a history of using euphemisms to speak in code so as to avoid outing themselves,[25] as well

The Euphemisms Chapter

as to be ironic and humorous.[26] While Stuart in *Queer as Folk* invariably found some of the euphemisms he listed to be offensive, he may have been more comfortable with others; some words, in fact, are likely to be used frequently and even *favorably* in certain contexts. For heterosexual characters such as Murray, Joe, and Gene to use these euphemisms, however, while irony and humor might be rationales, it is much more likely that they were intending to *insult*; their goal was to *malign* homosexuality. Had Gene simply wanted to state that Stephen Warren (Tom Mannion) was homosexual, he could have done so in one single word. Had Murray wanted to refer to Cher's boyfriend as gay, he, too, could have used the word. If Joe was trying to avoid controversy, he could have stopped after he asked whether his client were gay. *Instead*, these characters used a broad range of euphemisms—most of which have a history of serving as slurs—thereby highlighting that homosexuality is still a characteristic that has varying degrees of public loathing associated.[27] Othering is about making a person—or a group of people—feel different from the majority. By using vivid language that focuses on the often stigmatized sexual practices of a minority, the *homosexual* gets portrayed as more heinous and sexual preference becomes a defining and limiting attribute, in turn demonizing homosexuality.

In Stuart's *Queer as Folk* monologue, he used a number of different euphemisms for homosexuality. While, as noted, he might consider many of these terms to be offensive, there is also the possibility of considering some to be sexy, or at least sexy when deployed during intimacy or heated passion. This possibility is discussed in the next section.

THE LANGUAGE OF AROUSAL

Euphemism is frequently thought of as a technique used to temper a sensitive subject matter; euphemisms tend to be words that are *less* inflammatory and, therefore, less likely to evoke extreme reactions. This, however, is not always the case: the lyrics of Khia and Peaches discussed earlier highlight that sometimes euphemisms are chosen specifically *because* of their dirty talk connotations.

In my book *Part-Time Perverts: Sex, Pop Culture, and Kink Management*, I extensively discussed dirty talk, noting that such dialogue "can be instrumental in perverse sex"[28]: "Inherent in the concept of dirty talk is that the language used differs markedly from the dialogue of daily life; it is sexy because people do not usually speak this way."[29]

While *penis* might be the clinical term, it is less sexy, and certainly less kinky than a word like *cock*. In *Bachelorette* (2012), for example, when

Trevor (James Marsden) said, "Shut up, Cunt," to Regan (Kirsten Dunst) during a passionate sex scene, the word *cunt* did not appear to be an accidental choice. If the speaker intends to arouse a lover or themselves, clinical terms have much less passion and urgency attached than euphemism. This is a point sex writer Tracy Quan made in her chapter on prostitution and euphemism: " 'Whore' is an angry insult during a marital row or, in bed, a spicy term evoking erotic abandon ... Try to imagine a passionate lover replacing 'whore' with 'sex worker' during an exchange of erotic sweet-nothings."[30]

Jay similarly discussed this issue by noting that "[e]rotic words are certainly not the same as clinical or technical terms. The erotic relies on slang and euphemism."[31] In a sex scene from *Sideways* (2004), the following dirty talk transpired in a sex scene between Cammi (Missy Doty) and her husband (MC Gainey):

Husband: You picked him up and you fucked him, didn't you, bitch?
Cammi: I picked him up and I fucked him. I'm a bad girl.
Husband: And you liked fucking him, didn't you, you fat little whore?
Cammi: I liked it when you caught me fucking him.

While a word like *whore* is sexy because it is less polite and *dirtier* than an established word like *prostitute*, part of the thrill—part of the titillation—comes from using language that would be unacceptable in any other context, and notably one that is inextricably bound up with power. *Whore* is sexy *because* it conjures the extreme emotions that more clinical terms are unable, something I discussed in *Part-Time Perverts*: "Dirty talk can help create power dynamics which otherwise do not exist in a relationship and which facilitate both power loss or gain that differ (often quite markedly) from what is experienced in real life."[32]

Words such as *cunt* and *whore* are effective in dirty talk because they have political gravitas: they are insulting, subordinating, and inflammatory, but notably they are *evocative*. Such words can be arousing because they are distanced from the language of real life and simultaneously fetishize subordination.

While dirty talk frequently eroticizes and fetishizes the politics of euphemism, *diluting* politics can also be a central rationale for euphemism, as discussed in the next section.

CORRECTING THE POLITICS

Art critic Robert Hughes condemned politically correct language, facetiously describing it as "a linguistic Lourdes where evil and misfortune are dispelled by a dip in the waters of euphemism."[33] His words constitute a theatrical description but nonetheless provide a useful allusion to a central rationale for euphemism: political correctness. Political correctness describes the process whereby efforts are made to phrase things without exhibiting bias or judgment; *differently abled*, *vertically challenged*, and *plus-size* are examples. While class, race, religion, and physicality are a few of the many realms where political correctness has influenced language, sexuality is one area where the impact is both rife and extensively discussed. In *The Routledge Companion to Feminism and Postfeminism*, for example, it was contended that political correctness was born from American feminism in the 1980s and constitutes "a serious attempt to challenge habitual assumptions encoded in speech and tradition."[34] While political correctness is highly contentious—some feminists describe it as puritanical and a straitjacket,[35] while others praise it as liberating[36]—its influence on popular parlance is undeniable. In this section I examine the political correctness surrounding *prostitution*.

One of the central aims of political correctness is to avoid terms that reinforce prejudice. In recent years the phrase *sex work* has come to be extended to all people who work in the sex industry, most notably prostitutes. *Sex work*, while a popular euphemism—as Quan notes, in some circles, the phrase is mandatory and *prostitution* is frowned upon[37]—it is not without contention. In his work on prostitution and policy, criminologist Roger Matthews outlined some of the consequences of using the word: "The adoption of terms like 'sex work' is in fact a mode of distancing, sanitizing and rationalizing prostitution."[38] Matthews discussed that its use removes stigma and is less essentialist. Quan similarly noted that *sex work* is "associated with acceptance of the prostitute and prostitute power."[39] While there are benefits, theorists also spotlight a number of problems. Matthews, for example, noted that *sex work* muddies the waters, making it difficult to distinguish between prostitutes and other kinds of sex industry workers.[40] Quan similarly noted that *sex work* "ignores or undercuts the emotions that surround prostitution—and prostitutes."[41] Just as political correctness may be construed as a kind of linguistic whitewash, the use of euphemisms for prostitution conceal the politics surrounding sex work, thereby rendering euphemism use controversial. They may be controversial in this context perhaps, but such euphemisms are identifiable throughout popular culture.

Prostitute is named explicitly in a number of songs: Frank Zappa had a song "Teen-Age Prostitute" (1982), Tom Waits had "I'm Your Late Night Evening Prostitute" (1991), and Guns 'n' Roses had "Prostitute" (2008). Far more common, however, is the cavalcade of euphemisms used in place of this term.

Hooker and *ho* are common substitutions and are apparent in a wide variety of songs, from Waits's "Christmas Card from a Hooker in Minneapolis" (1978), to Randy Travis's "Three Wooden Crosses" (2002) ("A farmer and a teacher, a hooker and a preacher / Ridin' on a midnight bus bound for Mexico"), to Ludacris's "Ho" (2000) ("You doin' ho activities with ho tendencies / Hoes are your friends, hoes are your enemies"). *Streetwalker*, also common in popular parlance, appears in Ryan Adams's "Tina Toledo's Street Walkin' Blues" (2001) ("Hard on the knees, money in the bag"), Delta Spirit's "Streetwalker" (2008) ("Old men like to rape her in the red light"), and Time Again's "Streetwalker" (2006) ("now she's on the corner twenty dollars at a time"). Simon and Garfunkel used the popular *whores* euphemism in "The Boxer" (1969), where the protagonist "took some comfort there." Hall and Oates used the same word in "I'm Watching You (A Mutant Romance)" (1974) ("I can usually find you near 42nd and 8th / A whore in a doorway (yeah)"), and Kid Rock used it in "Desperate-Rado" (1993) ("and I'd kill for a cheap whore and a barrel of cold beer").

Words such as *hooker*, *streetwalker*, and *whore*—while predictable—are less about being politically correct and, in fact, function more as synonyms. Music, however, also offers a variety of other euphemisms whereby the intention centers on eschewing judgment, in line with the objective of political correctness.

Cole Porter's "Love for Sale" (1930) is a prostitute's tout to customers: "appetizing young love for sale / love that's fresh and still unspoiled / love that's only slightly soiled." "Love for sale" is similarly offered in Donna Summer's "Lady of the Night" (1974). In Janis Ian's "Pro-Girl" (1967), she describes the work of a prostitute: "you work your way on through the streets of hell." This popular *streets* metonym is evident in Arctic Monkeys' "When the Sun Goes Down" (2006), where a woman is said to have "had to roam the streets." *Painted lady* substitutes for *prostitute* in Elton John's "Sweet Painted Lady" (1973); in John's 1975 "Island Girl," he refers to prostitution as "turning tricks." The *hustle* is sung about in Lou Reed's "Walk on the Wild Side" (1972), where listeners are told "Ev'rybody had to pay and pay / A hustle here and a hustle there." The Police's "Roxanne" (1978) again eschewed *prostitution* and instead offered lyrics such as "You don't have to sell your body to the night" and "You don't have to wear that dress tonight." Prostitutes are referred to as *bad girls* in Summer's song of the same name (1979). In Iron Maiden's "22 Acacia Avenue" (1982), the "looking for a good time" euphemism is used. In ZZ Top's "Mexican Blackbird" (1987), a prostitute is referred to as a "honey": "dancin' and a-lovin's her trade." In Snoop Dogg's "Pay for Pussy" (1998), prostitution is referred to as "the world's oldest profession." In Salt 'n' Pepa's "None of Your Business" (1993), it is spoken of with the euphemism "sell it on the weekend." Cage the Elephant's "Ain't No Rest for the Wicked" (2008) refers to prostitution as "use a little company."

Euphemisms such as *honey* and *painted lady* are much gentler—and certainly less politically loaded—than *prostitute*. Similarly, such examples frequently dodge politics by focusing on the work of the prostitute; *love for sale*, *hustling*, *selling it*. By focusing on the work, the euphemism can be construed as less of an indictment of the woman and more a description of her labor, functioning the way euphemisms are assumed to in an attempt to neutralize politics and downplay sting. Similarly, in songs that explore a man's use of a prostitute, such euphemisms can moderate his purchase of sex; by eschewing explicit and loaded words such as *prostitute* and *whore*, the transaction can, in some way, be romanticized.

In the next section the idea of euphemisms deployed for entertainment purposes is explored.

EUPHEMISM AND LAUGHTER

As highlighted by many of the euphemisms discussed thus far, while achieving a variety of purposes including arousal and sugar-coating, euphemisms can also entertain. In fact, a euphemism is often chosen *because* it is simply funnier than the more clinical term. As linguist Barry Blake notes, while terms such as *special* for those at the lower end of the ability spectrum and *vertically challenged* for short are motivated by political correctness, such terms are also frequently used jokingly.[42] In an episode of *How I Met Your Mother* (2005–), for example, Barney (Neil Patrick Harris) termed a vibrator "a battery-powered adult recreational fake penis." The elaborate euphemism is funnier as opposed to being more politically correct or less offensive. In the British sitcom *Are You Being Served?* (1972–1985), a constant stream of jokes were centered on Mrs. Slocombe's (Mollie Sugden) persistent reference to her *pussy*:

Mrs. Slocombe: (Removes her gas mask) What about this fog! My pussy's been gasping all night.
Mrs. Slocombe: It's a wonder I'm here at all, you know. My pussy got soaking wet. I had to dry it out in front of the fire before I left.
Mrs. Slocombe: You're lucky to have me at all, Captain Peacock. I had to thaw my pussy out before I came. It had been out all night.

While *pussy* as a euphemism for *vagina* is very common in popular parlance, Mrs. Slocombe was actually talking about her pet cat. In this context, the use of *pussy* worked as a double entendre rather than as a euphemism: *pussy* simply made every cat comment appear salacious, thereby soliciting laughter. There are many other examples were euphemisms for genitals are specifically used for comedy. On the website TVTropes.com, the phrase "Hurricane of Euphemisms" describes the tactic used in film and television whereby a barrage of euphemisms is used for effect.[43] Earlier in this chapter I discussed examples from *Clueless*, *Philadelphia*, *Life on Mars*, and *Queer as Folk* to illustrate some more serious applications of stacked euphemisms as related to homosexuality. In this section I examine the hurricane of euphemisms used in comedy as related to genitals.

In the film *Teen Witch* (1989), a hurricane of euphemisms was used when a sex education teacher asked her students to guess what an umbrella will represent in her demonstration. One student, Rhet (Noah Blake), raised his hand and answered, "A roger. A love one. Joystick, dong, zipper-lizard, tallywhacker, trouser-snake, schlong!" The hurricane of euphemisms for *penis* was taken substantially further in the film *Four Rooms* (1995) during a heated discussion between Sigfried (David Proval) and his wife Angela (Jennifer Beals), who had been trying to enrage Sigfried by talking about the penis of the bellhop (Tim Roth):

Sigfried: Please stop talking about his cock!

Angela: Well, it's hard to stop talking about something that's so huge. I mean, I could go on and on about his cock ... his bone ... his knob ... bishop, wang, thang, rod, hot rod, hump-mobile, Oscar, dong, dagger, banana, cucumber, salami, sausage, kielbasa, schlong, dink, tool, Big Ben, Mr. Happy, peter, pecker, pee-pee, wee-wee, wiener, pisser, pistol, joint, hose, horn, middle leg, third leg, meat, stick, joystick, dipstick, one-eyed wonder, Junior, little head, little guy, Rumple Foreskin, Tootsie Roll, love muscle, skin flute, Roto-Rooter, snake ... Hammer, rammer, spammer, bazooka, rubber, chubby, sticky, stubby.

Angela's intent in this scene appeared neither to sugar-coat nor to offend. Instead, the stacked euphemisms were simply used for *comedy*: the sheer number of different euphemisms for penis was farcical and entertaining. This idea was also presented in Monty Python's *The Meaning of Life* (1983) when Eric Idle (playing Noël Coward) sang "The Penis Song," whose lyrics included "Your piece of pork, your wife's best friend, your percy or your cock." Lady Gaga's song "LoveGame" (2008) uses the equally humorous euphemism of *disco stick*.

In a hurricane of euphemisms scene from *Varsity Blues* (1999), euphemisms for erections were proposed: Miss Davis (Tonie Perensky) asked her class if anyone could suggest some "common slang" for the male erection. Jonathan (James Van Der Beek) offered the following answer:

> Pitchin' a tent, sportin' a wood, stiffie, flesh rocket, tall tommy, Mr. Morbis, the march is on, icicle has formed, Jack's magic beanstalk, rigor mortis has set in, Mr. Mushroom-head, mushroom on a stick, purple headed yogurt slinger ... Oh, and Pedro.

In the episode of *House* referred to earlier, a hurricane of euphemisms was used in the context of masturbation when Dr. House explained to Claire (Leigh-Allyn Baker) that her young daughter Rose (Amber DeMarco) had been masturbating:

House: In actuality, all your little girl is doing is saying "yoo hoo" to the hoo hoo.
Claire: She's what?
House: Marching the penguin. Ya-ya-ing the sisterhood. Finding Nemo.
Rose: That was funny.
House: It's called gratification disorder. Sort of a misnomer. If one was *unable* to gratify oneself, that would be a disorder.
Claire: (Covering the girl's ears) Are you saying she's masturbating?
House: I was trying to be discreet. There's a child in the room!

Masturbation was treated similarly in an episode of *Game of Thrones* (2011–) when Tyrion (Peter Dinklage) confessed to masturbation in his childhood: "I milked my eel, I flogged the one-eyed snake, I skinned my sausage, I made the bald man cry." In *Liar Liar* (1997), this hurricane technique was used to describe sex in a courtroom scene when lawyer Fletcher (Jim Carrey) asked about the sex life of a witness: "You slammed her, you dunked her donut, you gave her dog a Snausage! You stuffed her like a Thanksgiving turkey!"

While these examples give insight into the enormous variety of sex-themed euphemisms, in each case their deployment was primarily geared toward soliciting laughter; audiences are often entertained by linguistic gymnastics. The use of euphemisms in these examples is funny because euphemisms are stacked for comic effect; humor is borne from exaggeration and madcappery. Such examples are also entertaining because many of these descriptions are visually arresting and substantially more entertaining than use of the more clinical descriptors.

FEARING THE EUPHEMISM

While this chapter has focused on reviewing and explaining the wide variety of euphemisms connected to sex, worth pondering is whether we should be concerned by their use. Earlier, for example, I discussed Orwell's use of the expression "newspeak" in *Nineteen Eighty-Four*, where the aim was for the state to limit expression. In Orwell's novel, the Newspeak dictionary editor explained: "Don't you see that the whole aim of Newspeak is to narrow the range of thought? In the end we shall make thoughtcrime literally impossible, because there will be no words in which to express it."[44]

Given the dozens of euphemisms discussed throughout this chapter, it seems thoroughly *incongruous* that a narrowing of language might be occurring: if there are hundreds and thousands of euphemisms for sex and wanton woman, for example, surely the lexicon isn't actually shrinking. While a narrowing may not be occurring, use of euphemisms does raise some concerns, particularly when connected to crime. In Parker and Mahlstedt's work on language and rape, the authors posed the question: "Imagine a time when the terms 'date rape' and 'acquaintance rape' did not exist. What would you have called the experience of being raped by someone you were dating or knew as a friend?"[45] Following this theme, in historian Anthony Neal's book *Unburdened by Conscience*, he recounted an interesting story: "A revered historian of American slavery once asked me, 'Do we need to be told again that white men took sexual advantage of black women during American slavery?' I replied, 'Not exactly.' Depending upon how we interpret the phrase 'took sexual advantage of,' it could mean anything from a euphemism for rape to a misleading mischaracterization of it."[46] These examples highlight a problem that occurs in the absence of accurate and precise language: a minefield of ambiguity is created. While there are often serious reasons why someone might choose to eschew *rape* and use a euphemism instead, doing so has consequence: a central one is that meaning often gets muddled. Connected to this idea is that not only do euphemisms confuse events, but they also potentially confuse thinking. Carolyn Logan, in her book *Counterbalance: Gendered Perspectives for Writing and Language*, discussed this idea, contending that euphemisms confuse thinking and potentially *values*: "euphemisms are sometimes handy, but, if the habitual use of euphemisms causes us to forget that stealing is wrong or to ignore death as a part of life, the habit inhibits clear thinking and clear communications."[47] Logan's fear is that by making language gray, the concepts of right and wrong likewise become blurred. Discussed earlier were the examples of the songs "Runaway Love" and "Delilah," where rape is discussed with a variety of very watered-down euphemisms. A possible consequence is that instead of being explicit about the perpetrator being a rapist and the crime being heinous, the recounting of the story becomes modulated, gray, and confusing.

Not only does using a euphemism in the context of rape confuse thoughts and descriptions, but it helps reinforce the idea that frank discussion of rape is taboo. In his research, Jay contended that "[w]hen speakers refrain from talking about the taboo, they empower the taboo."[48] Continuing to use euphemisms instead of the more precise, clinical descriptions supports the idea that some words are too bad, too inflammatory, and too emotive to say aloud. When taboo exists around certain words, people may be afraid to say them, and thus be afraid to speak up about crimes or ask questions related to their bodies.

Instead of being explicit in dialogue about sex, humans often favor euphemisms. Such euphemisms are detectable throughout popular culture, notably in songs and on the screen. In this chapter I reviewed a wide variety of euphemisms, identifying that our reasons for their deployment are just as diverse as the many options at our disposal.

The Vegetarian Chapter: Introducing the Hippies, Sad Sacks, and Fundamentalists

Political research on food tends to restrict analysis to issues of ethical production, food security, marketing, and consumption. This chapter, however, examines the politics of representations of vegetarianism. While being a vegetarian is not a media taboo in the same way that cunnilingus and pregnancy termination are, vegetarianism is nonetheless an uncommon dietary choice and normally portrayed as fringe behavior. Karen Iacobbo and Michael Iacobbo, in their book *Vegetarians and Vegans in America Today*, contended that "[v]egetarians may be typical Americans, but their practice and philosophy of not eating meat ... sets them apart."[1] That vegetarians are *apart* from mainstream culture is something mirrored on screen, with most film and television examples portraying vegetarians as somehow different. The standard othering and stereotyping—if not outright *demonizing*—of vegetarian characters highlight that not only is eschewing meat considered unusual, but that it also raises a variety of social and political issues related to gender, patriotism, health, and intellect. This chapter begins with a discussion of the challenges that vegetarianism poses to American values and then examines the screen stereotypes, notably the hippies, sad sacks, and fundamentalists.

THE AMERICAN LOVE OF MEAT

In the documentary *No Cure for Cancer* (1992), comedian Denis Leary discussed vegetarianism:

> I tried eating vegetarian. I feel like a wimp going into a restaurant: "What do you want to eat sir? *Broccoli*?" Broccoli's a side dish, folks. Always was,

always will be, okay? When they ask me what I want, I say: "What do you think I want? This is America. I want a bowl of raw red meat right now. Forget about that, bring me a live cow over to the table. I'll carve off what I want and ride the rest home."

Here, Leary humorously alludes to the truism that meat-eating is essential to being American, that it is what *normal* Americans do. This idea—presented in a variety of ways—is a standard screen presentation. In 2006, the industry group Meat and Livestock Australia harnessed this idea and aired a television campaign with the slogan: "Meat. We were meant to eat it." In the film *Kama Sutra: A Tale of Love* (1996), the same idea was apparent when Raj (Naveen Andrews) remarked, "There is joy in three things: eating meat, riding meat and putting meat into meat." In *Halloween II* (2009), Sheriff Brackett (Brad Dourif) commented, "Man was meant to eat meat. We, all of us, have a little bit caveman in us." In *Revelation* (1999), during an argument with a vegetarian, Willie (Tony Nappo) retorted, "Yeah, well, if God didn't want us to eat animals he shouldn't have made them out of meat." Harland (Mike Connors) made a similar jibe in *Gideon* (1999): "Yeah, well, if God didn't want us to eat animals, why are they made out of meat?" In an episode of the animated series *The Simpsons* (1989–), Homer purported that "All normal people love meat." The Dutch businessman (Jan Vlasák) in the horror film *Hostel* (2005) proudly claimed, "I am a meat-eater. It is human nature." In an episode of the Australian crime show *Rush* (2008–2011), Lawson (Rodger Corser) argued that: "Killing animals for food is just the natural order of things." In an episode of the sitcom *Joey* (2004–2006), the title character (Matt LeBlanc) claimed: "It is natural for humans to eat meat, okay? We eat the cows; the cows eat the grass; we mow the grass, which makes us hungry for more cows." In *No Cure for Cancer*, Leary claimed, "Not eating meat is a decision. Eating meat is an instinct." In an episode of sitcom *Married with Children* (1987–1997), Peggy (Katey Sagal) served her husband Al (Ed O'Neill) lunch, to which he exclaimed: "Peg, this is just three pieces of bread. Where's the meat?" The same idea was apparent in an episode of *The Good Guys* (2010) when Dan (Bradley Whitford) remarked, "A sandwich without meat isn't a sandwich; it's just lonely bread." Each of these examples present the idea that eating meat is not merely normal, but it is what humans want, what they *crave*—that meat-eating is innate, God-intended behavior, and that meals devoid of it are incomplete.

Taking the meat-is-good truism further are narratives where a world without meat is considered to be a frightening, hellish dystopia. In the sci-fi series *SeaQuest DSV* (1993–1996), meat was outlawed. The same thing transpired in the futuristic worlds of *Demolition Man* (1993) and *Escape from LA* (1996), where meat was banned along with a variety of other practices including smoking, swearing, and premarital sex. The imposition of a vegetarian diet in these narratives was considered undemocratic and thoroughly un-American.

In claiming that eating meat is normal and *American*, the implication is that not doing so is somehow *un-American*. While contempt for vegetarians is normally conveyed on screen through the presentation of a vaguely loathsome caricature—and thus complying with the *show—don't tell* mantra of the screen—such contempt was actually spoken aloud in an episode of the television series *Sons of Anarchy* (2008–). In the pilot, a planned barbeque was discussed by Jax (Charlie Hunnam) and his mother Gemma (Katey Sagal). Jax commented that the "New kid doesn't eat meat," to which Gemma responded, "Don't patch him in; can't trust anyone who doesn't eat meat." While Gemma doesn't explain her position, she nevertheless conveys the idea that there is something *wrong* with vegetarians. Interestingly, she also presents a rarely articulated essentialist view: that vegetarians are— *by nature*—untrustworthy. Such comments are in line with a perception that not only is vegetarianism unusual, but that it conflicts with American values; to not eat meat and to not be *like everyone else* makes a person objectionable and suspicious. That *outlaw bikers* consider vegetarians as untrustworthy appears both ironic and telling.

Given the comparative strangeness of not eating meat, for a character to be a vegetarian means that his or her mere presence on the screen challenges American values and forces other characters to think about their own dietary practices. This challenge can be presented in numerous ways; in this chapter I focus on negative stereotyping. Jenna Torres, one of the authors of *Vegan Freak*, discussed stereotyping, claiming that "[b]ecause we challenge the status quo just by choosing not to eat the Standard American Diet, people think that vegans are self-righteous, crazy ideologues who are out to threaten everyone's way of life."[2] Bob Torres, *Vegan Freak*'s other author, presented a similar argument: "there's always a price to pay for going against social norms ... Though vegans and vegetarians aren't really breaking any rules, we do things that are contrary to what's expected in meat-eating America, and we pay for that by being ridiculed and/or mis-portrayed in the media, by being laughed at as crazies, or by being shunned during social occasions."[3]

Torres and Torres contend that demonization and mocking are motivated by the ethos that vegetarianism runs counter to the standard narrative which dictates that meat-eating is *what Americans do*. Margaret Puskar-Pasewicz, in her book on vegetarianism, took this idea further, contending that such stereotypes are partly the results of "million-dollar efforts of large-scale, industrial meat companies."[4] An example of such marketing was a 2004 advertisement for Ballpark Franks, which explicitly stated that "vegetarians are not only weird, but maybe un-American." Interestingly, the un-American position references the same allegations that have been hurled at hippies since the 1960s: in historian Stephen Oates's research, he noted, "Most often hippies were seen as degenerate and representative of all things godless and un-American."[5] It is therefore unsurprising that the hippie is one of the most common vegetarian stereotypes.

Discussed earlier was the apparent natural, God-sanctioned love of meat. Meat-love is a very obvious undercurrent in screen presentations: the supposed deliciousness of meat makes giving it up (almost) too arduous to consider.

UNATTAINABLE VEGETARIANISM

Mary Marginson, an animal rights activist and filmmaker, claims to have met "very few people who were actually against the idea of vegetarianism." Instead, she noted that far more frequently people claim, "I could never do that."[6] The idea here is that a consensus exists that while vegetarianism might be a lofty aspiration, *in practice* a person's meat-eating impulses will win out. This theme is apparent in a wide variety of screen examples where vegetarianism is alluded to through reference to its unachievability.

In the Russian film *Stalker* (1979), the character of The Writer (Anatoliy Solonitsyn) remarked, "My conscience wants vegetarianism to win over the world. And my subconscious is yearning for a piece of juicy meat." In *No Impact Man: The Documentary* (2009), the Conlin family tried to live sustainably, including reducing their meat consumption. In one scene Michelle Conlin remarked, "I *want* to be a vegetarian, but I want to have a hot dog now and then." In the pilot of sitcom *The Big Bang Theory* (2007–), Penny (Kaley Cuoco) claimed, "I'm a vegetarian. Except for fish. And the occasional steak, I love steak." In an episode of the sitcom *Roseanne* (1988–1997), Darlene's (Sara Gilbert) boyfriend David (Johnny Galecki) claimed to be "vegetarian-*like*" based on "eating a lot more chicken." In the sitcom *Bored to Death* (2009–2011), Jonathan (Jason Schwartzman) lamented, "In my heart I'm a vegan, but in my mouth I lack discipline." In the British documentary *Bill Bailey: Live at the Apollo—Part Troll* (2004), the comic joked, "I'm a vegetarian, I'm not strict. I eat fish. And duck, but they're nearly fish aren't they?" In an episode of the British sketch comedy series

The Fast Show (1994–2001), the schoolgirl character "Our Janine" (Caroline Aherne) commented, "I've gone vegetarian now. I mean, I know I had a sausage roll yesterday, but it's not really meat, is it, y'know? I mean, there's no animal called a *sausage*."

Sociologist Donna Maurer has discussed the difficulty of obtaining data on vegetarianism, writing that "many more people identify as vegetarians than adhere to the standard definition."[7] One explanation for this discrepancy is that vegetarianism is often *aspirational*; thus people's self-labeling is indicative of wishful thinking and an idealized identity rather than a dietary reality. In the examples discussed previously, a range of characters implied that while they believed that vegetarianism was something noble and something that they should *want* to be, in practice it is difficult; notably, they claimed that meat just tastes too good to give up. The difficulty of vegetarianism is depicted on screen in a number of ways; two discussed in this section are the tempted vegetarian and the ordeal of vegetarians living among nonvegetarians.

The Tempted Vegetarian

In the animated film *Barnyard* (2006), the character Pig the Pig remarked, "Vegetarians have to eat in the dark, right?" While Pig in this scene is confusing vegetarianism with *vampirism*, a possible alternative reading of his comment is the presumed clandestine behavior of some vegetarians; that is, the difficulty of vegetarianism makes temptation inevitable. In the sitcom *Unhappily Ever After* (1995–1999), the youngest son Ryan (Kevin Connolly) wanted to win a young environmentalist award, so he tried to convince his household to join him in giving up meat as his project. It was exposed in the episode that Ryan couldn't stick to vegetarianism himself and was shown secretly eating meat. The sitcom *Dharma & Greg* (1997–2007) centered on the very different lifestyles of Dharma's (Jenna Elfman) hippie family and Greg's (Thomas Gibson) straight-laced upper-middle-class family. Dharma's father Larry (Alan Rachins) is a good example of a tempted vegetarian: because of his wife Abby's (Mimi Kennedy) vegetarian convictions, Larry generally lived as a vegetarian but, when given the opportunity, succumbed to temptation—in one episode he ate mini-hotdogs at a party.

While Larry's vegetarianism appears largely motivated by appeasing his wife, Abby is a *devout* vegetarian nearly throughout the series. *Nearly*, because during one season she was pregnant and briefly succumbed to meat temptation. The same storyline transpired in sitcom *Friends* (1994–2004), when vegetarian character Phoebe (Lisa Kudrow) submitted to her pregnancy cravings for meat. While pregnancy provided both women with the opportunity to take respite from their diets, the fact that two staunch—and political—vegetarian characters were successfully tempted conveys an essentialist understanding of meat-eating: that it is what our bodies "naturally" want. Such ideas, of course, are in line with the dominant thesis that *vegetarianism* is the true aberration. This is certainly how the character of Detective Holder (Joel Kinnaman) was presented in *The Killing* (2011–). Early into the series he identified as a vegetarian but in a later episode was seen eating ham, eggs, and sausage. His colleague, Detective Linden (Mireille Enos) asked, "What happened to your whole lacto-ova-vegan thing?" to which he responded, "Nothing. I'm just ready to embrace meat again."

While Abby and Phoebe returned to their vegetarianism, the fact that they deviated during pregnancy alludes to another incarnation of the tempted vegetarian on screen: the *kind of* vegetarian. In an episode of *NCIS* (2003–), the following exchange occurred between Abby (Pauley Perrette) and her colleague Timothy (Sean Murray):

Abby: Do you know what my biggest pet peeve is, McGee?
Timothy: People who say they're vegetarians but eat chicken?

In this scene, Timothy facetiously referenced the type of vegetarian that Maurer defined as not adhering to the "standard definition": the *flexitarian*—or flexible vegetarian. In Robin Asbell's recipe book *New Vegetarianism*, she described flexitarians as "folks who eat a lot of vegetarian food, but when the moment suits them, they eat meat or fish."[8] Asbell's definition is politically neutral, but in practice flexitarians are susceptible to criticism as lacking in commitment or, even worse, being construed as cheats or hypocrites.

A number of flexitarian characters are detectable on screen. David on *Roseanne*, for example, considered himself "vegetarian-*like*" based on his high consumption of chicken (presumably *instead* of red meat). Larry on *Dharma & Greg* more explicitly suits the label: he was vegetarian for most of the time, but occasionally strayed. While Holder declared his vegetarianism early into *The Killing*, as discussed earlier, in one episode he was shown eating ham and sausage; as colleague Linden described him, he is a vegetarian "who eats pork rinds." In the Canadian animated series *What about Mimi?* (2000–2003), Mimi's mother, Saffron, was a vegan and the family lived as vegans. In one episode Saffron went away for the weekend and

Mimi's father, Marvin, secretly ate meat. In an episode of *Sabrina, the Teenage Witch* (1996–2003), Sabrina's (Melissa Joan Hart) friend Roxie (Soleil Moon Frye) was an activist vegetarian. When Roxie and Sabrina appeared on MTV's *Total Request Live* (1998–2008), while Roxie *intended* to convey an anti-meat message, she became so starstruck by host Carson Daly that she failed to deliver her message. The next day, Roxie saw Daly on television and was again so distracted that she ate a turkey sandwich.

Like the tempted vegetarians discussed earlier, in these examples a more fickle incarnation is presented: opportunity or even mere *distraction* can motivate a character to stray. One reading is the perpetuation of the idea of vegetarians as untrustworthy and disingenuous; another is the "fad" idea. Vegetarians, for example, often report that upon declaring their vegetarianism, those around them assume that their decision will be fleeting, that it is something they will *grow out of*. Certainly this idea is promoted by promeat groups: Maurer, for example, noted that "[i]nterest groups such as the National Cattlemen's Beef Association argue that vegetarian diets are a passing fad, bound to go in and out of style like bell bottoms, new-wave music, and mood rings."[9] Characters whose vegetarianism is flexible or faddish work to perpetuate the idea that vegetarianism doesn't need to be taken seriously—most certainly not if vegetarians *themselves* can't do so.

Vegetarians in a Nonvegetarian World

In my book about infidelity, *Cheating on the Sisterhood: Infidelity and Feminism*, I discussed the issue of feminists often finding it difficult to stick to their principles in a world that is otherwise *nonfeminist*: "Small numbers of feminists may have the opportunity to live entirely within a feminist community, but most reside in environments not conducive to, or potentially even hostile to, feminism and thus find only 'intermittent' practice of their politics possible. For these feminists, adapting their identities to prosper is likely an attractive solution."[10]

As related to a discussion of vegetarianism, given that the vast majority of vegetarians reside in a nonvegetarian world, they need to manage their beliefs and politics within a hostile environment. For many, this is a struggle— a topic that feminist and animal rights advocate Carol Adams devotes her book *Living Among Meat Eaters* to exploring. In the aforementioned episode of *Roseanne*, Darlene criticized David for eating meat and in reply he challenged her convictions, arguing that she was a hypocrite because her family made its income from *selling* meat: Darlene's mother ran a loose-meat diner. The episode focused on Darlene's struggle to manage her vegetarian identity within a household—and lifestyle—that was supported by the very meat she so abhorred. A similar struggle transpired in the Canadian series *Ready or Not* (1993–1997): in one episode Laura (Amanda Zimm) became a vegetarian but her best friend Busy (Lani Billard) couldn't join her because Busy's father was a butcher and she had a part-time job selling hotdogs. In an episode of *The Simpsons*, the same struggle unfolded when Lisa became a vegetarian: she had to contend with her meat-loving family—at one point, violently throwing away a roasted pig and storming out of a barbeque—but eventually learning to tolerate the opposing views of others, notably through the examples set by Apu, the vegan convenience store owner, and activists Paul and Linda McCartney.

Another way that the "vegetarian in a nonvegetarian world" narrative is presented is through portrayals of vegetarianism as something foreign: something well illustrated in films *My Big Fat Greek Wedding* (2002) and *Everything Is Illuminated* (2005) as well as in episodes of *The Simpsons* and *Friends*. In *My Big Fat Greek Wedding*, Toula's (Nia Vardalos) fiancé Ian (John Corbett) is a vegetarian. When Toula's Aunt Voula (Andrea Martin) discovered this, she exclaimed "What do you mean, he don't eat no meat?" The room fell silent and she then conceded, "Oh, that's okay. I make lamb." In *Everything Is Illuminated*, the following conversation transpired between Jonathan (Elijah Wood), Grandfather Safran (Stephen Samudovsky), and his friend Alex (Eugene Hutz):

Jonathan:	I'm a vegetarian.
Alex:	You're a what?
Jonathan:	I don't eat meat.
Alex:	How can you not eat meat?
Jonathan:	I just don't.
Alex:	(To Grandfather, in Russian) He says he does not eat meat.
Grandfather:	(To Alex, in Russian) What?
Alex:	No meat?
Jonathan:	No meat.
Alex:	Steak?
Jonathan:	No.
Alex:	Chickens?
Jonathan:	No.
Alex:	And what about the sausage?

Jonathan:	No, no sausage, no meat.
Alex:	(To Grandfather, in Russian) He says he does not eat any meat.
Grandfather:	(To Alex, in Russian) Not even sausage?
Alex:	(To Grandfather, in Russian) I know!
Grandfather:	(To Alex, in Russian) What is wrong with him?
Alex:	What is wrong with you?
Jonathan:	Nothing, I just don't eat meat!

While in both scenes Ian and Jonathan are portrayed as peculiar—and even slightly *otherworldly*—neither character was actually ridiculed; rather, their choices were simply not understood. In fact, these scenes could actually be interpreted as ridiculing the *meat-eating* characters: by suggesting she cooks lamb for Ian, Voula appears vaguely idiotic; Alex and Grandfather Safran similarly appeared unsophisticated. Such an analysis is certainly applicable to the scene from *The Simpsons* when Lisa declared her vegetarianism and her father, Homer, queried whether she would still eat bacon, ham, or pork chops. A similar—if slightly more mean-spirited—idea was apparent in an episode of *Friends* when Rachel (Jennifer Aniston), her father Leonard (Ron Leibman), and friend Phoebe were at restaurant:

Leonard:	How about I order everyone the Moroccan chicken?
Phoebe:	Oh, I—I don't eat meat.
Leonard:	It's chicken.
Phoebe:	Yeah, I don't eat that either.
Leonard:	I'll never understand you lesbians.

While Leonard, a doctor, is not portrayed as necessarily *naïve* in this scene, he nonetheless comes across as vague, dismissive, and even slightly arrogant.

Introduced earlier were the vegetarian characters of Phoebe on *Friends* and Abby on *Dharma & Greg*. Not only vegetarians, these characters exemplify perhaps the most common vegetarian portrayal on screen: the hippie.

HIPPIES AND THE NEW AGE

In an episode of the British series *A Very Peculiar Practice* (1986–1988), Professor Furie (Timothy West) remarked, "I need meat, I'm not a sociologist! I can't work on hippie food!" Here, Professor Furie highlights the most common stereotype of the vegetarian on screen—that not eating meat renders a person as *hippie-like*. In Puskar-Pasewicz's research, she identified that vegetarian characters are frequently presented as "engaged in a variety of New Age "alternative" practices."[11] This perception certainly plays out on screen. In the romantic comedy *How to Lose a Guy in 10 Days* (2003), after Andie (Kate Hudson) faked being a vegetarian, her unsuspecting new boyfriend Ben (Matthew McConaughey) took her to a vegetarian restaurant: sitar music played, wheatgrass grew in pots on the counter, and the staff were all presented as pierced and tattooed. In the comedy *The Dictator* (2012), Zoey (Anna Faris) ran a vegan co-op: she was a hippie feminist, complete with underarm hair. Both were the screen's typical alternative characters who notably *look* different.

While the left-leaning, crunchy granola, New Age, free-spirit stereotype may seem rather obvious, the hippie vegetarian serves a number of functions other than to merely visually encapsulate counterculture values. In this section I discuss the hippie vegetarian as presented (1) as charmingly offbeat, (2) as a manipulative poser, (3) as sexually liberated, and (4) as a pacifist. In each example, the character is an aesthetic presentation of vegetarianism but also embodies varying degrees of contempt and mockery, in line with dominate—and negative—attitudes toward vegetarianism.

The Quaintly Offbeat Vegetarian

In the British sitcom *The Young Ones* (1982–1984), Neil (Nigel Planer) was a student, a vegetarian, and the archetypal hippie: long hair, a penchant for conspiracy theories, and the butt of his housemates' jokes. In *Dharma & Greg*, Dharma's hippie parents, Abby and Larry, were casual, sexually liberated, bohemian-style dressers, preoccupied with conspiracy theories and left-of-center pursuits such as tarot. Phoebe in *Friends* was similarly portrayed as the archetypal flaky hippie: she was a sometimes-masseuse and an aspiring—albeit not very talented—musician with an unconventional dress sense. While Neil, Abby, and Phoebe were presented as slightly dippy, they were nonetheless kind-hearted characters whose lifestyle choices—while often ribbed by those around them—functioned to contrast with the characters around them: Neil contrasted with his violent punk housemate Vyvyan (Adrian Edmondson); easygoing Abby contrasted with Greg's uptight and conservative mother Kitty (Susan Sullivan); free-spirited Phoebe contrasted with her neurotic and obsessive-compulsive friend Monica (Courtney Cox) and materialistic friend Rachel. In these examples, the characters' vegetarianism was less about animal rights and more a way to present the characters as different, offbeat, and peace-loving; their vegetarianism was just as "zany" as Vyvyan's antiestablishment values or Rachel's penchant for high-end fashion.

The Hippie Poser Vegetarian

While Neil's, Abby's, and Phoebe's flakiness were mocked in their respective narratives, the mocking of the vegetarian is taken substantially further in *High Fidelity* (2000). Tim Robbins played Ian, a character described by cultural theorist Kristina Nelson as "an aging yuppie with a sitar-loving, Gandhiesque demeanor"[12] and as a "terrifying amalgamation of New Age odiousness"[13] by film critic Chris Barsanti. Rob (John Cusack) was the film's protagonist and Ian was his love rival: Ian was a ponytailed, vegetarian hippie and the new boyfriend of Rob's ex-girlfriend, Laura (Iben Hjejle). Describing Ian, Rob spotlighted "his stupid clothing, his music—Latin, Bulgarian, whatever fucking world music was trendy that week—stupid laugh, awful cooking smells. I can't remember anything good about him at all." Whereas vegetarianism helped to embellish Neil, Abby, and Phoebe as good-natured hippies, Ian's vegetarianism was largely presented as yet another thing that made him weird, repellant, and worth hating. Interestingly, while Ian fulfilled the hippie stereotype *aesthetically*—as well as in regard to his world music and vegetarian lifestyle choices—those qualities also worked to help highlight that the character was manipulative and somewhat disingenuous. His New Age, hippie credentials were really just the façade of a sleaze; Ian used the *trappings* of vegetarianism as a way to appear peace-loving. Another way that the poser is presented is through vegetarians being portrayed as judgmental and preachy; not consuming meat, in this case, allows them a degree of superiority.

Hippies and Sexual Liberation

In the film *Shortbus* (2006), Justin Bond (playing himself) commented, "These bitches sucking cock and eating ass ... then they show up at the buffet and say they're vegan." While the quote is vaguely humorous within the narrative, it also presents a link between vegetarianism and sexual liberation. Abby and Larry's attitude toward sex was quite liberal: in one episode, they encouraged her daughter Dharma and husband Greg, "Feel free to have sex anywhere." In *Friends*, Phoebe was presented as similarly liberal: while generally presented as heterosexual, in one episode she appeared sexually attracted to her friend Monica's female cousin; in another she sang a song that included the lyrics "Sometimes men love women / sometimes men love men / then there are bisexuals." In an episode of *Bored to Death*, Allison (Parker Posey) was a "radical vegan" who, within minutes of meeting Jonathan, had sex with him. In the animated series *American Dad!* (2005–), daughter Hayley is the stereotypical marijuana-smoking, community-college student vegetarian who is also sexually promiscuous (and hinted to be bisexual). In the British soap *River City* (2002–), Jennifer (Lorna Craig) is presented as a modern-day hippie—preoccupied with animal rights, pacifism, and veganism—and is also a lesbian.

While historically meat-eating was thought to stir the passions and to lead to higher sex drives,[14] the "free love" movement of the late 1960s and 1970s permanently linked vegetarianism with the hippie movement, thereby creating an enduring connection between vegetarianism and sexual liberation. One explanation for this stereotype is that vegetarianism is often linked to a higher spiritualism and to heightened experiences including sexuality. Another reading—linked to the earlier discussion about vegetarianism conflicting with American values—is the assumption that to be a hippie and to be vegetarian is to shun American values: that vegetarianism, promiscuity, and nonmainstream sexuality are each equally horrible elements of the counterculture.

The Pacifist Vegetarian

In an episode of the British food-themed series *Gordon's Great Escape* (2010–2011), chef Gordon Ramsay was in South India, a place he described as a "hotbed of vegetarians." At one point, a food writer, Rashmi Uday Singh, told Ramsay, "We believe that [meat-eating] is what is responsible for your bad temper." To this, the chef snapped, "Eating meat makes you bad tempered? What a load of bollocks!" Encapsulated in this exchange is the idea that to be a meat-eater is to be a hothead.

Certainly presentations of vegetarianism as connected to the peace-loving, pacifist values of hippies are easily detected on screen. In *John Tucker Must Die* (2006), Beth (Sophia Bush) discussed her relationship: "We share a vegan nonviolent outlook on life." In an episode of *Futurama* (1999–), a hippie animal rights protester argued that you "shouldn't eat things that feel pain." In the animated film *Shark Tale* (2004), the shark protagonist Lenny fought his nature, refusing to participate in acts of violence. The same thing occurred in the animated series *Count Duckula* (1988–1993); according to the series' theme song, the title character "won't bite beast or man, 'cause he's a vegetarian." In an episode of the animated series *My Little Pony: Friendship Is Magic* (2010–), Pinkie Pie sang a song with the lyrics: "Both our diets, I should mention / Are completely vegetarian / We all eat hay and oats / Why be at each other's throat?" In the animated series *Avatar: The Last Airbender* (2005–2008), protagonist Aang was a vegetarian, consistent with the character's beliefs that all life is sacred. In an episode of *Buffy the Vampire Slayer* (1997–2003), the character of Annabelle (Courtnee Draper)—a slayer-in-training—claimed to be a "veggie." Annabelle was similarly reluctant to be involved in violence or to carry a weapon.

In each of these examples, an assumption is made that for a person to eschew meat means that he or she is a kinder, gentle soul, in line with hippie values and caricatures. The pacifist vegetarian, however, can also be presented as a gross caricature. In *How to Lose a Guy in 10 Days*, on her new boyfriend Ben, Andie tested out a variety of clichéd ways that women ruin relationships; Ben, meanwhile, was road-testing his own set of clichés designed to make women swoon. In one scene, Ben cooked Andie dinner: lamb. Andie sadly lamented that she only *wished* she ate meat and started to sing, in a baby voice, "Mary Had a Little Lamb." She then gagged. A similar, idiotic caricature was presented in *Notting Hill* (1999) with the character Keziah (Emma Bernard) who claimed to be a "fruitarian": "We believe that fruits and vegetables have feelings so we think cooking is cruel. We only eat things that have actually fallen off a tree or bush—that are, in fact, dead already." These two examples present exaggerations of the pacifist character—that being *so* gentle is stupid and insipid, working to yet again spotlight the contention that vegetarianism itself is bizarre and counter to the normal way of life and (certainly in these two examples) even *feminine*.

Connected to the idea of pacifism on screen is the explanation that a triggering atrocity is what propels a character to reform his or her meat-eating ways, that humans will resist their natural meat-eating impulses only if given the right motivation. A humorous example of this occurred in an episode of sitcom *3rd Rock from the Sun* (1996–2001) when Dick (John Lithgow) accidentally hit a chipmunk, thereby motivating his (temporary) vegetarianism. In an episode of the animated series *South Park* (1997–), Stan (temporarily) became a vegetarian after finding out about the cruel ways baby calves are treated in veal production. In *The Simpsons*, Lisa's vegetarianism was similarly motivated by her bonding with an impossibly cute lamb at a petting zoo. In other examples, pacifism is connected to more explicit atrocities. In an episode of *CSI* (2000–), for example, Sara (Jorja Fox) explained her vegetarianism: "I haven't eaten meat since we stayed up that night with that dead pig. It pains me to see ground beef." In an episode of *Bones* (2005–), protagonist Temperance (Emily Deschanel), became a vegetarian after visiting a pig farm and seeing how pigs were killed (and discovering her mother was killed the same way). In the Canadian cartoon *Braceface* (2001–2003), protagonist Sharon had a crush on Alden and got a part-time job working with him at his uncle's meat-packing plant. After seeing and hearing sad animals, Sharon became a vegetarian. In the horror film *Dread* (2009), Cheryl (Hanne Steen) connected the smell of meat to her father, who worked at a meat-packing plant and who had sexually abused her as a child: "I can hardly stand to look at a piece of meat now, let alone think about eating it." In these examples, atrocities served as "light bulb" moments for characters to connect their meat-eating to violence.

While Dick in *3rd Rock from the Sun* and Stan in *South Park* resumed eating meat by the end of their episodes, the fact that the other characters remained vegetarians implies that exposure to the realities of meat production can actually motivate dietary change. In Adams's research on vegetarianism, she spotlighted this idea through a discussion of the "absent referent": "The 'absent referent' is what separates the meat eater from the animal and the animal from the end product. The function of the absent referent is to keep our 'meat' separated from the idea that she or he was once an animal."[15] Here, Adams explains how humans are able to dissociate from the animal they are consuming through a variety of tools, including packaging and euphemism. These screen examples present an interesting example of characters who—when confronted by the realities of meat—can no longer dissociate nor convince themselves that meat-eating is justifiable.

Another obvious stereotype of the vegetarian on screen is the undernourished weakling. Refusing to eat meat, it seems, means to miss out on essential nutrients and in turn leaves a character emaciated.

THE SICKLY VEGETARIAN

Iacobbo and Iacobbo discussed the weak vegetarian stereotype, tracing it back to the 1830s when a prominent physician claimed that vegetarians were "weaklings."[16] Puskar-Pasewicz similarly discussed the vested interests of meat companies in promoting this stereotype.[17] While in reality vegetarians may not all be weak, on screen there remains a tendency for the archaic stereotype to proliferate.

In an episode of *Roseanne*, Roseanne (Roseanne Barr) commented on the dietary choices of her daughter Darlene and boyfriend David: "They're vegetarians so they don't have the strength to hold their heads up." In the film *Trainspotting* (1996), Sick Boy (Jonny Lee Miller) complimented the surprising strength of Rent Boy (Ewan McGregor): "For a vegetarian, Rents, you're a fuckin' evil shot." In an episode of *How I Met Your Mother*

(2005–), after Ted (Josh Radnor) suggested the lamb at a restaurant, his date Nora (Danneel Ackles) sarcastically said, "Oh, I'm a vegan. I wish I could tune out that moral voice inside me that says eating animals is murder. But, I guess I'm just not as strong as you are," to which Ted replied, "That's 'cause you need protein." In an episode of *Buffy the Vampire Slayer*, Principal Snyder (Armin Shimerman) referred to a protesting student—who had chained himself to a snack machine—as a "pathetic little no-life vegan." In an episode of *Futurama*, a vegetarian lion was presented as sad and emaciated.

While a simple explanation is that one way to demonize vegetarians is to present them as *less than*—as less strong and less healthy than meat-eaters—this stereotype also works as a health-based attack on vegetarians that validates meat-eating. Given that some meat-eaters likely feel guilty about their dietary choices—certainly those who claim vegetarianism but don't adhere to traditional definitions seemingly do—vegetarianism gets dismissed as unhealthy, thereby justifying meat consumption.

Connected to the idea of the sickly vegetarian is the weak vegetarian. In H. G. Wells's novel *The Time Machine* (1895), members of the vegetarian race, the Eloi, were described as superior and possessing "faint and delicate beauty,"[18] but were bred as food for the cannibalistic Morlocks. This same idea appears in various guises on screen. In an episode of the Canadian comedy series *The Red Green Show* (1991–2006), Reg Hunter joked: "*Vegetarian* is an old Indian word meaning 'I don't hunt so good.'" In the animated film *The Princess and the Cobbler* (1993), the character Phido the Vulture claimed, "I'm so hungry I could eat a vegetarian."

An extension of the undernourished vegetarian stereotype is the crazed, hungry vegetarian. In the film *Halloween: Resurrection* (2002), for example, Rudy Grimes (Sean Patrick Thomas) commented, "Never underestimate the effect of a poor diet . . . Next thing you know, you're cutting up bodies in the bathtub. I mean, look at Hitler. He was a vegetarian." In a scene from the German film *Der Untergang* (*Downfall*) (2004), Hermann (Thomas Kretschman) also discussed Hitler, remarking: "What do you expect from a teetotal, nonsmoking vegetarian?" While these quotes again highlight the presumed negative health connotations of vegetarianism via reference to history's most famous "vegetarian,"[19] they also allude to the possibility of a damaged psyche—the implication is that for a person to be a vegetarian, that there is something severely wrong with the individual; indeed, vegetarianism might even be linked to psychopathy. Another stereotype—certainly connected to their presentation as weaklings—is the killjoy, implying that vegetarians are negative, unhappy people.

KILLJOYS AND SAD SACKS

In an episode of sitcom *Scrubs* (2001–2010), the following exchange occurred between J. D. (Zach Braff) and Elliot (Sarah Chalke). The latter had been (unsuccessfully) searching for a roommate:

Elliot: I put all those flyers up and no one wants me to live with them.

J. D.: Oh, come on, Elliot, I'm sure you'll eventually find a roommate who's a clean nonsmoking vegetarian that rinses the shower thoroughly after each usage.

In an episode of the Australian sitcom *Acropolis Now* (1989–1992), Effie (Mary Coustas) tried to convince her cousin Jim (Nick Giannopoulos) not to get involved with colleague Liz (Tracey Callander): "Think about it. Life with Liz. Vegetarian food, no TV, just books with no pictures in them."

While *Halloween: Resurrection* and *Der Untergang* (*Downfall*) exaggerated it, *Scrubs* and *Acropolis Now* comically presented the truism that a vegetarian is someone staid and difficult—if not neurotic—and is generally unlikeable. In their research, Iacobbo and Iacobbo noted that "the term *strict vegetarian* carries a negative connotation in pleasure-seeking America."[20] Certainly the idea that to be a vegetarian is synonymous with being difficult —if not also unhappy—exists in numerous screen examples.

In an episode of the animated series *O'Grady* (2004–2006), Kevin remarked, "Vegetarians are just mad that they can't eat meat." In *Bored to Death*, Lisa (Jenn Harris)—after hearing about Allison's veganism—remarked, "I know a lot of radical vegans. She must be an unhappy person." While Allison doesn't actually seem overtly unhappy, she is nonetheless presented as overprotective and neurotic and in a codependent relationship with her son. She also comes across as thoroughly *unlikeable*. She appeared motivated to have sex with Jonathan purely to cajole him into investigating her son's stolen skateboard, for example, but when he returned to visit her she quickly took the board from him and shut the door in his face. In the sitcom *The Office* (2005–2013), Angela (Angela Martin) is a vegetarian who is also a control freak: for her, vegetarianism appears to be a manifestation of her controlling tendencies and an additional characteristic that makes her unlikeable. Kevin in *O'Grady* provided the most obvious rationale for the unlikeable vegetarian on screen: battling the naturalness and deliciousness of meat makes a character crotchety.

In the film *About a Boy* (2002), Fiona (Toni Collette) was a vegetarian single mother who also happened to be clinically depressed, even attempting suicide in one scene. Interestingly, once Fiona recovered, she suggested a trip to McDonald's to her son. One interpretation of her behavior is that her depression was somehow connected to her vegetarianism, either as a symptom of, reason for, or contribution to it. Once better, Fiona saw the error of her ways. Mentioned earlier was the character of Neil on *The Young Ones*. While a hippie, Neil was also clinically depressed, shown to have attempted suicide in a number of episodes. In the animated series *Danny Phantom* (2004–2009), Sam was a vegetarian goth. While perhaps not as miserable as other screen goths, Sam was nonetheless portrayed as a depressive character, at one point acknowledging, "I'm usually the sour one around here." As with the unlikeable characters discussed earlier, depression in these cases can be considered as motivated by the difficulties of vegetarianism as well as undernourishment; a more cynical explanation is that depression is considered the consequence of fighting biology—that characters are punished for going against their dietary nature. Another possible explanation is that certain kinds of characters—innate sad sacks, for example—are attracted to the discipline, self-control, and "flavorless" food of vegetarianism as some kind of self-punishment and masochism.

For the characters mentioned earlier, their misery was largely inwardly directed. Another screen stereotype is the preachy vegetarian who makes the lives of *others* horrible through his or her efforts at guilt-tripping and evangelizing.

THE PREACHY VEGETARIAN

In a scene from *Scott Pilgrim vs. the World* (2010), Todd (Brandon Routh) and Envy (Brie Larson) explained their veganism:

Todd: I partake not in the meat nor breastmilk or ovum of any creature that has a face.
Envy: Short answer: being vegan just makes you better than most people.

In a similar-themed scene from *The Simpsons*, Lisa met Jesse, an activist with the ecoterrorist group Dirt First:

Lisa: You do yoga?
Jesse: Yeah, but I started before it was cool.
Lisa: My name's Lisa Simpson. I think your protest was incredibly brave.
Jesse: Thank you. This planet needs every friend it can get.
Lisa: Oh, the earth is the best! That's why I'm a vegetarian.

Jesse: Ha. Well, that's a start.

Lisa: Uh, well, I was thinking of going vegan.

Jesse: (Chuckles) I'm a level five vegan: I won't eat anything that casts a shadow.

Lisa: Wow. Um ... I started an organic compost pile at home.

Jesse: Only at home? You mean you don't pocket-mulch? (Takes out pocket mulch for Lisa to touch.)

Lisa: Oh, it's so decomposed! Do you think I could join Dirt First?

Jesse: Well ... we might have an opening at the poser level.

Lisa: Oh, thank you. Thank you!

A similar idea was apparent in *Transamerica* (2005): the hitchhiker (Grant Monohon) claimed, "I'm a Level 4 Vegan. I don't eat anything that casts a shadow."

These scenes present excellent examples of preachy, holier-than-thou vegetarians, whose vegetarianism is centered on self-aggrandizing, linking back to the poser hippies discussed earlier. Such examples are relatively easily detected on screen, with preachy, unlikeable characters being a common screen demonization of vegetarianism. In an episode of *True Blood* (2008–), for example, vampire Amy (Lizzy Caplan) claimed, "I am an organic vegan and my carbon footprint is miniscule." In the sitcom *Community* (2009–), Britta (Gillian Jacobs) is permanently crusading so it is unsurprising that vegetarianism is also one of her issues: in the episode that she declared her vegetarianism, her classmates feigned surprise and Troy (Donald Glover) facetiously mocked, "Shocker!" Britta then preached, "If you guys knew how they treated the animals that you're eating, you would eat them faster just to put them out of their misery. And then you would throw up." In the *How I Met Your Mother* episode discussed earlier, Ted's date articulated her vegetarian philosophy through passive aggression and inflammatory language. In each of these examples, vegetarianism is presented as extreme, if not *fundamentalist*, and designed to make other people feel bad about their dietary choices. The connection between vegetarianism, righteousness, and preachiness was articulated particularly well by food writer Tara Austen Weaver: "Not eating meat is like a guilt-free pass. I can sleep knowing that I'm not contributing to the ethical and environmental issues brought on by meat consumption ... Being a vegetarian earns you a health serving of virtuosity. This can also creep into a distressingly common case of vegetarian self-righteousness, it must be said."[21] Torres and Torres make a similar point, contending that "For those couch potatoes who've never met a vegan, vegan now means 'judgmental asshole' and nothing else. And sadly, many people live their lives using TV as an educator."[22]

More prevalent than a vegetarian being stereotyped as preachy, however, is the vegetarian portrayed as overtly *hostile*.

THE HOSTILE VEGETARIAN

There are many politically motivated and politically *active* vegetarians on screen who are *not* actually presented as hostile. In an episode of *Miami Vice* (1984–1990), for example, Detective Tubbs (Philip Michael Thomas)—after declining ham for breakfast—stated, "I'm a vegetarian by conviction. I'll never change my view." Tubbs articulated his position and left it at that. In *Did You Hear about the Morgans?* (2009), Meryl (Sarah Jessica Parker) divulged her vegetarianism and claimed that she was a member of PETA (People for the Ethical Treatment of Animals). Again, she disclosed her politics but in a manner that was not hostile. These are characters who are indeed political vegetarians but who are neither aggressive nor missionary about their beliefs. Such examples, however, are outliers: the politically active vegetarian is generally presented as substantially more hostile. In the horror movie *Saw* (2004), Adam (Leigh Whannell) commented, "My last girlfriend was a feminist vegan punk who broke up with me because she thought I was too angry." Adam's inference is that a feminist vegan punk will always be angry and militant—that a person *can't* be a feminist or a vegan or a punk *without* high-level rage. On screen, such vegetarian rage is routinely presented through diatribes, stunts, and coercive tactics.

In *The Simpsons*, when Lisa became a vegetarian, she tried to force everyone not to eat meat at Homer's barbeque by discarding his roasted pig. In an episode of the sitcom *Living Single* (1993–1998), when Regina (Kim Fields) became a vegetarian, she cleared the house of all meat, expecting her housemates to follow her new diet. In *Roseanne*, Darlene organized for white chalk-line drawings of two cows—with red faux-blood painted at their heads—to be drawn outside her mother's meat sandwich stand at a local carnival. In an episode of *Danny Phantom*, the vegetarian character, Sam, smuggled live frogs out of the biology lab. Such stunts were parodied in the comedy spy film *Leonard Part 6* (1987), where a vegetarian was presented as evil and as involved with brainwashing animals to kill people. In an episode of the animated series *King of the Hill* (1997–2010), Bobby's teacher—Mr. McKay—was portrayed as a fanatical environmentalist who made students report to him any nongreen acts of their family; at one point the teacher visited Bobby's home and berated the family for eating meat.

Such examples present vegetarians negatively by depicting their evangelizing and arrogance. While such characters are unlikeable because of their dogma, they are presented more strongly as conflicting with the prized American liberal value of freedom of choice and with people's beliefs that they should be able to eat whatever they want free from guilt-trips and lectures. By presenting vegetarians as permanently on soap boxes, these depictions perpetuate the idea of vegetarianism as cultish,[23] missionary and generally unpleasant.

Discussed earlier were characters such as Larry from *Dharma & Greg* and Marvin from *What about Mimi?* who were vegetarians because of the convictions of their partners. In the next section, the idea of circumstantial vegetarianism is discussed, whereby characters become vegetarians only because of their situation.

CIRCUMSTANTIAL VEGETARIANS

In my book *Part-Time Perverts: Sex, Pop Culture, and Kink Management* I discussed the idea of circumstantial homosexuality: "Circumstantial homosexuality ... describes gay sex engaged in when circumstances dictate that same-sex partners are all that are available; such behavior commonly occurs in boarding schools, mining hostels, on ships, in the army and notably in prison ... It is this idea of perversion being circumstantial or temporary that alludes to its potentially fleeting nature and provides an explanation for why the practice might only be dabbled in."[24]

Something similar occurs on screen in the context of vegetarianism, whereby some vegetarians avoid meat temporarily because of their circumstances. An obvious way this is illustrated is through supposedly vegetarian pets. In the aforementioned episode of *Futurama*, a hippie activist argued that meat-eating is not natural by claiming, "We taught a lion to eat tofu!" A pitiful, undernourished, cowering lion was then shown. In *Seven Pounds* (2008), Emily (Rosario Dawson) claimed her Great Dane was a vegetarian who ate only tofu and steamed broccoli. The dog seemingly disagreed, eagerly eating the meat Ben (Will Smith) offered it. In *Legally Blonde* (2001), Elle (Reese Witherspoon) introduced herself and her dog: "Hi. I'm Elle Woods and this is Bruiser Woods. We're both Gemini vegetarians." While Elle is a vegetarian by choice, it is unlikely that Bruiser chose his diet. These three examples present animals that are vegetarians not of their own choosing, but rather because of the decisions made by those around them. While in these examples pet *owners* make the animals vegetarian, in other cases loved ones do the coercion.

In a scene from *Pulp Fiction* (1994), Jules (Samuel L. Jackson) discussed the deliciousness of a hamburger:

> Well, if you like hamburgers, give 'em a try sometime. Me, I can't usually eat 'em 'cause my girlfriend's a vegetarian. Which more or less makes me a vegetarian, but I sure love the taste of a good burger.

In the episode of the sitcom *Unhappily Ever After* discussed earlier, Ryan coerced his father and older brother to become vegetarians so he could take credit for their green activism. In the episode of *3rd Rock from the Sun* discussed earlier, Dick—after his chipmunk epiphany—forced his family to stop eating meat. In an episode of *King of the Hill*, son Bobby dated Marie, who convinced him to become a vegetarian. After they broke up, he demonstrated that he was over her by eating a giant steak. Such presentations relate well to the underlying criticism of vegetarianism that it is merely a fad, a passing phase, and that no one needs to take it too seriously.

While politics and circumstance are two obvious reasons for vegetarianism, another is health. A vegetarian diet is often presented on screen as perceived to be healthier by those on health kicks.

VEGETARIANS FOR GOOD HEALTH

For a character to be vegetarian, there is an assumption that politics is involved, centered on pacifism and animal rights. While this might often be the case, another stereotype is also identifiable: the vegetarian motivated by health. In *Captain America: The First Avenger* (2011), the following exchange occurred between Dr. Arnim Zola (Toby Jones) and Colonel Chester Phillips (Tommy Lee Jones):

Zola: I don't eat meat.
Phillips: Why not?
Zola: It disagrees with me.

In an episode of the sitcom *Happy Days* (1974–1984), Fonzie's (Henry Winkler) long-lost brother Artie (Michael Holden) declared that he was a vegetarian: "For some people the ingestion of meats can cause fatty deposits to form in the arteries creating pustules ... One day you're reading the paper, the next day you're in it." In the pilot of *The United States of Tara* (2009–2011), Tara (Toni Collette), as her teenage alter ego T, claimed, "I'm a vegetarian now. I don't eat meat. Besides the hormones in that cluck cluck can make you get a third nipple." In an episode of *Roseanne*, Molly (Danielle Harris) told David, "I'm a vegetarian, too. I think anyone who cares about their body wouldn't poison themselves with that stuff." In an episode of the sitcom *The Jamie Foxx Show* (1996–2001), a visit from a vegetarian author, Kwame Cooper (Roy Fegan), coerced some characters to contemplate vegetarianism; at one point, when Fancy (Garcelle Beauvais) apologized to Cooper for having eaten meat the day prior, Kwame responded, "Don't apologize to me; apologize to your colon."

A much more vivid presentation of the health rationale was articulated in *The Road to Wellville* (1994), a film centered on health crusader Dr. Kellogg (Anthony Hopkins). When the doctor was asked about meat consumption, he gave the following response:

> Each juicy morsel of meat is alive and swarming with the same filth as found in the carcass of a dead rat. Meat eaters, sir, are drowning in a tide of gore. What is a sausage? A sausage is an indigestible balloon of decayed beef, riddled with tuberculosis. Eat and die! For I have seen many a repentant meat glutton his body full of uric acid and remorse, his soul adrift on the raft in the ocean of poisonous slime, sloshin' against the walls of the body's kitchen.

These examples present a (comparatively) politically neutral justification for vegetarianism—that it is not about saving the planet or sparing animals, but rather about preserving one's own health. Certainly this is one interpretation for characters such as politically conservative Angela in *The Office* or politically conservative Dr. Kellogg, who aren't typical tree-hugging liberals. For these individuals, their vegetarianism is centered on self-preservation.

In the aforementioned examples, a meat-is-unhealthy truism is presented. This is certainly a theme identifiable in health kick narratives, where meat is often the first thing dumped in pursuit of good health. In an episode of the sitcom *The Monkees* (1966–1968)—tellingly titled "I Was a 99-Lb. Weakling"—Micky (Micky Dolenz) temporarily became a vegetarian after meeting a charlatan body-building coach, Shah-Ku (Monte Landis), who advocated dietary change and Eastern mysticism. In an episode of *Married with Children*, Peggy went on a health kick that involved eschewing meat and insisted that her family do the same. In the sitcom *Blossom* (1990–1995), the same thing transpired: father Nick (Ted Wass) decided that the family needed to go on a health kick via a vegetarian diet. This also happened in the sitcom *What I Like about You* (2002–2006) when Valerie (Jennie Garth) embarked on a meat-free health kick after breaking up with her boyfriend.

Interestingly, in *The Monkees*, *Married with Children*, *Blossom*, and *What I Like about You*, the characters all returned to their meat-eating ways by the end of the episode. Vegetarian was once again portrayed as too difficult to stick to and presented merely as a passing phase. Worth noting, something highlighted in these examples—as well as in the vegetarian restaurant scene in *How to Lose a Guy in 10 Days* and Rob's "awful cooking smells" comments in *High Fidelity*—is the idea of vegetarian food being *horrible*, that the unappealing nature of such foods is what makes vegetarianism difficult and what makes vegetarians joyless. In an episode of the sitcom *That '70s Show* (1998–2006), for example, Kitty (Debra Jo Rupp) put her husband Red (Kurtwood Smith) on a low-protein, meatless diet after his heart attack. Red was clearly unhappy and criticized the food: "This is not food, this is what food eats." Such an idea again reiterates the normalcy of meat-eating meat, the freakishness of eschewing this behavior, and the supposed unappealing self-sacrifice of vegetarianism.

THE ENLIGHTENED VEGETARIAN

Earlier the idea of vegetarianism as connected to intelligence and as an enlightened state was alluded to through a discussion of scenes from *Friends*, *The Simpsons*, *Everything Is Illuminated*, and *My Big Fat Greek Wedding*, where the meat-eating characters were presented as naïve compared to the vegetarians. Earlier I quoted Professor Furie from *A Very Peculiar Practice*, who remarked "I need meat, I'm not a sociologist!," implying that vegetarianism was something that only hippie academics were involved with. One interpretation of Furie's comment is the linking of vegetarianism with intellect. Puskar-Pasewicz identified that the half-human, half-Vulcan Mr. Spock (Leonard Nimoy) from the original *Star Trek* (1966–1969) television series was the first regularly occurring vegetarian character on screen, something attributable to the fact that "Vulcan characters are often portrayed as vegetarian because of their logical reasoning to eat healthy foods."[25] Mr. Spock embodies the idea of vegetarianism being connected to intellect, but also emphasizes that vegetarianism can be construed as an *enlightened* state of being and reflecting futuristically advanced cognitive functioning. In *Veronica Mars* (2004–2007), Veronica's (Kristen Bell) computer genius friend Mac (Tina Majorino) was also a vegan. In *Glee* (2009–), the over-achieving Rachel (Lea Michele) is a vegan. While potentially able to be construed as control freak neurotics, another interpretation is that such characters are smart enough—are *evolved* enough—to understand the harms of animal consumption.

Earlier I discussed *SeaQuest DSV*, *Demolition Man*, and *Escape from LA* as examples where futuristic worlds were presented as ones without meat.

While certainly in *Demolition Man* and *Escape from LA* the meatless societies were presented as less progressive and more authoritarian, there are other examples depicting meatless futures as being *more* evolved and less accepting of practices such as animal farming. *Logan's Run* (1976), for example—like *Demolition Man* and *Escape from LA*—was about a dystopic future. In one scene, some characters discovered a "sort of breeding pen" and the following exchange occurred between Logan (Michael York) and Jessica (Jenny Agutter):

Logan: They say people used to breed animals, fish, anything. To eat, you know?
Jessica: Must have been a savage world.

Here, while the *Logan's Run* vision of 2274 might appear awful and akin to the futures found in *Demolition Man* and *Escape from LA*, Jessica's comments also highlight a level of futuristic enlightened thinking: that the future may involve a time when meat might be missed, but where farming animals is construed as abhorrent.

An obvious link between vegetarianism and enlightenment is that cultures that place a strong emphasis on spirituality and enlightenment tend to be vegetarian; thus on-screen characters connected to Asian cultures are often presented as vegetarian. Earlier I discussed Aang from *Avatar: The Last Airbender*; his vegetarianism was grounded in his Taoist and Buddhist beliefs. In *The Monkees* episode where Shah-Ku's vegetarian lifestyle was touted, it was also noted that he practiced Eastern mysticism. In the series *Kung Fu* (1972–1975), the protagonist Kwai Chang Caine (David Carradine) was a vegetarian whose dietary choices were connected to his spiritualism; his character was a Shaolin Monk. While Aang, Shah-Ku, and Caine might be considered as *other* because they are ethnically and spiritual "different," they were also portrayed as peaceful and wise—two comparatively *positive* connotations of vegetarianism on screen.

While Aang, Shah-Ku, and Caine were portrayed as physically strong characters who also purported to be vegetarian pacifists, they are outlier examples. Discussed earlier was the idea that vegetarians are invariably portrayed as weaker and wimpier. One explanation for this perspective, explored in the next section, relates to the gendered connotations of vegetarianism: that real men eat meat and that vegetarianism is somehow feminine.

GENDER AND VEGETARIANISM

In this section, the idea that meat consumption is masculine, and thus to eschew meat equates to effeminacy is explored.

Real Men Eat Meat

In an episode of the animated series *Ben 10: Ultimate Alien* (2010–), Ben commented, "Come on, Kevin. Meat is man food." In 2006, the fast-food restaurant chain Burger King ran a series of television advertisements titled "I Am Man," where the lyrics to Helen Reddy's feminist anthem "I Am Woman" (1970) were rewritten and sung as "I am man, hear me roar, in numbers too big to ignore / And I'm way too hungry to settle for chick food." These examples represent the "meat and potatoes" stereotype of the all-American guy, the inference being that men eat meat and women choose the salad. Adams's book *The Sexual Politics of Meat* focuses on this very topic, explaining that "[m]anhood is constructed in our culture, in part, by access to meat eating"[26] and that "[a]ccording to the mythology of patriarchal culture, meat promotes strength; the attributes of masculinity are achieved through eating these masculine foods."[27] For a man to become a vegetarian, he challenges the "real man" stereotype: "Men who become vegetarians challenge an essential part of the masculine role. They are opting for women's food. How dare they? Refusing meat means a man is effeminate, a 'sissy,' a 'fruit.'"[28]

Certainly the idea of vegetarianism as connected to diminished masculinity is evident on screen. Earlier I discussed Leary's *No Cure for Cancer* where the comic commented: "I tried eating vegetarian. I felt like a wimp." In the Hungarian film *Sajtóvadászat* (*Press Hunting*) (2006), journalist Rezsõ (Dávid Szöllõskei) commented, "I don't eat meat, I'm a vegetarian," to which his colleague, András (Gergely Molnár), responded, "Vegetarian? What are you, a fag?" In an episode of *Doctor Who* (2005–), the Dream Lord (Toby Jones) insulted The Doctor (Matt Smith) by speculating that he was a vegetarian and calling him a "flop-haired wuss."

In the episode of *South Park* discussed earlier, after Stan refused to eat meat, he contracted a condition that resulted in open wounds on his skin. His doctor explained:

> He's very lucky you got him here when you did. He was in a very advanced state of vaginistis ... It occurs when a person stops eating meat. Those sores on his skin were actually small vaginas. If we hadn't stopped it in time, Stan would have eventually just become one great big giant pussy ... We've got an IV of pure beef blood pumping into Stan's veins and the sores are fading.

The *South Park* episode makes explicit what is merely implied in the other examples (and discussed at length by Adams): that avoiding meat makes a man not only less masculine, but also notably more *feminine*. There are, of course, departures from this stereotype. Earlier I discussed Detective Tubbs in *Miami Vice*. In *The Killing*, Detective Holder, like Tubbs, was a heterosexual detective—and in no way able to be construed as feminine—but nonetheless identified as a vegetarian (even if, as noted, his vegetarianism wasn't permanent).

Interestingly, there also appears to be a trend on screen in which vegetarianism is linked to lesbianism—a particularly peculiar relationship given the routine association of lesbianism with *masculinity* on screen,[29] but nevertheless perhaps predictable given the fringe connotations of both. Earlier, for example, I mentioned the scene from *Friends* where, after Phoebe told Leonard that she was a vegetarian, he responded, "I'll never understand you lesbians." The vegan character, Jennifer, on *River City* was also a lesbian. In the film *Butch Jamie* (2007), Jill (Michelle Ehlen) remarked, "I've never met a man who was a vegetarian before—only lesbians." In a scene from *Not Another Teen Movie* (2001), the following exchange occurred between Janey (Chyler Leigh) and her brother Mitch (Cody McMains):

Janey: I read Sylvia Plath, I listen to Bikini Kill, and I eat tofu. I am a unique rebel.
Mitch: It sounds more like you're a lesbo.

Even vegetarian Hayley in *American Dad!* was presumed to be bisexual, a possibility that also existed for Phoebe on *Friends*.

These scenes can be read in numerous ways. Discussed earlier in the context of hippies was the idea that being a hippie is synonymous with shirking conservative values. Another explanation is the idea of compound negativity: that lesbianism is *just another thing* that makes a vegetarian loathsome.

The last presentation of vegetarians discussed in this chapter encompasses those difficult to classify—that is, those vegetarians whose dietary choices aren't connected to free love or politics or health, but rather are just an unexplained facet of identity.

THE NONPOLITICAL, NONSTEREOTYPED VEGETARIAN

While this chapter has largely focused on stereotypical portrayals of vegetarians, there are also examples in which the food choices of vegetarians are portrayed as neither connected to politics nor health, rather are simply just an unexplored fact.

Discussed earlier was the film *Everything Is Illuminated*, notably the scene where Jonathan had to explain to his grandfather and Alex that he didn't eat meat. When Alex asked, "What is wrong with you?" Jonathan responded,

"Nothing, I just don't eat meat!" Jonathan's answer encapsulates how vegetarianism is presented in *Everything Is Illuminated*: Jonathan *just doesn't eat meat*; the audience is not told why, it is just a fact of his identity. In the sitcom *The Office*, Angela is a conservative character, loathing of anything liberal (she is, for example, vocally homophobic)—as distanced as possible from the hippies discussed earlier—and yet she is a vegetarian. Her choice is not explained, and while we could speculate—maybe it is because she is a generally holier-than-thou character or because she really loves her cat—a rationale is never articulated.

In the film *The Contender* (2000), Laine Hanson (Joan Allen) was a Democratic senator running for vice president. At one point, at a restaurant, when her Republican dining companion ordered the porterhouse steak for her, she said, "No, I don't eat meat," and then selected the penne. Laine's vegetarianism was not discussed, and it was not a plot point. While one might speculate that it had something to do with her Democratic politics—and that vegetarianism was a way to contrast her with her Republican companion—Laine's reasons for not eating meat were not explained.

The same thing occurred in an episode of animated series *The Powerpuff Girls* (1998–2004):

Buttercup: You stole my side of beef!

Bubbles: I did not! I'm a vegetarian! Besides, you took my drawing.

In *Dawson's Creek* (1998–2003), Henry (Michael Pitt) was a vegetarian; the origins of his vegetarianism were not discussed. In *Will & Grace* (1998–2006), Grace (Debra Messing) dated Nathan (Woody Harrelson), a vegetarian, whose food choices also weren't discussed. In *Gosford Park* (2001), it was noted that Mr. Weissman (Bob Balaban) "won't eat meat," although it was not explained why. In an episode of *Buffy the Vampire Slayer*, Buffy (Sarah Michelle Gellar) was offered a guidance counselor job by the principal (D. B. Woodside). Buffy sarcastically asked, "Were you impressed by my work at Doublemeat Palace?" to which Principal Wood replied, "No, I'm a vegetarian." Mentioned earlier were the characters of Fiona in *About a Boy* and Allison in *Bored to Death*: while both explicitly articulated their vegetarianism, audiences were not told the source from which it stemmed. While assumptions might be drawn from their attire—that both women were left-leaning and ascribed to hippie philosophies—none of this was explained.

While ordinary vegetarians—that is, characters whose vegetarianism is simply part of their personality—are not a common screen feature, their existence nonetheless is worth analysis. First, it might be contended that the presence of such characters is connected to an increased incidence of vegetarianism in American society; such an assertion is, however, problematic. Maurer identified the problematic nature of obtaining accurate information on vegetarianism: longitudinal data is not available to prove such an increase; similarly, collecting data on this topic is fraught with difficulty. While we might not be able to argue that mainstream vegetarian characters reflect any growth in vegetarianism, they nevertheless highlight a growth in acceptance. Most restaurants now cater to vegetarians in a way that would have been unthinkable a generation ago, something well highlighted by Johanna McCloy, an actor and activist: "Think about Gardenburger. It's no longer considered 'weird' to the public. It's almost expected on a menu. Think about soy milk. It's offered at every Starbucks. Times are changing."[30]

Another explanation is that real-life vegetarians and vegan actors and producers are actually creating—or at least influencing—roles whereby characters share their politics. This is something Puskar-Pasewicz discussed via examples including Pamela Anderson, who is a real-life vegetarian and who starred in, as well as was an executive producer on, the series *V.I.P.* (1998–2002), where she played a vegetarian character. Similar clout can be illustrated when Paul and Linda McCartney lent their voices to the episode of *The Simpsons* when Lisa became a vegetarian; apparently a condition of their appearance was that Lisa's character *stayed* a vegetarian.[31]

This chapter has explored the wide variety of stereotypes of vegetarians on screen. While they are frequently demonized and feminized and presented as preachy and annoying, also highlighted were those occasions where they are portrayed as smart, if not *enlightened*.

The Alcohol Chapter: The Drunk in Film and Television

While characters desperately craving a drink or drowning sorrows are screen staples, and while alcohol consumption is frequently the go-to activity for fun and socializing, this chapter focuses on the *alcoholic*: the addict who can't simply imbibe recreationally, but rather who is demonstrably out of control of his or her drinking and who regularly drinks to excess. This chapter explores the wide variety of alcoholic archetypes, including the (seemingly) happy drunks, the sad drunks, the female lushes, and the ritually demonized "bad moms."

DEFINING ALCOHOLISM

Alcohol is often at the forefront of social events in the United States; thus it is unsurprising that characters are frequently shown drinking. Some narratives—sitcoms *Archie Bunker's Place* (1979–1983), *Cheers* (1982–1993), and *It's Always Sunny in Philadelphia* (2005–), for example, and films *Cocktail* (1988), *Road House* (1989), and *Coyote Ugly* (2000)—are set around bars; alcohol consumption forms the backdrop for the action and drinking is presented as perfectly normal. Merely consuming alcohol, of course, is not enough to warrant the label *alcoholic*. While definitions of alcoholism are heatedly contested, the one used in this chapter is the one approved by the National Council on Alcoholism and Drug Dependence as well as the American Society of Addiction Medicine: "[alcoholism] is characterized by continuous or periodic: impaired control over drinking, preoccupation with the drug alcohol, use of alcohol despite adverse consequences, and distortions in thinking, most notably denial."[1] While many other definitions focus on harm—be it mental, physical, or social—the preceding definition emphasizes the inability to control one's drinking and a preoccupation with its consumption. Characters experiencing this affliction—be they suffering or seemingly enjoying it—are a staple of the screen.

THE HAPPY DRUNK

When thinking about drunk characters—such as Barney from the animated series *The Simpsons* (1989–), Arthur (Dudley Moore) from *Arthur* (1981) and *Arthur 2: On the Rocks* (1988), and Billy (Adam Sandler) in *Billy Madison* (1995)—the happy drunk stereotype often comes to mind: alcohol consumption appears to make these individuals joyful and fun to be around. While such characters are routinely presented as inebriated and engaged in reckless behavior, their intentions are never malicious; they are stupid but nevertheless *good-natured* drunks. Such portrayals contrast markedly with a character such as Willie (Billy Bob Thornton) in *Bad Santa* (2003), who was a drunk but also a devious criminal.

In film theorist Norman Denzin's work on presentations of alcoholism, he discussed the well-established role of the "comic drunk" in comedy. Two characters he focused on—Arthur from the *Arthur* films and Elwood (James Stewart) from *Harvey* (1950)—were characters he claimed enacted "the belief that alcohol can produce positive effects for certain drinkers, even when the drinker is defined as an alcoholic or chronic drunk."[2] Arthur's prostitutes and partying and Elwood's rabbit hallucinations, for example, are presented as positive experiences facilitated by alcohol.

While a cursory reading of characters such as Barney, Arthur, Billy, and Elwood might construe them as *happy* drunks, as each narrative unfolds, alcohol is presented as concealing a darker turmoil. Denzin, for example, noted that both Arthur and Elwood "are sorrowful, lonely men. Elwood longs for friendly companionship ... Arthur pines for true love."[3] The putatively happy drunk who uses alcohol to conceal other problems is an archetype rife throughout screen narratives: Barney, Arthur, Billy, and Elwood drink because they are, in varying degrees, lonely.

While the common portrayal of the happy drunk is a person possessing an undercurrent of sadness, there are a small number of happy drunk characters who are actually genuinely joyful in their inebriation (or, at the very least, the audience is never given any reason to doubt this). Two examples are Fun Bobby (Vincent Ventresca) from the sitcom *Friends* (1994–2004) and John (John Belushi) from *Animal House* (1978). Fun Bobby, one of Monica's (Courtney Cox) boyfriends on *Friends*, perfectly illustrates the happy drunk archetype: his inebriation made him entertaining and appeared to be a trait completely disconnected from any obvious internal melancholy. When Bobby and Monica reunited after a break-up, Monica's brother Ross (David Schwimmer) excitedly declared, "I love this guy. Hey, I was so psyched to hear you're back with my sister!" Later—after Bobby's alcohol consumption was tallied—Ross realized, "I don't think I've ever seen Fun Bobby without a … a drink in his hand." Monica eventually convinced Fun Bobby to give up drinking; the result was that he was no longer fun. "Turns out that Fun Bobby was fun for a reason," she lamented. Friend Chandler (Matthew Perry) went so far as renaming him "Ridiculously Dull Bobby." Fun Bobby was fun when he was drunk and far less so when he was sober. John (John Belushi) in *Animal House* was another example of the happy drunk whose drinking was not portrayed as symptomatic of any other obvious demons; he was presented as a typical drunken frat boy who drank simply because drinking is what men apparently do at college.

Fun Bobby and John are rarities, however. More common are attempts to *explain*, if not pathologize and rationalize, drunkenness. An obvious reason for this is that alcoholism is generally construed in broader society as bad, if not a taboo; thus presenting an alcoholic as someone who is happy—and who is motivated to drink excessively purely out of enjoyment and with no ill effects—is likely construed by audiences as (1) unrealistic, (2) unsustainable, and (3) dramatically contrary to popular understandings of addiction. Prohibition in the 1920s and early 1930s stemmed from pressure exerted by religious groups who were convinced that alcohol consumption caused social degradation. The idea that drinking—or at least *excessive* alcohol consumption—is immoral and uncouth persists. In turn, while happy drunk characters can be detected, their happiness is rarely presented as genuine, but rather as merely a façade, in turn confirming the idea that excessive alcohol consumption is inextricably linked to social problems. Such a presentation is in line with what film theorist Mike Lewington termed the "moral model" of alcohol portrayals, where drunkenness is construed as "an immoral activity" and "as being the result of a moral flaw or spiritual degeneracy" and presented on screen accordingly.[4]

Lewington noted that one obvious consequence of excessive drinking is the "dereliction of responsibility in the home and the workplace."[5] Such derelictions notably lead to another popular stereotype: the Skid Row drunk.

THE SKID ROW DRUNK

One extreme presentation of alcohol abuse on screen occurs when a character's drinking is presented as not only out of control, but as causing a character to "hit rock bottom" and head to Skid Row. Sociologist Earl Rubington provided a definition of Skid Row useful for this discussion: "Skid Row stands in our society as the most dramatic symbol of a general failure of socialization and a particular failure to learn moderate drinking customs."[6] *Skid Row* is frequently used to describe a place—generally a metaphoric one—where drunkards end up; it is a place of despair and is, as Rubington notes, defined by "degradation, hopelessness and denial of human aspirations."[7] Lewington discussed the Skid Row drunk, noting that the presentation "usually entails a decline in dress and personal hygiene and a rise in offensive drunken behaviour sometimes leading to incarceration."[8] The presentation of a drunk character's life unraveling—evidenced by declines in dress and hygiene along with an escalation in bad behavior—is easily detected on screen.

In *Party of Five* (1994–2000), a clear sign that Bailey's (Scott Wolf) alcoholism was steering him toward Skid Row occurred in an episode where he agreed to serve as the clown at his younger brother's birthday. Bailey was drunk, dropped the cake, and got into an altercation with his older brother, in turn ruining the party. Something similar occurred in the film *28 Days* (2000), when drunken bridesmaid Gwen (Sandra Bullock) was dancing and fell into her sister's wedding cake; later she stole a car and crashed it. In *Californication* (2007–), Hank's (David Duchovny) life started to spiral out of control when his excessive drinking led to brawling and an arrest. In *Crazy Heart* (2009), the alcoholism of country music artist Otis (Jeff Bridges) led to multiple bad marriages, a nonexistent relationship with his son, and a tattered career.

While in these examples, drinking led to bad consequences, in each case the characters reformed: Bailey, Hank, Gwen, and Otis sobered up. They ultimately *didn't* actually end up on Skid Row; Skid Row just existed as a threat as to what *might* happen, in turn motivating reform. This, however, is not always the case—some characters' journeys do end at Skid Row.

Lewington discussed a number of films where alcoholism led characters to disastrous, destructive consequences. In *What Price Hollywood?* (1932), for example, Max (Lowell Sherman) was an alcoholic who eventually killed himself. In *Come Fill the Cup* (1951), Lew (James Cagney) was an alcoholic who lost his job and became destitute. The same bad Skid Row ending is identifiable in more recent films. *Ironweed* (1987), for example, centered on the life of two Skid Row drunks, Francis (Jack Nicholson) and Helen (Meryl Streep); Helen ended up dying from her affliction. *Barfly* (1987) was a film about Henry (Mickey Rourke), an alcoholic writer, whose drinking led him to Skid Row, to poverty, and to a missed opportunity to get his work published. In *Leaving Las Vegas* (1995), Ben (Nicolas Cage) drank himself to death.

Similar to the happy drunk portrayals discussed earlier, an obvious explanation for the Skid Row drunk archetype is the "moral model." Folklorist David Emery described the *cautionary tale* in literature as follows: "a fable with a moral message warning of the consequences of certain actions or character flaws."[9] As related to portrayals of alcoholism, these moral stories function to warn of looming disaster (an idea readily detectable in the teen drunk portrayals discussed later in this chapter).

Henry's alcoholism in *Barfly* is thought to stem from his inability to generate an income from his writing. In this film, he illustrated another alcoholic archetype: the drunken writer. *Lost Weekend* (1945), *In a Lonely Place* (1950), *Mrs. Parker and the Vicious Circle* (1994), *Henry Fool* (1997), *Leaving Las Vegas*, *Wonder Boys* (2000), *Sideways* (2005), *Factotum* (2005), *Californication*, and *Seven Psychopaths* (2012) all included drunken writers as central characters, each of whom complied with the cliché of the tortured artist. While writing is frequently presented as a profession strongly linked to alcoholism, another with even stronger connections is police work, manifested as the archetypal drunk cop character.

THE DRUNK COP

In his discussion of cinema, Lewington explored sociological approaches to alcoholism, identifying several circumstantial factors such as careers that can serve as risk factors. He referred to *The Squeeze* (1977) and the British series *Hazell* (1978–1979), both of which presented drunk cop characters who worked to perpetuate the myth that "policemen are driven to alcoholism by the stressful nature of their work."[10] The idea of cops battling alcoholism can be detected in innumerable screen narratives. Jim (John Nettles) in *Bergerac* (1981–1991), Matthew (Jeff Bridges) in *8 Million Ways to Die* (1986), Lennie (Jerry Orbach) in *Law and Order* (1990–2010), The Lieutenant (Harvey Keitel) in *Bad Lieutenant* (1992), Gary (Nicholas Lamont) in *Pie in the Sky* (1994–1997), Donald Cragen (Dann Florek) in *Law and Order: Special Victims Unit* (1999–), Jericho (Arnold Schwarzenegger) in *End of Days* (1999), Rebus (Ken Stott; John Hannah) in *Rebus* (2000–2007), Brian (Alun Armstrong) in *New Tricks* (2003–), Andy (Dennis Franz) in *NYPD Blue* (1993–2005), Fritz (Jon Tenney) and Provenza (G.W. Bailey) in *The Closer* (2005–2012), Jack (Bruce Willis) in *16 Blocks* (2006), Jimmy (Dominic West) in *The Wire* (2002–2008), Eddie (Richard Gere) in *Brooklyn's Finest* (2009), and Ronnie (Bradley Walsh) in *Law & Order: UK* (2009–2011) are but a small sample of the very wide range of law enforcement characters who are also alcoholics.

Lewington's explanation of job stress could be one rationale for this depiction; research does, indeed, document a link between police work and alcoholism. While accurate figures are difficult to source given that alcoholics tend to try and conceal—if not outright *deny*—their problems, psychologist William Kroes et al. estimated that 25 percent of police officers have an alcohol problem.[11] Other research has noted that police are more than 300 times more likely than the average person to be an alcoholic[12] and that 67 percent of officers have reported drinking on the job.[13] Such figures imply that there is something unique about police work that makes employees more inclined to drink than other professionals. While academic research on alcoholism and law enforcement points to this tendency being connected to industry camaraderie and social interaction,[14] in screen narratives alcoholism is normally presented as an extreme response to the equally extreme things that law enforcement officers have witnessed. Cops in screen narratives are invariably portrayed as investigating gruesome crimes; thus it is perhaps no surprise that some seek solace in addictive substances.

Returning to Lewington's discussion, another sociological factor he identified as connected to alcoholism was ethnicity. One screen stereotype exploiting this risk factor is the drunken Irishman.

THE DRUNKEN IRISHMAN

Lewington noted high rates of alcoholism among the Irish, something that certainly appears to inform screen presentations: Irish characters are frequently portrayed as inebriated. This was an issue discussed by cultural historian Lawrence Mintz in his work on the stereotypes used in vaudeville and early burlesque: "The Irish characters are drunk belligerent, and dumb ... The Italians are happy rascals, promiscuous, profligate, and irresponsible, comically hyperemotional—and dumb ... Blacks are lazy, dishonest, promiscuous, profligate, irresponsible and—guess what—dumb."[15]

The drunken Irishman appears in numerous guises on screen; an obvious way is in the punch line of jokes. In a St. Patrick's Day-themed episode of

The Simpsons, for example, news reporter Kent Brockman discussed footage of the day's events:

> Ladies and gentlemen, what you are seeing is a total disregard for the things St. Patrick's Day stands for. All this drinking, violence, destruction of property. Are these the things we think of when we think of the Irish?

In this scene Brockman highlights the tropes that audiences *do* indeed think of when they think of the Irish: in this scene—and as often evident on screen—the Irish drunkard is a caricature who is frequently the butt of jokes. In a scene from *Postcards from the Edge* (1990), the same punch line was present: Doris (Shirley MacLaine) remarked, "And now I just drink like an Irish person!" In *The Ghost and the Darkness* (1996), John (Val Kilmer) claimed, "God invented liquor so the Irish wouldn't rule the world." In an episode of the sitcom *Just Shoot Me!* (1997–2003), Eliot (Enrico Colantoni)—accused of illegal gambling—defended himself arguing, "Well, my mother is half-Irish, so I must have been drunk when I did it!" In the comedy *Keeping the Faith* (2000), Father Brian (Edward Norton) was accused of being drunk, to which he responded, "I'm Irish! This is milk to me, baby! Milk!" In the pilot of the series *The Black Donnellys* (2007), in the narration Joey (Keith Nobbs) stated:

> The Irish have always been victims of negative stereotyping. I mean people think we're all drunks and brawlers. And sometimes that gets you so mad all you wanna do is get drunk and punch somebody.

In episode of the animated series *Archer* (2009–), Malory remarked, "The classic Irish man's dilemma: do I eat the potato or do I let it ferment so I can drink it later?"

While the Irish drunkard stereotype is often referenced, it is also a depiction that frequently appears outside of punch lines and gets embodied in narratives. In an article in *Empire* magazine on stereotypes in cinema, Helen O'Hara discussed the "bar propper" character:

> As any Hollywood screenwriter/producer knows, Ireland is full of alcoholics. It stands to reason, therefore, that any male over the age of 50 to be found anywhere on the island will spend most of his time in his local drinking establishment, red-nosed face in a pint of the black stuff. This character is most likely good-natured and amiable (especially if the visiting lead buys him a drink) and probably owns a fiddle that will be put to good use in the final ceile around the pub.[16]

O'Hara's examples include "most of the cast of *Waking Ned Devine* [1998], the supporting cast of *Leap Year* [2010], most of the cast of *The Quiet Man* [1952], Darby O'Gill in *Darby O'Gill and the Little People* [1959]."[17]

There are, of course, many more examples outside of O'Hara's list. Marty (Colin Farrell) in *Seven Psychopaths*, for example, occupied the drunken Irish writer role. The short-tempered Irish drunkard role was filled by Frank (Jack Nicholson) in *The Departed* (2006), Jimmy in *The Wire*, Nate (Timothy Hutton) in *Leverage* (2008–), and Ted (Peter Midlan) in *War Horse* (2011). Irish drunks more akin to the happy drunk stereotype are also identifiable. In the animated series *Family Guy* (1999–), for example, Peter's real father turned out to be an Irishman, Mickey McFinnegan, and together the two sang a song called "My Drunken Irish Dad": "Oh, we Irish lads are all infirm and our moods infect us like a germ, 'cause we're all the spawn of a pickled sperm!" The sober alcoholic character Sam Malone (Ted Danson) on the sitcom *Cheers* was equally presented as a happy man of Irish origins; his happiness was based on his status as a *ladies man*.

One explanation for the Irish drunkard caricature is that, like the drunk cop, it references a cultural truism. In public health researcher Roger Blaney's work on alcoholism in Ireland, he exhibited skepticism about whether alcohol abuse is more of a problem for the Irish than for other cultures, but noted that it is nevertheless *still* a problem. Blaney pointed to a number of historical factors, including climate, bad food, a lack of alternative activities, availability, and low price as contributors to alcoholism in Ireland.[18] Given that alcohol is a problem for the Irish—as it is for many cultures—perhaps its frequent presentation on screen is to be expected. That said, given that alcoholism does plague many other populations, other explanations are likely culpable.

As in any racial stereotyping, the objective in depicting the drunken Irishman is to mock and render the race as inferior. Returning to Mintz's discussion cited earlier, he noted that it is common for stereotypes to be used to cast a race as dumb. By continually portraying the Irish as alcoholics, any number of other negative stereotypes follow: the Irish are construed as stupid, reckless brawlers and ultimately uncivilized; in turn, a justification is created for prejudice and distrust, if not also *demonization*.

Discussed earlier was John from *Animal House*, who was the happy drunken frat boy, and Bailey in *Party of Five*, who was the alcoholic heading for Skid Row. These two characters both reflect another popular screen portrayal: the drunken teen.

ALCOHOLIC TEENS

An episode of *Law and Order: Special Victims Unit* centered on "floating parties" where kids moved from one house to the next while getting progressively drunker; at one party, a murder occurred. While teen drinking was identifiable in this storyline, alcohol *abuse* among teenagers is more commonly tackled in Very Special Episodes. Such episodes are described by media theorists Robert Abelman and David Atkin as being defined by "a key dramatic moment in the program—a birth, a death, a recovery from illness—that has built for several weeks and stands a good chance of generating a particularly large audience."[19] Tara Ariano and Sarah Bunting in their book *Television without Pity* are a little more biting in their definition: "a Very Special Episode is an episode that feels more like school than like escapist television ... If it's got a lecturing tone, feels like a PSA [public service announcement], and presents an overly simplistic picture of a complex issue, it's probably a Very Special Episode ... VSE topics often include drug or alcohol abuse; bad touching; war, death, and grief; homosexuality ... They customarily conclude with a Very Valuable Lesson."[20]

As Abelman and Atkin, and Ariano and Bunting, note, teen alcohol abuse is a topic often tackled in Very Special Episodes and is rarely readdressed in subsequent episodes. In an episode of the sitcom *Growing Pains* (1985–1992), for example, Carol's (Tracey Gold) boyfriend Sandy (Matthew Perry) died after a drunk driving accident. In an episode of the sitcom *Family Matters* (1989–1998), Steve Urkel (Jaleel White) got drunk after a drink-spiking incident, leading to all kinds of "hilarious" accidents and bad behavior. In an episode of *Saved by the Bell* (1989–1993), a car accident occurred after Zack (Mark-Paul Gosselaar) drove drunk.

While each of these examples involved teen drinking, none was actually about teen *alcoholism*; rather, each was simply a cautionary tale as to why alcohol should be avoided. Some examples of teen alcoholism are however, identifiable. Discussed already in this chapter was Bailey, an alcoholic teen in *Party of Five*. In the sitcom *Blossom* (1990–1995), the oldest brother Tony (Michael Stoyanov) was a recovering alcoholic. Dylan (Luke Perry) in *Beverly Hills, 90210* (1990–2000) was an alcoholic, and in *Girls* (2012–), Adam (Adam Driver) has been a recovering alcoholic since he was 17. In *Weeds* (2005–2012), teenager Shane (Alexander Gould) battled alcoholism across the course of the series. While an unusual presentation, the teen alcoholic is the ultimate cautionary tale and serves as an ongoing warning of what happens when alcohol is consumed by young people: the unsubtle Very Valuable Lesson is that when young people drink, addiction is a likely consequence.

That the teen drunk is frequently served a Very Valuable Lesson is also in line with the U.S. reality that it is illegal for teenagers to purchase alcohol. Thus it is unsurprising that if underage drinking occurs, a punishment narrative ensues.

Thus far in this chapter I have discussed archetypes of alcoholics that seem to almost exclusively involve male characters. This issue was spotlighted by sociologists Judith Harwin and Shirley Otto in the late 1970s, when they discussed the issue of gender and screen portrayals of alcoholism. These authors noted that very few films had been made about female alcoholics: "such women remained hidden from public view and therefore, in effect, limited the possibility of any broader portrayal than that derived from a minority of highly atypical women who drank in public, such as actresses and prostitutes."[21]

This situation changed markedly during the 1970s. While perhaps not present in the same numbers as alcoholic men, female drunks are now relatively easily detected in contemporary screen narratives. Sociologist Elizabeth Ettorre, for example, documented a variety of negative images attached to drunken women, including the lush, the drunken whore, and the bad mother.[22] These three images are explored in the following sections.

THE LUSH

While female drunks are frequently condemned on screen with a variety of other negative attributes—commonly promiscuity or bad parenting—on some rare occasions the lush gets to partake of alcohol without being a whore or a bad mother; instead, she is just a lush, characterized simply by overindulgence and eccentricity. Fran (Tamsin Greig) in the British series *Black Books* (2000–2004), for example, was an often acerbic and aggressive character who overindulged in both alcohol and cigarettes. Aunt Lily (Swoosie Kurtz) in *Pushing Daisies* (2007–2009) was an alcoholic who, like Fran, was also often acerbic and lived largely as a shut-in. In *The Simpsons*, Eleanor Abernathy—otherwise known as the Crazy Cat Lady—is an alcoholic who is also seemingly mentally ill. Aside from their shared overindulgent personalities, something else uniting these female characters is that each is presented as varyingly *strange*; they do "weird" things. For instance, Fran ran a store that sold gifts that she dismissed as a "wank," Aunt Lily was obsessed with cheese and birds, and Eleanor hordes cats. Thus their alcoholism was presented as just another trait that marked these characters as odd.

Another incarnation of the lush—in line with Harwin and Otto's identification of "atypical" women such as drunk actresses—is the faded beauty drunk. Harwin and Otto discussed cinema portrayals of women who turn to drink after their beauty fades: "As the mask of youth and good fortune deserts them ... [they are] exposed as helpless, passive and vulnerable individuals."[23] Their examples included Diana (Dorothy Malone) from *Too Much, Too Soon* (1958), Lillian (Susan Hayward) from *I'll Cry Tomorrow* (1955), and Kirsten (Lee Remick) from *Days of Wine and Roses* (1962); each woman was a glamorous celebrity who, in the twilight of her career, turned to drink. Other examples include Norma (Gloria Swanson) in *Sunset Boulevard* (1950), Alex (Jane Fonda) in *The Morning After* (1986), and more recently the drunken former model Nina (Wendie Malick) on sitcom *Just Shoot Me!* The faded beauty drunk is an archetype that is very gender specific, reflecting that for women beauty is a commodity prized excessively highly; when it fades, then, the consequences can be psychologically devastating. That such women are considered as pathetic characters likely stems from audiences being unlikely to relate to them or to feel much sympathy for their plights: this kind of beauty is likely unfamiliar to audiences, so these women's despair is construed as peculiar, if not histrionic and self-indulgent.

Much like the presentations of alcoholic characters for whom explanations for their substance abuse are generally provided, for the female characters eccentricity or lost looks is emblematic of the trend to *explain* alcoholism. Characters are perceived as needing a good reason to drink to excess; otherwise, their condition doesn't make sense to audiences. Put simply, the taboo of alcoholism needs to be breached for a decent *narrative* reason.

As noted, the presentation of the lush often also involves promiscuity: a woman who overindulges in alcohol does so as readily as she overindulges in other "immoral" behavior such as sex. Thus both behaviors work in tandem as character indictments. In Lewington's discussion, he noted that of the alcoholic women in the films he discussed—*Too Much, Too Soon* and *Days of Wine and Roses*—they exhibited a "prodromal obsession with sex and chocolate respectively,"[24] and that while alcoholism for men invariably leads to aggression, for women it leads to "acts of promiscuity."[25] Such ideas underpin the popular portrayal of the promiscuous drunk on screen.

THE PROMISCUOUS DRUNK

Psychologist Melinda Kanner's discussion of sexual politics and popular culture explored the inextricable link between the female drunk and sexuality, noting that alcoholic women "are still configured in terms of their sexuality and their sexual and romantic interests to men."[26] While in *Black Books*, *Pushing Daisies*, and *The Simpsons*, the *absence* of enduring (or quality) relationships with men might be construed as one explanation for each woman's alcoholism, these characters were not portrayed as overtly promiscuous. Promiscuous lushes, however, are effortlessly detected.

In *Opening Night* (1977), much like the faded beauties discussed earlier, Myrtle (Gena Rowlands) was a former nightclub singer and dancer who, in the twilight of her career, became both alcoholic and promiscuous. In the British sitcom *Absolutely Fabulous* (1992–), Edina (Jennifer Saunders) and Patsy (Joanna Lumley) are best friends and both alcoholics; Patsy, however, is portrayed as the far more overindulgent character, depicted as both alcoholic and *promiscuous*. In *Just Shoot Me!*, Nina was a former model who in her 50s was presented as promiscuous, frequently discussing dalliances with a variety of celebrities, including Mick Jagger; in some episodes, subtle allusions were even made to the possibility that she was bisexual. In sitcom *Will & Grace* (1998–2006), Karen (Megan Mullally) was alcoholic and promiscuous. Like Nina, she was also presumed to be bisexual: in different episodes she referred to relationships with women including Martina Navratilova and Goldie Hawn. Like Nina and Karen, Meredith (Kate Flannery) in *The Office* (2005–2013) is an alcoholic and is presented as sexually inappropriate and promiscuous: her drinking has resulted in her forgetting the men she has slept with. In one episode, Meredith even divulged a pornography addiction. Like the lushes discussed earlier, these characters are all presented as eccentric, but their promiscuity is of equal importance to their identity.

The coupling of alcohol and promiscuity on screen is hardly surprising: both are "vices" that function to demonize women and to portray them as threatening because they are seemingly out of control. A drunk woman, it seems, is unreliable and potentially untrustworthy, shirking the mandates associated with her gender. The drink is her true love. There also appears a cause-and-effect relationship between the two vices: alcohol leads to promiscuity, while promiscuity is further evidence of the loathsomeness of the lush. Again, each behavior functions as an explanation for female drunkenness: "normal" people don't drink to excess, so there must be something wrong, damaged, or venomous about the female alcoholic who clearly lacks ladylike decorum and self-restraint.[27]

Nina and Meredith are interesting characters because while they fill the lush *and* drunken whore stereotypes, both also fill another requirement for the female drunk: they are *bad mothers*.

THE BAD MOTHER

If the *good* mother—as defined by sociologists Susan Chase and Mary Rogers—is "selfless ... [h]er children come before herself and any other need or person or commitment, no matter what"[28]—then the *bad* mother is the opposite. In geographer Robyn Longhurst's discussion of gender and maternity, she discussed mothers who comply with society's description of "bad": "Mothers involved in the sex industry and disabled mothers ... teenagers, lesbians, drug users, addicts, alcoholics, violent mothers, ill mothers, single mothers."[29] Her discussion, in fact, included a reference to Edina from *Absolutely Fabulous*, whose drunkenness earned her the bad mother indictment: "Edina is undoubtedly a bad mother who is far more interested in living it up with her chain-smoking, hard-drinking, drug-imbibing, schooldays chum Patsy ... than she is in caring for her daughter."[30]

The alcoholic bad mother is a portrayal readily identified on screen. In *Just Shoot Me!*, it was discovered that Nina gave a child up for adoption as a teenager; Nina evidently demonstrated the *ultimate* of bad mothering—complete dereliction of duty. In *The Office*, Meredith has custody of only one of her children; one might suspect that this has something to do with her drunkenness. While Karen in *Will & Grace* wasn't biologically a mother, she was nevertheless involved (at least putatively) with looking after her husband Stan's children, a task that she was comically terrible at it: she referred to one child as "the fat one" and another simply as "The Girl." Karen had no aptitude for motherhood and admitted to taking employment with Grace (Debra Messing) purely to "get away from Stan and the kids."

In these examples, Nina, Meredith, and Karen were characters not primarily defined by mothering—Nina was never a mother in any ways beyond biology; Meredith was defined as an alcoholic employee rather than an alcoholic mother; and Karen was very committed to the idea that the children were *Stan's*. In such cases, bad parenting is simply another aspect of their drunkenness that renders a female drunk eccentric and entertaining in the context of sitcoms. By comparison, in some other narratives the female alcoholic is defined by her mothering—something that gets compromised by her alcoholism.

As identified earlier, Edina in *Absolutely Fabulous* is a comic example of the bad mother: her daughter Saffron (Julia Sawalha) is the comparatively sensible character. Kitty (Debra Jo Rupp) from *That '70s Show* (1998–2006) operated in a similar comic fashion: she was presented as perpetually—albeit subtly—inebriated, although there was little consequence to her behavior other than her character existing as an *unusual* example of a television mom.

Taking the drunk mom a few steps further was Sue-Ellen Ewing (Linda Gray) from the television series *Dallas* (1978–1991). Sue-Ellen complied with the faded beauty archetype discussed earlier—she was, after all, a former Miss Texas—and is also well-suited to the drunk mom label. A similar drunk mom/socialite was Letitia Darling (Jill Clayburgh) in *Dirty Sexy Money* (2007–2009): she was suspected throughout the series of murder *and* infidelity. The infidelity theme—referencing women's apparent failure to remain appropriately restrained and chaste—is also apparent in *The Graduate* (1967). Mrs. Robinson's (Anne Bancroft) bad mothering manifested as promiscuity: she seduced the son (Dustin Hoffman) of her husband's business partner and manipulated her young lover's relationship with her daughter.

The film *When a Man Loves a Woman* (1994) centered on Alice (Meg Ryan), a drunk mother: her bad mothering was shown when she frequently neglected her children and, at one point, even slapped her daughter. In *Veronica Mars* (2004–2007), the alcoholism of the title character's (Kristen Bell) mother, Lianne (Corinne Bohrer), led to her abruptly leaving the family and, like Nina in *Just Shoot Me!*, abandoning her parenting duties all together. Such neglect was similarly presented as part of the back story of the character of Lilly (Kathryn Morris) in the drama series *Cold Case* (2003–2010): her alcoholic mother, Ellen (Meredith Baxter), frequently left her alone to care for her sister. In *House* (2004–2012), Dr. Chase's (Jesse Spencer) neglectful alcoholic mother used to lock him in the study when she was unable to care for him; at other times she required him to be *her* caretaker. In *Orange County* (2002), Shaun's (Colin Hanks) mother Cindy (Catherine O'Hara) was an alcoholic: her bad mothering centered on her emotional fragility.

In *Spanking the Monkey* (1994), the alcoholism of Ray's (Jeremy Davies) mother Susan (Alberta Watson) underpinned a substantial demonstration of bad parenting: mother and son were sexually involved. In the sitcom *Arrested Development* (2003–2006), while Lucille (Jessica Walter) can be read as a comic drunk mom akin to Edina in *Absolutely Fabulous* or Kitty in *That '70s Show*, her bad mothering can also be interpreted as much more problematic, something I discussed in my book *Part-Time Perverts: Sex, Pop Culture, and Kink Management*: "The relationship between Buster (Tony Hale) and his mother, Lucille (Jessica Walter), is smother/mother ... exemplified well when Lucille takes Buster to the annual 'Motherboy' dance. Their relationship is further complicated when Buster gets sexually involved with his mother's nemesis (and contemporary) 'Lucille Two' (Liza Minnelli)."[31]

The drunk mom is the perfect embodiment of a number of social transgressions. She is overindulgent, something considered to be a breach of femininity mandates as related to being self-sacrificing, self-abnegating, self-restraining, and self-denying.[32] Most notably, she allows a vice to control her behavior and lead her to neglect her responsibilities as a mother. Society attaches all kinds of virtues to the mother; for a mother to breach them and become an alcoholic presents a substantial on-screen scandal and taboo breach.[33]

Just as the drunk mom is a screen staple, so too is the drunk dad.

THE DRUNK DAD

Just like the drunk moms discussed previously, the drunk dad epitomizes bad parenting. While there are different social expectations made of mothers and fathers, the drunk dad fails to set a good example to his children, he can be construed as drinking family resources, and oftentimes he is physically and verbally abusive. In film theorist Marcus Grant's discussion of alcohol and film, he noted that the man who can drink frequently but hold his drink is considered more manly and as substantially different to the drunkard.[34] With the drunk dad on screen, however, the character is not defined by manliness, but rather is a family failure.

Already in this chapter I have discussed a number of characters who are not only drunks, but drunk fathers. Hank in *Californication*, Francis in *Ironweed*, and Lennie in *Law and Order*, for example, were all drunks who also had children. Akin to Lilly's back story in *Cold Case*, in *The Mentalist* (2008–), Teresa's (Robin Tunney) past involved a drunken father who abused her and who ended up committing suicide. In *Cherrybomb* (2009), Luke's (Robert Sheehan) father was a drunk who attempted to kill himself. In the film *Forrest Gump* (1994), Jenny's (Robin Wright) father (Kevin Mangan) was an alcoholic and similarly presented as sexually abusive.

Given that drunk characters are most likely to be men, it probably comes as no surprise that drunk dads are more common on screen than drunk mothers. While the drunk mom is more of a taboo breach than the drunk dad, nonetheless the drunk dad breaches a number of expectations related to his role and gender. In human development theorist Rob Palkovitz's discussion of fatherhood, he detailed the attributes of good fathers:

> A good father is someone who is there for his children. He is caring and loving. His children know he is committed to them. He is available to them and

he spends quality time with them. His time with them shows he is genuinely interested in them ... A father's behavior and attitudes unmistakably show he is child centered and willing to sacrifice his own goals and career in order to actively do things for his children ... A good father is a provider.[35]

For a father to prioritize his drinking, he has put his family and their needs *after* his substance abuse problem.

While in this chapter I have focused largely on drunk characters who are portrayed negatively, worth noting is that sometimes alcohol is presented as providing a character with special skills and attributes beyond social lubrication.

ALCOHOL AND SUPERPOWERS

While not necessarily alcoholics, there are examples of characters for whom alcohol provides special powers. In the sitcom *The Big Bang Theory* (2007–), for example, Raj (Kunal Nayyar) is able to charm to women only when he is under the influence of alcohol. In one episode he was able to chat up a woman on a train because he *thought* he was drunk; it turned out he had actually been drinking low-alcohol beer thus indicating that his bravado stemmed from the power of suggestion. The drunken superpowers idea was taken further in the Chinese film *Jui kuen* (*Drunken Master*) (1978), whereby Beggar Su Hua Chi (Yuen Siu-tien) taught a secret style of martial arts in which inebriation was key. In *Old School* (2003), Frank (Will Ferrell) became a very good debater when drunk. In *The Drew Carey Show* (1995–2004), the boss Mr. Wick (Craig Ferguson) could only give speeches when slightly inebriated. In the sitcom *Raising Hope* (2010–), tone-death Jimmy (Lucas Neff) can only sing well when drunk. In the sitcom *Happy Endings* (2011–), Penny (Casey Wilson) can speak Italian, but again, only when drunk and Peter in *Family Guy* can play the piano but only when inebriated. It is no surprise that these examples all involve *comedies*; the idea of drunkenness giving someone a "special" ability seems farcical. Such stupidity—each example situated inside a comedy—can be construed as *reiterating* that drinking to excess is a *bad* thing.

An interesting paradox exists in our culture whereby alcohol is considered an essential part of socializing, yet alcohol*ism* is considered a substantial social problem. Such ideas play out on screen where male and female drunks are frequently considered as loathsome, leading to a variety of negative consequences and thereby reinforcing the taboo of alcoholism.

The Drugs Chapter: Advertising Mother's Little Helper

Prescription medicines are unlike any other product: they are considered serious enough to be restricted in sale and their consumption is something most people would assume should be recommended by doctors and not by television commercials. Yet, in the United States and New Zealand, a strange situation exists where prescription medication is peddled mercilessly on television—*direct to consumers*—to the tune of billions of dollars; this practice is prohibited in every other country in the world. From weight-loss drugs to sleeping aids to erectile dysfunction remedies, this chapter explores the techniques used to help market prescription medications. Using appeals to guilt, fear, nostalgia, and lifestyle, a variety of marketing tools are deployed to make potentially dangerous prescription medications seem necessary, desirable, and completely normal. The legislative landscape and the frequent broadcast of such advertisements spotlights the strange situation in which use of prescription medication is presented as akin to use of any other product. Misuse and abuse of prescription medication are as a big a problem for society as abuse of illegal drugs,[1] yet the former is legitimized by advertising, while the latter is construed as heinous.

THE TABOO OF PRESCRIPTION MEDICATION

To include a chapter on prescription medication in a book on taboos in popular culture might seem like an anomaly. Other chapters in this volume explore topics wherein the taboo lies in a subject's absence or, alternatively, where something is routinely demonized or mocked to maintain a taboo.

In the case of prescription medication, no taboo actually exists in the United States surrounding the advertising of such drugs: doing so is perfectly legal. Similarly, no taboo exists around the *consumption* of such drugs: research indicates that more than half (51%) of all Americans take at least two prescription medications every day,[2] with this percentage ever rising.[3] Consumer expenditures on pharmaceutical drugs exceed $200 billion annually,[4] and pharmaceutical manufacturing is considered one of the most lucrative industries in the United States.[5] The true taboo, in fact, lies in the discussion of the connection between persistent pharmaceutical advertising and high-level drug use: it is taboo in contemporary culture to blame advertising for the enormously high consumption of potentially dangerous products. It is estimated that direct-to-consumer drug advertising expenditures amounted to $12 million in 1989; by 2001 this sum had increased to $2.3 billion and in 2008 this figure was pegged at $4.4 billion.[6] Drug advertising is common and, according to the industry, enormously effective: for every dollar spent on drug advertising, an extra $4.20 in drug sales is reaped.[7]

This relationship highlights the taboo related to prescription drugs. Doctors spend several years in medical school as well as participate in innumerable professional development courses throughout their careers so that they can adequately diagnose and treat patients. While advertising messages are not entirely replacing the doctor-patient relationship, with so many pharmaceuticals advertised, it is now very common for patients to visit their doctor with a diagnosis and remedy already in mind. Research indicates that among consumers who request a drug they saw advertised, more than half actually receive a prescription for that product.[8] The idea that consumers are influenced by advertising, and that doctors are influenced by advertising *and* by patients, presents an interesting situation. It could be contended that it is problematic for the sanctity of the doctor-patient relationship to be compromised by television advertising. Of equal concern is *over-prescription* and the question of whether the 51 percent of Americans taking two or more prescription medications daily really need them.[9]

Herein lies the taboo: having the conversation about the role of advertising in both the doctor-patient relationship and in over-prescription. This chapter focuses on a topic frequently considered taboo in the face of a multibillion-dollar pharmaceutical industry and in a country where so many people take pharmaceuticals daily—namely, that advertising has substantial complicity in this situation. This chapter focuses on the *how* of creating the landscape of a highly medicated America, examining the techniques used by pharmaceutical companies to create and maintain the enormous market for drugs.

THE ROLE OF ADVERTISING

Advertising is about persuasion, about getting people to desire a product or service. Much marketing, most notably the advertising of nonessential products and services, relies on guiding viewers to identify a problem—be it a physical or lifestyle imperfection or deficiency—and then offering them purchasable solutions.

Advertising is routinely criticized by scholars on several fronts: (1) it coerces unnecessary purchases, (2) the images used create unrealistic beauty standards, (3) some advertisements are age inappropriate, and (4) deliberately offensive images are frequently deployed to attract attention and controversy.[10] Such criticisms are, of course, routinely directed at prescription medication commercials. In addition, however, drug ads draw their own, more specific complaints: (1) they compromise the doctor-patient relationship, (2) encourage demand for unnecessary medication, (3) lead to overprescription, and (4) cause health-related neurosis and hypochondria. The pharmaceutical industry would, of course, counter such claims, alleging that a variety of *good things* emerge from patient-targeted television advertising, including (1) the provision of consumer information, (2) alerting consumers to new treatments, (3) encouragement of patients to become involved in their own care, and (4) destigmatization of medical conditions.

Regardless of whether we believe that advertising is likely to help or harm, the idea that it has the power to do *anything* is a highly controversial idea debated under the communications studies banner of *media effects*.[11] In some areas such as sex or violence, the effects of portrayals—as related to instigating harm—are extensively contested. By comparison, in advertising, the effect is much easier to predict and measure: two obvious indicators are the dollars spent on advertising and product sales. Billions of dollars are spent on advertising prescription medications: pharmaceutical companies would not continue to spend this way if they did not believe advertising has a positive effect on their brands and, in turn, their sales. While many factors other than advertising influence purchases—for example, personal experience, peer group, and the purchasing environment—advertising is assumed by the industry to play a pivotal role. It is the idea that drug advertising influences consumer behavior that underpins the need to investigate how these products are marketed on television.

CREATING A DRUG MARKET

A key purpose of advertising is to create a market filled with consumers; companies advertise because they want to conjure up a demand for their products. While for some products a natural market exists—hunger or thirst, for example—the market for a new drug isn't always obvious; people don't always instinctively know that they "need" medicine. In the context of pharmaceuticals, advertising has a primary function of helping viewers to self-diagnose and notably to *self-prescribe*.[12]

Self-Diagnosis and Self-Prescription

The diagnosis and treatment of fibromyalgia highlights well the role of advertising in helping consumers to self-diagnose ailments and to desire a promoted solution. In medical researcher Nortin Hadler's book *Worried Sick*, the author explored topics such as over-prescription and its connection to widespread pharmaceutical advertising. In discussing fibromyalgia, Hadler noted that it is a diagnosis that "denotes nothing more than persistent widespread pain."[13] Given that there are no tests to diagnose this condition, the label—one repeatedly coupled with vague but common symptoms in commercials—potentially applies and appeals to those persons suffering from the generic "widespread pain" complaint. While an imprecise diagnosis perhaps, such commercials nevertheless aid in self-diagnosis and self-prescription, something that lies at the heart of all marketing: the drive to help consumers identify that something is wrong with them and then offer a remedy. Marketing theorists Charles Lamb et al. discussed the connection between fibromyalgia and the persistent marketing of the drug Lyrica: "There are no biological tests to diagnose fibromyalgia, and the condition has not yet been linked to any environmental or biological causes. But worldwide sales of Lyrica reached $1.8 billion in 2007 ... helped by consumer advertising."[14]

Advertising for Lyrica most certainly illustrates the self-diagnosis and self-prescription cycle. In one commercial, a woman explains, "I kept feeling this radiating ache everywhere; the pain was so frustrating." In another, a woman describes: "I was living with this all-over pain. A deep, throbbing persistent ache." In both commercials, symptoms that could be associated with any number of conditions are diagnosed *in seconds* as fibromyalgia; in both cases, the characters reveal that they "learned Lyrica can provide significant relief from fibromyalgia pain." In short, their pain suddenly had both a label *and* a treatment.

In his book *Brandwashed*, marketing theorist Martin Lindstrom discussed these same themes, identifying that commercials don't merely help with self-diagnosis, but also aid in the *pathologization* of a variety of traits that outside of the pharmaceutical industry would simply be considered quirks or variants. Lindstrom argued that the effect of such commercials is that they come to dictate that normal variances are not merely unpalatable but are, in fact, *medical problems* necessitating pharmaceutical remedy: "Do you suffer from shyness? Apparently shyness isn't just a personality trait but an actual pathology, and one that Paxil can cure. What about acid reflux disease, formerly known as heartburn? Today there are over a dozen drugs, from Nexium to Prilosec to Zantax, available to treat it. Who knew that irritable bowels weren't just the unfortunate repercussions of a spicy Mexican dinner but were actually a 'syndrome'?"[15]

Such ideas play out extensively in advertising. In a Paxil commercial, a variety of characters were shown as uncomfortable in social situations such as parties. The voiceover pitched Paxil as the solution for "the many who suffer from overwhelming anxiety and intense fear of social situations with unfamiliar people." The subtext is that shyness isn't *merely* a personality trait, but rather a medical condition that can be remedied through use of pharmaceuticals. Similar examples of pathologized personality deviations are identifiable in commercials for Strattera and Effexor. In the Strattera commercial, the audience is asked, "What's it like to have adult attention-deficit disorder? You often feel distracted, disorganized, unable to finish things." What might seem like rather general symptoms are diagnosed as something *medical*: someone who experiences distraction or procrastination is now a patient with adult attention-deficit disorder. An Effexor antidepressant commercial similarly opens with this text: "Do you feel alone? Do you feel everyone else is far away from you? You could be depressed." Again, symptoms that are vague are quickly pathologized and pharmaceuticals are recommended as the remedy.

Another way markets are created or expanded is through promotion of products' side effects. That is, the unanticipated consequences of a drug can lead to off-label usage and, therefore, potentially to new customers.

OFF-LABEL MARKETING

Lumigan was a drug originally prescribed to treat glaucoma. A side effect for many users was the growth of longer eyelashes. This side effect created the possibility of a new market: the side effect could be repurposed as a "cure" for short lashes. Lumigan became Latisse and is now marketed exclusively for cosmetic purposes. In the Latisse commercials, actors including Brooke Shields and Claire Danes display their long lashes and advise that Latisse is "The first and only FDA-approved prescription treatment for inadequate or not enough lashes." Suddenly, shorter lashes aren't just an individual trait—aren't just something distinguishing one person from another—but rather constitute a condition that can be overcome through medical intervention. Greg Critser, in his book *Generation Rx*, presented a similar story as related to Viagra. Originally created to treat angina, this medication demonstrated a tendency to produce erections. Thus the manufacturer, Pfizer, had a highly marketable side effect; it just needed to find a disease that erections would cure: "The answer was a condition dubbed 'erection dysfunction,' or ED."[16]

The longer lash side effects of Lumigan and the erection opportunities offered by Viagra highlight a frequent occurrence in the pharmaceutical industry: the truly *lucrative* market for a drug emerges from its off-label uses. While Lumigan and Viagra eventually got formal FDA approval for their off-label uses, most such uses have not—and do not—ever receive such official approval. One way pharmaceutical companies help create and expand their markets, therefore, is by making allusions—with varying degrees of subtlety—to nonapproved uses. This is a successful strategy: it has been estimated that one in four prescriptions written in the United States is for a drug that will be used on an off-label basis.[17] While the overt promotion of off-label uses is illegal,[18] an obvious way to circumvent this constraint is simply mentioning such uses among a drug's side effects. In commercials for Wellbutrin, for example, repeatedly mentioned was the fact that the drug has "low sexual side effects." While Wellbutrin has FDA approval as an antidepressant, the repeated mentioning of the low sexual side effects hints at an off-label sexual stimulant use for the product.[19] Advertising in this manner helps quietly expand a market beyond the putatively intended recipients. Sociologist Mary Ebeling discussed this issue as related to the off-label uses of Sculptra, a drug approved to treat facial fat loss in HIV patients; Sculptra is now used on an off-label basis for cosmetic purposes.[20]

Drug Market Expansion

Noted earlier was that a fundamental objective of advertising is to create new markets. For many products, a natural market exists and so the task of advertising is either getting people to switch brands or to expand a market. Selling Sculptra to a market *beyond* HIV patients is an obvious example.

Another example is the advertising of contraceptive pills. Given that the Pill has been around for more than half a century and virtually all women know about its role in preventing conception, pharmaceutical companies have to tout "new" features to make their products appear distinct and to appeal to those women who are either not using a contraceptive pill or are unaware of their products' "unique benefits." Historian Aharon Zorea, for example, explored the marketing of contraceptive pills to very young women: "The ad campaigns always mentioned the contraceptive use but often placed greater emphasis on premenstrual dysphoric disorder or acne fighting in order to distinguish itself from its competitors."[21]

That these advertisements are for contraceptive pills is obvious—after all, birth control is what these drugs have FDA approval for—but it is often the positive *side effects* such as mood stabilization or clear skin that are pitched. In the process, girls potentially too young to be in the natural market for contraception are targeted. Such techniques are easily detected in contemporary advertising. In a commercial for Yaz, for example, a young woman joins her female friends at a bar. One friend greets her: "Wow! Look who's here." The new arrival responds, "This time last month I'd never have made it." The new arrival discloses that she has recently explained to her doctor that she is an "emotional wreck a week or so before my period," so her doctor prescribed Yaz. While the birth control function of Yaz is briefly mentioned, the advertisement focuses on the product's mood-stabilizing functions. The same off-label use promotion is evident in comments made in a commercial for the Beyaz pill:

> Like all birth control, Beyaz is effective in preventing pregnancy and may give you lighter periods. And if you choose Beyaz for birth control it may help treat moderate acne and premenstrual dysmorphic disorder.

Again, birth control is mentioned but the focus is on the lifestyle-enhancing side effects that young women—who might not even be sexually active—desire.

Another technique of creating and expanding markets is normalization—that is, normalizing certain medical conditions and normalizing the use of pharmaceuticals to treat them.

PHARMACEUTICAL ADVERTISING AND NORMALIZATION

In cultural theorist Linda Seidel's research on the body, she noted how pharmaceutical advertisements reinforce stigmas associated with age and disability and, in turn, establish the young and able body as the standard to aspire to: "the ordinary slowing of sexual response as one ages becomes medicalized as a condition to be treated. The decline in athleticism that even the physically fit are liable to experience as they grow older is to be staved off as long as possible through the correct pill, lest they have to admit the advance of age or disability."[22] While commercials frequently present versions of "normal" to entice consumers to obtain products promising to help them reach this mythic state, there are two other ways that advertising functions to normalize: normalizing medical conditions and normalizing the consumption of prescription medication.

Noted earlier was a defense that pharmaceutical companies use to justify their marketing techniques—namely, that they are removing stigma from medical conditions. *Removing stigma* basically involves making something—in this case, a sickness—seem less freakish or less of an outlier condition. One way this is done is through the *you are not alone* appeal.[23] While this might be construed as something positive—that sufferers no longer need to feel like pariahs—from a marketing perspective, having people feel less stigma and shame also means that they are more likely to feel comfortable about seeking help from a medical practitioner, and therefore more comfortable with the thought of acquiring medication.

Normalizing Medical Conditions

Seidel discussed the role of advertising in making medical conditions seem common: "Whether we have to urinate too often, need to monitor our diabetes, can't become erect, or no longer move with the agility of youth, we know that we have plenty of company. All those people in the ads tell us so."[24] Earlier I discussed a Paxil advertisement that employed the *you are not alone* appeal: the voiceover asked if the viewer was "one of the many" who suffers from anxiety. A Plavix commercial similarly revealed that "millions of us are hospitalized with heart-related chest pain." A Zoloft antidepressant commercial opened with a voiceover that explained: "You know when you feel the weight of sadness. You may feel exhausted, hopeless and anxious ... These are symptoms of depression, a serious medical condition affecting over 20 million Americans." An advertisement for Rozerem sleep medication claimed that "More than half of adults report experiencing some sort of insomnia at least a few nights a week." By alerting audiences to the fact that many—if not *millions*—of people are suffering *like you*, the cited statistics validate a malady and private concerns appear common.

The *you are not alone* appeal also transpires in more personalized approaches. In an advertisement for Cauduet, for example, a woman asks the viewer, "Are you like me? I have high blood pressure *and* I have high cholesterol." Again, the suffering viewer is made to feel that his or her condition is common; the suffer feels validated and more importantly *normal*—and certainly normal enough to see a doctor and buy medicine.

Advertising can also normalize medical conditions through the use of celebrity spokespeople. Golfer Jack Nicklaus has touted the blood-pressure medication Altace, actor Sally Field has spoken on behalf of the osteoporosis drug Boniva, and actor Jane Seymour has helped advertise diabetes medicine Avandia. Celebrities help to normalize medical conditions by reminding audiences that *no matter who you are*, you, too, can suffer from a condition that needs medical intervention and that no shame should be felt. This idea was actually presented in the narrative of a Lipitor commercial: a glamorous older woman got out of a car and walked the red carpet at a premiere. Her statistics appeared on the screen—height, weight, dress size, and so on—and then her cholesterol figure was presented and the woman stumbled over. The voiceover stated, "High cholesterol doesn't care who you are." The message is that any one—celebrity *or* viewer at home—can succumb to sickness, but fortunately (pharmaceutical) help is available.

While drug advertisements help normalize medical conditions, they also can help normalize the taking of prescription medication.

Normalizing Drug Use

In communication theorists Robin Andersen and Jonathan Gray's discussion of pharmaceutical advertising, the authors considered the role of commercials in normalization of both diseases and the use of medicine: "While DTCA [direct-to-consumer advertising] can help to 'normalize' previously misunderstood or stigmatized medical conditions, the proliferation of advertising for medical conditions across a spectrum of seriousness can also lead to a tendency to diagnose even the most minor of medical ailments as being suitable for prescription treatment."[25] Health researchers Gordon Edlin and Eric Golanty similarly explained how very normal it is for Americans to now view prescription medication as the solution to health concerns:

> Many Americans have come to accept pharmaceutical solutions (called lifestyle drugs) for symptoms, behaviors, and moods that are caused by unhealthy behaviors (smoking, drinking alcohol, overeating, lack of exercise) or from the stress and anxiety of daily living. Instead of changing unhealthy behaviors or seeking nonchemical ways to reduce excessive stress and anxiety, many people prefer to pop a pill. They are encouraged to do so by an unrelenting barrage

of drug company advertising urging them to use drugs as the best way to solve life's problems.[26]

Pharmaceutical executive Thomas Picone presented an interesting example of how such attitudes are manifested in daily practices: "it is not uncommon to hear that consumers with an allergy to cats would take a product such as Zyrtec or Claritin daily to suppress their allergy because of their love of cats or because of their love of someone else who loves cats."[27] Writer Gayle Greene discussed these ideas in the context of sleep medication advertisements, noting that the effect is to make taking such medicine "seem like the most 'natural' thing in the world."[28] Legal scholar Patricia Peppin similarly noted that "the earliest advertisements for Prozac used the same legitimization technique to normalize the expression of depression—along with the remedy."[29] These practices help to highlight that a fundamental task of prescription medication marketing is to present drug consumption as *perfectly normal* so as to "empower" the viewer to make a pharmaceutical purchase.

Perhaps one of the most common lines used in prescription medication advertising is "diet and exercise may not be enough." This statement is used to justify a variety of drugs, invariably those in the lifestyle category. While this statement might be accurate, it also potentially implies that drugs can *compensate* for—or even *substitute* for—a bad diet or insufficient exercise. A commercial for Avandia, for example, opened with an overweight man explaining that he has diabetes and is committed to diet and exercise. He is still noticeably overweight, however, so diet and exercise *haven't* been enough; Avandia is the promised solution. The same thing transpired in an advertisement for Onglyza: diet and exercise clearly were insufficient for the overweight male character, and medicine was the solution. In an advertisement for the erectile dysfunction medication Levitra, a man tried unsuccessfully to throw a ball through a hoop; the voiceover reassured him, "Sometimes you need a little help staying in the game." The man was middle-aged. As noted by Seidel, it might be perfectly normal for a man's sexual response to have slowed with age; nevertheless, such an advertisement implies that it is more normal *not* to acquiesce to nature, but to take medicine instead. Sociologist Chris Wienke discussed this Levitra commercial in his work on masculinity: "It is through the imagery and message of ads like this one that Levitra is constructed as a lifestyle drug. Such ads are intended to appeal to not only men with impotence but also large segments of the male populace, whether or not they have bona fide medical problems."[30]

In the next sections, I explore a variety of techniques used within the narratives of advertisements to entice audiences into thinking that they need the promoted drug.

FEAR APPEALS

An emotional manipulation technique frequently deployed in advertising is fear; when stimulated, such an emotion is powerful in promoting change in attitude or behavior. Psychologist Bernardo Carducci explained how the appeal works:

> The basic principle upon which anxiety is used in advertising can be summarized in a two-step process. The first step involves the advertisement creating a sense of anxiety, either by utilizing the anxiety that is already present in most people (e.g., fear of rejection) or by creating a state of anxiety (e.g., you could die prematurely). The second step involves providing a message (e.g., "our mouthwash reduces plaque") or a course of action (e.g., "act now and receive our bonus coverage") designed to reduce anxiety. Thus, the basic role of anxiety in advertising is to make you feel uneasy so the product being advertised can make you feel good.[31]

Fear appeals are used throughout advertising: marketing researchers John Rossiter and Larry Percy, for example, discussed the use of this technique in advertising for American Express traveler's checks, where the fear of robbery was exploited. The authors also discussed fear appeals in commercials for Prudential Insurance, where life insurance was marketed with images of a mother drowning and a father dying on an operating table.[32] It is no surprise that fear is one of the most common devices used in pharmaceutical advertising: fears related to life and death have a natural home in the marketing of products intended to help mitigate health problems. Whether it is fears of allergies or angina, bladder leakage or erectile dysfunction, prescription medication advertisements routinely remind viewers that these conditions are genuine and worrisome, but for which treatment is available. In the next sections, fear appeals including those related to fear itself, death, and lost attractiveness are explored.

Fear of Fear

In his inaugural presidential address, Franklin D. Roosevelt mentioned the "fear of fear," defining it as a "nameless, unreasoning, unjustified terror which paralyzes needed efforts to convert retreat into advance."[33] It is this anxiety—vague, nonspecific, and potentially paralyzing—that is frequently appealed to in advertising. A good example occurs in an advertisement for the antidepressant Paxil, where a variety of characters mused on their condition: "It's like I can't participate in life. Like I'm too busy worrying ..."; "I can't control it and I'm always worried about it." In the advertisements for Strattera and Effexor, vague if not thoroughly ordinary symptoms such as distraction, disorganization, and loneliness are also depicted as something that fear might exacerbate. Such advertisements present a series of common and nonspecific fears and then offer prescription medication as the solution.

The undercurrent of fear appeals is that the thing being feared may expand. A worst-case scenario in the context of health is death, a fear frequently harnessed in pharmaceutical advertising.

Fear of Death

Fear of death is a normal fear harbored by humans. This fear can be easily exploited by pharmaceutical corporations by suggesting that death is imminent but fortunately can be staved off with the right prescription.

In an advertisement for Plavix—an antiplatelet drug—a middle-aged sports coach was shown talking to his team; the voiceover narrated: "Bill is a formidable man but he was no match for something smaller than a bead of sweat. It K-Oed him so fast he didn't even see it coming. It was a clot." In the Plavix commercial discussed earlier—showing a busy city scene—a voiceover revealed, "Millions of us are hospitalized with heart-related chest pain ... Think aspirin and your other heart medications alone are enough? One more thing could help make a difference." In a Lipitor advertisement, a man divulged: "Talk about a wake-up call. I had a heart attack at 57. My doctor told me I should've been doing more for my high cholesterol. What was I thinking?" In the Lipitor advertisement discussed earlier, a glamorous celebrity stumbled on the red carpet; the voiceover stated, "High cholesterol doesn't care who you are." In each of these examples, allusions were made to very close calls—miniscule clots, chest pain, high cholesterol—each functioning as a "call to arms" for pharmaceutical intervention.

Sometimes fear of death appeals are made much more literally and employ devices normally witnessed in horror films, whereby death is either overtly prophesized or given form and presented as physically encroaching. In an advertisement for the cholesterol drug Zocor, for example, the voiceover warned, "You just never know what high cholesterol and heart disease really mean until someone you love has a heart attack"; the footage showed a panicked wife tending to her severely ill husband while frantically making an emergency phone call. In a Lipitor commercial, a middle-aged man raced his bicycle through a forest while an elevated cholesterol number chased him. In a Plavix commercial, a woman moved around a golf course while a hospital gurney chased her; the voiceover warned, "If you've had a heart attack caused by a completely blocked artery, another heart attack could be lurking waiting to strike ... One that could be fatal." A Pravachol cholesterol drug commercial opened by asking, "Who knows how long you'll live? Who knows when you'll die? If you have high cholesterol, will a heart attack make your life run out before it has to?" In each of these examples, death is presented as a highly likely consequence if individuals don't "take control" of their health and buy some medicine.

Fear of Lost Attractiveness

A common fear harnessed by advertising is declining desirability. By reminding audiences that they might go bald, grow fat, lose skin elasticity, look old, and ultimately get closer to death, advertisers imply that viewers might become *less attractive* and, in turn, that the quality of their relationships—thus their *quality of life*—might decline. Psychiatrist Richard Rosse contended that losing attractiveness is one of the most common human anxieties: "You feel that your attractiveness display is in danger. The fear is that your mate and others will discover that you really are not as attractive as they initially thought you were, and as a consequence the relationships will suffer."[34]

Appeals that center on fears of lost attractiveness remind audiences of what might happen to negatively affect desirability and then, predictably, offer a solution. In a Propecia advertisement, for example, the voiceover asked, "Are you concerned about losing more hair?" The footage showed a man looking into a variety of mirrors and seeing a balding version of himself. In an advertisement for Detrol LA, a woman is at a party and the voiceover says, "Having a bladder control problem is bad enough. What makes it worse is the constant worry. The worry that your problem is as obvious as if you'd announced it to the world." The female party guest is then shown holding a sign disclosing her bladder problem. Both advertisements harness the perception that hair loss or bladder leakage will make a person less desirable; in both cases, pharmaceuticals are offered as the solution.

Erectile dysfunction advertisements target a number of fears—impotence, failure, and so on—but the fear of being perceived as less desirable to one's partner is highly notable. Advertisements for medications such as Cialis and Levitra repeatedly show women caressing the faces of their male partners, holding hands with them, and sharing their umbrella—in essence, *loving them* and thus confirming his desirability. In a Levitra commercial, for example, a woman—appearing bare-legged and dressed in a man's shirt—is shown seated on a sofa. She asks the viewer, "Can I tell you a secret? My man takes Levitra." Flashback footage shows intimacy between her and her partner; he is wearing the shirt that she dons in her monologue. In each of these advertisements, the implicit message is that if a man is able to sexually perform, his partner will continue to find him attractive; if not, he jeopardizes his relationship. Pharmaceutical intervention is thus essential.

GUILT APPEALS

Like fear, guilt is another emotion frequently targeted in advertising as a way to manipulate audiences and to motivate purchases. Marketing theorist Terence Shimp explained the guilt appeal: "Appeals to guilt are powerful because they motivate emotionally mature individuals to undertake responsible action leading to a reduction in the level of guilt."[35]

Seidel discussed this issue as related to pharmaceutical advertising, noting that such drug ads invite us to believe that "Oh *I am* that person who must try to stay fit—for my family, my students, my co-workers."[36] Certainly the idea of audiences being guilt-tripped into staying healthy so that they can continue with their caring duties is evident in a variety of commercials. In an advertisement for Vioxx, for example, a middle-aged woman is in a classroom; she tells the audience "after all these years, I still look forward to going to school, and I'm pretty sure the kids do, too." Another Vioxx advertisement shows a grandmotherly woman being led up the stairs by a young boy; she then bathes him. In the voiceover, she says, "I don't want to run a marathon, I don't want to go skydiving ... not feeling ancient would be nice. All I really want is to be able to climb the stairs and give Michael a bath." In another Vioxx commercial, a middle-aged man and some younger boys are assembling furniture; the voiceover says, "I don't want to build a skyscraper, I don't want to bench press two-fifty ... all I want is to hang out with my guys." While these advertisements are open to interpretation as being concerned with promoting lifestyle, they can also be construed as being centered on guilt: these characters *have* to stay well for those around them; their students, children, and grandchildren *need them*.

Guilt as related to caring—notably in the context of participating fully in a relationship—is an appeal alluded to in the aforementioned erectile dysfunction advertisements: men are encouraged to pharmaceutically improve their sexual functioning to do *the right thing* by their partner and their relationship. Such sexual/relationship guilt is equally evident in advertisements for Wellbutrin. Characters talk to the camera about the benefits of controlling their depression; they are then shown with their partners and the commentary explains the drug's low sexual side effects. The subtext is that depression can make a person a bad partner; that ineffective treatment or nontreatment of depression can result in *high* sexual side effects, which can be alleviated with the right product guilt; that relationships can be salvaged. Such themes are also detected in an advertisement for Chantix: a woman discusses her smoking addiction and simultaneously plays with her wedding ring. The unspoken message here is that she needs to give up smoking *for the sake of her relationship*.

In some advertisements, the guilt is far less coded. In an advertisement for the cholesterol medication Zocor, a grandpa is shown teaching his grandson how to ride a bike; the voiceover asks, "Aren't there enough reasons to talk to you doctor about Zocor? ... Zocor: be there." An advertisement for Imitrex shows a woman clutching her head, with her young daughter standing nearby. Via voiceover, the woman says, "I'd made a promise to Janie; her new bike had to be ready, but my migraine wouldn't go away." A Valtrex treatment advertisement details all the ways that genital herpes can be spread; a female character then reveals, "Now I take once-daily Valtex to reduce my risk of passing it on." This woman has a disease but she is doing *the right thing* by making sure she doesn't spread it. The guilt-trip is even more explicit in a Cymbalta antidepressant advertisement: the voiceover asks, "Where does depression hurt? Everywhere. Who does depression hurt? Everyone." The footage cuts from a woman looking miserable to her worried-looking children. The same thing transpires in an advertisement for the Abilify antidepressant: a mother stands at the window looking miserable; her husband and daughter watch her, looking fearful. An advertisement for the cholesterol medication Pravachol opens with various characters directing messages to relatives (i.e., "This is a message for my grandpa Leon"). The characters then say, "Remember, I'm your kid brother" and "It's hard for me to imagine you not being here in my world"; each character pleads his or her case or guilt-trips the relative into not dying and abandoning the family.

While thus far I have focused on guilt and fear—devices that are able to be construed as primarily negative—in the next sections, comparatively more positive and feel-good techniques such as appeals to nostalgia, empowerment, and lifestyle are explored.

NOSTALGIA APPEALS

Nostalgia in advertising is about using idealized elements from the past to appeal to a viewer's sense of sentimentality and reminiscence. Such devices can infuse a brand with history and endurance and can make a product seem dependable and solid. As economist Petr Král explained: "In today's world, when people worry about so many things, such as terrorism, job reduction or global warming, an old brand gives people the feeling of comfort and security and reminds them of times when they felt better."[37]

In the context of pharmaceutical advertising, nostalgia appeals are very much centered on reminding audiences—particularly older audiences—of a time when they *felt better*—that is, when they felt healthier and more energetic. Given that many pharmaceutical advertisements promise to return users to their "prime," it is unsurprising that such advertisements routinely deploy nostalgic themes.

A commercial for the cholesterol drug Zocor opens with a rock-n-roll style dance venue supposedly in the 1950s or 1960s; the voiceover reveals, "I could dance all night back then." A commercial for the Enablex bladder medication shows a "Class of '68" reunion sign and the voiceover claims, "There are moments you look forward to and you shouldn't have to miss out on them." A Propecia commercial follows the changes in hairstyles of three male friends through different stages of their life—leaving school, traveling abroad, attending a school reunion. An advertisement for the antidepressant Zoloft shows an adult man—wearing a tie-dyed T-shirt—riding a bike and doing tricks on it; the Bobby McFerrin song "Don't Worry be Happy" (1988) plays in the background. In these three advertisements, positive aspects of the past—rock-n-roll dance halls, high school, wacky hairstyles, tie-dyed T-shirts and 1980s music—are used to remind audiences of better, simpler times, when they were less affected by worry or illness, in turn presenting the fondly recalled state as an incentive to use the marketed drug.

Another way nostalgia is deployed is through the simpler objective of coercing audiences to yearn to return to a nonspecific time when they simply felt better—that is, an idealized time *before* age or illness. In a Cymbalta antidepressant advertisement, for example, one of the sufferers muses, "I'd like to enjoy things again." A Prozac antidepressant advertisement opens with a woman making her way through a tunnel of darkness; she then emerges into the light and finds herself on a bright, sunny beach. The commercial ends with the phrase "Welcome back." Another Prozac advertisement shows a woman in a darkened house; she eventually opens up the blinds and lets the light in. Again, the closing message is "Welcome back." In these examples, the appeal is to a time *before* depression: welcome back to your *true self*. A Paxil advertisement similarly harnesses these ideas; in one, a female character claims, "I feel like me again." Such commercials coerce audiences to desire to feel *as they once did*.

Nostalgia is used in advertising to establish that a time before now—a time *before* stress and anxiety and depression—was a better, more golden time. In turn, the past is depicted as a state that a person should desire to reprise through medication.

EMPOWERMENT APPEALS

An identifiable trend in modern advertising is the coupling of purchases with empowerment—that consumption is the road to true independence and self-realization. This style of advertising has been extensively criticized. Feminist theorist Susan Bordo, for example, critiqued the *for me* and *my choice* arguments by contending that they routinely forget to mention that such purchases are rendered necessary "for me, in order to feel better about myself in this culture that has made me feel in adequate as I am."[38] Such *for me* and *my choice* appeals are easily detected. In this section I examine empowerment appeals as related to choice, health information, and individualism.

Empowerment through Choice

An idea central to marketing theory is to make consumers feel empowered by their choice: to make them feel that not only was their decision to purchase *their own idea*, but also that even though they had many different options they *actively chose* the right one, the smart and sensible one, and that doing so was a good, if not *noble* decision.

In an advertisement for Yasmin birth control, a woman is shown on a variety of unsuccessful dates with men, each ending with her rebuffing his sexual advances and getting out of his car. The voiceover says, "It's nice to know that you have a choice when it comes to the guy. Wouldn't it be nice to feel that way about your pill?" While choice exists in nearly all commodities, choice in the Yasmin commercial is presented as something empowering and as something that, if acted on, gives a woman liberation and control.

Choice is notably evident in advertisements for products deemed controversial or at least—in a time of feminist enlightenment—potentially coerced. Earlier I discussed Bordo's criticism of the *for me* and *my choice* arguments;

her comments were made in the context of discussing women's justifications for cosmetic surgery—that women routinely claimed that they were having surgery *for me*. When women make such arguments, they are doing so in a culture that is skeptical; there is a widespread belief that such surgeries are undertaken solely to be more appealing to men, so the *for me* argument is a way for women to acknowledge and then counter such arguments. Instead of being cultural dupes or pandering to patriarchal fantasy, then, these women are presenting themselves as empowered and self-determined. Such ideas are easily illustrated in an advertisement for Botox, in which a variety of women reveal why they decided to pursue Botox: "This is my time" and "I did it for me." Again, rather than the women appearing like dupes, the advertisements reference the idea of women wanting to feel in control, empowered, and *savvy*. Thus having Botox is depicted as something they chose to do *for themselves* and at *their* optimal time.

Empowerment through Health Knowledge

Discussed earlier was a defense frequently used by pharmaceutical companies—namely, that their advertisements help patients get information and become empowered about their health care. This is a narrative idea frequently exploited in advertising. Given that nearly all drug advertisements end with an appeal to viewers to visit their doctor for a prescription, it is unsurprising that the possibility of empowerment offered by health information is a device frequently used. Earlier I discussed advertisements for Lyrica where patients "learn" about their fibromyalgia condition—and about treatment—from medical practitioners. Such narratives involve patients receiving information—and thus *health epiphanies*—from their doctors; for television audiences, the same epiphany is delivered through the commercial. This technique is illustrated well in a Lipitor advertisement in which a middle-aged man looks out from a cliff top: "I can't believe I used to swing over those rocks. I took some foolish risks as a teenager. But I was still taking a foolish risk with my cholesterol." This man has become *enlightened* through receipt of health information and the use of cholesterol medication. In an advertisement for Yasmin birth control, young women are shown whispering secrets, passing notes, and writing on one another's hands. Each time the message is the same: "Have you heard about Yasmin?" This advertisement again harnesses the idea that knowledge—and being privy to health information—is the key to empowerment. The Yasmin advertisement notably taps into the idea of how integral it is for young women to keep abreast of health information, particularly amidst their peer groups.[39]

Such appeals are made more obvious when having health information, taking control, and taking prescription medication are each presented as being essential to wellness. Neulasta, a drug targeted at cancer patients, is advertised with a variety of characters telling the camera, "I'm ready to fight my cancer" and "I'm to begin chemotherapy." An ad for Zyban—an anti-smoking drug—begins with the voiceover telling audiences, "You are in the fight of your life. Just you against your smoking addiction. One on one." In an advertisement for Gardasil, women give their reasons for being vaccinated, including "I chose to get vaccinated because I'll do everything I can to help protect myself from cervical cancer." In each of these examples, medicine is presented as the key to empowering a person to be healthy: that empowerment comes from a person's proactive decision to pursue use of pharmaceuticals. A Zoloft advertisement epitomizes these ideas: "Zoloft: when you know more about what's wrong, you can help make it right." Just as with the women who undertake Botox treatment *for me*, taking Neulasta and Zyban and having the Gardasil vaccination are presented as the key to health-centered empowerment; the decision to be medicated is *righteous*.

Empowerment through Identity and Individualism

The *for me* and *my choice* appeals are underpinned by the notion that the self—understanding it, tending to it, advancing it, *indulging* it—is at the true center of happiness and fulfillment. Such ideas are perfectly in line with individualism and the self being all important. The Botox advertisement discussed earlier demonstrates this point as women explain their use of the product: "This is *my* time" and "I did it for *me*."

Such appeals are also tied to the idea that formation of the self is connected to purchases—that the true self can only be fully realized through consumption. In an ad for the Ortho Tri-Cyclen-Lo contraceptive pill, for example, the voiceover encourages viewers, "Be true to yourself with a birth control pill that gives you a high level of effectiveness and a low level of hormones." Apparently a *true self* is sourced through buying the right contraception. This idea is taken further in an advertisement for the Nuva Ring contraceptive: it opens with women doing a synchronized swimming routine and the voiceover suggests, "Maybe it's time to break free from the pack." *The pack* refers not only to the birth control pack, but also to the pack—*the herd*—of other women. Individuality is thus promoted: *self* comes from the right prescription medication, which is right for you and sets you apart from those around you.

Worth noting, appeals to the self can also be somewhat nostalgic. For example, it may be implied that illness or age has diluted one's authentic self and that medicine can help a person return to his or her *true self*; as the woman in the Paxil advertisement claims, "I feel like me again." The subtext is that drugs can help retain or resurrect identity.

THE MALLEABLE SELF

An identifiable message in pharmaceutical advertising is the notion of the self—of one's body, health, and appearance—as being a permanent work-in-progress; there's no option to ever consider oneself as *finished* or *complete*, as there is always more to be done, be it maintenance or prevention. While such techniques could be interpreted as guilt appeals—that is, guilt-tripping audiences into believing that they are never doing enough for their health—in this section I contend that this kind of appeal is more about indoctrinating audiences into thinking of their body as something that is always able to be improved, notably through pharmaceutical intervention. Psychiatrist Anne Becker discussed this idea in her work on the body: "The culture validates this ethic of intensive investment in the body as a key to the projected self-image, suggesting that the goal is not necessarily to attain a particular physical feature, but rather to signal participation in the process of body work and image-making."[40]

Ideas about *body work* are ever present in pharmaceutical advertisements, where medicine is presented as a way to ensure that the *best version of yourself* is promoted. An advertisement for Celebrex pain medication, for example, shows a middle-aged woman jumping on a trampoline: "Ageing is inevitable; getting old doesn't have to be. Outsmart old. Celebrex." In another Celebrex commercial, candles on a birthday cake set off a fire alarm, but the voiceover says, "Your true age can't be measured in candles. Outsmart old. Celebrex." An ad for Zocor similarly suggests, "Ask yourself if you're doing enough to protect your heart." Earlier I discussed the Propecia advertisement where a man looks in mirrors and sees balding versions of himself: the message is that he needs to stay vigilant about his appearance (through pharmaceuticals). Feminist theorist Susan Bartky discussed self-surveillance as related to women's bodies: she contended that women are taught to constantly survey and patrol their appearance to make sure that they are always aesthetically appealing.[41] In pharmaceutical advertisements, bodily self-surveillance is something encouraged and promoted *for everybody*: it is right, justified, and empowering to remain vigilant about health.

THE PEDDLING OF LIFESTYLE

The last narrative device I discuss in this chapter is appeals to lifestyle—that is, the contention that through the right drugs, the *good life* can be reaped. Advertising researchers William Leiss et al. discussed this lifestyle appeal: "Lifestyle ads commonly depict a variety of leisure activities (entertaining, going out, holidaying, relaxing). Implicit in each of these activities, however, is the placing of the product within a consumption style by its link to an activity."[42] This was a topic similarly addressed by marketing theorist Sean Brierley: "Rather than focusing on the product, it focuses on consumers, their lifestyle, values and beliefs. Lifestyle advertising involves the reinterpretation of the consumer's self-image."[43] Marketing theorist Matthew Healey also discussed this idea: "Many advertisements for pharmaceuticals, real estate, and financial services paint a rosy picture of the retiree lifestyle, in which fit and smiling 60-somethings enjoy life to the fullest, usually outdoors. The implication is that the product being sold will contribute to this mythic sense of comfort and wellness at any age."[44] These theorists each highlight that products often get marketed through appeals to a way of life: that the product offered is a necessary stepping stone to achieving the *good life*.

In a Vioxx advertisement, U.S. figure skater Dorothy Hamill—now middle-aged—skates across the ice, touting the benefits of the drug. Apparently she wouldn't be able to continue skating if it wasn't for the drug; in other words, her life would be worse without it. Discussed earlier were the Levitra and Cialis advertisements in which couples are presented as happy and affectionate: a good relationship is evidently maintained by pharmaceuticals. An advertisement for Boniva—an osteoporosis treatment—shows a group of older women readying themselves for exercise. In another ad, a group of happy, active older women are shown chatting at a café, again discussing the product. In an advertisement for Dulera asthma medication, a young woman is shown on holiday in Costa Rica. In each of these examples, a life of wellness and continued participation in activity—in *life*—is promoted; the subtext is that such situations are possible only because of prescription medicine.

Appeals based on lifestyle also emphasize convenience: lifestyle is enhanced by the utilization of products that make life easier. The Beyaz pill discussed earlier promises lighter periods (the inference being that menstruation is a hassle).[45] In a Diflucan advertisement, a woman discusses the prescription yeast infection medication: "there may be an easier way ... a pill that's as effective as the leading seven-day creams without the mess." In an advertisement for the Mirena contraceptive pill, a woman is in a supermarket and asks herself,

"Did I take my pill this morning?" The voiceover advises, "There's birth control you don't have to think about taking every day." In each of these examples, pharmaceuticals are promoted as enhancing convenience; they help free up time for things that you enjoy, and they give a person more time for the good life.

This chapter has explored a variety of devices used to create—and then ultimately *satisfy*—a market for prescription medications. By appealing to our fears and guilt as well as our penchant for empowerment, individuality, and quality of life, such advertisements dare to suggest that *television* is as important a source for health information as a medical practitioner, in turn presenting the idea that medicine is good and that questioning this is taboo.

The Abortion Chapter: Back Alleys and Back Stories on Screen

References to abortion on screen trace back to films such as *Where Are My Children?* (1916), *The Road to Ruin* (1928), and *Ann Vickers* (1933) and are readily identifiable in contemporary narratives. While allusions to abortion may be easily detected on screen, the topic nevertheless remains a taboo—a subject invariably treated with proverbial *kid gloves*—because off screen it fiercely polarizes. In this chapter I examine the broad range of portrayals of abortion. Predictably, most examples present abortion as something *negative*—think backyard abortions and botched operations, leading to permanent infertility, if not death. Alternatively, it is presented as something persistently divisive and political. There are, however, some examples of positive, or at least comparatively even-handed, presentations whereby abortion is presented as a reality and as a common back story for women. This chapter examines and analyzes these presentations to investigate how the abortion taboo is both maintained and challenged on screen. While Christian antiabortion groups have funded the production of a number of overtly antichoice narratives—for example, *Come What May* (2009), *Sarah's Choice* (2009), and *October Baby* (2011)—this chapter focuses on mainstream examples where the motives are less explicit.

THE CONTINUATION OF THE TABOO

In this chapter I refer to dozens of examples of abortion references in film and television. That so many examples exist raises the question of whether it is still appropriate to consider abortion to be a screen taboo. In my book

Periods in Pop Culture: Menstruation in Film and Television, I analyzed more than 200 scenes of menstruation in film and television. While many scenes were detected, menstruation nonetheless remains a taboo because the vast majority of presentations uphold the idea that menstruation is something disgusting that needs to be separated from the private sphere.[1] Something similar transpires with representations of abortions: many portrayals doesn't mitigate the reality that the taboo still exists. The fact that most presentations reinforce the notion that the topic is at best highly contested, and at worst life-threatening and soul destroying, demonstrates that the abortion taboo remains active—a perception that popular media helps to maintain.

In philosopher Al-Yasha Ilhaam's examination of the abortion-themed comedy *Citizen Ruth* (1996), she discussed the fraught nature of presenting abortion diplomatically: "Owing to the highly personal and sexual nature of abortion ... [it is nearly impossible] to state one's views without offending anyone."[2] The real-life and highly divisive politics pervading abortion render any portrayals potential threats to network sponsors and audiences. In sociologist Steven Dubin's research on politics and visual culture, for example, he discussed abortion presentations and highlighted the concerns that such portrayals create for television networks: "while abortion may have emerged from the back alley, it has remained in the shadows of dramatic TV. The rarity of references to abortion on TV belies its ubiquitous presence in modern American life. Characters in regular television series seldom mention it; when they do, there is the ever-present risk of sponsor defections."[3]

Dubin illustrated his ideas with two television examples where abortion portrayals jeopardized network advertising revenue. In an abortion-themed episode of *China Beach* (1988–1991)—when Holly (Ricki Lake) got an illegal abortion—sponsors failed to support the episode, which in turn prevented it from being rebroadcast the following summer. Dubin also discussed the made-for-television film *Roe vs. Wade* (1989), which necessitated more than 20 drafts before the NBC network approved it; the film still ended up having great difficulty attracting advertising revenue.

While Dubin was writing in the early 1990s—making it tempting to speculate that the situation may have improved—more contemporary work contends that abortion not only remains taboo, but that American popular culture may have become even *more conservative*. Writing for the British paper *The Guardian*, Hadley Freeman discussed the teen-pregnancy-themed film *Juno* (2007): "after *Waitress* [2007] and *Knocked Up* [2007], *Juno* (which received a best picture Oscar nomination last week) completes a hat-trick of American comedies in the past 12 months that present abortion as unreasonable, or even unthinkable—a telling social sign. Each of these films present situations where women do not consider abortion as a feasible possibility and dismiss it."[4] Philosopher Kelly Oliver made a similar point in her discussion of pregnancy-themed films including *Fools Rush In* (1997) and *Knocked Up*: "Even while these films embrace a woman's right to choose, they still expect women to choose babies and not abortions ... Although in these films women have the right to choose, they are expected to make the *right* choice, which is always to have their baby."[5] Writer Eve Kushner also drew attention to this topic, identifying the propensity for Hollywood to appear to consciously acknowledge that abortion exists as an option but to present it as one that is invariably *not* taken:

> Unexpected conceptions occur onscreen with surprising frequency, but filmmakers routinely play it safe, avoiding substantial discussions of a pregnancy's pros and cons. They keep abortion out of plots and even out of dialogue, ensuring that movies end with a heartwarming birth. Female characters rarely feel any ambivalence about carrying unplanned pregnancies to term—and why should they, when life always works out so perfectly? ... Abortion exists only as a faux option—something to choose *against*.[6]

The 2004 remake of *Alfie* (1966) is often considered a good example of Hollywood becoming more *not less* conservative as related to abortion. In the 1966 film, Alfie (Michael Caine) was visibly distressed when he saw the fetus he had fathered in a bucket. In the 2004 version, while an abortion still transpired, Alfie (Jude Law) didn't actually ever confront it himself—he certainly didn't *see* the fetus—and in turn the film focused less on the abortion issue and more on the broader issues of Alfie's anomie. While it could be contended that abortion is simply less controversial in 2004 than it was in the 1960s because of the changed legal situation—the abortion in 1966 was illegally performed in an apartment as opposed to legally in a clinic in 2004—and thus it need not have been made a "big deal" on the screen, an equally viable interpretation is that the topic is dodged in the newer film because today it is more inflammatory, certainly so for a film marketed as frothy.

The examples of *Fools Rush In*, *Juno*, *Waitress*, and *Knocked Up* highlight a pattern of abortion presentations that present the topic by *avoiding it*. This is interesting and coincides with the way menstruation frequently enters film and television narratives: many menstruation references transpire on screen through the absence of a period and a suspected pregnancy.[7] The next section explores the idea of abortions being alluded to on screen through their circumvention.

THE ABORTION CLINIC EPIPHANY

Kushner argues that abortion exists as a *faux-option*, an idea that certainly plays out on screen. In contemporary narratives, pretending that abortion does not exist as a real option would be fraudulent. Even in narratives where abortion is clearly off the table, such as in *Waitress*, the option—even if not named explicitly—was nevertheless briefly alluded to. This was apparent in a conversation between pregnant Jenna (Keri Russell) and her doctor Jim (Nathan Fillion):

Jim: So ... What seems to be the problem?
Jenna: Well, I seem to be pregnant.
Jim: Good. Good for you. Congratulations.
Jenna: Thanks, but I don't want this baby.
Jim: Oh, well, why don't we perform ... uh ...
Jenna: No, I'm keeping it, I'm just telling you I'm not so happy about it like everybody else might be. So maybe you can be sensitive and not congratulate me and make a big deal every time you see me. I'm having the baby, and that's that. It's not a party, though.

Jim suggests the option of performing *something*—we assume he means an abortion—but clearly Jenna is not interested.

Many narratives present the abortion "option" much more explicitly—by having characters actually *visit* the abortion clinic—only to then show them reaching an epiphany about not continuing. Abortion clinic epiphanies transpire in a very wide variety of narratives. In *Juno*, Juno (Ellen) changed her mind about her scheduled "hasty abortion" while actually at the abortion clinic; she was unable to forget the words of a protestor who harangued her about the fetus' fingernails. An abortion clinic visit also convinced Charlie (Ruth Negga) to change her mind about her planned abortion in the British film *Breakfast on Pluto* (2005). In an episode of drama series *Felicity* (1998–2002), Ruby (Amy Smart) decided she couldn't go through with an abortion while at the clinic. Miranda (Cynthia Nixon) opted against an abortion on *Sex and the City* (1998–2004) at the abortion clinic, as did Joan (Christina Hendricks) on *Mad Men* (2007–) and both Amy (Shailene Woodley) and Adrian (Francia Raisa) in episodes of *The Secret Life of the American Teenager* (2008–). Cindy (Michelle Williams) was on the actual table at the abortion clinic when she changed her mind in *Blue Valentine* (2010). This idea—albeit presented humorously—was also apparent in a controversial episode of animated series *Family Guy* (1999–): apparently when Lois was pregnant with Meg, she went to get an abortion, but upon arriving at the clinic—and discovering that the abortionist had only one arm—she changed her mind.

These examples work to highlight that in contemporary Western culture it would be disingenuous not to have unexpectedly pregnant characters—even if only with varying degrees of seriousness—consider an abortion. Having characters acknowledge abortion as an option could be considered progressive as well as more reflective of reality and thus enables a narrative to be construed as credible by audiences. Nevertheless, that these characters *change their minds*—that being in the clinic convinces them that abortion is the *wrong* path—renders them as examples of how antichoice messages are often packaged in modern screen narratives: they are made palatable, made *progressive*, by presenting characters who weigh their options and eventually choose *the right one*. Abortion in these examples is not overtly demonized, but rather by virtue of it being the path *not chosen*, it is presented as the less desirable option.

Another way abortion is avoided on screen is via the abortion aborted narrative. In the next section I discuss a variety of narratives whereby the woman does not go through with her pregnancy, but also does not actually have an abortion, thereby dodging any associated ethical or moral stigma.

ABORTION ABORTED

In *Periods in Pop Culture*, I discussed the issue of Maddie's (Cybill Shepherd) miscarriage in *Moonlighting* (1985–1989) and Julia's (Neve Campbell) miscarriage in *Party of Five* (1994–2000). In both narratives, the characters did not want to proceed with their pregnancies but were spared from actually having abortions (Julia, in fact, had her miscarriage *at* the abortion clinic):

> In *Party of Five*, the pregnancy was unwanted; in *Moonlighting* it was inconvenient: actual abortions in both narratives would have been controversial—likely too much so given the youth audience of *Party of Five* and the political climate in the era of *Moonlighting*—so instead both pregnancies were handled in a socially acceptable way. Rather than Julia or Maddie becoming "baby killers", they were "gifted" miscarriages which cast them as figures of sympathy; the ending of their pregnancies was taken out of their hands and thus the woman was (albeit temporarily) transformed into a tragic figure.[8]

The carefully circumvented abortion is identifiable in a number of other examples. In *Citizen Ruth*, for example, Ruth (Laura Dern) eventually decided to have an abortion—something she was undecided about for most of the film—but miscarried on the day it was scheduled. In *Grey's Anatomy* (2005–), Cristina (Sandra Oh) scheduled an abortion but ended up having an ectopic pregnancy and miscarried. In *South of Nowhere* (2005–2008), Chelsea (Aasha Davis) decided to have an abortion and then changed her mind; she then miscarried after a car accident. Something similar happened in *Big Love* (2006–2011): Sarah (Amanda Seyfried) got pregnant, decided not to go through with the abortion, and then had a convenient miscarriage.

As I suggested with the *Moonlighting* and *Party of Five* narratives, abortions would have been a much more controversial way to deal with an unwanted pregnancy. Thus the pregnancy was *dealt with*, in turn liberating the woman from the stigma of being complicit in "baby killing."

Aborted abortions also transpire in narratives where the character gets murdered *before* she has the opportunity to terminate. In *A Place in the Sun* (1951), for example, a poor girl—Alice (Shelley Winters)—got pregnant. Her lover, George (Montgomery Clift), wouldn't marry her, so she sought an abortion. Her doctor refused to give her one; George ended up murdering Alice. In *Brick* (2005), teenager Emily (Emilie de Ravin) was pregnant and was considering abortion but was killed beforehand. Sheryl Crowe's song "Hard to Make a Stand" (1996) explores this same theme, telling the story of a woman shot on her way to have an abortion.

One reading of these narratives centers on punishment: girls who not only dare get pregnant out of wedlock but dare to consider abortion will receive their due punishment. This narrative can likewise be construed as potentially conveying a much more horrific reality: *audiences* are comparatively more comfortable with homicide than pregnancy termination; homicide is a much less divisive topic—and certainly much less of a taboo—than abortion.

These narratives—much like the abortion clinic epiphanies discussed earlier—ultimately avoid abortion. While they present abortion as a choice, it is always the choice *not taken*.

In the next section, the predictable—and overtly negative—portrayals of abortion are explored, beginning with a discussion of the back alley termination.

THE BACK ALLEY ABORTION

In Cyndi Lauper's song "Sally's Pigeons" (1993), she sang of a friend who "was lost from some back alley job." This idea of a "back alley"—or illegal—abortion is the most common negative way that abortion is presented on screen. While the back alley abortion doesn't always end in death (as it did for the girl in Lauper's song), the idea of back alley abortions as something gritty and grimy and performed by sleazy opportunists—and frequently botched—is a common portrayal on screen. In her discussion of abortion in cinema, Oliver notes: "Many films that do seriously raise the issue of abortion have a scary dimension that makes them feel more like cautionary warnings than pro-choice alternatives."[9]

While reading many of the back alley abortion scenes as cautionary tales is certainly possible, these are not the only worthwhile interpretations.

The Nightmarish Providers

Back alley abortions transpire in circumstances where legal and safe abortions are unavailable. While practitioners of illegal abortions are not always nefarious—abortionist Vera (Imelda Staunton), in the 1950s-themed British film *Vera Drake* (2004), was an example of a kindly, if not *saintly* provider—in most cases such characters are presented, to varying degrees, as *sinister*. Such providers are shown as preying on the desperate circumstances of pregnant women and doing so in invariably unsanitary locales, such as the derelict building where Angie's (Natalie Wood) abortion was scheduled in *Love with the Proper Stranger* (1963).

In the original *Alfie*, the abortionist (Denholm Elliott)—while on screen only briefly—was presented as a sleazy character. This idea is taken further in the television series *American Horror Story* (2011–) and the film *The Cider House Rules* (1996). In *American Horror Story*, Dr. Montgomery (Matt Ross) worked from home and in association with his wife Nora (Lily Rabe), performed illegal abortions on girls in the early 1900s as a way to make money to support the couple's lavish lifestyle. Dr. Montgomery's creepiness manifested in him routinely taking drugs and notably dabbling in Dr. Frankenstein-esque experiments: in one episode he stitched his murdered baby back together using various animal parts. In *The Cider House Rules*, abortionist Dr. Larch (Michael Caine) was shown repeatedly inhaling ether. These two characters are presented, to varying degrees, as *unhinged*, in turn creating the possibility of determining that these men have some moral ambiguity about their role as abortionist; drugs, it is suggested, are necessary to numb the reality of their tasks.[10] Such presentations could be construed as being *antichoice*: these doctors harbor a quiet belief that abortion is wrong, is heinous, and that they need to self-medicate to cope.

Worth noting—and something relevant to *all* seemingly negative abortion portrayals on screen—illegal abortions performed in filthy locales and by disreputable practitioners do not always have to be read as an antichoice narratives. It could, in fact, be contended that it is only when abortions are restricted or made illegal that the practice is driven underground, leading to such ugly exploitation. Therefore, such narratives could be construed as strong cases *in favor* of safe and legal abortions.

The abortionists in *Alfie*, *American Horror Story*, and *The Cider House Rules* are presented as sleazy and unhinged. More common, however, is the idea of the abortionist as *opportunistic*.

In *Vera Drake*, Vera's friend-since-childhood Lily (Ruth Sheen) acted as the liaison between Vera and the pregnant girls. Lily was shown—without Vera's knowledge—to be taking payment for the abortions. This (comparatively) low-level opportunism was also engaged in by Nora in *American Horror Story*; Nora collected money from the desperate girls and administered the anesthetic. It is interesting that in both of these examples it is *women* who are profiting from the desperation of other women. These women are presented as doubly heinous because (1) they are seen as profiting from other women's circumstances and (2) they are shown to be involved in facilitating the abortion of fetuses and thus engaged in very *unmaternal*, unwomanly behavior. Nora, for example, was presented as much more heinous than her husband: she was shown collecting the money and throughout the season appeared much more preoccupied with lifestyle than him. Similarly, even though Vera performed the abortions, it was Lily who was presented as heartless, hard, and calculating, as well as deceitful for not divulging the profits to Vera.

While in these examples Nora and Lily financially profited from being involved in illegal abortions, this might actually be expected given that the act was illegal at the time that each narrative was set and thus anyone providing such a service might expect to be compensated for taking such risks. There are, of course, some far more egregious examples of the exploitation of young pregnant women on screen. In the French film *Amok* (1944), a woman was denied an abortion by the island doctor; later he suggested that he might do it in return for sexual favors. The same quid pro quo arrangement was apparent in the Romanian film *4 luni, 3 saptamâni si 2 zile* (*4 Months, 3 Weeks, 2 Days*) (2007): Găbiţa (Laura Vasiliu) was pregnant and she and her friend Otilia (Anamaria Marinca) organized for her to meet Mr. Bebe (Vlad Ivanov) in a hotel for an illegal abortion. It soon became apparent that Mr. Bebe expected the two women to have sex with him. Again, as in the examples of the sleazy and drugged abortionists discussed earlier, these characters emphasize the notion that abortion is heinous and that the providers are miscreants. The narratives are however, again also open to being read as further evidence of the necessity for safe and legal abortions.

The Dangerous Back Alley Abortion

A bigger problem than sleazy, drugged, or opportunistic abortionists are those who simply do not know what they are doing—who do a bad job and thus risk the health of the woman. Mr. Bebe in *4 Months, 3 Weeks, 2 Days*, for example, wasn't a doctor. Neither was the abortionist in *Love with the Proper Stranger*. In *Dirty Dancing* (1987), Penny's (Cynthia Rhodes) back alley abortion went life-threateningly wrong and Baby's (Jennifer Grey) father Dr. Houseman (Jerry Orbach) had to tend to her. Dr. Houseman reassured Penny that she could still have children; this, however, was not the outcome for many female characters who receive botched abortions.

In television's first abortion storyline—in an early episode of the soap opera *Another World* (1964–1999)—Pat (Susan Trustman) had an illegal abortion that she feared left her infertile. While Pat later discovered that she was wrong, many characters are indeed left infertile. In *Days of Our Lives* (1965–), Mimi (Farah Fath) had an abortion and ended up getting a pelvic inflammatory disease and was left infertile. In an episode of series *Cold Case* (2003–2010), a backyard abortion left a woman infertile. In *Dogma* (1999), Bethany (Linda Fiorentino) worked as an abortionist: she was infertile because the doctor who had given her an abortion as a teenager had botched it. The same thing transpired in *Palindromes* (2004): the abortion undergone by teenager Aviva (played in the film by several different actresses) rendered her unable to have children. In *The Yellow Handkerchief* (2008), May's (Maria Bello) miscarriage was explained as attributable to an abortion she had in her youth. The same thing was alluded to in *21 Grams* (2003): Mary (Charlotte Gainsbourg) admitted to her doctor that she had an abortion when he asked her why her fallopian tubes appeared damaged.

While it is tempting to interpret these presentations through the same antichoice/pro-choice lenses discussed earlier, such presentations lend themselves to being construed as more cautionary tales—as warnings *against* any kind of abortion, illegal or not. While in the *Another World* and *Cold Case* examples the abortions were illegal, in the other examples the time frames lend themselves to being *legal* abortions. The idea that legal abortions can lead to negative consequences is very much an *antichoice* presentation. In real life, abortion is considered to be a very safe procedure—according to *The Johns Hopkins Manual of Gynecology and Obstetrics*, "abortion is very safe in the United States, with the legal abortion mortality rate of 0.6/100,000"[11]—and there is apparently "no evidence that abortion causes infertility."[12] Nevertheless, the linking of abortion and infertility occurs frequently in anti-choice rhetoric. By presenting the idea that there is a physical downside to abortion—however overblown or inaccurate—such narratives work as cautionary tales that warn women to *very carefully* consider their options before aborting.

The Deadly Back Alley Abortion

In *If These Walls Could Talk* (1996), Claire (Demi Moore)—in a vignette set in 1952—died as a result of a botched abortion. In the Mexican film *El crimen del padre Amaro* (*The Crime of Father Amaro*) (2002), the title character (Gael García Bernal) got a teenage girl, Amelia (Ana Claudia Talancón), pregnant. He arranged for her to have an illegal abortion; she began bleeding uncontrollably and died before reaching a hospital. As powerful a cautionary tale as death might serve as, it is equally worth considering whether these scenes deliver powerful pro-choice messages. *If These Walls Could Talk*, for example, was an overtly pro-choice narrative: the film opened with a montage of footage showing activism on women's reproductive rights. Oliver, however, criticized the "supposedly feminist film," contending that it "connects abortion and death both visually and in terms of its narrative. Barbara (Sissy Spacek), the only woman who decided to have her baby, is safe, while the other two are traumatized or die."[13]

While the film *could* be construed as a cautionary tale, I suggest that those viewers attracted to an overtly abortion-themed film such as *If These Walls Could Talk* would likely view it as a reminder of the need for safe, legal abortion. While the legal abortionist Dr. Thompson (Cher) was shot in the modern-day vignette, rather than necessarily signaling punishment for the provider—although, granted, this is one interpretation—this narrative could be read as showing the necessity for women to continue to fight for rights that can't be deemed fixed. As apparent in *If These Walls Could Talk*, the idea of extremist antiabortionists threatening the safety of legal abortion through attacks on clinics and providers is identifiable in a number of narratives. In *Palindromes*, an abortion doctor was murdered in his home. In an episode of *Law and Order* (1990–2010), a late-term abortion provider was shot and killed while in church; the same character had apparently also been shot the year prior. In an episode of *Law and Order: Special Victims Unit* (1999–), an abortion clinic had bulletproof glass; a sniper had previously shot and wounded the receptionist. An episode of the British series *Spooks* (2002–2001) focused on an antiabortion terrorist leader visiting the United Kingdom to establish a series of terror cells. Mudhoney's song "F.D.K. (Fearless Doctor Killers)" (1995) and Ani DiFranco's song "Hello

Birmingham" (1999) are both about this same topic. These examples all cast antiabortion activists as zealots, highlighting that even in a time of safe and legal abortion, the right to access it is permanently under threat.

While in the examples discussed in this section illegal abortion is framed negatively due to its connection to nefarious providers and unhygienic conditions, the next section explores the notion of abortion being connected to *punishment*.

THE PUNISHMENT NARRATIVE

As discussed in the previous section, in screen examples with a historical focus—or those with a setting in countries where abortion is illegal—the punishment is connected to the back alley nature. In essence, a wayward girl is punished for (1) having sex and (2) even considering termination; her sentence is to have an abortion performed by a creepy practitioner in a scary locale. There are, however, a variety of narratives where punishment is meted out in other guises, including in hauntings and in death.

The Tortured Woman

While having to seek an illegal abortion is something that could be construed as torturous for the woman—illustrated on screen by the often shady providers and unhygienic locales discussed earlier—even in situations where abortions are legal, they are often presented as thoroughly unpleasant. A good example of this occurred in *Wild at Heart* (1990). In a flashback scene to an abortion that Lula (Laura Dern) had when she was younger, the camera zoomed in on Lula's terrified face, with a soundtrack reminiscent of a blender. In a more recent example from the television series *The L-Word* (2004–2009), when Kit (Pam Grier) had her abortion—for reasons that were not explained in the narrative—she went to a very conservative clinic that showed her photos of fetuses before the procedure, evidently in an attempt to force her to think carefully about the seriousness of her situation.

In both situations we assume Lula and Kit had *legal* abortions, yet the characters and the audience were still offered insights into the "horrors" of legal abortions. On the one hand, such narratives can simply be construed as presenting abortion as something serious and needing to be thought through carefully. On the other hand, given that legal abortions in the United States are widely considered to be very safe, that these narratives present abortion as something distressing certainly leaves them open to being construed as antichoice narratives, or at best cautionary tales.

The Haunted Woman

In psychologist Tadeusz Grygier's work on oppression, he discussed popular understandings of criminality: "One of our sentimental clichés about the criminal is that he is haunted by the vision of his victim, haunted until remorse drives him to reformation or despair."[14]

While Grygier noted that real criminals rarely feel this way, this *sentimental cliché* nevertheless pervades popular culture. The idea of a character being haunted by his or her criminal actions has a long history. Shakespeare's character Lady Macbeth, for example, was tormented by her involvement in the murder of Duncan. In more recent incarnations, the same idea is detectable. In *The Bells* (1926), the struggling innkeeper Matthias (Lionel Barrymore) murdered a wealthy merchant, whose ghost then haunted him. In the French film *Un prophète* (*A Prophet*) (2009), Malik (Tahar Rahim) murdered a man in prison and was then haunted by his ghost. In the Spanish film *Crimen ferpecto* (*Ferpect Crime*) (2004), salesman Rafael (Guillermo Toledo) killed his colleague Don Antonio (Luis Varela), who then haunted him. In *Voice from the Grave* (1996), the murder suspect ended up pleading guilty during his trial after his victim appeared to him in the courtroom. Many of the subplots of *American Horror Story* similarly involved victims haunting their murderers.

Marc Moskowitz's book *The Haunting Fetus* is about fetus-ghost hauntings in Taiwanese culture.[15] While Moskowitz's book centers on Asian culture, a connection between abortion and "hauntings" can also be detected on screen. In the aforementioned narratives such as *The Bells*, *Un prophète* (*A Prophet*), and *Crimen ferpecto* (*Ferpect Crime*) (2004), it was argued that ghosts are a manifestation of a murderer's guilt. Given the antichoice lobby's routine coupling of abortion with murder, it is no surprise, then, that such themes are detectable in some abortion narratives, with a woman sentenced to feeling forever guilty for her choices.

Oliver briefly discussed the film *The Unborn* (2009), noting that "images of unborn children certainly suggest that we are haunted by anxieties over abortion."[16] While *The Unborn* was not actually about abortion, the notion of a woman being haunted by an aborted fetus is certainly easily detected and open to an interpretation of cultural anxiety, if not also character guilt. Feminist writer Andi Zeisler discussed the "ghost child" approach to abortion presentations: "a character has an abortion and is then haunted by a specter of the little lost soul."[17] Zeisler illustrated this idea with a scene from the series *Six Feet Under* (2001–2005), when the abortions that Nate (Peter Krause) had been responsible for came to him as children in a dream.

The same idea was used in another episode: Claire's (Lauren Ambrose) aborted child appeared to her in a hallucination carried in the arms of her brother Nate. The Thai horror film *Gwai wik (Re-cycle)* (2006) was about Lee (Angelica Lee), a woman was helped/haunted throughout by a little girl. At the end of the film, the girl was revealed to be the child that the woman aborted years prior. In the thriller *The Life Before Her Eyes* (2007), Diana (Evan Rachel Wood) had an abortion and was haunted throughout the narrative with physical guilt pangs; she was often shown writhing in pain and experiencing visions of disapproving nuns. The film title puts these pangs and visions into context. Less about a ghost and more about an actual monster, this haunting idea was taken substantially further in the horror film *The Suckling* (1990): an aborted fetus was washed down a toilet and ended up mixing with toxic waste. After becoming a monster, the creature wreaked havoc on everyone, including the woman who had aborted it.

While ghosts and monsters are one way for the woman to be haunted by her "dastardly" deeds, another way is simply for her to be stricken with guilt afterward, either immediately post abortion or potentially for the decades that follow, in line with the idea of abortion grief.[18] In *Things You Can Tell Just by Looking at Her* (1999), Rebecca (Holly Hunter) had an abortion. When she returned to her car, she broke down in tears; she was clearly devastated. In the Australian series *The Secret Life of Us* (2001–2005), Alex (Claudia Karvan) had an abortion. While she was presented as believing she had made the right decision, she was also portrayed as initially suffering great sadness. In sitcom *Scrubs* (2001–), Jordon (Christa Miller) revealed a past abortion and seemed—years later—to still be somewhat stricken. In *Last Chance Harvey* (2008), Kate (Emma Thompson) mentioned an abortion she had had when in college: it wasn't a major plot point, although she nevertheless exhibited some remorse.

One example where 15 years of a woman's life were presented as ruined by an abortion transpired in the comedy *Bachelorette* (2012): Gena (Lizzy Caplan) was a woman in her early 30s who was presented as depressed, relatively unhinged, and a substance abuser. Her first appearance in the film was when she woke up in bed with a man she didn't know. These issues were connected to the abortion she had as a teenager—an abortion that, seemingly, set her life on an awful trajectory.[19]

Abortion grief is also readily identifiable in song. Cold Chisel's "Choirgirl" (1979) is about a man trying to console his distressed girlfriend about her abortion. Ben Folds Five's "Brick" (1997) is about the same theme. In Nicky Minaj's song "Autobiography" (2008), abortion grief is identifiable at the end of the song: "Mommy was young, mommy was too busy trying to have fun ... wish I could touch your little face and hold y'little hand."

While these songs focus on female abortion grief, there are also examples of men sharing such sentiments. Joni Mitchell's "The Beat of Black Wings" (1988) is about a man discovering his girlfriend had an abortion without telling him. Kid Rock's song "Abortion" (2000) centers on a man who contemplates suicide following his girlfriend's abortion.

Later in this chapter I discuss a variety of narratives where characters disclose abortions as part of their back stories. That these characters divulged these abortions in later life may be interpreted as indicative of long periods of suffering—of punishment—post abortion; the pain of their abortion apparently never left them.

Whereas the shady providers and botched abortions discussed earlier could be interpreted as cautionary tales, the hauntings offered in these examples are much more explicit. They appear to acknowledge that in contemporary culture physically surviving an abortion is highly likely, yet the idea that a woman will be forever haunted—that the psychological effects may be devastating—is a far scarier cautionary warning for contemporary audiences.

The Executed Mother

The screen has a long history of punishing women who breach mandates associated with their gender; women who commit adultery, who are promiscuous, or who neglect their responsibilities as mothers or, as discussed earlier, even dare to *consider* abortion often receive punishment on the screen. It is therefore unsurprising that women who abort in narratives are punished for their terminations. In *If These Walls Could Talk*, Claire got pregnant from a one-night stand; she was duly punished with a botched back alley abortion culminating in her death. In *Revolutionary Road* (2008), married April (Kate Winslet)—feeling trapped in her marriage and wanting an exit—gave herself an abortion; she botched it and died. In the Russian film *The Banishment* (2007), a wife was pregnant by someone (seemingly) *other* than her husband. She eventually decided to abort but died during the procedure. In the teen drama *Jack and Bobby* (2004–2005), Missy (Keri Lynn Pratt) had an abortion and was killed in a car accident in the next episode.

While it could be contended that such narratives are simply about compounding the tragedy of these women's lives—that their death is the character's ultimate demise and that the stacked tragedies work for narrative purposes—another interpretation is that the character is simply being

The Abortion Chapter 167

punished. In other words, these women are delivered the ultimate sentence for their ultimate crime: they are executed. Worth noting, from a production perspective, having such characters get killed also means that they no longer have to exist on screen as Characters Who Aborted (i.e., as an embodiment of "sin") and, therefore, no longer have to serve as a permanent reminder of a taboo breach.

While thus far I have discussed abortion narratives centered on negative associations such as guilt, pain, and punishment, in the next section some comparatively positive narratives are explored in which the portrayal is less cautionary tale and more reflective of the reality of abortion.

ABORTION AS BACK STORIES

In the Alcohol Chapter, I noted that alcoholism—notably the alcoholism of a parent—is a common back story for characters. Interestingly, abortion is also frequently presented this way—as something that happened in a character's past. There are many screen examples where, while it may not be part of the immediate narrative, an abortion will be mentioned as something that once happened to a character.

An early example of this occurred in *Detective Story* (1951): detective (Kirk Douglas)—who had been investigating a backyard abortionist—discovered that his wife Mary (Eleanor Parker) actually had had an abortion performed by that very doctor prior to their marriage. In an episode of sitcom *Roseanne* (1988–1997), Roseanne's (Roseanne Barr) grandmother, Nana Mary (Shelley Winters), divulged having had two abortions. In *Naked* (1993), Sophie (Katrin Cartlidge) briefly mentioned the abortions of her past. In *Sex and the City* (1998–2004), Carrie and Samantha both disclosed past abortions. In an episode of *The West Wing* (1999–2006), a Supreme Court nominee—Baker Lang (Glenn Close)—divulged an abortion as part of her back story. In *High Fidelity* (2000), part of Laura (Iben Hjejle) and Rob's (John Cusack) back story was that he cheated on her while she was pregnant and she had an abortion. As discussed earlier, in the sitcom *Scrubs*, Jordon revealed a past abortion. In *Series 7: The Contenders* (2001), Dawn (Brooke Smith) briefly mentioned an abortion. Tina (Laurel Holloman) on *The L-Word* had abortions in her past and Emily (Paget Brewster) in *Criminal Minds* (2005–) had an abortion as a teenager. In *Match Point* (2005), Nola (Scarlett Johansson) revealed having had two previous abortions; this formed part of her justification for not wanting to go through with a third when lover Chris (Jonathan Rhys Meyers) suggested it. In *Hidden Secrets* (2006), Sherry (Tracy Melchior) revealed having had one—and was committed to the belief that she would eventually be punished for it. As noted earlier, in *Last Chance Harvey*, Kate mentioned an abortion that she had in college. In *Margaret* (2011), Lisa (Anna Paquin) also claimed to have had an abortion.

There are a number of ways to read these scenes. As noted earlier, the fact that these characters even *mention* their abortion can be construed as indicative of them continuing to feel some guilt or remorse. That said, this is not the only interpretation. One reading is simply that—given that abortion is something relatively common—these characters are simply divulging their abortion as an aspect of their past. Discussing the *High Fidelity* example, gender researcher Audry Fisch contended that the depiction delivered "the more radical message that abortion doesn't have to be the stuff of tragic melodrama."[20] A more pro-choice interpretation is that divulging abortions means that these characters are taking ownership of them and choosing *not* to feel shameful; in essence, they are participating in a normalization of it. The idea of confessing to an abortion as being part of both healing and activism is well illustrated in the documentary film *I Had an Abortion* (2005). This film focused on 10 women telling their real-life stories of abortion to highlight the importance of ensuring access to safe and legal abortions and to alert women that they are not alone—that abortion is, in fact, *common*.

In these examples, abortions are referred to as something occurring outside of a narrative and as part of the characters' back stories. Another way they are presented is within the narrative but, as Fisch discussed, not necessarily the makings of melodrama.

THE NONTRAGIC ABORTION

Earlier, I mentioned the abortion that Lisa divulged in *Margaret*: in a scene occurring after she had sex with her teacher (Matt Damon), she approached him on the street and told him that she had an abortion. While the audience doesn't know if her assertion is true—Lisa telling him is the first the audience has heard about this event, and the character is somewhat unhinged so skepticism is justified—that she simply divulged it matter-of-factly alludes to the idea that it is possible for an abortion to be something that *just happens*. In other words, abortion doesn't have to lead to guilt or to hauntings or to any other tragic consequences; an abortion may simply transpire and characters then move on with their lives. While this might be one way to interpret the back story abortions discussed earlier, it is also a way to interpret the abortions that occur within narratives. In *Fast Times at Ridgemont High* (1982), for example, Stacy (Jennifer Jason Leigh) got pregnant and had an abortion. In *Coach Carter* (2005), Kyra (Ashanti) got pregnant and had an abortion, deciding that she (1) was too young to be a mother, (2) had drifted away from her boyfriend, and (3) had other priorities. In the British drama *Skins* (2007–), young musician Jal (Larissa Wilson) had an abortion so that she could go to university. In *Six Feet Under*, Claire's abortion was similarly noncontroversial. In these narratives, like Lisa in *Margaret*, the girls involved were teenagers. Discussing the *Fast Times at Ridgemont High* example, cultural theorist Dina Smith argued, "The scene renders abortion as a naturalized part of the teenage girls' experiences."[21] Certainly this was Katie's (Isla Fisher) take on it in *Bridesmaids*: when Regan (Kirsten Dunst) let slip that she had driven Gena to have her abortion in high school, Katie appeared aggrieved that she wasn't invited along, implying that she considered an abortion akin to any other teenage adventure. In each example, the character's youth made abortion appear a sensible decision. While abortion is rarely a noncontroversial decision on screen, abortions had by very young women likely makes sense to audiences, particularly for the target audiences of these narratives.

Of course, characters don't choose abortions only when they are young, but in fact have them across the life-course. It is here where the presentation of abortion becomes somewhat more complicated. In *The Secret Life of Us*, discussed earlier, Alex was a doctor: part of her abortion decision was underpinned by consideration of her career. In an early episode of *All My Children* (1970–2011), Erica (Susan Lucci) had an abortion so not to compromise her modeling career. In an episode of the soap opera *As the World Turns* (1956–2010), careerist Ellie (Renee Props) discovered she was pregnant with a deformed fetus and aborted it, believing that she would be unable to care for a disabled child. In the television series *Maude* (1972–1978), the title character (Bea Arthur) decided to abort the pregnancy that she conceived in her mid-40s, believing she was too old to have a baby. In *Cabaret* (1972), Sally (Liza Minnelli) had an abortion; her motives were never entirely clear, but her career certainly appeared one explanation. In *The Godfather II* (1974), Kay (Diane Keaton) claimed to have aborted as a way to get out of her marriage to Michael (Al Pacino). In *Fame* (1980), dancer Hillary (Antonia Franceschi) had an abortion so that she could advance her ballet career. In the Australian comedy series *Frontline* (1994–1997), ambitious news reporter Brooke (Jane Kennedy) was pregnant and was told that she wouldn't get a starring role in a new show if she was pregnant. Brooke took a day off for a "funeral" and was assumed to have aborted. In the British mini-series *Prime Suspect IV* (1995), the unmarried careerist detective Jane (Helen Mirren) had an abortion. In *Greenberg* (2010), Florence (Greta

Gerwig) had an abortion; it was presented as thoroughly matter-of-fact and noncontroversial. In each of these examples, abortions were not presented as great traumas for the women involved. Rather, they were depicted as simply choices related to lifestyle: to further careers, because the women couldn't care for a deformed baby, because they wanted out of their marriages, or because they just simply didn't want to be pregnant.

One way to read these narratives is as conscious attempts to be cutting edge and to push boundaries—not necessarily to be confrontational (although that is certainly an interpretation), but rather to be *of the Zeitgeist* and to present reality, even if gritty. Of course, while these narratives highlight the array of abortion rationales, construing them as being necessarily received by audiences as noncontroversial would be premature. In political scientist John Gray Geer's book on public opinion, he noted that the public is generally unsympathetic toward "lifestyle abortions": "For instance, 62 percent believe it should be illegal for a woman to abort her pregnancy solely because she cannot afford the child. Similarly ... most favor outlawing abortions performed because tests show the baby will be mentally impaired ... A recent study also reveals only about one-quarter support abortions that are performed to ensure motherhood does not interfere with the woman's career."[22] This information highlights that abortions that are deemed to take place for "lifestyle" reasons—as opposed to preserving the health of the mother or because of rape, for example—remain controversial. With this controversy in mind, it might be contended that such presentations are conscious attempts to create controversy: to get the film or episode spoken about. (This style of marketing is discussed further in the Rude Gestures chapter.) For some narratives, the depiction might also be stylistic: *Six Feet Under* and *Greenberg*, for example, were examples of narratives that were overtly concerned with appearing cutting edge, alternative, and at the vanguard, so they may be interpreted as modern and hip, pro-choice narratives.

Keeping in mind Geer's research on the unpopularity of so-called lifestyle abortions, having female characters abort for reasons potentially construed as "fickle" might be read as ways to demonize them: to cast these women as driven, unsympathetic, selfish, and egotistical—if not, as in the case of Kay in *Godfather II*, potentially even desperate or cruel. Having a woman abort for lifestyle reasons also casts her as unfeminine and certainly unmotherly: putting her own needs first is the *antithesis* of good mothering. (This topic is discussed further in the Alcohol Chapter.)

Noted at the beginning of this chapter was the nature of abortion as being controversial and highly emotive. A common way abortion appears in screen narratives is simply by referencing the abortion debate—a debate that has been waging for decades in the United States and that will no doubt endure.

ABORTION: *THE* SOCIAL AND POLITICAL DEBATE

Mentioned already in this chapter were the films *Citizen Ruth* and *The Cider House Rules*. While abortion was at the forefront of both narratives, neither presented strong pro-choice or antichoice messages. *Citizen Ruth*, for example, stereotyped people on both sides of the debate: from the hymn-singing pro-lifers to the New Age lesbian abortion rights activists. *The Cider House Rules* offered a much more sober take on the topic but similarly presented the debate relatively even-handedly. A number of media depictions also attempt to provide a fair overview: the TV film *Roe vs. Wade* was such an example. *Absolute Strangers* (1991) was another relatively diplomatic made-for-TV docudrama about a husband wanting to get his comatose and brain-damaged wife an abortion to save her life. *A Private Matter* (1992) was also a made-for-TV film about the legal battles of a woman who sought to abort her severely deformed fetus in the 1960s, and *Hush-a-Bye Baby* (1990) was about the battles of abortion in Ireland in the 1980s; both focused on the issue without any side being prioritized. An episode of sitcom *Seinfeld* (1990–1998) also focused on the controversy of abortion: Elaine (Julia Louis-Dreyfus) was committed to not frequenting businesses where the owners were antichoice. In one scene, she discovered that restaurateur Poppie (Reni Santoni) was antichoice: she made a dramatic exit that forced the other patrons to confront—and articulate—their politics. The focus—and the humor—was on abortion as a lightning rod and not about any specific political view. Such a portrayal was also apparent in an episode of *The Simpsons* (1989–), when aliens Kodos and Kang tried to take over the government. In one scene, Kang addressed a crowd by shouting, "Abortions for all!" The crowd booed. Kang then suggested, "Very well, no abortions for anyone." The crowd again booed. The concession Kang then offered was, "Hmm ... Abortions for some, miniature American flags for others." The crowd cheered. In the *Seinfeld* and *The Simpsons* episodes, the arguments for or against were sidelined; the focus was on just how inflammatory the topic is.

While both sides of the debate could, of course, claim these narratives either help or hinder their causes, the overarching theme is controversy. Rather than overtly demonizing abortion or lauding it as a viable option, these narratives instead focus on abortion existing as a continually divisive issue, mirroring how the debate plays out in reality.

While abortion is defended by feminists on the grounds of bodily rights and reproductive choice, some screen examples present narratives where abortions are taken out of the hands of women and become someone else's choice.

FORCED ABORTIONS

Abortion is perpetually framed as a women's rights issue—particularly in narratives where the legal option doesn't exist, the struggle is about the need for *choice*. In some narratives, however, abortion is presented as actually *not* the choice of the pregnant woman at all. In such narratives an abortion is *imposed* on the pregnant woman; *her* choices are subordinate to the choices of others.

In *Expecting Mary* (2010), teenage Mary (Olesya Rulin) became pregnant and her wealthy parents tried to coerce her to have an abortion; instead, she ran away and went through with the pregnancy. Something similar happened in an episode of *Private Practice* (2007–): Maya (Geffri Maya) was pregnant and her mother wanted her to abort; Maya chose to continue with the pregnancy. In *Harsh Times* (2005), Marta (Tammy Trull) revealed she was pregnant and boyfriend Jim (Christian Bale) responded badly, telling her that she needed to abort and threatened to punch her in the stomach and shoot her in the head. While the abortion didn't occur in any of these narratives, it was certainly something threatened. The coerced abortion did transpire in *Starting out in the Evening* (2007): Casey (Adrian Lester) coerced his partner Ariel (Lil Taylor) to abort. In the Australian film *The Delinquents* (1989), Lola (Kylie Minogue) was forced by her mother to have an abortion. In *Palindromes*, 13-year-old Aviva was forced into an abortion by her mother. The same thing occurred in *Venus* (2006): Jessie (Jodie Whittaker) mentioned her mother forcing her to have an abortion when she was younger. In the South Korean film *Hae anseon* (*The Coast Guard*) (2002), a forced abortion was performed on a woman who had had sex with a number of soldiers.

This forced abortion idea was presented in a "humorous" way in the comedy film *MacGruber* (2010). MacGruber spoke about his relationship with Casey (Maya Rudolph), whose previous relationship was with Cunth (Val Kilmer): "She was actually carrying his child at the time. I asked her to terminate it obviously, so we could start fresh. And she agreed." In the aforementioned *Seinfeld* episode, the topic of forced abortion was similarly presented as something funny: Jerry (Jerry Seinfeld) asked restaurateur Poppie for his thoughts on abortion, to which Poppie responded:

> When my mother was abducted by the Communists she was with child . . . but the Communists, they put an end to that!

While these narratives could be interpreted as making light of abortion and more broadly as trivializing the politics of choice, another interpretation is that they—like *The Simpsons* episode discussed earlier—are simply about just how inflammatory the debate is. In other words, the ease with which the abortion topic fires people up is the real source of comedy, rather than abortion itself.

The notion of forced abortion doesn't necessarily lend itself to being construed as either a pro-choice or antichoice position, given that both sides of the debate would agree that *any* kind of *forced* medical intervention is problematic. Nevertheless, these narratives do reference one of the antichoice lobby's concerns with legalized abortions: that they can be forced—or at least strongly insisted upon—for women who don't actually want them. Much like the arguments against euthanasia—which propose that once it is legal, it can be subjected to misuse—arguments based on abuse are routinely cited to oppose abortion.

This chapter has provided an overview of the presentation of abortion on screen. In real life, abortion remains an emotive and conflict-ridden issue; thus it comes as no surprise that such controversies play out in contemporary screen narratives. While the abortion topic remains taboo, it is frequently considered difficult to present in mainstream film and television for fear of incurring the wrath of audiences and sponsors. As demonstrated in this chapter, abortion is relatively easily identified on screen but is presented in a wide variety of ways, many of which lead to fraught consequences.

The Penis Chapter: Undressing Male Nudity

While the penis is frequently referred to in mainstream popular culture through jokes and references to size, and while the male body has increasingly become something to be desired and objectified on screen, its unsheathed display remains a rarity in American film and television. While the exposed penis might be standard for pornography—and is certainly a sight most people would have had real-life exposure to—full frontal male nudity remains taboo in mainstream screen narratives. Many times when films have dared to break this taboo—think *Caligula* (1979), *Salo—120 Days of Sodom* (1975), and the French film *Anatomie de l'enfer* (*Anatomy of Hell*) (2004)—it was the visibility of the penis that prompted critics to contend that the film should be reclassified as pornography.

This chapter focuses on occasions when the penis taboo is breached, and explores what such representations mean as related to filmmaking as well as to sexual politics. Director Peter Greenaway—famous for frequently including uncovered penises in his films—once claimed that a large penis on screen represents "aggressive sexuality, the male principle, penis-worship, the male ego, penis-envy, exhibitionism, arrogance, dominance."[1] In this quote, Greenaway highlights a variety of narrative purposes that the exposed penis serves; his suggestions, as well as numerous others—ranging from comedy through to madness—are explored in this chapter.

PEAK-A-BOO PENISES AND SHEATHED ERECTIONS

While male nudity is relatively common on screen—bare torsos and even bare buttocks get extensive screen time—full frontal male nudity remains rare. James Wolcott, in his *Vanity Fair* article, discussed this point: "Directors play peekaboo with it, dodging an R rating or worse by deploying a variety of cute fig leaves, such as a hurriedly grabbed teddy bear as an emergency groin protector. Steam discreetly clouds it in the gym shower and sauna. Bedsheets are draped with the care of Saks window displays to shelter the little fella from view even as the actress in the scene goes total nudie."[2] Wolcott's discussion highlights the most obvious way the penis is "presented" on screen: as routinely *obscured* by props. In *The Simpsons Movie* (2007), this idea actually formed the basis for a lengthy joke: while Bart's penis was eventually shown, in the lead-up—while he skateboarded naked through town following a dare from his father—his penis was obscured by a wide variety of objects. Such depictions are the standard ways that male nudity is portrayed: the male character is quite obviously naked but his penis is concealed by props.

Equally common is the display of the penis to other characters within a narrative but shielded from audiences. In such scenes, the reactions of the other characters guide the audience response. Film theorists Santiago Fouz-Hernández and Alfredo Martinez-Expósito, for example, discussed the Spanish teen-comedy *XXL* (2004), where the penis of protagonist Fali (Óscar Jaenada) was constantly referred to but never actually shown to audiences: "despite the visual and verbal emphasis on Fali's organ, it is never shown in the film. Instead, its size is discussed by friends, lovers and middle-aged female customers."[3]

Rather than allowing audiences their own reactions to the sight of a bare penis, the "appropriate" reaction is instead provided to them via the responses of other characters. Films such as the British film *The Full Monty* (1997) or more recently *Magic Mike* (2012)—both which were about male stripping—intriguingly completely avoided showing full frontal nudity and instead, as in *XXL*, focused on character reactions.[4] Discussing this idea in the British newspaper *The Guardian*, Olly Richards wrote that both films "obeyed the first rule of male screen stripping: nobody wants to see the bits."[5] This question of whether *nobody wants to see the bits* is addressed later in this chapter, but certainly avoiding the penis is a rule that most films and television programs seem to adhere to.

Another way that the penis is presented without actually being made visible is through the sheathed erection. In films such as *Road Trip* (2000),

Tomcats (2001), and *Anchorman* (2004), and in the sitcom *Curb Your Enthusiasm* (2000–) and the drama series *Californication* (2007–), erect penises are presented via tented fabric. The vague idea of the erection is displayed—that is, an obvious bulge at the crotch is identifiable—but there is not enough detail provided for it to be easily identified as a penis. Instead, it appears more simply—and less seemingly offensively—as just a *caricature* of an erection.

While there are lots of reasons why penises are made invisible on screen, perhaps the most obvious explanation for obfuscation is *classification*, something Wolcott alluded to. Suzanna Andrews discussed this perspective in *The New York Times* when she contended that the attitude of the Motion Picture Association of America "seems to be that male nudity is fine as long as it's obscured."[6] While the issue of classification is addressed later in this chapter, suffice it to say that avoiding unnecessary audience restrictions is one obvious explanation for the concealed penis.

On occasions when penises are displayed to audiences, the most common way this is done is via the glimpse—the blink-and-you'll-miss-it presentation, where freeze-framing is often required.

THE BLINK-AND-YOU'LL-MISS-IT PENIS GLIMPSE

In a broad range of films, extremely brief glimpses of penises are provided. Films such as *Altered States* (1980), *All the Right Moves* (1983), *American Flyers* (1985), *About Last Night* (1986), *Blue Velvet* (1986), *Terminator 2: Judgment Day* (1991), *Armed for Action* (1992), *Damage* (1992), *Color of Night* (1994), *The Governess* (1998), and *Wild Things* (1998) all included rapid-fire shots of full frontal male nudity.

Feminist philosopher Susan Bordo discussed such brief glimpses and identified what she determined to be the trend toward increased displays of them, something she traced back to the brief exposure of Lewis's (Tom Berenger) penis in *At Play in the Fields of the Lord* (1991): " 'Flashing' is more accurate, as some man streaked across the screen, en route and with great dispatch: into the lake, scurrying to the bathroom."[7] Bordo noted that while these mere glimpses—or *flashes* as she termed them—might be the most common presentation of bare penises on screen, this trend of providing penis glimpses was occurring at the same time as a gender double standard was emerging: "more and more movies seemed *constructed* in order to get some entirely naked female in full frontal view."[8]

The first explanation for the brief penis shots is that this tactic enables a film to avoid being dubbed gratuitous or pornographic and, in turn, avoid stricter classification or edits. As these examples testify, brief glimpses of penises can be included without NC-17 or X ratings, a point that film theorist Peter Lehman discussed: "Showing the male genitals does not mean an automatic X or NC-17 rating if the context is not one of explicit lovemaking, and nearly all the Hollywood films that contain frontal male nudity are R-rated."[9]

In each of the brief-glimpse scenes referenced earlier, penises weren't made visible because of sex, but rather because of brief incidental nudity (a topic discussed in greater detail in the next section). This situation aptly illustrates Lehman's point: a glimpse of a penis can circumvent stricter classification if the penis display is not about sex—that is, if the penis can be construed as just being about nudity.[10] (This idea also references why the *erect* penis is almost never seen in non-X-rated cinema.)

Another explanation is that the blink-and-you'll-miss-it presentation enables the mystique of the penis to be maintained. A prime reason for keeping the penis out of cinema is because doing so enables its specialness to be maintained: by providing only a glimpse, a film is able to gently break a taboo and in turn benefit from additional attention while *simultaneously* avoiding a stricter classification. On lists of most paused scenes from films,[11] two frequently mentioned are (1) when Dirk's (Mark Wahlberg) enormous penis is unveiled in *Boogie Nights* (1997) and (2) the very briefly spliced penis shot in *Fight Club* (1999). The use of subliminal images in film has often been associated with advertising and attempts to surreptitiously encourage product sales,[12] but writer and film editor Gael Chandler noted that this technique can also be deployed to "ratchet up the tension to help make the audience uneasy."[13] While a penis shot doesn't necessarily make an audience feel *uneasy*, it certainly can affect tension: by providing a glimpse of an image that is unusual for the screen, the mood is changed and intrigue is generated. The knowledge that such subliminal scenes exist can create attention and curiosity around a film and potentially even lead to increased DVD sales. This latter issue was something alluded to by director Noam Gonick in an interview about his film *Hey, Happy!* (2001); "on the DVD you can freeze-frame the penises," he suggested.[14] Just as the infamous penis "secret" of *The Crying Game* (1992) was one of the key selling points—and exists as an example of another frequently paused scene—the incorporation of subtle taboo breaches can deliver a film extra attention.

Taking the glimpse a little further is the incidental penis, whereby it is simply exposed in the course of a man going about his daily routine. The penis in such examples is not engaged in sexual activity or presented as hilarious, but rather is just shown as a body part that is simply made visible because of nudity. In such a case, the penis has entered the public sphere because the camera is filming a male character's daily routine and not because he is being an exhibitionist.

THE INCIDENTAL PENIS

In his discussion of penises on screen, Lehman contended that "penises cannot simply be shown as penises in ordinary contexts."[15] When thinking about the "grand reveals" of the penis in *The Crying Game*, for example—where Dil's (Jaye Davidson) penis exposed the character as biologically male—or the much discussed giant-penis exposures in *Boogie Nights* or *The Brown Bunny* (2003), the idea of an exposed penis being a substantial "to-do" is easily detected. In such narratives, the penis is part of the narrative and is an important storytelling device. This, however, is not always the case; sometimes penises on screen are just another body part.

First, to contend that an exposed penis can ever be *incidental* is by no means effortless: given the taboo, when a film does include an exposed penis, it is difficult to completely overlook the possibility of a statement being made. That said, there are a number of scenes where, regardless of what the image might convey on a filmmaking or sociological level, in the context of the narrative it can simply appear incidental. In such cases, the image is not explicitly a statement or a plot point, but rather just a bare bodily reality. As noted, the films of Peter Greenaway—such as *The Cook, the Thief, His Wife & Her Lover* (1989), *Prospero's Books* (1991), and *The Pillow Book* (1996)—often include scenes of incidental nudity. In *The Piano* (1993), George's (Harvey Keitel) penis was visible when he was cleaning the piano while naked. In *Color of Night*, Bill's (Bruce Willis) penis was briefly visible while he was in the pool naked. In *Wild Things*, Ray's (Kevin Bacon) penis was visible while he was showering. In *Young Adam* (2003), while Joe's (Ewan McGregor) penis was avoided in all of the sex scenes, it was indeed made visible in a scene where he got out of bed after having slept naked. In *Shame* (2011), protagonist Brandon (Michael Fassbender) walked around naked in several scenes readying for his day, his penis clearly visible (as Wolcott described, Brandon's penis is simply "a plain, plump fact of life"[16]).

The incidental penis can also appear through no fault of the character; rather, narrative events have simply dictated that external forces put the man in a position of having to make public his penis to other characters and in turn the audience. The Mexican film *El Topo* (1970), for example, opened with a young boy (Brontis Jodorowsky) left naked in the desert by his father; the young boy's penis was clearly visible. The boy didn't *choose* to display it, but it got displayed due to his naked abandonment. In a scene from *Fargo* (1996), Carl (Steve Buscemi) was interrupted during sex; as he tried to flee from his attackers, his penis was exposed. Something similar occurred in the Israeli film *Lirkod* (*The Belly Dancer*) (2006): Yaki (Yuval Segal) was apprehended during sex and thus his penis was visible. In *American Psycho* (2000), a prostitute decided during sex that she didn't want to remain in the home of protagonist Patrick (Christian Bale); Patrick had other ideas and chased her, naked, through the house with a chainsaw, his penis being visible. In an episode of the television series *Big Love* (2006–2011), Wanda's (Melora Walters) newborn baby boy was shown; he was naked and his penis was visible. In *Eastern Promises* (2007), Nikolai (Viggo Mortensen) was in a sauna when he got attacked; his penis was visible during the fight scene.

While the penis in these scenes is open to a number of interpretations as to the *why* of its showing—as opposed to concealed, as is normally the case—another interpretation is that such images highlight the character's vulnerability. The penis is again incidental in these scenes; it is shown simply because the character is otherwise naked. As in the penis-glimpse scenes discussed earlier, the penis display is not overtly relevant to the narrative, but the penis is exposed because the character is put in a position where his nakedness is made public. While such scenes might cast a film as arty or cutting edge or facilitate it reaping additional publicity, ultimately these penises were not central to the narrative and were made visible simply because of nudity.

Another way the penis appears on screen is in comedies, whereby the sexual—and thus potentially challenging, threatening, or confronting—connotations are sidelined and the penis is made visible because it is (apparently) something funny.

THE FUNNY PENIS

Noted in the introduction was that penises are often present in narratives via dialogue, inevitably through penis-related humor.[17] Comedy, however, is also commonly the backdrop for actual penises to appear on screen in what is often simply a *live action* penis joke. Wolcott discussed this issue in his *Vanity Fair* article, writing that "In American film, the penis ... remains mostly a comic prop, the little brother that insists on tagging along."[18] Richards made a similar point, noting, "We all know the nude male form is essentially ridiculous, built only for floppy comedy. Hollywood recognised this quickly."[19] Sociologist Travis Kong also made this point in relation to the penis in Hong Kong cinema, noting that full frontal nudity traditionally appeared only in comedies.[20] When the penis is present in American cinema, often it is included as a sight gag: as a joke without words.

In a scene from the comedy *There's Something about Mary* (1998), Ted (Ben Stiller) got his penis stuck in a zipper. The audience saw some bloated genital flesh trapped in his zipper; his exposed penis made Ted the object of ridicule by a very large number of characters. In *Borat* (2006), a naked wrestling scene occurred between the title character (Sacha Baron Cohen) and his producer Azamat (Ken Davitan); the scene was intended to be funny, something compounded by the hairiness of both men, the obesity of Azamat, and notably the sight of flopping penises. In *2 Days in Paris* (2007), a photograph was perused by the parents of Jack's (Adam Goldberg) partner Marion (Julie Delpy): in it, Jack was presented as completely naked with helium balloons holding up his penis. Jack was humiliated. A similar scene transpired in the British film *I Give It a Year* (2013) where Josh's (Rafe Spall) penis was accidentally shown to his in-laws through some honeymoon photography.

In the opening scene of the comedy *Forgetting Sarah Marshall* (2008), Sarah (Kristen Bell) broke up with her boyfriend Peter (Jason Segel); Peter was wearing only a towel at the time and it fell off during the scene: the entire break-up was played out while he was naked, his penis visible.

The most obvious element of these scenes is that each moves the penis out of a sexual context and presents it as just like any other body part. Of course, because audiences know that—given the extensive taboo attached—the penis is *not* just an ordinary part, its visibility in these scenes makes it look out of place. The visibility of the exposed penis, therefore, makes these scenes particularly awkward and awkwardness makes them funny. Humor can make difficult or controversial subjects more palatable or more acceptable; for a penis to appear in a comedy, the kind of tension, disgust, or controversy that is normally attached to a taboo can be mitigated.

The humor surrounding these scenes can also reduce some of the homosexual anxieties as well as size concerns that frequently prevent penises from being shown on screen. Humor can be disarming, so presenting penises as funny can mean that the audience doesn't (necessarily) need to think of them as sexual, nor do they need to conduct a comparison. Rather, audience attention is directed to the funniness and awkwardness of the scene—the situation of the penis being exposed—rather than the penis as a sexual or aesthetic object. While some audiences will, of course, be looking at—and appreciating—the penis for what it is, its presence doesn't *have* to be construed as erotic.

THE VULNERABLE PENIS

The exposed penises in scenes from *Eastern Promises*, *Fargo*, and *Lirkod* (*The Belly Dancer*) were incidental in that the characters were naked—in a sauna and having sex, respectively—thus forcing the man's nakedness into the public sphere. While these scenes can be classified as incidental as discussed earlier, worth examining is their function in spotlighting male vulnerability. In other words, a penis can be exposed to make a male character appear vulnerable, both physically and emotionally.

Physical vulnerability was an issue discussed by Bordo: "Nonerect, the penis has a unique ability to suggest vulnerability, fragility, a sleepy sweetness. It's not just soft; it's really soft . . . it *is* more easily hurt than other parts of the body."[21] A similar point was made by Wolcott in his discussion of *Eastern Promises* and the naked male wrestling scene in *Women in Love* (1969): "No matter how bull-strong the late Oliver Reed was, no matter how topographically muscular Mortensen is, the male viewer is always apprehensively aware of how vulnerable the little guy is in a fight, the testicles even more at mercy, clenched or swaying like tiny twin punching bags—one hard tap and Hercules himself would fold in two, unless he were wearing a bronze cup."[22] Here, Bordo and Wolcott present the idea that the exposed penis makes a male character *physically* vulnerable: direct contact can be excruciating, such that an exposed penis can function to highlight the extent to which a character is physically in peril. Such a presentation can motivate the audience to be fearful for the character's safety by their recognition that this normally protected body part is perilously out in the open.

While such vulnerability is evident in *Eastern Promises*, *Fargo*, and *Women in Love*, the exposed penis can also function as a clue to forthcoming vulnerability. In *American History X* (1998), for example, a prison shower scene showed the penises of a number of inmates. Moments later, there was a brutal rape scene; the vulnerability of the penis was symbolic of the vulnerability of men in prison. Something similar occurred in the Chinese film *Night Fall* (2012): the film opened with a very brutal naked fight scene occurring in a prison.

While in these scenes the penis was not overtly attacked, there are examples where a direct onslaught against a man's genitals does actually become the man's downfall. Most often this occurs with a direct strike to a clothed penis. In the final scene of comedy *What Happens in Vegas* (2008), for example, Tipper (Lake Bell) punched her ex-boyfriend Mason (Jason Sudeikis) in the genitals, causing him to collapse in pain. In *Something to Talk About* (1995), Emma Rae (Kyra Sedgwick) similarly kicked her cheating brother-in-law in the genitals and he collapsed to the ground in agony. While in these examples the assaults were on genitals, clothing was present, in turn conveying the idea of a modicum of protection; without clothes, bare genitals leave a man much more exposed.

In *Snakes on a Plane* (2006), a man used the toilet on the plane—his penis was exposed, although audiences couldn't see it—and it was then attacked by a snake. This idea was made more explicit in the horror films *Piranha* (2010) and *Teeth* (2007), when actual penises were shown. In *Piranha*, for example, Derrick (Jerry O'Connell) was attacked by piranhas and his bare penis was actually bitten off and then shown floating in the water, where it was seized on by more piranhas. The premise of *Teeth* centered on the psychoanalytic idea of *vagina dentata* or the "toothed vagina." In this film, penises were made vulnerable to a variety of things—vaginas with teeth as well as attack by crabs and dogs. In these examples, exposed penises put men in positions of physical jeopardy.

The exposed penis can also indicate vulnerability *metaphorically*: audiences know that an exposed penis can make a man physically vulnerable, so its display can serve as a clue to other kinds of vulnerability. For Ted in *Something about Mary*, his penis conveyed his vulnerability in terms of his flailing social standing. For Peter in *Forgetting Sarah Marshall*, his exposed penis could be interpreted as a visual clue to his vulnerability as a boyfriend, as a man. For Brandon in *Shame*, his penis alluded to his susceptibility to be governed by his sexual impulses; he is so beholden to the needs and wants of his penis that his happiness is being sabotaged.

A final way vulnerability is conveyed through an exposed penis is via the display of a naked corpse; a *dead penis* is the ultimate sign of life termination and the ceasing of a man's functioning. Lehman discussed the full frontal nudity of male corpses in a variety films including *In the Realm of the Senses* (1976), *Basic Instinct* (1992), *Shallow Grave* (1994), *Se7en* (1995), *This World, Then the Fireworks* (1997), and *Munich* (2005), as well as in television shows including *Oz* (1997–2003) and *Six Feet Under* (2001–2005). In such scenes, the flaccid penis worked to encapsulate the loss of life: in the display of a relatively small piece of flesh, the pitifulness and vulnerability of the inactive penis demonstrated the end of life, functionality, and masculinity. Presenting a penis this way is not only thoroughly *nonsexual*—and, therefore, can avoid the wrath of censors—but more importantly reduces the penis to meat, eliminating all the mystical and taboo properties that it is often anointed with.

Exposing a penis can also illustrate another kind of vulnerability, whereby full frontal nudity can be used to convey the mental instability of a character.

PENISES AND MADNESS

In a culture where covering the penis in public is mandatory, its exposure on screen can be a way to connote a kind of madness. Exhibitionism is a mental disorder characterized by a compulsion to display one's genitals, generally to unsuspecting strangers. While there are exhibitionist and flasher characters in film and television—for example, the exhibitionist Mark (Karlheinz Böhm) in the thriller *Peeping Tom* (1960) or The Flasher (John Waters) in *Hairspray* (2007)—audiences don't actually *see* penises in either example. Given the rarity of unsheathed penises on screen, when a character does expose himself, this action can be construed as flashing. The act of exposure can nonetheless be construed as symptomatic of a kind of madness; only a *crazy* character would expose himself.

An episode of *Law and Order: Special Victims Unit* (1999–) opened with a man running naked through Central Park: he was then arrested and institutionalized. In a scene from *The Deer Hunter* (1978), a drunken Michael (Robert De Niro) ran through the streets naked—inexplicably—and his penis was visible. This scene certainly provided a substantial hint to the character's mental instability. In the final scene of *2 Days in Paris*, Jack and Marion passionately discussed their relationship. Marion narrated the scene, telling the audience that evidently neither character really knew the other. At one point Jack undid his pants and exposed his penis; Marion narrated that he was showing "himself totally bare to me." Jack's penis display—compounded with him shaving an "M" into his chest hair—seemed to indicate a kind of madness, or at the very least *desperation*. In a scene from the Australian film *Dead Europe* (2012), after taking drugs three characters were shown racing through a forest, naked, penises visible: the nudity was connected to a kind of drug-fueled loss of inhibition, if not drug-fueled madness.

Taken a step further, this idea played out in *Bad Lieutenant* (1992) when the title character's (Harvey Keitel) drinking, drug use, and corruption reached breaking point: he was shown naked, gritting his teeth, his arms outstretched, making pained noises, with his penis clearly visible. This scene is open to a number of readings—the character's nakedness can be construed as showing his vulnerability or as a reference to a request for redemption in a Christ-like sense, but notably appears indicative of just how mad he has become. This idea was presented much less subtly in *The Fisher King* (1991): in one scene, the homeless man Parry (Robin Williams) danced naked in Central Park at night with his penis visible; associate Jack (Jeff Bridges) screamed at him, "You're out of your fucking mind!" Evidently only a crazy person would engage in such behavior. While Patrick in

American Psycho was incidentally nude because he had just been having sex, to watch Patrick race around the house with a chainsaw certainly functioned as a perfect illustration of insanity. Patrick's nudity took the presentation of his craziness to the next level: the character appeared even more frightening because he was naked. That Patrick would murder while naked shows his insanity as escalating.

Such scenes seem to—in varying degrees—show a character at or exceeding madness; exposing one's penis means a character challenges societal expectations by putting all of himself completely *out there*.

THE COCK-CENTRIC CHARACTER

Communications theorists Brian Ott and Robert Mack defined *phallocentrism* as "a social condition where images or representations of the penis carry connotations of dominance and power."[23] For a film to be phallocentric, the presentation of a penis is not always necessary; visual culture has a long history of depicting phallocentricity in a variety of other ways, notably through props. Guns are an obvious example of this and something discussed by cultural theorist Josephine Metcalf: "Guns and their phallocentric associations have long been used to demarcate and assert maleness, with the gun metaphorically reinforcing both the power and sexuality of men."[24] Bordo similarly explored this idea in her discussion of artwork from romance novels: "If you can't show a hard penis on the cover, show a hard body."[25] Certainly the preponderance of bare male chests in cinema—particularly in films such as *Magic Mike* and *The Full Monty* discussed earlier—presents this idea to be a truism; the penis is routinely avoided but a substitution, such as a bare chest, is routinely offered.

Just as phallocentricity can be conveyed with objects and without a penis, an exposed penis on screen doesn't *necessarily* convey phallocentricity. Ted's exposed penis in *Something about Mary* and Peter's penis in *Forgetting Sarah Marshall* were actually demonstrations of masculinity *in crisis*, about the penis potentially meaning nothing, of being *depleted* of its power. In a world of greater gender equality, such scenes can be construed as downplaying penis reverence and potentially downplaying patriarchy.

While the penis doesn't necessarily work to convey phallocentricity on screen, it certainly can. In *The Crying Game*, the big "reveal" scene was when Dil—a character assumed by Fergus (Stephen Rea) to be a woman—undressed and exposed a penis. Suddenly Fergus's understanding of Dil as a woman was completely shattered; the presence of the penis forced Fergus to think about Dil differently, to consider whether Dil's penis was at the center of her identity, her sex. *American Psycho* and *Shame* presented this idea much more explicitly. In *American Psycho*, Patrick's identity was very much shaped by his sense of himself as a sexual being. In one scene—when he was having sex with one prostitute while being filmed by another—Patrick's focus was not on either woman, but rather on his image in the mirror: he thrust and posed, flexed his muscles, and ran his fingers through his hair. Patrick was aroused by the idea of himself as a man who fucks. In the scene where Patrick was running around naked with the chainsaw, the display of his penis was one way to convey to the audience that this is a character who is *cock-centric*; he is a man not necessarily *ruled* by his penis, but who certainly deems it central to his identity. The film *Shame* focused on Brandon's sex addiction. It stands to reason that for a man so shaped by penis-centric activities—whose leisure time largely centered on attending to his penis—the audiences actually got to see it; in a classic *show—don't tell* cinema move, the audience saw Brandon's penis because it was every bit as important to his character as his face.

An extension of the idea of a character being cock-centric is the notion that his penis is out of control—that its wants are jeopardizing a character's health or happiness. Certainly for Brandon, the wants of his penis appeared to have left him as a depressed, anomic character. For Patrick in *American Psycho*, the wants of his penis seemed to have left him insane. The *penis out of control* idea was presented literally in the fantasy/horror film *Bad Biology* (2008): Batz's (Anthony Sneed) snake-like penis literally had a mind of its own. In much of the film Batz was shown trying to tame his wayward penis, but in one notable scene it detached and wreaked havoc on an apartment building. In Wolcott's discussion of the penis, he discussed this *mind of its own* idea: "It is the one part of an actor's equipment that doesn't answer to commands, instructions, suggestions, cajoling, or subtle fine-tuning; its range of expression is rather limited, its freedom of motion restricted."[26]

While Wolcott was largely discussing the challenges of the penis *for actors*, certainly the penis poses very similar challenges for male characters: it doesn't answer to commands and often has a mind of its own. The inability for the penis to stay hard at will, for example, was well illustrated in *Hope Springs* (2012), when middle-aged Arnold (Tommy Lee Jones) battled with being unable to maintain an erection. The inability of the penis to deflate at will was equally well illustrated by the inconveniently timed erections of Andrew (Ryan Reynolds) in *The Proposal* (2009) and Matt (Josh Hartnett) in *40 Days and 40 Nights* (2002). While these three films didn't actually expose the penis, they nevertheless highlighted the issue of the penis being—as discussed already in this chapter—*vulnerable*, in that it is rarely compliant to the instructions of the brain, in turn creating substantial anxiety for a man.

While thus far in this chapter I have focused on screen examples of the exposed penis and explored ways of interpreting its presentation, bare penises are still incredibly rare on screen. The standard avoidance of them raises a number of interesting topics for discussion; the remainder of this chapter centers on exploring why the bare penis is invariably eschewed.

FULL FRONTAL NUDITY AND THE GENDER DOUBLE STANDARD

Earlier I discussed Bordo's comments about the burgeoning double standard of showing only glimpses of a penis while dwelling on the naked bodies of women. In an article in the Australian newspaper the *Sydney Morning Herald*, Douglas Rowe similarly discussed the full frontal nudity in *The Dreamers* (2003): "scenes with full-frontal male nudity usually can be timed with a stopwatch while those with nude women can be measured with a sundial ... Pop-culture observers maintain that's because a de facto sexism still exists in Hollywood, where women can parade around in the altogether but men can't."[27]

Both Bordo and Rowe allude to a double standard that exists where more full frontal *female* nudity is shown on screen than male nudity.[28] A feminist interpretation for this appears in film theorist Laura Mulvey's seminal work on spectatorship in the cinema, where she identified that women in film are defined by their "to-be-looked-at-ness": women are routinely used as a decorative device and are the object of the audience's gaze.[29] Women's studies researcher Elayne Rapping similarly discussed this idea as related to the rarity of full frontal male nudity: "For a man to reveal his private parts is to be reduced to the position that women have always been reduced to—which is to be examined, to be judged. And I think that's a scary thing."[30] Bordo has presented a similar argument, contending that the bare penis "is a symbol for male exposure, vulnerability to an evaluation and judgment."[31]

Given that the audience gaze is often assumed to be male—either actually male or more generally just primed to view women as sexual objects—full frontal female nudity is thus more in line with what an audience is assumed to *want* to look at.

This double standard links to a bigger issue of whether the penis is an aesthetically pleasing object; this idea was alluded to earlier when Richards in *The Guardian* claimed that "nobody wants to see the bits."[32] Laurent Allary from the French film export union Unifrance referred to this issue in comments he made about the censorship of *The Crying Game*: "a naked woman is more easily accepted as artistic. A naked man is perceived as more unnatural and more aggressive, and it is difficult to convince old-fashioned censors, who are not used to seeing such things, that it is art."[33] Encapsulated in this statement is a very well-established idea that the penis is not artistic, is not *beautiful*; instead, that the nude male form is—as Richards claimed—*essentially ridiculous*.[34] While it is impossible to determine whether people *actually* believe the penis is attractive (as disconnected from a culture convincing them that this is so), nevertheless the screen reiterates this idea by predominantly choosing *not* to expose the penis and, therefore, choosing not to anoint it with the status of being considered beautiful. In my book on advertising, *Sex in Public: Women, Outdoor Advertising and Public Policy*, I noted that a side effect of the routine absence of women who are not young, thin, and white in the media is that women who exist outside of this narrow aesthetic are assumed as less attractive. When media routinely eschew showing penises, the similar inference is that penises are deemed less desirable and less worth looking at than other body parts.

FILMMAKING CONSTRAINTS

A central explanation for why penises tend to be avoided on screen relates to a range of factors centered on the process of filmmaking more so than on narrative.

Censorship and Classification Concerns

As mentioned repeatedly in this chapter, an obvious explanation for the avoidance of penises on screen is to avoid having a film classified in a way that would restrict audiences. While plenty of research addresses the politics and machinations of censorship and classification in cinema,[35] in this section I am more interested in attempts to avoid NC-17 and X ratings.

While some theorists have contended that a film with a less restricted rating is able to be marketed in more places—and, therefore, is more likely to fare better at the box office[36]—others have noted that a *somewhat* restricted rating actually *helps* with ticket sales. Communications theorist Stephen Vaughn, for example, discussed a variety of films where profanity—generally swearing—was *added* into films so that they could avoid a G-rating: "the G was undesirable because it was associated with older Disney films and 'the kind of entertainment' young people had 'grown out of.' ... The G rating became almost as undesirable for large-budget films as the X."[37] A similar point was made by historian John Semonche, who noted that "Ratings at both ends of the spectrum played poorly at the box office. Well over 60 percent of films received an R rating, apparently the most profitable rating."[38] Here, Vaughn and Semonche identify an apparent "sweet spot" in regard to ratings: there is sense in inserting *just enough* raunchy material to have the film's audience *somewhat* restricted, but not so much as to prohibitively limit distribution and revenue.

While making a film slightly raunchy—without making it too much so—likely explains the brief glimpse and incidental nudity offered, it also alludes to why showing much more than this could be problematic. This was a point made by cultural theorist Udo Helms, who noted that it is very difficult to *subtly* photograph male genitals without being explicit: "Pubic hair hides female genitalia; were it shaved, or were the crotch shot in a position that clearly exhibits the vulva, it would still be considered obscene … A nude male body, however, cannot be shot without its protruding genitalia."[39] This point was also made by actor James Spader when he was asked about the lack of full frontal male nudity in his film *Crash* (1996): "The nudity takes place during sex scenes. At such times, male nudity is not visible—if you're any good at all."[40] Helms and Spader highlight that there is a very fine line between showing male nudity subtly and being obscenity.

Avoiding the Penis Distraction

In my book *Periods in Pop Culture: Menstruation in Film and Television*, I noted that menstruation is often absent from narratives because it can prove distracting for audiences: "Having a character participate in something widely considered taboo, however, can distract an audience (and also commentators) and thus potentially derail a narrative."[41] Film critic Robert Ebert presented a similar argument as related to the presence of genitals on screen: "Genitals, of either sex, reduce any scene to a documentary. Nudity below the waist is fatal to the dramatic impact of any scene, drawing attention away from the characters, dialogue, and situation."[42]

By including a full frontal image, attention is directed to the penis. Because the penis is such an unusual presentation, it would be naïve to think that audiences would not be distracted by this uncommon sight. As noted in relation to the brief-glimpse penises discussed earlier, knowing that an audience can be distracted by a penis can be part of a marketing strategy, premised on the fact that audiences are often captivated by its presentation and might elect to see a film *because* of such depictions.

When Ebert noted that genitals reduce a scene to a documentary, one possible extension of this comment is that the audience can no longer relax and simply enjoy a scene as erotic; instead, the "shock" of the penis distracts them. Feminist theorist John Stoltenberg discussed this issue as related to the male gaze and pornography: "The straight male viewer wants to imagine himself in the sex scenes and he does not particularly care to be distracted by the phallic competition."[43] For a penis to be visible in a scene, the man in the audience is not only unable to fantasize that he is in the scene, but more importantly his spectatorship enjoyment is potentially disrupted because he now has to confront questions of whether the scene is enjoyable *because* of the presence of the penis or in spite of it.

Reluctant Actors

A small number of actors have, in fact, embraced exposing their penises. Actor Ewan McGregor, for example, gloated about it having been *his* idea to expose his penis in the film *Velvet Goldmine* (1998): "I was only meant to show my arse, but I managed to get my penis in as well. Too good an opportunity to miss."[44] Fouz-Hernández and Martinez-Expósito, in their discussion of Spanish cinema, similarly noted: "Most major male stars have agreed to full-frontal exposure albeit often only from a distance in medium-long or long shots."[45] While McGregor and Spanish male film stars might be comfortable with displaying their penises, I suggest that this is not the case for the vast majority of actors. Cultural theorist Gwendolyn Audrey Foster addressed this issue in her work on the body and Western cinema, writing: "Male actors are not only prudish about exposing their genitalia, but they vocalize their discomfort with exposing their backsides as well."[46] An actor might resist exposing his penis for any number of reasons, including personal values, morality, and prudishness, but two important ones likely relate to the penis mystique and the comparison factor.

In *Periods in Pop Culture*, I discussed the absence of menstruation scenes in film and television, proposing that this omission is, at least partly, attributable to the disinclination of actors being involved with material that might possibly "cheapen their brand."[47] Wolcott made a similar point, contending that "an actor's mystique is part of his capital."[48] By exposing his penis, an actor leaves nothing to the imagination. Discussed later in this chapter is the idea of the mystique attached to the penis, but suffice it to say for this section—and to quote film theorist Richard Dyer—"The limp penis can never match up to the mystique that has kept it hidden from view for the last couple of centuries."[49] Arguably—unless substantially well endowed, such as Michael Fassbender, Jason Segel, and Ewan McGregor—an average-sized penis will typically appear *underwhelming* and anticlimactic when exposed. While this might suit male audiences—who might, in fact, *appreciate* a downward comparison—this is unlikely to value-add to an *actor's* mystique or star power.

Reluctant Directors

In *Periods in Pop Culture*, I suggested that filmmakers might eschew a presentation of menstruation because "focusing too keenly on such a topic may be viewed as limiting one's opportunities as a producer or filmmaker."[50] As related to full frontal male nudity, for some directors there is potentially a fear that by presenting it, they—while not necessarily limiting opportunities—are potentially having their careers *defined* by such displays. Numerous theorists, for example, have drawn attention to director Peter Greenaway's use of penises.[51] According to John Walsh, writing for the British newspaper *The Independent*, "Greenaway's fascination with nudity borders on monomaniacal."[52] While the perception of him as *monomaniacal* appears not to concern Greenaway, some directors no doubt would be concerned with such a label.

Another explanation for why male directors might avoid full frontal nudity derives from their concerns with homosexuality or, at least, *homoeroticism*. In Rowe's *Sydney Morning Herald* article about *The Dreamers*, he noted that filmmaking "is still a male-dominated business, and men are more likely to show female nudity."[53] Here, Rowe makes the assumption that filmmakers are most likely to be male heterosexuals, or at least men who prefer looking at the female form. For such directors to include male full frontal nudity, suspicions might then arise about their sexual inclinations. This issue was addressed, albeit cheekily, by Michael Ferguson in his book *Idol Worship*:

> Find a film with lots of male nudity, especially frontal stuff, and you're damned likely to find a gay director ... This isn't to suggest that gay directors are preying upon their male stars any more than hetero directors are preying upon their female stars, just that only gay men are sweet enough and thoughtful enough to think about their brethren out there in the dark waiting for that extra-special moment to take home with them.[54]

It might be speculated that male directors don't want to brand themselves as gay filmmakers and thus avoid the penis display.

HOMOSEXUAL PANIC

Homosexual panic is a legal defense often deployed to try and excuse behavior such as gay bashing: "The term homosexual panic has been loosely defined as a state of rage, mixed with anxiety and tension, experienced by an individual with latent homosexual tendencies and that are aroused by a homosexual advance."[55] As related to a discussion of popular culture, the idea helps explain the anxiety and tensions that are often included in narratives in which men are put in situations where their sexuality is challenged based on the presence of another man's exposed penis.

A scene from *Crazy. Stupid. Love.* (2011), for example, illustrated this point well: Cal (Steve Carell) and Jacob (Ryan Gosling) were in the gym locker-room after their workout. Cal, fully dressed, sat talking to a naked Jacob, who was standing; Jacob's genitals were positioned parallel with Cal's face throughout the scene:

Cal: Could you put on some clothes please?

Jacob: Oh, I'm sorry. Is this bothering you?

Cal: (Sarcastically) No, it's not.

Jacob: Cal, my schvantz is in your face for twenty minutes. If it's not bothering you, we got a bigger problem.

While the audience doesn't see Jacob's penis, Cal does and is forced to confront his discomfort with it—a sentiment Jacob was actually trying to encourage in him, apparently to make him more *manly*.

A similar scene transpired in *Hall Pass* (2011), where penises were actually made visible to the characters *and* the audience. In one scene, Rick (Owen Wilson) fell asleep in a hot tub and was helped to his feet by two naked men; Rick was visibly uncomfortable with having a very large penis in his face.

The discomfort of Cal and Rick in these scenes provides a good insight into why exposed penises are largely absent from the screen: there is an assumption that the heterosexual male audience is made uncomfortable by them. Lehman discussed this idea in his work on male nudity: "the representation of the penis creates a great deal of anxiety for homophobic men who may become intensively disturbed at finding themselves fascinated by it or deriving pleasure form looking at it."[56]

While in this section I propose that being exposed to a bare penis might force a man to confront homosexual feelings and in turn might be anxiety producing, another explanation is that being faced with such a vision may force a man to do a comparison. While Rick might have been uncomfortable having a very large penis in his face for any number of reasons, one is that the size of the other man's penis might have made him feel inferior.

Earlier I quoted Rapping, who identified the reluctance of men to appear naked on screen as indicative of their disinclination to place themselves in a position of being "examined, to be judged."[57] While fear of being scrutinized and assessed likely contributes to some male actors' disinclination to participate in full frontal nudity, it also may explain why male nudity is not frequently included: it is assumed that audiences will, perhaps unhappily, participate in this examination and judgment. Lehman discussed this point: "Men fear that the representation of the penis gives women a basis for comparison and judgment and, although men have long engaged in such behavior toward women, the thought of the tables being turned on them is close to unbearable."[58]

Given that filmmaking is still a male-dominated profession, those involved in the industry are likely considering their own concerns with comparison as well as the concerns of their target audience.

MAINTAINING THE MYSTICISM

Earlier I discussed that the revelation of normal-sized penises on screen will likely prove underwhelming and anticlimactic. This idea alludes to some central facets of filmmaking, whereby tension can often be *destroyed* by a big reveal. In discussing his regrets on including the bus explosion scene in his film *Sabotage* (1936), director Alfred Hitchcock explained: "The bomb should never have gone off. If you build an audience up to that point, the explosion becomes strangely anticlimactic."[59] Tension, allusions, and subtlety have generally been considered Hitchcock trademarks. Hitchcock frequently *alluded to* violence and horror without actually showing it; when he did do so—as in *Sabotage*—he felt that the revelation was anticlimactic.

Similarly, it could be contended that by avoiding actual presentations of a penis, the sexiness and erotic possibilities of a scene are retained without the threatened anticlimax of an actual reveal. When actor Jennifer Love Hewitt discussed her show *The Client List* (2012–), she alluded to this issue: "I think that it's sexier not to show everything. I feel that people's imaginations can do way more."[60] By keeping the penis hidden, there is the possibility of imagining something greater (read: bigger) than the reality. Foster discussed this in her work on nudity, where she contended that maintenance of the penis taboo in Hollywood prevents the "demystification of the penis."[61] The same idea has been echoed by other theorists. Fouz-Hernández and Martinez-Expósito, for example, contended that focusing on buttocks rather than showing full frontal male nudity works to "somewhat preserv[e] the phallic mystique."[62] Lehman similarly noted that "the awe we attribute to the striking visibility of the penis is best served by keeping it covered up."[63]

Keeping the penis obfuscated could be construed as not only about maintaining the mystique of the character or the actor, but of maleness more broadly.

As highlighted in this chapter, full frontal male nudity is indeed identifiable on screen. Of course, while examples are readily sourced, these images are nevertheless *rare*: exposed penises might be everywhere in pornography but in mainstream cinema they are inevitably avoided or shown only briefly. By eschewing the bare penis or by presenting male nudity with strategically placed props, the idea that audiences should not be exposed to the penis is reinforced, as is the idea that the penis is not suitably attractive to display, in turn raising a number of interesting points about the agendas that maintaining such a taboo serves.

The Circumcision Chapter: Capturing Cuts in Popular Culture

In an episode of *The Late Late Show with Craig Ferguson* (2005–), the host discussed the film *The Changeling* (2008) with actor John Malkovich. Referencing a circumcision-themed plot point, Ferguson remarked, "A movie's not a movie unless you've got a circumcision." While the host was being funny, he also inadvertently highlighted a strange reality: circumcisions *are* a very common screen inclusion. Such a situation is interesting because while in real life the ethics of the practice is heatedly debated—medical historian David Gollaher, for example, dubbed circumcision "the world's most controversial surgery"[1]—on screen the topic is far less contentious. While there are certainly narratives that spotlight the debate—the film *What to Expect When You're Expecting* (2012) is a recent example showcasing parents with differing views—circumcision is more often portrayed as about the finished product and about the *normal* circumcised penis rather than the process. From the demonization of foreskins to the supposed aesthetic superiority of a circumcised penis, this chapter examines the wide range of television and cinema presentations of male circumcision, analyzing the debates surrounding a topic that remains highly controversial *off* screen.

In his discussion of circumcision in popular culture, Hugh Young contended that several themes occur in circumcision presentations, most notably that infant circumcision is presented as *inevitable*.[2] This idea of inevitability—of circumcision being *normal*—is presented on screen in a number of different guises. This chapter begins with its justification on the grounds of circumcision denoting *civility*.

CIRCUMCISION AND CIVILITY

Gollaher reflected on late 19th- and early 20th-century views on circumcision and identified the views that have come to shape popular understanding of the normal—and in turn the *deviant*—penis: "the foreskin ... commonly came to indicate ignorance, neglect, and poverty. As white middle-class Gentiles adopted circumcision, those left behind were immigrants, people of color, the poor, and others at the margins of respectable society. These were the groups imagined to have filthy, malodorous bodies: people who lacked culture, manners, intelligence, and in a word, civilization."[3]

On-screen examples of the class connotations of uncircumcised men are certainly identifiable. In an episode of the sitcom *30 Rock* (2006–2013), for example, the bumpkin character Kenneth (Jack McBrayer) proclaimed, "We Parcells are neither wealthy nor circumcised but we are proud." In an episode of *Sex and the City* (1998–2004), when Charlotte (Kristin Davis) was dating the uncircumcised Mike (Alex Draper), she lamented his foreskin to her friends: "He's a nice WASPy guy, what went wrong?" Her friend Carrie (Sarah Jessica Parker) speculated, "Maybe his parents were hippies." In the Mexican roadtrip film *Y tu mamá también* (*And Your Mother Too!*) (2001), Tenoch (Diego Luna) referred to Julio (Gael García Bernal)—whose penis was intact—as "white trash" and "a peasant." In each of these examples, the foreskin was associated with a lack of refinement: something must be "wrong"—poverty or antiestablishment values, for example—that would justify parents not circumcising a son.

In real life, circumcision does indeed have deep class connections. Physician Morris Sorrells noted that circumcision has always been far more common among middle- and upper-class families. He suggested that part of this trend can be explained by the middle-class preoccupation with *conformity*.[4] The idea of the middle class being comparatively more concerned with what other people think—notably as related to circumcision—is certainly detectable on screen. In *Desperate Housewives* (2004–2012), for example, Bree's (Marcia Cross) justification for supporting circumcision was grounded in conformity: "I do not want our son to be teased for being different. Do you?" Evan (Matthew Morrison) in *What to Expect When You're Expecting* exhibited similar fears, justifying his desire to circumcise as being about not wanting his son teased. The fears harbored by Bree and Evan do actually play out on screen, as evidenced by the abundance of narratives where the uncircumcised penis is repeatedly mocked and maligned. While an uncircumcised penis might not necessarily be something mocked in real life—particularly given *declining* rates of circumcision in the United States[5]—the story told by popular culture seems to indicate that such teasing is inevitable and that Bree's and Evan's fears are well grounded. If we are to believe that Hollywood wants to present the idea that circumcision is the norm—certainly something that Young suggested[6]—then showing characters fearing the negative consequences of failing to circumcise, along with narratives where the foreskin is actually demonized, certainly makes sense.

A similar conformity theme helps interpret scenes whereby the justification for circumcision is grounded in ensuring that a son looks like his father *all over*. In a scene from the comedy *Flirting with Disaster* (1996), while dining in a restaurant, FBI agent Tony (Josh Brolin)—while nursing a baby—asked the baby's parents:

> So where did you folks come down on the big circumcision controversy? 'Cause, you know, there's a movement afoot these days to keep the foreskin and, personally, I think a boy's penis should look just like his father's.

The same idea was alluded to in an episode of sitcom *Scrubs* (2001–2010). Dr. Cox (John C. McGinley) and his wife Jordan (Christa Miller) were arguing, and Cox alluded to his wife having previously won the circumcision debate:

> I mean, come on, Jordan, you haven't let me make one decision about our son. Which is why, by the way, you'll be doing the answering when he asks why daddy's wee-wee doesn't have a turtleneck on it like his.

In another episode of *Scrubs*, new father Mr. Marrick (Don Tiffany) was advocating for his son to be circumcised so that he looked like him; his wife, however, was opposed. Dr. Kelso (Ken Jenkins) reassured him, "Even if your son isn't circumcised, he will still look like you." Mr. Marrick remained unconvinced.

As distinct from Bree's and Evan's concerns that teasing might occur, in these *Scrubs* scenes the anxiety centered on *ego*: that a father attached a sense of esteem to his penis and wanted to ensure that his son's penis resembled his own. These fathers apparently considered their own penis as something special—they attached some sense of identity and self to it—and in turn wanted their son to look similar. A noteworthy subversion of this idea occurred in the film *Deconstructing Harry* (1997). In one scene, Hilly (Eric Lloyd) asked his father Harry (Woody Allen), "Dad, why doesn't my penis look like yours?" Harry explained that "it's because your mother and I never had you circumcised." In another scene, Helen (Demi Moore)—Hilly's mother—complained to Harry, "I rue the day that I listened to you and didn't have him circumcised." Helen's quote indicates that it was (seemingly) *Harry's* decision to opt *against* circumcision and in turn *against* having his son look like him. While such a scene might indicate that not all fathers want their sons to have penises that look like theirs—or at least, that not all fathers are *preoccupied* by this—another interpretation is that some fathers, in fact, actively want their son's penises to look different. Like most of Woody Allen's characters, Harry is highly neurotic. Not having Hilly circumcised, therefore, might be read as Harry's attempt to have his son grow up *without* some of his own neuroses—neuroses Harry may have connected to his penis. Certainly the connection between circumcision and neurosis for Jews has been speculated on elsewhere.[7]

The idea of the ego as related to circumcision was also raised in an episode of the U.S. version of the series *Queer as Folk* (2000–2005). Brian (Gale Harold) interrupted the bris of his son—who was being raised by two lesbians, Lindsay (Thea Gill) and Melanie (Michelle Clunie)—and articulated his opposition to the circumcision:

Lindsay: Why does it matter to you if Gus is circumcised?

Brian: It matters that he's been in this world less than a week and already there are people who won't accept him for the way he is. Who'd even mutilate him rather than let him be the way he is. The way he was born. Well, I'm not gonna let that happen.

While Brian might just be expressing his views that circumcision is a form of child abuse, another explanation is that he is simply using the bris as a way to exert his parental rights. Perhaps it is not so much the *circumcision* that he abhors, but rather that his connection to his baby is seemingly slipping from his fingers; stopping the bris is a way for him to be involved; his son's penis, at least, is *something* he can exercise control over. Returning to the feuding parents scenes discussed earlier, this battle could similarly be interpreted as a power-play between parents, as opposed to a true battle over circumcision.

In the Penis Chapter, I discussed the interpretation of penises as being out of control and nonresponsive to instructions. Another reading of Harry's and Brian's reactions in these scenes is that perhaps neurosis-filled Harry and homosexual Brian have deemed their penises as something that they haven't been able to control—that its wants have led to their adult problems. Sparing their sons a circumcision, therefore, enables them to both control someone else's penis—if only temporarily—and facilitate a future where their sons might have more control, or at least not battle the penis-centered demons they have faced themselves.

In Gollaher's explanation of the origins of the class-based connotations of circumcision, he referred to "filthy, malodorous bodies." The idea of circumcision being connected to cleanliness and hygiene is an idea commonly expressed on screen, where civility is presented as synonymous with cleanliness, and by extension the pursuit of cleanliness is something that necessitates circumcision.

CIRCUMCISION AND CLEANLINESS

Hygiene has been a standard justification for circumcision historically, and it is a theme that underpins many screen portrayals. In an episode of *Dexter* (2006–), for example, Mazuka (C. S. Lee)—a character renowned for his "colorful" and explicit language—remarked, "The coroner can suck my uncircumcised penis if he doesn't rule this as a homicide!" That the word *uncircumcised* was added to the typical *suck my dick* insult could be interpreted as a reference to size. It is more likely, however, that Mazuka was suggesting that his foreskin would make sucking his penis a particularly egregious task, that the foreskin makes his penis *disgusting*. While disgust—as related to aesthetics—is addressed later, here I focus on disgust centered on an assumed lack of cleanliness.

Bree defended circumcision in *Desperate Housewives* by claiming, "It's a simple surgery meant to promote lifelong masculine hygiene." In the circumcision-themed episode of the sitcom *Seinfeld* (1990–1998), George (Jason Alexander) defended the practice to Kramer (Michael Richards) by saying, "But Kramer, isn't it a question of hygiene?" In an episode of sitcom *'Til Death* (2006–2010), Kenny (J. B. Smoove) considered having adult circumcision. One of his friends—horrified that Kenny still had his foreskin—commented, "I can't believe you're not taken care of down there. That's disgustin'!" The same idea was apparent in the British film *East Is East* (1999) when Maneer (Emil Marwa) claimed, "Foreskins are dirty."

In an episode of sitcom *Married with Children* (1987–1997), after Al (Ed O'Neill) was mistakenly circumcised, his wife Peggy (Katey Sagal) felt guilty.[8] Neighbor Marcy (Amanda Bearse) reassured Peggy by explaining the benefits of circumcised men: "They're healthier, the sex is better."

Each of these narratives presents the idea that not being *taken care of*—not being circumcised and, therefore, apparently not paying due attention to personal hygiene—is something heinous. In each of these examples, circumcision is assumed to be the *hygienic* option.

Worth noting as related to this issue of civility are the double standards apparent concerning gender. Circumcision is an ancient practice, tracing at least as far back as the Old Testament.[9] While some groups defend its continued practice on the grounds of tradition, an interesting paradox exists where *female* circumcision is widely considered to be barbaric and *antiquated* in modern, civilized society; these are the very same arguments that are used to *defend male* circumcision.[10]

Mentioned several times already—and certainly something alluded to in Mazuka's comments in *Dexter*—is that much of the disgust associated with the foreskin derives from it being considered ugly.

THE AESTHETIC HORROR OF THE FORESKIN

In a scene from *Fargo* (1996), police chief Marge (Frances McDormand) interviewed two prostitutes. One prostitute (Larissa Kokernot) described the suspect as "kinda funny-lookin'." When Marge prompted the woman to be more specific, the prostitute said, "I couldn't really say ... He wasn't circumcised." While it's not entirely clear whether *funny-lookin'* was connected to the man's intact penis, this is certainly one interpretation, and certainly a reading in line with the routine portrayal of the foreskin as something visually repellant. In the aforementioned episode of the sitcom *'Til Death*, Eddie (Brad Garrett) discussed his own penis and claimed that he was "cute as a button down there." Eddie's inference in this scene was that cuteness—aesthetic *tidiness*—was connected to circumcision; he is cute and neat because he has been circumcised. The idea of the foreskin being *funny-looking* and *not cute* is presented frequently in film and television.

In the *Sex and the City* episode discussed earlier, when Charlotte was in bed with Mike for the first time, she reached into his pants:

Charlotte: Oh! You're ... It's ...
Mike: Uncircumcised. Is that okay?
Charlotte: No ... Sure ... Of course it is.

Charlotte, of course, was lying. As Carrie narrated: "It was not okay. The only uncut version of anything Charlotte had ever seen was the original *Gone with the Wind* [1939]." Later Charlotte bemoaned to her friends, "There was so much skin. It was like a shar pei!" and justified her concerns by saying, "Aesthetics are important to me." A similarly negative *shar pei* allusion was made in the series *Nip/Tuck* (2003–2010). When teenaged Matt (John Hensley) and his girlfriend Vanessa (Kate Mara) were about to have sex for the first time, she said, "It looks like a shar pei. Are you part-Arab or something?" In an episode of the British series of *Eastenders* (1985–), Jodie (Kylie Babbington) ran screaming from the bedroom after seeing Darren's (Charlie G. Hawkins) intact penis. In these examples, women rejected men based on their anatomy, notably at a time when penis-related sensitivity was likely heightened.

Such insults occur in a variety of other examples. In the *'Til Death* episode discussed earlier, one of Kenny's friends claimed, "I saw a [uncircumcised] man at the gym once. I almost passed out." In an episode of the reality show *The Simple Life* (2003–2007), Nicole Richie spoke of having once visited a nude beach: "Yeah, and some of the guys were uncircumcised, and it was fucking disgusting." In the aforementioned episode of *Desperate Housewives*, Bree described foreskins as "unsightly." In *Y tu mamá también* (*And Your Mother Too!*), Tenoch claimed that "Julio has a really ugly cock … It looks like a deflated balloon. It has a hood on it; it's really gross."

The episode of *Seinfeld* discussed earlier included a variety of conversations that presented the foreskin as ugly. This transpired, for example, in a conversation between Jerry (Jerry Seinfeld) and his friend Elaine (Julia Louis-Dreyfus):

Elaine: Hey Jerry, you ever seen one?
Jerry: You mean that wasn't uh—
Elaine: Yeah.
Jerry: No. You?
Elaine: Yeah.
Jerry: What'd you think?
Elaine: (Shakes her head) It had no face, no personality. It was like a Martian. But hey, you know that's me.

Later Elaine and Kramer discussed the uncircumcised penis:

Elaine: Hey have you ever seen one of those?
Kramer: No.
Elaine: Well I have and believe me, it's no picnic.

The same theme was evident when George and Kramer spoke about it:

Jerry: Hey George, have you ever seen one?
George: Yeah, my roommate in college.

Jerry: So what'd you think?

George: I got used to it.

In the horror film *Hostel* (2005), the Scandinavian character Oli (Eythor Gudjonsson) offered to show Josh (Derek Richardson) his newly shaved scrotum. Josh responded, "You're not ... no ... I'm good, I'm good. Put your anteater away. It's totally creepy."

In each of these examples, the circumcised penis was presented as unsightly and, apparently, as *uncommon*. When characters were exposed to uncircumcised penises, they were seemingly shocked and appalled; evidently exposure to the intact penis was something they needed to *get used to*.

While the horror of the foreskin is one way to convey the notion that uncircumcised penises are aesthetically preferable, this can also be accomplished by sexualizing the circumcised penis. In *State and Main* (2000), for example, Claire (Sarah Jessica Parker) asked Joe (Philip Seymour Hoffman) whether he was Jewish. He said that he was and Claire cooed, "I love Jewish men." When Joe asked why, she said, "You know why." The inference here is that because Joe was Jewish and because Jewish men are (often) circumcised,[11] he matched her aesthetic preference.

One interpretation of this narrative theme is that it works to reiterate that the circumcised penis is the *normal penis*; those who deviate are abnormal, are heinous. Such an idea may also contribute to the middle-class anxieties discussed earlier, whereby parents fear that their son will be mocked for his foreskin. Another interpretation is while the real-life rates of circumcision in the United States are declining, the fact that characters find the foreskin horrible—notably that *women* find it so—is certainly in line with popular sentiments. A small amount of research, for example, contends that women prefer a circumcised penis; this preference is grounded in the idea that such penises apparently look cleaner and sexier and feel nicer to touch.[12] It could be contended that such presentations reflect the reality of women's aesthetic preference, or at the very least, the *cultural myth* that such preferences exist based upon repetition of this idea; the latter is something discussed in Young's work.[13]

An undercurrent of Claire and Joe's exchange in *State and Main* is the contention that there is something sexy about a circumcised man, or at least something particularly desirable about having sex with him.

CIRCUMCISION AND SEXUAL PROWESS

Discussed earlier were Marcy's comments in *Married with Children* about circumcision being something that adds to the sexual pleasure for women; Marcy was implying that men last longer because they are less sensitive, the inference being that lasting longer is a good thing. This *reduced sensitivity* issue is also alluded to other narratives. In *East Is East*, for example, when Meenah (Archie Panjabi) asked her brother Tariq (Jimi Mistry), "Why do they cut it off?," he responded, "It lessens the feeling in y'knob." The same idea was alluded to in an episode of *Weeds* (2005–2012), when Shane (Alexander Gould) contended that circumcision "decreases pleasure." This issue was also referred to by Orson (Kyle MacLachlan) in *Desperate Housewives*, who claimed, "It's a traumatic procedure, which reduces the male's capacity for sexual pleasure by desensitizing the tip." Kramer on *Seinfeld* made the same claim: "Besides, you know, [the foreskin] makes sex more pleasurable."

While it is certainly possible to construe the desensitizing of the penis as barbaric, the comments of Marcy, Tariq, Shane, and Orson allude to a possible *positive* of the procedure, or at least a popularly construed positive: enhanced sex. When Claire in *State and Main* claimed that she loved Jewish men, one possible interpretation is that she loves them because they are circumcised and because circumcision leads to decreased sensitivity and thus longer-lasting sex.

While in this case Claire was construed as the beneficiary of a circumcision —and certainly Marcy in *Married with Children* implied that Peggy would similarly benefit—the idea that there is also benefit for the man is identifiable. After Mike's adult circumcision in *Sex and the City*, he clearly benefited from a new sexual outlook—so much so that after his circumcision he couldn't commit to Charlotte: "There's a whole new me happening. I should get out there and share it ... I mean I feel like I owe it to myself to take the doggie out for a walk around the block ... you know?" For Mike, the removal of his foreskin sexually liberated him. His foreskin had, seemingly, made him feel self-conscious; thus it came as no surprise that with it gone, he was able to relax and enjoy sex more. Improved sexual self-esteem certainly appeared to motivate Kenny to seek adult circumcision in *'Til Death*. In one scene he spoke about his visions for his life post circumcision: "I'm going to nude beaches, make love with the lights on. I'm gonna get a pair of jeans with a zipper."[14] Certainly enhanced esteem played out for Matt in *Nip/Tuck*: he had already been teased at school and called "Anteater" based on his intact penis; his girlfriend similarly seemed appalled. After Matt had the surgery, he was instantly more sexually confidant. In *Romance and Cigarettes* (2005), Nick (James Gandolfini) got a circumcision, something motivated by his girlfriend's repeated mentions of his foreskin. After his circumcision the two had passionate sex. This outcome might be attributable to the removal of his foreskin or, at the very least, to his girlfriend's enthusiasm and flattery that he did this for her.

The idea that the circumcised penis is normal, that it boasts hygiene benefits, that it is aesthetically preferable, and that it enhances sexual performance underpins another theme identifiable in circumcision narratives, whereby adult men undergo the procedure *electively*.

ADULT CIRCUMCISION

In an episode of sitcom *Dharma & Greg* (1997–2002), at one point Dharma (Jenna Elfman) decided against circumcising her newborn son and instead thought she would let him decide for himself. Her mother-in-law Kitty (Susan Sullivan) rebuffed this idea, contending that he would never choose to do so himself. Dharma ended up circumcising her son. While Kitty's point—that circumcision would be something that no man would ever *choose* for himself—might be largely accurate, there are nevertheless numerous examples of adult men *electively* going under the knife on screen.

In *Undressed* (1999–2002), Brett's (Wolé Parks) girlfriend was unimpressed with his foreskin. Her attitude prompted him to seriously consider adult circumcision. Discussed earlier was the episode of *'Til Death*: Kenny got a circumcision after his girlfriend saw his intact penis and considered it as ugly. The same thing transpired in *Sex and the City*: Mike ended up getting a circumcision after Charlotte's unfavorable reaction—a reaction we assume he had experienced with other women, too. This theme—of men getting circumcisions for displeased women—is identifiable in many narratives. Discussed earlier was the storyline in the U.K. soap *Eastenders* in which Darren's girlfriend ran screaming from the room after seeing his penis, in turn prompting him to get circumcised. While being teased at school contributed to his foreskin-related low self-esteem, it was Matt's girlfriend Vanessa's negative reaction on *Nip/Tuck* that motivated Matt's circumcision. In *Romance and Cigarettes*, Nick similarly got his circumcision after his girlfriend kept mentioning his foreskin.

While adult circumcision narratives can be construed as being underpinned by men's internalized middle-class anxieties and their desire to be "normal," there are other ways to interpret these scenes. In each of the aforementioned examples, the adult men were motivated to have their surgeries because of women—more specifically, because of *women's* displeasure. Such scenes, therefore, can be construed as attempts to cast women as not merely exhibiting an aesthetic preference for the circumcised penis, but being shallow and demanding to the extent that they would encourage their partner to pursue *surgery*. In presenting women as proverbial *ball-breakers*, however, worth considering is whether those men who acquiesce to the demands of their girlfriends are perceived as weak-willed. While the women in these scenes seemed largely flattered that their men would go to such lengths for them, nevertheless, that a man would actually have part of his penis removed for a woman casts him as someone who, while not necessarily *pussy-whipped*, is certainly evidently *swayed* by her.

While Matt on *Nip/Tuck* ended up getting a surgical circumcision, he initially attempted to perform his circumcision *himself*: his desire to be free of his foreskin was so strong that he attempted to perform the procedure with a pair of nail scissors. This idea of men so desperately wanting to be circumcised that they undertake the procedure themselves is identifiable in a number of narratives.

Self-Circumcision

In an episode of the sitcom *The Office* (2005–2013), Dwight (Rainn Wilson) claimed to have performed his own circumcision as a baby. While audiences might infer that Dwight was being hyperbolic—if not blatantly *lying*—as shown in *Nip/Tuck*, male characters have indeed been known to attempt self-circumcision. In *Drowning by Numbers* (1988), the disturbed boy Smut (Jason Edwards) circumcised himself after a girl suggested that a circumcised penis was desirable. In an episode of *ER* (1994–2009), a young man (Drew Ebersole) was admitted to a hospital after trying to cut his foreskin off to please his female partner; as in *Nip/Tuck*, the procedure then needed to be performed surgically in the hospital. In an episode of *House* (2004–2012), a man (Randall Park) also tried to circumcise himself, again for the benefit of his girlfriend who had never been with a circumcised man. While the man botched the surgery, unlike in the *ER* episode, Dr. House (Hugh Laurie) did not finish the task surgically; instead, he arranged for a plastic surgeon to put the "Twinkie back in the wrapper." The enormously strong desire for circumcision among these men likely gives some credence to Young's idea that the inevitably *positive* portrayal of the circumcised penis in American popular culture influences audiences' perceptions of what constitutes normal.

Discussed earlier was the perception of adult men who get circumcisions as weak-willed. For those men who try to do the circumcision themselves, rather than merely being pussy-whipped, they are construed as—in the case of Smut—psychotic, or at the very least as weird or naïve, if not completely *stupid*.

Also worth considering is whether these scenes may be about horror rather than taking a stance on circumcision: they tap into men's fears of castration by showing the horror of botched circumcisions. Instead of dealing with the politics of circumcision, these scenes are more about the scariness of blades being placed near men's genitals. Interestingly, the idea that for adult men blades near penises is frightening, but the same thing is somehow perfectly justifiable for babies, highlights a double standard that is effortlessly detected on screen. Indeed, circumcision is presented as justifiable for babies because, apparently, the pain is quickly forgotten.

CIRCUMCISIONS AND PASSING PAIN

In a circumcision-themed episode of the sitcom *Being Erica* (2009–), Erica (Erin Karpluk) vocally opposed circumcision. Erica's best friend Ethan (Tyron Leitso) argued with her, defending the procedure by saying, "So, it's two seconds. Who cares?" The idea of the pain being something temporary is strongly connected to the screen presentation of circumcision being—at least for babies—routine and without lasting negative effect. In an episode of *Judging Amy* (1999–2005), for example, the judge (Amy Brenneman) granted permission to a father who wanted to circumcise his son; as Amy explained to the opposing mother: "It's a standard medical procedure; it's done all the time. It's relatively short and painless." The same argument was mounted by Bree in *Desperate Housewives*: "That's why the procedure should be done on babies; they won't remember." In an episode of sitcom *The Big Bang Theory* (2007–), the fleeting nature of circumcision pain was briefly alluded to: the Jewish character Howard (Simon Helberg) exclaimed, "Ouch! Damn! Paper cut! Nothing worse than a paper cut!" His Hindu friend, Raj (Kunal Nayyar), responded, "Well, obviously you don't remember your circumcision." The same idea was also apparent in the comedy *But I'm a Cheerleader* (1999) when, in a group therapy session, the characters were asked to speculate on the root of their homosexuality. Joel (Joel Michaely) offered, "traumatic bris." The other characters gave other seemingly stupid reasons—for example, "I was born in France"—with the inference being that the idea of an adult remembering his bris is laughable.

While such presentations can be construed as reiterating the point that circumcision is normal—as well as working to justify its continuation by downplaying a baby's pain (in turn distancing it from the barbarism that opponents often try to associate with it)—another interpretation is that these scenes are indicative of *gallows humor*. Gallows humor is about finding the funny side of an inevitably bad situation; the gallows refers to hanging and thus focuses on finding humor in something awful, such as an execution. This is certainly Young's reading of the bris episode of *Seinfeld*: even though the bris is botched and Jerry—who was holding the baby—ended up having *his* finger circumcised instead of the baby's penis, there is an air of inevitably to it. All the men in the episode *had* been circumcised themselves; while the experience might be awful, the characters were largely resigned to it because circumcision is what *has* to be done, because it is what's *normal*.[15]

Thus far I have focused on presentations that depict the circumcised penis as normal and preferable and, in turn, foreskins as ugly and unhygienic. In the next section I explore narratives whereby the situation is presented as less clear-cut. From narratives focused on dueling parents to those presenting circumcision as barbaric, the remainder of this chapter highlights narratives that are less obvious about support for circumcision, and instead spotlight the contestation.

TO CIRCUMCISE OR NOT CIRCUMCISE

The *'Til Death* episode discussed earlier was titled "Circumdecision": for Kenny, as an adult, the decision of whether to circumcise needed to be made very carefully. While in the previous section I discussed narratives that presented circumcision as routine and noncontroversial, an equally wide variety of media depictions present the *circumdecision* as heatedly debated. Mentioned in the introduction was the film *What to Expect When You're Expecting*: in it, two parents argued about whether to circumcise their unborn child (assuming it was a son). The mother's anticircumcision opinions were so strong that she appeared on the front of health magazine opposing the practice (in turn, causing dramatic conflict in her relationship). The *to circumcise or not circumcise* debate plays out in a number of other narratives.

The *Desperate Housewives* episode mentioned throughout this chapter focused on Bree and Orson arguing about whether they should get their grandson circumcised. In the episode Orson mentioned how his own parents had disagreed about his circumcision. In the *Scrubs* episode, the Marricks argued about whether to circumcise their son, as apparently did Dr. Cox and Jordan. In the series *thirtysomething* (1987–1991), Hope (Mel Harris) and Michael (Ken Olin) argued about the circumcision of their newborn son. In the aforementioned episode of *Queer as Folk*, Brian argued with the mother of his son, Lindsay, about whether their son should be circumcised. In an episode of *ER*, new parents Carla (Lisa Nicole Carson) and Peter (Eriq La Salle) had the circumcision fight, as did Kevin (Stephen Rannazzisi) and Jenny (Katie Aselton) in *The League* (2009–) and Bessie (Nina Repeta) and Bodi (Obi Ndefo) in *Dawson's Creek* (1998–2003).

The circumcision debate can be an obvious way to present tension between new parents. Despite this wonderful new birth, it seems, some kind of conflict needs to enter the narrative to make it interesting; the circumcision debate is one way to provide this conflict. Something particularly interesting, however, is that in a number of these examples it is *women* who are the vocal opponents of circumcision: the mother in *Judging Amy*, Bessie in *Dawson's Creek*, Jordan and Mrs. Marrick in *Scrubs*, and Jules (Cameron Diaz) in *What to Expect When You're Expecting* each opposed the procedure. In an episode of sitcom *Arrested Development* (2003–), it was similarly Lindsay (Portia de Rossi) who got involved with a group called HOOP, an acronym for Hands Off Our Penises. Of course, if two people are debating the issue, there is a 50/50 chance as to who will oppose the procedure—after all, there wouldn't be a conflict if the parents didn't disagree—but it is interesting that women would take such an impassioned stance. If the father is advocating for a circumcision, it is highly likely he has had one himself and thus the mother is, presumably, having sex with a circumcised man; she has at least *tacitly* supported circumcision. Such examples might work to disprove the assumption that women actually prefer the circumcised penis, but more often these depictions represent mothers embodying maternal virtues—namely, that a mother is supposed to want to protect her baby from physical harm. A female character's stance on circumcision can, therefore, give insight into the values of that character. When Bree secretly got her grandson circumcised (by *lying* to a mohel that she was Jewish), she was portrayed as domineering, duplicitous, and not stereotypically *motherly*. This reading equally applies to the lesbian mothers in the *Queer as Folk* scene discussed earlier, who might be construed as eschewing traditional gender norms related to motherhood—if not also engaging in some symbolic castration—through their decision to circumcise their son.

In these examples, circumcision is presented as contentious. In the next section I focus on examples where it is presented as *barbaric*.

THE BARBARIC CUT

The idea of circumcision being something cruel is apparent in a number of narratives. In this section I explore (1) those that present circumcision as something barbaric and anachronistic and (2) those in which characters openly consider the procedure as a kind of *abuse*.

The Anachronism of Circumcision

Earlier I discussed the paradox of differing attitudes toward male and female circumcision based on tradition. The idea of male circumcision as being anachronistic is certainly identifiable on screen. In a scene from the comedy *Year One* (2009), the biblical character Abraham (Hank Azaria) proclaimed that he would circumcise himself as well as Zed (Jack Black), Oh (Michael Cera), and Isaac (Christopher Mintz-Plasse), along with the other males:

Abraham: Therefore, to signify my covenant with the one true God, I shall on this day circumcise the flesh of my penis. And of you. And you, and of you, and every male who dwelleth hereby.

Zed: Excuse me?

Oh: I don't know what you mean.

Abraham: We shall grasp the foreskins of our penises and we shall cut therefrom the extra flesh. Amen.

Zed: Oh. I don't think I have any extra.

Oh: Couldn't we pierce our ears or something?

Abraham: No, no, no. So it shall be written, and so it shall be done.

Zed: Let me get this straight. You're saying you have too much and you want to—(makes a scissors hand gesture). And you wanna... You know, Abe, it's been a long day, we've all had a lot to drink. And I know that this foreskin thing sounds like a good idea now but you might wanna sleep on it. We can always cut it off in the morning. But if we do it now, there's just no way to get it back on there.

Abraham: No, no, no, trust me, it's gonna be a very, very sleek look. This is gonna catch on. I'm gonna go get my good knife. Just wait right there. I'll be right back to cut your penises. Not the whole thing, you understand. Just the very tip. And after, we're all gonna have wine and sponge cake.

Zed and Oh hurriedly escape and hear Isaac screaming in pain.

The same anachronism theme was alluded to in the bris episode of *Seinfeld*, when Kramer (Michael Richards) discussed circumcision with Elaine and new father Stan (Tom Allan Robbins):

Kramer: A bris? You mean snip snip?

Stan: Yeah.

Kramer: I would advise against that.

Elaine: It's a tradition.

Kramer: Well, so was sacrificing virgins to appease the gods, but we don't do that anymore.

The antiquated notion of the practice was also referred to in the same *Seinfeld* episode when the mohel (Charles Levin) tried—unconvincingly—to justify the practice: "This is a bris. An ancient, sacred ceremony, symbolizing the covenant between God and Abraham ... or something."[16]

In another *Seinfeld* episode, the bris was likened to another outdated practice, a *public execution*:

Elaine: I could've been at my boss's son's bris right now.
George: You're supposed to do that?
Elaine: Yeah. What makes you think anyone would want to go to a circumcision?
George: I'd rather go to a hanging.

In each of these examples—with varying degrees of seriousness—the idea presented is that circumcision is something from the past and not relevant to contemporary culture. In *Year One*, Abraham was presented as thoroughly ridiculous and—as evidenced by the bemusement *and* terror of Zed, Oh, and Isaac—the idea that the practice might *catch on* seemed laughably preposterous. Of course, tapping into the gallows humor discussed earlier is the idea that while the practice might appear cruel and horrible—certainly so if presented in the *wine and sponge cake* way that Abraham did—there is nevertheless some inevitability about it. When presented as a skit as in *Year One*, it might seem ridiculous; several thousand years on, however, and Zed, Oh, and Isaac's horrified reactions in fact seem more unusual than the desire for the "sleek" look that Abraham promised.

In an episode of the British sitcom *'Til Death Do Us Part* (1965–1975), Warren (Alf Garnett) remarked, "It's y'Jews, innit ... getting their tribal mutilations on the NHS [National Health Service]." The depiction of circumcisions as *tribal* is an idea that reflects the notion that they are outdated, but it is Warren's *mutilations* description that notably alludes to another popular way that anticircumcision narratives are presented: by depicting the practice as *child abuse*.

Circumcision and Child Abuse

In *Desperate Housewives*, Orson stated that he didn't want to attend the bris of a friend's baby: "I just don't care to watch them ritually mutilate their child." In an episode of *Weeds*, Shane referred to circumcision as "a barbaric ritual." In *Dawson's Creek*, Bessie termed circumcision "barbaric" and a "human rights issue." In *Being Erica*, the title character opposed circumcision, claiming, "I don't know why I'm the only one who thinks that circumcising a baby is brutal, violent, and wrong." In the *Judging Amy* episode, the mother raged against circumcision, arguing, "You're mutilating my son!" and "It's child abuse!" In the bris episode of *Seinfeld*, Kramer claimed:

> Don't believe them when they tell you it doesn't hurt. It hurts bad. It hurts really bad. Imagine, this will be his first memory. Of someone yanking the hat off his little man. I know you love your baby, but what kind of perverts would stand idly by while a stranger rips the cover off his 9-iron and then serves a catered lunch?

Kramer actually attempted to kidnap the baby to protect his foreskin. Something similar happened in an episode of the sitcom *Cheers* (1982–1993), when Frasier (Kelsey Grammer) whisked his son away before he could be circumcised. In each of these examples, characters—both of whom were circumcised themselves—expressed vocal opposition to circumcision, framing the practice as heinous and as a form of child abuse.

What is most interesting in these cases is that in *Desperate Housewives*, *Being Erica*, *Seinfeld*, and *Cheers*, the bris actually went ahead. In *Judging Amy*, the judge ruled in favor of the father who wanted to circumcise, implying that this procedure would eventually transpire. Despite the protests and theatrics, all of the boys were circumcised in these episodes. One interpretation of these examples is that while the narratives highlighted that the topic can be divisive, circumcision was still presented as the *right* thing to do, even if it was acknowledged that it is not entirely pleasant. Worth noting, Frasier was presented as acting irrationally when he tried to kidnap his son and Kramer throughout *Seinfeld* was always presented as harebrained. The impulsiveness and craziness of these characters devalue the strength of their anticircumcision positions, if not also present them as laughable and notably as *immature*.

Connected to the idea of the pain of circumcision are narratives centered on those occasions when circumcisions go wrong.

THE BOTCHED CIRCUMCISION

In the bris episode of *Seinfeld*, Jerry's finger was cut instead of the baby's foreskin. Jerry later called the mohel "Butcher Boy," the inference being that the mohel was savage and incompetent. In *Seinfeld* the botched circumcision was presented as funny—a style similar to the framing of botched circumcisions in the series *Californication* (2007–) and in the film *Meet the Fockers* (2004). In *Californication*, Charlie (Evan Handler) argued with Hank (David Duchovny), contending, "How many times I got to tell you, I am not uncircumcised! The mohel left just a little too much foreskin, just a smidge." In *Meet the Fockers*, Gaylord's (Ben Stiller) parents told the story of their son's botched bris: "he wound up with a semicirc," apparently "a cross between an anteater and a German Army helmet."

Interestingly, while technically botchings, these narratives nevertheless function less as indictments of circumcision—in each narrative the man survived and thus the necessity of circumcision was maintained—and more as a source of comedy. Insulting a man by making negative reference to his penis is an obvious gag.[17] In *Californication* and *Meet the Fockers*, the humor was premised on the thoroughly bizarre thought of a half-circumcised penis; it was a reason to see the character as pitiful rather than to create any lasting doubt about the sense of the procedure. (The comedy here is reminiscent of Ted's [Ben Stiller] zipper-trapped penis in *There's Something about Mary* [1998], discussed in the Penis Chapter.) The botched circumcision joke is also detectable in a scene from *Samurai Cop* (1989). The title character (Matt Hannon) was propositioned by a nurse and circumcision became the basis for a size-themed slur:

Nurse: Would you like to fuck me?

Joe: Bingo.

Nurse: Well then, let's see what you've got … (Squeezes his genitals) Doesn't interest me. Nothing there.

Joe: Nothing there? Just exactly what would interest you? Something the size of a jumbo jet?

Nurse: Have you been circumcised?

Joe: Yeah I have, why?

Nurse: Well your doctor must have cut a big portion of it off.

While less about appearance and more about size, the theme of circumcision as a way to emasculate a man is evident.

While in these examples the botched circumcision was presented as funny, in episodes of *Chicago Hope* (1994–2000) and *Law and Order: Special Victims Unit* (1999–), the botched circumcision was actually presented as something much more tragic. In the hospital drama *Chicago Hope*, a patient sought reconstructive surgery: it was discovered that the doctor—when performing his circumcision—actually removed his penis in its entirety.

Something similar transpired in *Law and Order: Special Victims Unit*: a botched circumcision coerced parents to remove the mutilated penis of their baby son and raise him as a daughter. While these botched circumcision scenes showcased a dramatic downside of the procedure, both were presented as isolated incidents—something that likely mitigated just how much of a political message was being transmitted.

In psychologist Mark Blumberg's research, he contended, "With so many circumcisions performed each year by physicians and non-physicians alike, it is inevitable that some will be botched."[18] Here, Blumberg highlighted a reality that all medical procedures are subject to varying degrees of danger; even circumcision—a rarely dangerous procedure—has an element of risk and, while rare, mistakes occur. Neither *Chicago Hope* nor *Law and Order: Special Victims Unit* implied that circumcisions were inherently dangerous; rather, they focused on cases—each presented as isolated—where the outcomes were horrific. In fact, in both cases the botched circumcisions had transpired years prior, implying that such errors are associated with *historic* malpractice and are substantially less relevant concerns today.

While the botched circumcision narrative might be considered as putting a slight chink in the armor of the circumcised norm, this is done much more obviously—and notably more *convincingly*—in narratives where the intact penis is something actually *celebrated*.

THE SEXUALIZED FORESKIN

Discussed earlier were scenes where women expressed horror at the sight of the intact penis. In this section I present the counter case: narratives where the intact penis is actually considered as aesthetically pleasing. In a scene from *Wassup Rockers* (2005), for example, Jade (Laura Cellner) was about to have sex with Jonathan (Jonathan Velasquez). When Jonathan's pants came off, the following dialogue transpired:

> Jade: You're not circumcised.
> Jonathan: No. I'm Latino. Why? Do I look different?
> Jade: Looks dangerous!

Jade smirked, appeared impressed and the two continued kissing.

In *Undressed*—discussed earlier—Annie (Rachelle Lafevbre) asked to see her friend Brett's uncircumcised penis, claiming she hadn't seen one before. He showed her, she said it was beautiful, and they had sex. In *Arrested Development*, Lindsay articulated her support for the intact penis at a

HOOP meeting, claiming, "I think it looks frightening when it's cut off. It's a Doberman; let it have its ears!" Discussed already in this chapter was Julio and Tenoch teasing each other about their respective penises in *Y tu mamá también* (*And Your Mother Too!*). After Tenoch maligned Julio's uncircumcised penis, Luisa (Maribel Verdú) responded, "Mmm, yummy. Foreskins. I love them!" In the aforementioned episode of *Sex and the City*, Samantha (Kim Cattrall) expressed great enthusiasm for the intact penis: "Personally, I love an uncircumcised dick. It's like a Tootsie Pop. Hard on the outside, with a delicious surprise inside." Later, she said, "Uncut men are the best. They try harder."

These scenes could be interpreted as testifying to the fact that women don't necessarily have an aesthetic preference for the circumcised penis, as is often assumed. One problem with such a contention, however, is that the women in these scenes aren't merely expressing a tolerance for the intact penis but are actually *celebrating* it: they seem to find it *particularly* attractive. Two possible explanations for this idea proposed in this section are that the intact penis is presented as (1) something exotic and (2) something larger in size.

The Exotically Uncut

In an episode of sitcom *Two and a Half Men* (2003–), Evelyn (Holland Taylor) discussed her love of travel: "Yes, I love it. The classical architecture, the exotic cuisine, the uncircumcised men ... Although one could make a case that falls under exotic cuisine." In the comedy *Harold and Kumar Escape from Guantanamo Bay* (2008), Kumar (Kal Penn) teased Harold (John Cho) about the object of his affection—who was on holiday in Europe—by saying, "Right now, she's probably got two uncircumcised dicks dangling in front of her throat." In *Jennifer's Body* (2009), Needy (Amanda Seyfried) commented, "There's Ahmet, the exchange student from India." Jennifer (Megan Fox) responded, "I wonder if he's circumcised. I've always wanted to try a sea cucumber." In each of these examples, the intact penis was construed as something sexy and exotic.

For women who have only—or mostly—been exposed to circumcised penises, the intact penis might seem foreign, exciting, or—as Jade in *Wassup Rockers* claimed—*dangerous*. In a world where there is a preoccupation with hygiene and cleanliness, sex with an uncircumcised penis might seem like a renegade detour. In my book *Part-Time Perverts: Sex, Pop Culture, and Kink Management*, I discussed this idea as connected to sexual tourism: "Sex can function as a vacation or retreat, but sex—notably perverse sex—can also be a destination; as a place to go to experience something very distanced from normal life."[19]

An assumption in each of the aforementioned scenes is that the uncircumcised penis is exotic. Exoticness, however, is a quality that can exist only if it is not experienced regularly. Thus, while the intact penises in these scenes are presented as sexy, their sexiness primarily derives from their *unusualness*. Such an interpretation, therefore, paints circumcision as a norm, a standard, and implies that the intact penis is merely a detour or a fetish. This interpretation is further bolstered by the fact that all of the women expressing delight in an intact penis were sexually liberated characters, implying that an intact penis was just another thing on their list of sexual things they'd like to try.

The Size Thing

In *Y tu mamá también* (*And Your Mother Too!*), after being teased about his foreskin by Tenoch, Julio claimed that his friend was just jealous " 'cause I'm bigger." In a scene from *Quinceañera* (2006), Gary (David W. Ross) boasted about the penis size of a recent lover: "Yeah, and he's 8 inches uncut." In the Australian film *The Adventures of Priscilla, Queen of the Desert* (1994), Mitzi (Hugo Weaving) and Bernadette (Terence Stamp) discussed Bernadette's deceased partner "Trumpet." Bernadette explained the origins of the nickname: "Trumpet didn't have a single musical bone in his body. No, Trumpet had an unusually large foreskin. So large, in fact, that he could wrap the entire thing around a Monte Carlo biscuit."

In these examples, characters are presented as eroticizing the size of the uncut penis. Highlighted is the very simple appeal of the uncircumcised penis: it is marginally bigger than the circumcised penis. This appetite for a bigger penis has prompted men in real life to engage in a variety of lengthening and widening procedures, but can also be construed as one explanation for men pursuing foreskin restoration. Among the supposed benefits of restoration—along with increased sensitivity—are increases in length and girth. Culturally the large penis is something widely considered as desirable by both men and women. When a man goes through foreskin restoration, evidently he is attempting to emulate what the intact man has: *more penis*.

As discussed in this chapter, many adult male characters have pursued circumcision; despite what Kitty suggested in *Dharma and Greg*, such characters *did* choose to have their foreskin removed. At the opposite end of the spectrum are male characters who lamented the *loss* of the foreskin and who—with varying degrees of seriousness—sought its return.

FORESKIN RESTORATION

In the film *28 Days* (2000), in a scene at the rehabilitation clinic, a woman found a stray eyelash and insisted everyone make a wish. One patient, Gerhardt (Alan Tudyk), wished for "My foreskin back. No one asked before they took it; they just took it. They had no right to take it." The other characters guffawed; patient Oliver (Mike O'Malley), for example, remarked, "Way to share, Gerhardt, way to share." The scene, and notably Gerhardt's comments, seemed farcical and reminiscent of the "traumatic bris" mentioned in *But I'm a Cheerleader*. In *A Very Harold and Kumar Christmas* (2011), the character Goldstein (David Krumholtz)—a Jew who recently converted to Christianity—claimed, "Next week I have an appointment to get uncircumcised. That's right, I'm gonna get my schnozzle." In an episode of the hospital drama *St. Elsewhere* (1982–1988), Victor (Todd Susman) was a patient seeking foreskin reconstruction. In an episode of the series *Children's Hospital* (2008–), Owen (Rob Huebel) wanted a foreskin restoration; at one point he screamed at the doctor, "Stop talking and start sewing that deli meat on." In the New Zealand medical soap *Shortland Street* (1992–), Rex (Alvin Fitisemanu) actually had a foreskin graft.[20]

There are a number of ways to interpret these scenes. First, in line with the scene from *But I'm a Cheerleader* discussed earlier, the idea that circumcised men really feel aggrieved at not having a foreskin—and that there could possibly be any long-term consequences of circumcision—is presented as laughable. Second, even in the comparatively more serious examples such as *St. Elsewhere*, the patient was presented as peculiar for even wanting a foreskin. Such narratives, therefore, tend not to actually demonize the circumcision, but rather focus on pathologizing the man who wants a foreskin as though he is somehow developmentally stunted. Just as Frasier and Kramer were presented as foolish to try and kidnap babies to spare them from circumcisions, the men in these scenes were interpreted as idiots, further legitimizing circumcision as the norm.

In real life, circumcision is highly contested in the United States and rates of this procedure are declining. While the debate is sometimes hashed out on screen as in *Scrubs* or *What to Expect When You're Expecting*, circumcision is generally presented as the norm and the aesthetic standard and intact penises are presented as hideous at worst and a novelty at best.

The Vibrator Chapter: That Buzzing Sound in Film and Television

In the pilot episode of the television series *The Unusuals* (2009), Detective Casey Shraeger (Amber Tamblyn) defensively claimed, "I have secrets," to which her colleague Detective Jason Walsh (Jeremy Renner) responded, "A vibrator in your bedside table is *not* a secret." Here, Walsh implied vibrators are no longer an enormous taboo or source of shame, but instead are something common, if not completely *normal*. Certainly examples from popular culture could be used to substantiate this case. In the first season of *Sex and the City* (1998–2004), Charlotte (Kristin Davis) got her first vibrator—The Rabbit—which led to it becoming the world's best-selling sex toy.[1] In 2005, Siobhan Fahey had a song "Pulsatron," which was an ode to her vibrator. By 2010, vibrators hit primetime when Trojan began advertising its new Tri-Phoria "massager." In 2011, a feature film about the history of the vibrator—*Hysteria* (2011)—first screened.

While these are examples of vibrators leaving sex shops and pornography and entering the mainstream—notably in a sex-positive way—to contend that vibrators are no longer controversial would be premature. Although vibrators may no longer be a secret—in fact they are actually common and one of the most popular items in a multimillion-dollar sex industry—this does not mean they are without controversy. Vibrators have an inextricable link to female masturbation, a topic that remains shrouded in cultural anxieties. While positive portrayals of vibrators might exist, equally widespread are examples where their connotations are more negative and associated with embarrassment and loneliness. In this chapter, the range of vibrator presentations are explored, highlighting that while examples are easily sourced, rarely is the presentation incidental.

VIBRATOR EUPHEMISMS

In the Euphemisms Chapter, I discussed the sex-themed euphemisms frequently deployed to enable uncomfortable topics to be discussed. Just as the Tri-Phoria was advertised using the phrase *vibrating massager*, euphemisms are a common way vibrators are presented on screen. In an episode of *Mad Men* (2008–), for example, the "Electrosizer" was a vibrating weight-loss gizmo that Peggy (Elisabeth Moss) was assigned to market. After trying it on, Peggy soon realized that the belt was actually far more marketable as a sex toy. Explaining this to her colleagues—given that it was the 1960s—proved difficult. Peggy stammered through a euphemistic explanation to her boss: "You definitely feel something ... that I think some women ... would like to feel." In an episode of sitcom *How I Met Your Mother* (2005–), instead of using the word *vibrator*, Barney (Neil Patrick Harris) used the elaborate—and funnier—expression "a battery-powered adult recreational fake penis" to discuss a vibrator purchased for a bachelorette party.

In an episode of *Sex and the City*, Samantha (Kim Cattrall) attempted to do a store return at The Sharper Image. This scene highlighted the clerk's (Peter Ratray) penchant for avoiding saying—or even *hearing*—the word *vibrator* and the use of one of the most common euphemisms—the *neck massager*:

  Clerk: Can I help you?
Samantha: Yes. I'd like to return this vibrator.
  Clerk: We don't sell vibrators.
Samantha: Yes you do. I bought it here six months ago.
  Clerk: That's not a vibrator. It's a neck massager.

While Samantha—being the most sexually liberal character on the show—was evidently very comfortable speaking frankly about her sex toy, the clerk—be it because he was personally uncomfortable with the word *vibrator* or because it was company policy not to acknowledge retail of a sex toy—preferred to use the euphemism *neck massager*.

The *massager* euphemism was also used in an episode of the sitcom *That '70s Show* (1998–2006), when Eric (Topher Grace) claimed, "Laurie saved up all her money so she could buy a back massager—which isn't fooling anyone, by the way." In *Brown Sugar* (2002), when Francine (Queen Latifah) found her cousin Sidney's (Sanaa Lathan) vibrator, Sidney tried to correct Francine by claiming, "It's a massager from Brookstone." The massager euphemism was humorously *subverted* in an episode of the sitcom *M*A*S*H* (1972–1983). Hawkeye (Alan Alda) watched Margaret (Loretta Swit) using an electric neck massager on Frank's (Larry Linville) neck and commented, "I've always said that behind every great man, there's a woman with a vibrator." A similar subversion transpired in the Taiwanese film *He liu* (*The River*) (1997) when Xiao-Kang (Kang-sheng Lee) used his mother's vibrator on his sore neck.

As discussed in the Euphemisms Chapter, euphemisms provide an opportunity to talk more safely about topics that frequently embarrass. In the context of vibrators, the word is actually much less taboo than what the device is most commonly used for: female masturbation. One way, therefore, that possession of a vibrator gets justified on screen—for example, by Laurie (Lisa Robin Kelly) in *That '70s Show* and by Sidney in *Brown Sugar*—is that the vibrator is not actually used for masturbation at all, rather is deployed for less taboo and more socially palatable purposes such as nonsexual massage. Historian Whitney Strub discussed sex toy retailing and noted that "emphasizing medical or therapeutic validations of such devices serves to reinforce the stigmatization of women's masturbation."[2] The film *Hysteria*—about the invention of the vibrator—notably focused less on the sexual satisfaction aspects of genital stimulation and orgasm and instead honed in on the supposed health benefits. Something similar was explored in the film *The Road to Wellville* (1994), which likewise depicted the Victorian method of electrical genital stimulation for good health. The reality that such devices continue to be marketed this way today serves as testimony to the fact that while we may be growing more comfortable with the existence of vibrators, it is still taboo to frankly discuss their use.[3]

THE VIBRATION ALLUSION

Like many topics discussed in this book, taboo topics are frequently presented in popular culture through allusions rather than explicit displays. It is unsurprising, then, that devices for sexual stimulation are more often referenced *indirectly*: rather than specific references to vibrators, the topic is spoken about using allusions to other objects that might sexually stimulate—notably other objects that *vibrate*—without any allusion to genitals or masturbation. In some of these examples, the reference is relatively subtle. For example, a woman may lean on a washing machine during the spin cycle—something

Betty (January Jones) did in an episode of *Mad Men*. In an episode of the sitcom *Will & Grace* (1998–2006), Jack (Sean Hayes) alluded to having used Will's (Eric McCormack) electric toothbrush for purposes *other* than brushing his teeth. In another episode, Karen (Megan Mullally) mentioned using a pulsating showerhead and described it as "smooth-talking." Something similar transpired in the comedy *The 40-Year-Old Virgin* (2005) when Beth (Elizabeth Banks) used her showerhead *sexually*, as did Diana (Melissa McCarthy) in *Identity Thief* (2013). Without any explicit mention of masturbation, the inference in these scenes is that the toothbrush and showerhead were used for masturbation.

More specific references to the sexual stimulation from vibration are evident in sexualized references to vibrating cellphones. In an episode of sitcom *King of Queens* (1998–2007), for example, Carrie (Leah Remini) asked her husband Doug (Kevin James) whether he received her phone message. Doug replied, "No, my phone's on vibrate. I left it in my pocket, and—do you have a cigarette?" While neither *vibrator* nor *masturbation* was mentioned, the notion of sexual stimulation resulting from something vibrating in a pants pocket provided an allusion to arousal; that Doug requested a postcoital, *postorgasmic* cigarette made this reference even more explicit. In the film *Wasted* (2002), a similar allusion—albeit more explicit—was made by Samantha (Summer Phoenix) when she remarked, "Owen keeps calling me. You know what? I'm gonna put my phone on vibrate—it'll be the most pleasure he's ever given me." The same link was made in *Valentine's Day* (2010): publicist Kara (Jessica Biel) remarked, "My closest relationship is with my BlackBerry; thank God it vibrates!"

In each of these scenes the humor is relatively gentle: each example provides a very tentative acknowledgment that vibrations can be pleasurable without any overt references to masturbation. There are, however, examples when vibrating phones are *actually* used for masturbation. In *Extreme Movie* (2008), Jessica (Rheagan Wallace)—after discovering that the batteries in her vibrator had died—used her mobile phone on the vibrate setting. It got lodged in her vagina, which later prompted her father (James Eckhouse) to ask whether her vagina was ringing. In *The Oh in Ohio* (2006), Priscilla similarly achieved sexual pleasure from her vibrating cell phone. In these scenes, the vibrating phone used for masturbation was less allusion—although it could indeed be interpreted as being a visual allusion to the common vibrating cell phone joke—and instead was an example whereby the euphemism was deployed for humor.

In the Euphemisms Chapter, I discussed occasions where euphemisms are used because they are actually funnier than the more clinical descriptions.

Something similar occurred in the *Extreme Movie* and *Oh in Ohio* scenes: a vibrating cell phone was funnier—and almost *kinkier*—than had an actual sex toy been used. In my book *Part-Time Perverts: Sex, Pop Culture, and Kink Management*, I discussed household objects being reappropriated as sex toys, noting, "for some it might be particularly kinky to use an object out of context."[4] This is certainly one interpretation for the use of cell phones as sex toys in these scenes. This kink factor was further bolstered in *Extreme Movie* when the use of the phone facilitated a situation where Jessica's father queried whether her vagina was ringing—a bawdy joke that would not have been possible had a real sex toy been used.

As discussed throughout this book, taboo topics are frequently made palatable on screen through their presentation in comedies. As noted in the preceding examples, allusions and euphemisms are frequently funny. Comedy, in fact, is a very common way that vibrators appear on screen: as something to laugh at.

VIBRATOR HILARITY

In this section the variety of ways vibrators are presented as funny are explored—from the funniness of their place of purchase to the humorous irritation of their interrupted use.

An obvious way that vibrators can be presented as humorous is through their depiction as couched in a broader joke about the "hilarity" of sex shops. While nowadays such items can be easily procured online, the *show—don't tell* mantra of the screen makes sex shops the preferable visual demonstration of sex toy purchase. A visit to a sex shop offers the opportunity to include the standard "rain-coated" sex shop pervert customer who serves as a predictable source of both loathing and mockery.

In a scene from the sophomoric comedy *The Party Animal* (1985), the sexually inexperienced Pondo (Matthew Causey) visited a sex shop and naively played with the toys, unsure of their function and overwhelmed by their size. The toys were presented as strange, dirty, and depraved. In a scene from *Ghost World* (2001), Enid (Thora Birch) dragged Seymour (Steve Buscemi) into a sex shop; she seemingly had long been curious about visiting. Inside, Enid laughed constantly and claimed, "This place is a total riot!" In a scene from *The Naked Gun 2½: The Smell of Fear* (1991), the investigation led Lieutenant Frank (Leslie Neilsen) and his officers to a sex shop; a similar investigation led Kate (Stana Katic) and Richard (Nathan Fillion) into a sex shop in an episode of *Castle* (2009–). The Norwegian film *Arme Riddere* (*Jackpot*) (2011) opened with a shootout at a sex shop. In each of these scenes, stores that sold sex toys became the backdrops for scenes of comedy. Such places are associated with deviance, transgression, and taboo and are usually in obscure locations, accessed by concealed entrances and inevitably populated by strange attendants and customers. The characters who find themselves in such shops—Pondo, Enid and Seymour, and Kate and Richard, for example—seem distinctly out of place. These shops are assumed to cater to people who are *not normal*. For audiences, watching "normal" characters in such "weird" locations can be funny and function as *fish out of water* narratives, a device often used in comedy: "Comedy thrives on taking people from one environment and placing them in another—the 'fish-out-of-water' narrative—and then watching the situations unfold."[5] Such scenes work both to make sex toys a potential source of comedy and to associate their owners with deviance, while presenting non-vanilla sexual interests as something to laugh at.

Another way vibrators are presented as a source of comedy is by introducing them in strange situations. Removing a vibrator from a private masturbatory context and relocating it into the public sphere is fundamentally funny. In an episode of *Degrassi: The Next Generation* (2001–), for example, Clare (Aislinn Paul) was caught with a vibrator at school after stealing it from a teacher's house. The scene was funny because the vibrator appeared in a location that seemed incredibly far removed from sex and masturbation: a classroom.

In the comedy *Whipped* (2000), in one scene Jonathan (Jonathan Abrahams) secretly retrieved his date Mia's (Amanda Peet) vibrator and played with it by rubbing it over his face and body. He then accidentally dropped it into a filthy toilet and attempted to retrieve it. *Whipped* was of the sophomoric genre, so the scene was heavily reliant on visual gags. Notably, the character was depicted as doing something he shouldn't—playing with the private property of a woman he was trying to seduce—and was punished accordingly. The humor wasn't actually based on the masturbatory connotations of the vibrator—although such connotations were, of course, referenced given that audiences needed a reason to find it funny to see Jonathan rubbing the vibrator on his face—but rather centered on Jonathan's evident lack of knowledge as to what vibrators are used for and the fact that he is manhandling a woman's *private* masturbation tool. Interestingly, Mia's possession of the vibrator casts her as (comparatively) sophisticated and sexually interesting.

A similar kind of humor transpired in the romantic comedy *The Ugly Truth* (2009). In the film, Abby (Katherine Heigl) put on a pair of "vibrating briefs" in preparation for a date with her boyfriend. Her date was cancelled when she had to attend a work dinner; she didn't have time to change out of the briefs. The remote controller for the briefs fell out of her handbag when she arrived at the restaurant and was seized by a young boy at another table, who proceeded to play with the buttons. Abby ended up having to give her work presentation while climaxing. In this scene, the comedy was centered on the idea of self-stimulation—of orgasm—occurring in such an unlikely location: a restaurant. Worth noting, the humor in this scene was also premised on the cruel as well as *voyeuristic* appeal that Abby's predicament presented to her colleague Mike (Gerard Butler), who had secretly gifted her the briefs.[6]

Just as interrupted intercourse is a popular joke identifiable in film and television—where children or parents "hilariously" interrupt sex—the same idea is used in the context of masturbation. Such scenes solicit humor from the annoyance of interruption as well as the potential for embarrassment. In *Not Another Teen Movie* (2001), for example, the film opened with Janey (Chyler Leigh) watching her favorite actor on TV and using a large vibrator. Her masturbation was repeatedly interrupted by a variety of characters, each of whom wanted to wish her a happy birthday. Something similar happened in a scene from *Dirt* (2007–2008): Lucy (Courtney Cox) was shown in bed masturbating—the buzz of her vibrator was clearly audible—but she was interrupted by a phone call from her mother. In both scenes the humor came from sexual frustration: these women wanted to orgasm, so it was presented as funnily irritating that they were prevented from doing so.

While in these examples the interruptions were from people, worth nothing are other kinds of interruptions. Discussed earlier was the scene from *Extreme Movie* when Jessica ended up masturbating with a vibrating cell phone after her vibrator's batteries ran out. The humor of dead vibrator batteries was also used in the film *How the Garcia Girls Spent Their Summer* (2005), when Lolita (Elizabeth Peña) found her vibrator's batteries had ran out and she had to steal a pair from a remote control. In the horror film *Alive or Dead* (2008), after Maria's (Ann Henson) vibrator fell out of her handbag and out of her reach, she used her phone charger to masturbate with while driving. In these scenes, the humor centers on audience familiarity with horniness and the idea of sexual frustration when a person is thwarted in their pursuit of orgasm.

While in this section I proposed that the humor of the masturbation-interrupted scenes center on sexual frustration, such scenes can also be read as funny in the *American Pie* (1999) caught-masturbating style, tapping into adolescent anxieties predicated on shame.

In *Brown Sugar*, when Francine discovered Sidney's vibrator, she seemed primarily entertained by her cousin's embarrassment and vehement denial: "Come on, Sid, don't act like I don't know what a—." Sidney cut her cousin off however, clearly mortified. In a scene from the comedy *Parenthood* (1989), a blackout occurred during a family dinner. While the lights were out, Gil (Steve Martin) went searching for a flashlight. When the lights came back on, he was shown holding his sister Helen's (Dianne Wiest) buzzing vibrator, which he had mistakenly retrieved—in the dark—instead of a flashlight. Helen was mortified; Gil found the whole thing hysterical. In the episode of *Degrassi: The Next Generation* discussed earlier, Clare was caught with a vibrator at school. She was forced to take it out of her bag in front of the class: everyone laughed when the vibrator was exposed and was assumed to be hers. In an episode of the series *The L-Word* (2004–2009), Dana's (Erin Daniels) sex toys were exposed when she had to open her bags at airport security: their contents included a strap-on dildo and nipple clamps. In *Dedication* (2007), Carol (Dianne Wiest) found her daughter Lucy's (Mandy Moore) vibrator hidden in the freezer. When Carol confronted Lucy, Lucy just covered her face and said, "Oh God. Oh my God."

In the Flatulence Chapter, I discussed the concept of *schadenfreude* as related to the comic appeal of farting jokes. It is likely something similar is at play here—that audiences are laughing because it is the *character* who is suffering and notably not the audience member; the humiliation is relatable but pleasingly experienced by someone else. Another aspect of the humor relates to the characters being embarrassed that their sex toys (or at least, as in the case of Clare in *Degrassi*, the sex toy in her possession) were exposed, whereby something intrinsically private—masturbation—was made public. A connected idea is the humor centered on the discomfort of other characters who are exposed to a family member's masturbatory life. In an episode of *Archer* (2009–), for example, Sterling—while searching in his mother's desk—found her vibrator and said, "There's not enough liquor and therapy in the world to undo that." Sterling's comments perfectly highlight why the *Parenthood* and *Dedication* scenes are so awkward, and also why audiences find them so funny: it is unlikely the family members want to know anything at all about one another's masturbation; finding out about it is thoroughly awkward, if not mortifying. A scene from the comedy *The Change-up* (2011) referenced such ideas. The premise of the film was that Mitch (Ryan Reynolds) and Dave (Jason Bateman) swapped bodies. At one point Dave—while in the body of Mitch—was trying to prove to his wife Jamie (Leslie Mann) who he really was by revealing something only he could know:

Mitch: I know! You once took your vibrator into the bathtub. You then got electrocuted while using it and now you have a bald spot on your vagina.

Jamie: (Slaps Dave) How dare you tell him!

Jamie clearly perceived vibrator use as something private, so its public discussion appeared both a breach of privacy and thoroughly embarrassing.

A different kind of example occurred in the film *The Stepford Wives* (2004). After patiently listening to a boring conversation about holiday decorating with pinecones, Bobbie (Bette Midler) interjected by saying, "I'm going to attach a pinecone to my vibrator and have a really merry Christmas." Bobbie was using the idea of her vibrator—and the taboo notion of daring to talk about it—to shock the others. A similar example occurred in the British sitcom *Mrs. Brown's Boys* (2011–). In a scene in a pub, four female friends were sitting at a table and elderly Winnie (Eilish O'Carroll) remarked, "Well nowadays, that's what the women's do get, them vibrators." The title character, Agnes (Brendan O'Carroll), quieted Winnie by saying, "Shut up," and covered her friend's mouth with a handkerchief. As in the *Stepford Wives* scene, humor stemmed from the notion of something private becoming public through dialogue.

Bobbie in *The Stepford Wives* and Winnie in *Mrs. Brown's Boys* were both married. Their interest in vibrators therefore raises questions about the use of vibrators within relationships. While we don't know if Winnie ever got a vibrator—nor do we see Bobbie use hers—the issue of vibrators within relationships is a narrative identifiable on screen.

VIBRATORS AS MARITAL AIDS

In an episode of *My So-Called Life* (1994–1995), Brian (Devon Gummersall) complained that his parents owned a vibrator that sounded "like a lawnmower." While Brian was seemingly embarrassed about being exposed to his parents' sex life—his comment was both a confession and a lament—useful for this section was his reference to vibrator use inside a couple. While vibrators are routinely assumed to be something that aids *solo* sex pursuits, in a small number of mainstream examples sex toys are actually used by couples. In *The Kids Are Alright* (2010), for example, Jules (Julianne Moore) and Nic (Annette Bening) used a vibrator on each other. In a scene from *The Sopranos* (1999–2007), Janice (Aida Turturro) was shown penetrating Ralph (Joe Pantoliano) with a vibrator while talking dirty to him ("Work that arse you little cunt ..."). While we don't know much about the sex life of Brian's parents in *My So-Called Life*, of the very few examples of vibrators used outside of masturbation—such as in *The Kids are Alright* and *The Sopranos*—these couples were engaged in what queer theorist Gayle Rubin would call *bad sex*, the kind that is routinely demonized: "Bad sex may be homosexual, unmarried, promiscuous, non-procreative, or commercial. It may be masturbatory or take place at orgies, may be casual, may cross generational lines, and may take place in 'public' or at least in the bushes or the baths. It may involve the use of pornography, fetish objects, sex toys or unusual roles."[7]

In *The Kids Are Alright*, the couple were lesbians who were having sex with a vibrator while watching gay male pornography; in *The Sopranos*, Janice and Ralph were not merely engaged in an affair but were dabbling in *unusual roles* with sex toys. The implication in these scenes is that to use sex toys within a relationship means that the couple is—in varying degrees—kinky (or as Janice says to Ralph postcoitally, "We're so naughty ... We're so wacky"). Thus such presentations are in line with the sex shop deviant portrayals discussed earlier and work to cast those associated with vibrators as perverted.

This idea of vibrator use within marriage being conceived of as kinky was actually referenced in the film *She's the One* (1996). Renee's (Jennifer Aniston) husband Francis (Mike McGlone) apparently no longer wanted to have sex with her. Renee threatened Francis that unless he had sex with her, she was going into the bathroom to masturbate with a vibrator. The following exchange transpired:

Renee: Wake up your libido, or I'm in that bathroom in minutes. Hey, better yet, I could go get it and we could play with it together.
Francis: Very funny.

Francis at one point also said, "We have sex like normal people. In a bed, laying down. We don't masturbate like animals in bathrooms with vibrators." For Francis, the very existence of a vibrator in his house was construed as preposterous; that his wife would dare suggest the device be brought into the bedroom was considered so outlandish as to be laughable.

In these examples, vibrator use was presented as somehow revealing about the characters' sexual penchants. This idea is discussed in more detail in the next section, whereby the exposure of a vibrator user often implies that the character is *defined* by his or her sexuality.

VIBRATORS AND THE SEXUALLY ADVENTUROUS

In the episode of *Degrassi: The Next Generation* discussed earlier, after Clare's mother, Helen (Ruth Marshall), found out about the vibrator, she assumed Clare was having sex. Evidently, being in possession of a vibrator meant that her daughter was sexually active (*beyond* assumed masturbation). A similar—and equally erroneous—assumption was made in *Dedication*. When Carol found her daughter's vibrator hidden in the freezer, she asked, "Are you gay? ... If you are, just tell me." In this example, a vibrator was seemingly an insight into *homosexual* behavior.

The idea of "information" gleaned from vibrators also transpired in an episode of *CSI* (2000–). The crime scene investigator, Mia (Aisha Tyler), reported on some of the things she had found at the crime scene: "Nine vibrators, five plugs and four strands of beads." Mia would have been unlikely to have mentioned having found *nonsexual* household objects such as toothbrushes or cutlery—they wouldn't have seemed topical—but the mentioning of the sex toys was a way to highlight that people who aren't sexually *normal*—who aren't sexually *vanilla*—resided in the house; that their sexual depravity might, in fact, be relevant to the case. This idea was taken much further in the film *Hold Me, Thrill Me, Kiss Me* (1992): Sabra (April Rayne), remarked, "I know I seem a little bit on the kinky side, but deep down I'm a sensitive and vulnerable girl. Don't let my dildoes, vibrators, and handcuffs fool you." While Sabra was being factitious, she was also presented as the screen's typical vibrator user: Sabra was sexually adventurous.

In the episode of *Sex and the City* discussed earlier, when Samantha walked up to the counter at The Sharper Image to do her store return, she proudly—*loudly*—mentioned that her vibrator wasn't *getting her off*. She had no qualms: Samantha was the most sexually liberal character on the show; it would have been more surprising for her *not* to have owned a vibrator. In the film In *Slackers* (2002), Jeff (Michael C. Maronna) entered a dorm purporting to be looking for Angela (Jaime King) but instead encountered her roommate Reanna (Laura Prepon) using a vibrator:

Reanna: Do I fucking know you?
Jeff: Uh, I lent Angela my notebook, because I take such world famous notes. So I was wondering if I could ... Are you busy with something?
Reanna: Yeah. I was masturbating.
Jeff: Masturbating. In the dorms. Well, yeah, well when you go to art school.

Interestingly, Reanna continued to masturbate with a vibrator throughout the scene. In an episode of the sitcom *2 Broke Girls* (2011–), Max (Kat Dennings) made a jibe: "Tell that to my candy cane-shaped vibrator. I call it Santa's Big Helper." In another episode she yelled at her roommate Beth (Caroline Channing)—who assumed that she heard Max crying the night prior—"I was *masturbating*!" Max is the more sexually adventurous character of the two, so her possession of a vibrator—like Samantha and Reanna's—was a way to convey the character's sexually adventurous personality without saying so explicitly.

In an episode of *Two and a Half Men* (2003–), when the deceased character Charlie's (Charlie Sheen) belongings were being cleaned out of his home, his brother—Alan (Jon Cryer)—commented, "Let me just get Charlie's personal stuff out of here. Oh, here is some of his unfinished music. Um … panties. Panties … Panties … Waterpipe … Oh, vibrator." Charlie was always presented as a very sexually liberal character; that he was in possession of a vibrator—either because it was his or because it belonged to one of the many women he had slept with—is perfectly in line with his character.

While in these examples the vibrator is evidently an inclusion made on a production level to depict a character as sexually adventurous, there are occasions when characters actively display a vibrator *themselves* to convey their own sexual liberation. Renee—in *She's the One*—telling her husband that she has *needs* is an example of this, but the same idea is presented much more overtly in *Hurlyburly* (1998). In one scene, Mickey (Kevin Spacey) questioned Phil (Chazz Palminteri) about a vibrator:

Phil: It's a vibrator I carry around with me.
Mickey: You carry a vibrator around with you?
Phil: Yeah. As a form of come-on. So the girls can see I'm up for anything right away.

In this scene, Phil is verbalizing the more subtle connotations that vibrators are implied to have in the other scenes: that being in possession of a vibrator casts a character as kinky.

The coupling of vibrators with kinkiness might be construed as something negative if kinkiness is construed as a bad thing and as a character indictment. In such a case, vibrators being associated with nonmainstream sexuality could be interpreted as demonization. If, however, kinkiness is perceived as indicative of sexual liberation—as sexual interests simply being broader than just vanilla sex—then such portrayals could be considered as positive and these characters owning their sexual interests could be construed as evidence of their sexual liberation. In numerous scenes from *2 Broke Girls*, for example, Max's feminism was made explicit: an obvious example is the episode where she staged a protest against her boss's attempts to raise the price of the vending machine tampons. Max's possession of a vibrator—while casting her as sexually adventurous—can therefore be seen as a way to highlight her sexual liberation: she is a woman in control of her own sexuality and is not reliant on men to give her an orgasm. This idea of women choosing to partake in orgasm through masturbation—as opposed to foregoing orgasm because they don't have a man—is a theme detectable in vibrator portrayals on screen.

VIBRATORS AND MASTURBATION

Strictly Sexual (2008) opened with Donna (Amber Benson) tied up, breathing heavily and watching pornography; a vibrator dislodged from between her legs and fell onto the carpet. Donna wasn't merely masturbating, but was engaged in self-bondage, too; by the opening scene, she was cast as *sexually deviant*. In Rubin's discussion of *bad sex*, she noted that masturbation was part of this definition. While masturbation might be widely considered taboo[8]—or at best a *private* matter—it is a taboo that is routinely broken in a variety of screen narratives. While, as discussed throughout this chapter, representations of vibrators are relatively easy to detect on screen, rarely are these devices actually shown *being used*. Instead, they are discussed or displayed as *disconnected* from their genital stimulation functions. In this section, scenes where characters are shown actually using their vibrators for masturbation are discussed.

Noted earlier was the scene from *Dirt* when Lucy (Courtney Cox) was shown in bed masturbating with a vibrator before being interrupted by a phone call. In another episode, she used her vibrator while reading a celebrity gossip magazine. In *Not Another Teen Movie*, Janey's giant, brightly painted vibrator was displayed when she pulled off the sock that she had been sheathing it with; she then began using it. In a scene from the Canadian film *Year of the Carnivore* (2009), the sexually inexperienced Sammy (Cristin Milioti) was shown experimenting with a vibrator while babysitting twins. In a scene from *The Slums of Beverly Hills* (1998), Violet (Natasha Lyonne) was shown using a vibrator: not only did she use it through to orgasm, but the buzzing of the toy was clearly audible and the audience actually saw Violet's face transform as her pleasure increased and her toes curled. After she orgasmed, the large white vibrator was visible, clutched against her chest. A similar scene occurred in *How the Garcia Girls Spent Their Summer* when Lolita masturbated with a vibrator to orgasm. In a scene from the series *American Horror Story* (2011–), Vivien (Connie Britton) used her vibrator while fantasizing about Rubber Man. In the British film *9 Songs* (2004), Lisa (Margo Stilley) was shown masturbating with a vibrator; unlike the other examples—which were all cropped above the actor's waist—in this scene the audience was offered a full body shot and Lisa's genitals were visible.

There are a number of ways to read these scenes. On the one hand, they simply show vibrators used for the purposes in which they are intended. While they may be breaching a well-established taboo, these depictions are nevertheless just presenting *reality*: masturbation is common and sex toy sales are high, so showing masturbation with a vibrator is hardly an unrealistic display.

On the other hand, these scenes may be perceived as having voyeuristic connotations—an idea alluded to earlier as relevant to the reactions of the other diners witnessing Abby's orgasm in *The Ugly Truth*. In film theorist Laura Mulvey's seminal work on spectatorship in cinema, she identified that women on screen are often defined by their "to-be-looked-at-ness": they are routinely used as a decorative device and are the object of the audience's gaze.[9] As related to these portrayals of young, attractive women masturbating, it is possible to read these scenes as providing audiences with *voyeuristic* pleasure. The website BeautifulAgony.com, for example, is an online repository of videos of men and women—cropped around their faces—capturing sexual pleasure at orgasm from (mostly) masturbation: "Beautiful Agony began as an experiment, to test a theory that eroticism in human imagery lies not in the body, but in the face; that film of a genuine, unscripted, natural orgasm can succeed where the most visceral mainstream pornography fails, and that is, to actually turn us on."[10] The underlying premise of BeautifulAgony.com is that it is sexually stimulating for audiences to see the faces of characters as they masturbate. In the vibrator-masturbation scenes discussed earlier, the style in which they are filmed is actually very similar to the videos on BeautifulAgony.com, which are explicitly designed for arousal.

In my book *Periods in Pop Culture: Menstruation in Film and Television*, I proposed that menarche scenes often offer audiences an opportunity to think about the genitals of young girls: "[T]hrough the mentioning of menstruation, the audience was prompted not to simply think about the girl's genitals in an abstract sense, but about her bleeding vagina and her emerging sexuality more broadly."[11] Such an interpretation can be equally applied to these vibrator-masturbation scenes: while genitals might not be shown, audiences are nonetheless encouraged to sexualize young women and to think about their genitals.

Explored in this section was the notion of vibrators being useful in masturbation. The utility of vibrators in the context of masturbation—and the success they have in delivering orgasms to users—could be interpreted as raising questions about the usefulness and necessity of men.

VIBRATORS AND THE REDUNDANCY OF MEN

In a scene from the film *Sliver* (1993), Carly (Sharon Stone) commented, "You've been spending too much time with your vibrator," to which her friend Judy (Colleen Camp) responded, "I certainly have—I've been getting a plastic yeast infection!" In *The Oh in Ohio*, Priscilla had never had an orgasm until she got her vibrator. She then began to pursue orgasms at every opportunity; including with her vibrating cell phone during a work meeting. On the one hand, these examples can be interpreted as showing characters who have let their relationships with their sex toys get out of hand. On the other hand, another reading is that for Judy in *Sliver* and Priscilla in *The Oh in Ohio*, their vibrators are doing things for them that men never could.

This second argument alludes to a popular presentation of the vibrator on screen: as something that potentially renders men less essential. In an episode of *Sex and the City*, Miranda's (Cynthia Nixon) housekeeper Magda (Lynn Cohen) hid Miranda's vibrator, contending that owning one would decrease her chances of appearing wife-like: "It means you don't need him." In *Zack and Miri Make a Porno* (2008), Miri (Elizabeth Banks) remarked, "I've never met a man who can make me come like a vibrator does." In the comedy *There's Something about Mary* (1998), Mary (Cameron Diaz) similarly discussed her failed relationship with her friends and commented, "Who needs him? I've got a vibrator!" In a scene from the film *Men with Brooms* (2002), Chris (Paul Gross) lamented the demise of a local hardware store and said, "That hardware store was unique," to which Amy (Molly Parker) countered, "So was my husband. I'm still glad they came up with vibrators." In a scene from the television series *The Walking Dead* (2010–), a group of women were shown washing clothes in a quarry: Carol (Melissa McBride) mused, "I do miss my Maytag," and Jacqui (Jeryl Prescott) spoke about missing her "coffeemaker, with that dual-drip filter and built-in grinder." Andrea (Laurie Holden) divulged, "I miss my vibrator," a remark with which Carol agreed: "Me, too." For Andrea and Carol, evidently their vibrators were ranked as highly as the other possessions that they missed in their new post-zombie apocalypse world. In these scenes, the vibrator was presented as offering something special and something that, while not necessarily supplanting men, certainly limited women's reliance on them. This reality, of course, can prove threatening.

Discussed earlier was the scene from *She's the One* when husband Francis acted initially perturbed—and progressed to hostility—when wife Renee claimed to own a vibrator: "We do not have a vibrator in this home! Do we?" While Francis evidently didn't want to have sex with Renee himself, the thought that he might be superseded by a sex toy clearly perturbed him. It's quite possible that Frances viewed his wife achieving sexual pleasure from a vibrator as emasculating; sexual pleasure was construed as something that she should not experience outside of their marriage. A similar theme of emasculation was identifiable in *Rescue Me* (2004–2011): Lou (John Scurti) took the batteries out of Theresa's (Susan Misner) vibrator because the two had made an agreement to stop having sex in pursuit of getting to know each other better first; evidently Lou didn't feel that Theresa using a vibrator was in keeping with that agreement. The idea of a man being uncomfortable with women achieving sexual pleasure from sources *other* than his penis was discussed in the Oral Sex chapter but is made much more explicit in vibrator scenes on screen. In *The Oh in Ohio*, for example, despite being married for 10 years, Priscilla was unable to have an orgasm with her husband. A vibrator aided her in this endeavor, but her marriage was jeopardized as a result. In *9 Songs*, in one scene Lisa (Margo Stilley) was shown masturbating with a vibrator. Her partner Matt (Kieran O'Brien) stood in the doorway watching her doing this: her burgeoning sexual independence was a sign to him that she was pulling ever further away. In the series *Love Bites* (2011), Carter (Kyle Howard) arrived home to hear his fiancée Liz (Lindsay Price) moaning and groaning to discover that not only was she using a vibrator, but—far worse for his ego—she also claimed that she just had her first *real* orgasm.

In these scenes, the idea that vibrators can do things that men can't creates a dynamic where men may feel threatened. On the one hand, this might be construed as an accurate presentation—it is reasonable that a man might feel threatened by the functionality of a sex toy. On the other hand, it alludes to how men in the audience might feel when vibrators are put on the agenda, potentially highlighting a reason why vibrators aren't a common screen inclusion. In the Penis Chapter, I discussed how full frontal male nudity may force male audience members into conducting a comparison between their penises and those displayed. As related to this chapter, that a vibrator might make a man feel inadequate is worth considering.

Thus far I have explored scenes of masturbation and vibrator use that center on pleasure. The next section discusses the less positive connotations of vibrator use as related to it being all about solo sex—about sex *alone*.

VIBRATORS AND LONELINESS

In *Brown Sugar*, Sidney justified her ownership of the Brookstone "massager" by claiming, "Men take up too much of your time. Time I don't have." As the narrative progressed, it became evident that Sidney was lying; she routinely used her career as means to excuse her loneliness. Her owning a vibrator was apparently proof that she was a lonely spinster.

By its very nature, masturbation is stimulation of one's own genitals. While it can be done with someone else—as occurred in *The Kids Are Alright* or *The Sopranos*—invariably it is a solo pursuit. The idea that masturbation is primarily something done *without* a partner—and thus that such behavior might convey loneliness—is a common screen presentation.

The loneliness idea was alluded to in *Valentine's Day*, discussed earlier, when Kara remarked, "My closest relationship is with my BlackBerry; thank God it vibrates!" The same idea was presented slightly more explicitly in the sitcom *30 Rock* (2006–2013) when Jenna (Jane Krakowski) claimed, "Maynard was the longest relationship of my life, after Doug ... Doug is my vibrator." In *Rescue Me*, Lou similarly referred to Theresa's vibrator as her "little plastic boyfriend." In *The Slums of Beverly Hills*, Rita (Marisa Tomei) dubbed her vibrator as her "boyfriend." In *Parenthood*, while the fact that single mom Helen had a vibrator might be enough to convey the single/desperate female masturbator idea, Helen explicitly articulated this point herself during an argument with her daughter: "Do you know why I'm having sex with machinery? Because your father left to have a party and I stayed to raise two kids. I have no life." Earlier I discussed vibrators being a clue to a character's sexual liberation. In these examples, vibrators similarly clued audiences into a character's *loneliness*. Just as cats and alcohol frequently serve as the tropes of spinsterhood on screen, in these scenes the vibrator functions as an insight into just how desperate and sex starved these women are.

It is reasonable to assume that connecting vibrators to loneliness might have some grounding in the popular perception that masturbation is more common among single women than among those who are partnered. Similarly, this idea might have some basis in the perception of masturbation as a lackluster, *less fulfilling* substitute for intercourse. Regardless of whether vibrator use is actually more common among single, lonely women, such presentations work to demonize the vibrator owner by casting her as a figure of pity.

A connected presentation is the partnered-but-lonely woman. Renee in *She's the One*, for example, had a husband, but evidently he was no longer interested in having sex with her. Thus she had a vibrator; as she rationalized, "Occasionally I need sex. I'm married to a man who doesn't like to have sex anymore. So from time to time, I like to pleasure myself with a vibrator." In the *M*A*S*H* episode discussed earlier, Hawkeye's theory—"behind every great man, there's a woman with a vibrator"—could be interpreted similarly; that is, *great men* (interpreted, potentially, as busy, distracted, egotistical, or self-centered men) are disinclined, unable, or too busy to sexually satisfy their wives—hence the use of a vibrator. These examples—while working to convey loneliness—also function to signal *emasculation*: a husband is considered a failure if he cannot sexually satisfy his partner. In the Drugs Chapter, I discussed this idea as a narrative tool often used in advertisements for erectile dysfunction medication. In screen narratives, the same idea is detectable: a man is construed as a failure as a husband if he can't (or won't) have sex with his wife. Such ideas function as cautionary tales for women that their vibrator usage may threaten their relationships, but also direct a message to men that sex is a fundamental way to *retain* a relationship.

The final vibrator presentation discussed in this chapter is its depiction as a gift: a vibrator can become less controversial when *gifted*.

THE VIBRATOR GIFT

In *Part-Time Perverts*, I identified that one way to participate in nonmainstream sexuality is through a perverse gift: that special occasions such as birthdays or anniversaries might provide opportunities for couples—who otherwise engage in only vanilla sex—to dabble in something sexually unusual for them.[12] On screen, there are examples of vibrators being gifted that provide a way for a woman to have and use a vibrator without having to experience or endure the possible embarrassment or stigma of purchase. Ownership can then be easily legitimized and excused (*Oh, it was just a gift*).

At the beginning of this chapter, the Trojan Tri-Phoria vibrator was mentioned. One advertisement depicted a bridal shower at which one woman gave the bride-to-be a Tri-Phoria. The bride appeared elated; the vibrator appeared to be a gift that she was thoroughly delighted to receive but might have been otherwise reluctant to purchase. In screen narratives, this same idea is identifiable. In an episode of *How I Met Your Mother*, Robyn (Cobie Smulders) gave a vibrator as a bridal shower gift to Lily (Alyson Hannigan). In the comedy *Just Married* (2003), Kyle (David Moscow) gave newlyweds Tom (Ashton Kutcher) and Sarah (Brittany Murphy) a vibrator as a wedding present; the vibrator then ended up short-circuiting the electricity supply in their honeymoon hotel. In a scene from *Easy A* (2010), Brandon

(Dan Byrd) sent Olive (Emma Stone) a vibrator as a "thank you" gift to her for agreeing to be cast as the sex partner in a rumor he started to distract from his homosexuality.

In these examples, the vibrator gifted seemed appreciated: it is viewed as a quirky but nonetheless useful present. This was not the case, however, in the Australian film *Alexandra's Project* (2003). In a video message that Alexandra (Helen Buday) left for her husband Steve (Gary Sweet), she held up a vibrator and said:

> Nice birthday present, Steve, I really appreciated it . . . Do you know what this is, Steve? I'll tell you what this is. This is a machine. It's a machine you bought to go inside me so that you can get your rocks off. Don't say it was for me, because it wasn't. If I wanted one I would have bought myself one long ago.

In this scene, the voyeuristic connotations of vibrator use were highlighted. Discussed earlier was the idea of masturbation scenes being able to be read as about providing sexual arousal for an audience. In this scene, Alexandra evidently construed her husband's gift as something for *his* stimulation rather than hers.

The film *Friends with Money* (2006) opened with house cleaner Olivia (Jennifer Aniston) finding a vibrator in the drawer of a home she was cleaning. Olivia kept opening the drawer, eyeing the vibrator, and then closing it again: she was evidently very curious. In an episode of *Sex in the City*—in the Sharper Image store scene—Samantha ended up giving advice to other women about which items could be used for sexual stimulation purposes; the women were clearly *enthralled*. These two examples showcased women's intrigue with vibrators—an intrigue that is likely quite common in real life. Widespread vibrator use and curiosity about them are normal, yet this everydayness is rarely presented on screen. In *Periods in Pop Culture*, I presented the argument that menstruation—while thoroughly common in real life—is largely absent from the screen because it is considered both taboo and private. Something similar can be said about vibrator presentations: they are absent not because they are *rare* in real life, but rather because they are considered *personal*—that is, masturbation is considered *a private pursuit*.

In this chapter, the wide variety of presentations of vibrator scenes were explored—ranging from funny scenes, to scenes of sexual liberation, to those related to depression. These depictions highlight the variety of ways that sexual subjects such as masturbation continue to be inextricably linked to taboo and cultural anxieties.

Conclusion: The Rarely Simple Taboo Presentation

To dub something a taboo, the inference is that it can't be spoken about; that to do so is verboten or calamity inducing. As demonstrated across the course of the 12 chapters in this book, evidently taboo topics *are* actually spoken about. Quite often, in fact. While the controversies may not have yet evaporated—while such representations are still frequently construed as controversial, offensive or by many as thoroughly *inappropriate*—such examples do exist. *Hundreds of them.*

American Taboo has shined a light on a wide range of taboos related to the body. These are the taboos that create the most angst, outrage, and controversy in real life and that appear in a variety of guises in our popular culture.

While examples of taboos are easily detected, their presence is complicated. Two central points are made in *American Taboo*. First, just as opinions about taboo are diverse in real life, so, too, is their presentation in popular culture. Second, their appearance is nowhere near as common in popular culture as in real life: abortion and male circumcision and female masturbation are everyday happenings—engaged in frequently and often without controversy or punishment—yet they appear in popular culture comparatively rarely. This paradox raises some important questions about whether we expect—or even *want*—our popular culture to serve as a mirror on society rather than just offering us escapism. Equally worth discussing is the role of popular culture in substituting for serious and frank dialogue on some of these topics. It seems perfectly obvious that for many people, talking about topics such as abortion or cunnilingus is much harder than watching a fictional representation. For such people, participating in the debate or having vicarious access to it via popular culture is a way to have an association—to broach the topic tentatively—without actually having the difficult conversation. Worth asking is whether this is problem. Is it a problem, for example, that cunnilingus is infrequently presented on screen? Is it too big a call to connect this fact to women in real life finding it challenging to assert their sexual wants and needs to their partners? Is it a problem that full frontal female nudity on screen is much more common than full frontal male nudity? Is it over-reaching to argue that this perpetuates the idea of women's true value deriving from their appearance, their—to use film theorist Laura Mulvey's phrase—to-be-looked-at-ness?[1] Equally, does this imbalance contribute to *men's* anxieties about their penis size and functionality?

Popular culture is more than mere entertainment. Inherent in every film, every song, every sitcom, and every advertisement are fascinating insights—in varying degrees of seriousness, complexity, and nuance—into the topics that frighten, bewilder, fascinate, confuse, outrage, and arouse us. Spotlighted in this book is our enduringly complicated relationship with our bodies.

American Taboo provides some small insight into what's happening in our popular culture. No matter how controversial a topic might be, our cinema and television and music have invariably attempted to deal with it—*on our behalf*. This volume demonstrates that while in real life a variety of controversies plague how we use our bodies, expose our bodies, put things into them, do things to them, and give and draw pleasure from them, such controversies are not something popular culture has ignored. The hundreds of examples from film, television, music, and advertising discussed in this book highlight that controversial subjects make for very interesting popular culture and testify to the complexity of our relationships with our physical selves.

Media References

TELEVISION SHOWS

'Til Death (2006–2010)
'Til Death Do Us Part (1965–1975)
2 Broke Girls (2011–)
30 Rock (2006–2013)
3rd Rock from the Sun (1996–2001)
A Very Peculiar Practice (1986–1988)
Absolutely Fabulous (1992–)
Acropolis Now (1989–1992)
All My Children (1970–2011)
American Dad! (2005–)
American Horror Story (2011–)
Another World (1964–1999)
Archer (2009–)
Archie Bunker's Place (1979–1983)
Are You Being Served? (1972–1985)
Arrested Development (2003–)
As the World Turns (1956–2010)
Avatar: The Last Airbender (2005–2008)
Beavis and Butt-Head (1993–1997; 2011–)
Being Erica (2009–)

Ben 10: Ultimate Alien (2010–)
Bergerac (1981–1991)
Beverly Hills, 90210 (1990–2000)
Big Bang Theory, The (2007–)
Big Love (2006–2011)
Black Books (2000–2004)
Black Donnellys, The (2007)
Blossom (1990–1995)
Bones (2005–)
Bored to Death (2009–2011)
Braceface (2001–2003)
Buffy the Vampire Slayer (1997–2003)
Californication (2007–)
Casualty (1986–)
Cheers (1982–1993)
Chicago Hope (1994–2000)
Children's Hospital (2008–)
China Beach (1988–1991)
Client List, The (2012–)
Closer, The (2005–2012)
Cold Case (2003–2010)
Community (2009–)
Count Duckula (1988–1993)
Criminal Minds (2005–)
Crusader Rabbit (1949–1951; 1957–1958)
CSI (2000–)
Curb Your Enthusiasm (2000–)
Dallas (1978–1991)
Danny Phantom (2004–2009)
Dawson's Creek (1998–2003)
Days of Our Lives (1965–)
Degrassi: The Next Generation (2001–)
Desperate Housewives (2004–2012)
Dexter (2006–)

Dharma & Greg (1997–2007)
Dirt (2007–2008)
Dirty Sexy Money (2007–2009)
Doctor Who (2005–)
Drawn Together (2004–2007)
Drew Carey Show, The (1995–2004)
Eastenders (1985–)
ER (1994–2009)
Family Guy (1999–)
Family Matters (1989–1998)
Fast Show, The (1994–2001)
Felicity (1998–2002)
Flight of the Conchords (2007–2009)
Flintstones, The (1960–1966)
Friends (1994–2004)
Frontline (1994–1997)
Full House (1987–1995)
Futurama (1999–)
Game of Thrones (2011–)
Glee (2009–)
Good Guys, The (2010)
Good Wife, The (2009–)
Gordon's Great Escape (2010–2011)
Grace Under Fire (1993–1998)
Grey's Anatomy (2005–)
Growing Pains (1985–1992)
Happy Days (1974–1984)
Happy Endings (2011–)
Hazell (1978–1979)
Hey Arnold (1996–2004)
House (2004–2012)
How I Met Your Mother (2005–)
Howdy-Doody (1947–1960)
In Living Color (1990–1994)

It's Always Sunny in Philadelphia (2005–)
Jack and Bobby (2004–2005)
Jamie Foxx Show, The (1996–2001)
Jetsons, The (1962–1963; 1985–1987)
Joey (2004–2006)
Judging Amy (1999–2005)
Just Shoot Me (1997–2003)
Killing, The (2011–)
King of Queens (1998–2007)
King of the Hill (1997–2010)
Kung Fu (1972–1975)
Late Late Show with Craig Ferguson, The (2005–)
Late Show with David Letterman (1993–)
Law and Order (1990–2010)
Law and Order: Special Victims Unit (1999–)
Law and Order: UK (2009–)
League, The (2009–)
Leverage (2008–)
Life on Mars (2006–2007)
Living Single (1993–1998)
Love Bites (2011)
L-Word, The (2004–2009)
M*A*S*H (1972–1983)
Mad Men (2008–)
Married with Children (1987–1997)
Maude (1972–1978)
Mentalist, The (2008–)
Miami Vice (1984–1990)
Monkees, The (1966–1968)
Moonlighting (1985–1989)
Morning Show, The (2007–)
Mrs. Brown's Boys (2011–)
My Little Pony: Friendship Is Magic (2010–)
My Name Is Earl (2005–2009)

Media References 243

My So-Called Life (1994–1995)
Mythbusters (2003–)
NCIS (2003–)
Ned's Declassified School Survival Guide (2004–2007)
New Tricks (2003–)
Nip/Tuck (2003–2010)
NYPD Blue (1993–2005)
O'Grady (2004–2006)
Office, The (2005–2013)
Oz, (1997–2003)
Partridge Family, The (1970–1974)
Party of Five (1994–2000)
Pie in the Sky (1994–1997)
Powerpuff Girls, The (1998–2004)
Private Practice (2007–)
Pushing Daisies (2007–2009)
Queer as Folk [United Kingdom] (1999–2000)
Queer as Folk [United States] (2000–2005)
Raising Hope (2010–)
Ready or Not (1993–1997)
Real Time with Bill Maher (2003–)
Rebus (2000–2007)
Red Green Show, The (1991–2006)
Ren and Stimpy Show, The (1991–1998)
Rescue Me (2004–2011)
River City (2002–)
Roseanne (1988–1997)
Rugrats: All Grown Up (2003–2008)
Rush (2008–2011)
Sabrina, the Teenage Witch (1996–2003)
Saved by the Bell (1989–1993)
Scrubs (2001–2010)
SeaQuest DSV (1993–1996)
Secret Life of the American Teenager, The (2008–)

Secret Life of Us, The (2001–2005)
Seinfeld (1990–1998)
Sex and the City (1998–2004)
Simple Life, The (2003–2007)
Simpsons, The (1989–)
Six Feet Under (2001–2005)
Skins (2007–)
Sons of Anarchy (2008–)
Sopranos, The (1999–2007)
South of Nowhere (2005–2008)
South Park (1997–)
Spooks (2002–2011)
St. Elsewhere (1982–1988)
Star Trek (1966–1969)
That '70s Show (1998–2006)
Top Chef (2006)
Total Request Live (1998–2008)
True Blood (2008–)
Two and a Half Men (2003–)
Undressed (1999–2002)
Unhappily Ever After (1995–1999)
United States of Tara, The (2009–2011)
Unusuals, The (2009)
V.I.P. (1998–2002)
Venture Bros., The (2003–2012)
Veronica Mars (2004–2007)
Veronica's Closet (1997–2000)
Walking Dead, The (2010–)
Weeds (2005–2012)
West Wing, The (1999–2006)
What about Mimi? (2000–2003)
What I Like about You (2002–2006)
Will & Grace (1998–2006)

Media References 245

Wire, The (2002–2008)

Young Ones, The (1982–1984)

FILMS

A Place in the Sun (1951)

A Private Matter (1992)

A Very Harold & Kumar Christmas (2011)

About a Boy (2002)

About Last Night (1986)

Absolute Strangers (1991)

Adventures of Priscilla, Queen of the Desert, The (1994)

Alexandra's Project (2003)

Alfie (1966)

Alfie (2004)

Alive or Dead (2008)

Altered States (1980)

All the Right Moves (1983)

American Flyers (1985)

American History X (1998)

American Pie (1999)

American Psycho (2000)

Amok (1944)

Anatomie de l'enfer (Anatomy of Hell) (2004)

Animal House (1978)

Ann Vickers (1933)

Arme Riddere (Jackpot) (2011)

Arthur (1981)

Arthur 2: On the Rocks (1988)

Austin Powers: International Man of Mystery (1997)

Bachelorette (2012)

Bad Lieutenant (1992)

Bad Santa (2003)

Banishment, The (2007)

Barfly (1987)
Barnyard (2006)
Bells, The (1926)
Better Than Chocolate (1999)
Bill Bailey: Live at the Apollo—Part Troll (2004)
Billy Madison (1995)
Black Swan (2010)
Blazing Saddles (1974)
Blue Valentine (2010)
Blue Velvet (1986)
Boogie Nights (1997)
Borat (2006)
Boys Don't Cry (1999)
Breakfast Club, The (1985)
Breakfast on Pluto (2005)
Bring It On (2000)
Brooklyn's Finest (2009)
Brown Bunny, The (2003)
Brown Sugar (2002)
Bruce Almighty (2003)
Butch Jamie (2007)
Cabaret (1972)
Caddyshack (1980)
Caligula (1979)
Cannonball Run 2 (1984)
Captain America: The First Avenger (2011)
Carne trémula (Live Flesh) (1997)
Carpool (1996)
Changeling, The (2008)
Change-Up, The (2011)
Chasing Amy (1997)
Cherrybomb (2009)
Cider House Rules, The (1996)
Citizen Ruth (1996)

Click (2006)
Clueless (1995)
Coach Carter (2005)
Cocktail (1988)
Color of Night (1994)
Come Fill the Cup (1951)
Come What May (2009)
Coming Home (1978)
Contender, The (2000)
Cook, The Thief, His Wife & Her Lover, The (1989)
Cooler, The (2003)
Coyote Ugly (2000)
Crash (1996)
Crazy Heart (2009)
Crazy. Stupid. Love. (2011)
Crimen ferpecto (Ferpect Crime) (2004)
Crying Game, The (1992)
Damage (1992)
Dances with Wolves (1990)
Darby O'Gill and the Little People (1959)
Days of Wine and Roses (1962)
Dead Europe (2012)
Deconstructing Harry (1997)
Dedication (2007)
Delinquents, The (1989)
Demolition Man (1993)
Departed, The (2006)
Deer Hunter, The (1978)
Der Untergang (Downfall) (2004)
Desert Flower (2009)
Detective Story (1951)
Dictator, The (2012)
Did You Hear about the Morgans? (2009)
Dirty Dancing (1987)

Dogma (1999)
Dogtooth (2010)
Don't Look Now (1973)
Don't Tell Mom the Babysitter's Dead (1991)
Donnie Darko (2001)
Dr. T and the Women (2000)
Dread (2009)
Dreamers, The (2003)
Drowning By Numbers (1988)
Eastern Promises (2007)
East Is East (1999)
Easy A (2010)
8 Mile (2002)
8 Million Ways to Die (1986)
El crimen del padre Amaro (The Crime of Father Amaro) (2002)
El Topo (1970)
End of Days (1999)
Escape from LA (1996)
Everything Is Illuminated (2005)
Expecting Mary (2010)
Extreme Movie (2008)
Factotum (2005)
Fame (1980)
Fargo (1996)
Fast Times at Ridgemont High (1982)
Fight Club (1999)
Find Me Guilty (2006)
Fisher King, The (1991)
Flirting with Disaster (1996)
Fools Rush In (1997)
Forgetting Sarah Marshall (2008)
Forrest Gump (1994)
40 Days and 40 Nights (2002)
40-Year-Old Virgin, The (2005)

4 luni, 3 saptamâni si 2 zile (4 Months, 3 Weeks, 2 Days) (2007)
Four Rooms (1995)
Friends with Money (2006)
Full Monty, The (1997)
Funny People (2009)
Getaway, The (1994)
Ghost and the Darkness, The (1996)
Ghost Rider (2007)
Ghost World (2001)
Girl with the Dragon Tattoo, The (2011)
Glengarry Glen Ross (1992)
Go Fish (1994)
Godfather II, The (1974)
Gone with the Wind (1939)
Good Luck Chuck (2007)
Gosford Park (2001)
Governess, The (1998)
Graduate, The (1967)
Grease (1978)
Greenberg (2010)
Gwai wik (Re-cycle) (2006)
Hae anseon (The Coast Guard) (2002)
Hairspray (2007)
Hall Pass (2011)
Halloween II (2009)
Halloween: Resurrection (2002)
Hangover, The (2009)
Harold and Kumar Escape from Guantanamo Bay (2008)
Harold and Kumar Go to White Castle (2004)
Harsh Times (2005)
Harvey (1950)
He liu (The River) (1997)
Heartbreak Kid, The (2007)
Henry Fool (1987)

Hey, Happy! (2001)
Hidden Secrets (2006)
High Fidelity (2000)
Hold Me, Thrill Me, Kiss Me (1992)
Hope Springs (2012)
Horrible Bosses (2011)
Hostel (2005)
How the Garcia Girls Spent Their Summer (2005)
How to Lose a Guy in 10 Days (2003)
Hurlyburly (1998)
Hush-a-Bye Baby (1990)
Hysteria (2011)
I Give it a Year (2013)
I Had an Abortion (2005)
I'll Cry Tomorrow (1955)
Identity Thief (2013)
If These Walls Could Talk (1996)
In a Lonely Place (1950)
In the Cut (2003)
In the Realm of the Senses (1976)
Ironweed (1987)
Jay and Silent Bob Strike Back (2001)
Jennifer's Body (2009)
John Tucker Must Die (2006)
Jui kuen (Drunken Master) (1978)
Juno (2007)
Just Married (2003)
Kama Sutra: A Tale of Love (1996)
Ken Park (2002)
Kids Are Alright, The (2010)
Knocked Up (2007)
Last Chance Harvey (2008)
Laurel Canyon (2002)
Leap Year (2010)

Leaving Las Vegas (1995)
Legally Blonde (2001)
Leonard Part 6 (1987)
Liar Liar (1997)
Lie with Me (2005)
Life Before Her Eyes, The (2007)
Lirkod (The Belly Dancer) (2006)
Logan's Run (1976)
Lost Weekend (1945)
Love Stinks (1999)
Love with the Proper Stranger (1963)
MacGruber (2010)
Magic Mike (2012)
Margaret (2011)
Master, The (2012)
Match Point (2005)
Matrix, The (1999)
Meaning of Life, The (1983)
Meet the Fockers (2004)
Men in Black (1997)
Men with Brooms (2002)
Monsters Ball (2001)
Monty Python and the Holy Grail (1975)
Moolaadé (2004)
Morning After, The (1986)
Mrs. Parker and the Vicious Circle (1994)
Munich (2005)
My Big Fat Greek Wedding (2002)
My Science Project (1985)
Mystery Men (1999)
Naked (1993)
Naked Gun (1988)
Naked Gun 2½: The Smell of Fear, The (1991)
National Lampoon's Christmas Vacation (1989)

Night Fall (2012)
9 Songs (2004)
No Cure for Cancer (1992)
No Impact Man: The Documentary (2009)
Not Another Teen Movie (2001)
Notting Hill (1999)
Nutty Professor, The (1996)
October Baby (2011)
Office Space (1999)
Oh in Ohio, The (2006)
Old School (2003)
Opening Night (1977)
Orange County (2002)
Over Her Body (2008)
Palindromes (2004)
Parenthood (1989)
Party Animal, The (1985)
Peeping Tom (1960)
Philadelphia (1993)
Piano, The (1993)
Pillow Book, The (1996)
Play Misty for Me (1971)
Postcards from the Edge (1990)
Prime Suspect IV (1995)
Princess and the Cobbler, The (1993)
Proposal, The (2009)
Prospero's Books (1991)
Pulp Fiction (1994)
Quiet Man, The (1952)
Quinceañera (2006)
Remember the Daze (2007)
Revelation (1999)
Revolutionary Road (2008)
Road House (1989)

Road to Ruin, The (1928)
Road to Wellville, The (1994)
Road Trip (2000)
Rock of Ages (2012)
Roe vs. Wade (1989)
Romance and Cigarettes (2005)
Sabotage (1936)
Sajtóvadászat (Press Hunting) (2006)
Salo- 120 Days of Sodom (1975)
Sarah's Choice (2009)
Saw (2004)
Scary Movie 3 (2003)
Scott Pilgrim vs. the World (2010)
Series 7: The Contenders (2001)
Se7en (1995)
Seven Pounds (2008)
Seven Psychopaths (2012)
Shallow Grave (1994)
Shame (2011)
She's the One (1996)
Shortbus (2006)
Shrek Forever After (2010)
Sideways (2004)
Simpsons Movie, The (2007)
Sitter, The (2011)
16 Blocks (2006)
Slackers (2002)
Sliver (1993)
Snakes on a Plane (2006)
Something to Talk About (1995)
Somewhere (2010)
Spanking the Monkey (1994)
Speedy (1928)
Squeeze, The (1977)

Stalker (1979)
Starting out in the Evening (2007)
State and Main (2000)
Step Brothers (2008)
Stepford Wives, The (2004)
Strictly Sexual (2008)
Suckling, The (1990)
Sunset Boulevard (1950)
Superbad (2007)
Sweetest Thing, The (2002)
Teen Witch (1989)
Teeth (2007)
10 (1979)
Terminator 2: Judgment Day (1991)
There's Something about Mary (1998)
Things You Can Tell Just by Looking at Her (1999)
This is 40 (2012)
This World, Then the Fireworks (1997)
Thunderpants (2002)
Titanic (1997)
Tomcats (2001)
Too Much, Too Soon (1958)
Trainspotting (1996)
Transamerica (2005)
Tropic Thunder (2008)
True Romance (1993)
28 Days (2000)
21 Grams (2003)
2 Days in Paris (2007)
Two Girls and a Guy (1997)
Ugly Truth, The (2009)
Unborn, The (2009)
Un prophète (A Prophet) (2009)
Valentine's Day (2010)

Media References   255

Varsity Blues (1999)
Velvet Goldmine (1998)
Venus (2006)
Vera Drake (2004)
Voice from the Grave (1996)
Waitress (2007)
Waking Ned Devine (1998)
War Horse (2011)
Wassup Rockers (2005)
Wasted (2002)
Wet Hot American Summer (2001)
What Happens in Vegas (2008)
What Price Hollywood? (1932)
What to Expect When You're Expecting (2012)
When a Man Loves a Woman (1994)
Where Are My Children (1916)
Whipped (2000)
White Chicks (2004)
Wild at Heart (1990)
Wild Things (1998)
Women in Love (1969)
Wonder Boys (2000)
Wrestler, The (2008)
XXL (2004)
Y tu mamá también (And Your Mother Too!) (2001)
Year of the Carnivore (2009)
Year One (2009)
Yellow Handkerchief, The (2007)
Young Adam (2003)
Zack and Miri Make a Porno (2008)
Zoom (2006)

SONGS

2Pac, "Baby Don't Cry (Keep Ya Head Up II)" (1999)
Adams, Ryan, "Tina Toledo's Street Walkin' Blues" (2001)

Amos, Tori, "Me and a Gun" (1992)

Arctic Monkeys, "When the Sun Goes Down" (2006)

Autumn, Emilie, "Gothic Lolita" (2006)

Belle and Sebastian, "The Chalet Lines" (2000)

Ben Folds Five, "Brick" (1997)

Cage the Elephant, "Ain't No Rest for the Wicked" (2008)

Cold Chisel, "Choirgirl" (1979)

Crowe, Sheryl, "Hard to Make a Stand" (1996)

Delta Spirit, "Streetwalker" (2008)

DiFranco, Ani, "Hello Birmingham" (1999)

DiFranco, Ani, "Promiscuity" (2012)

Dresden Dolls, The "Mandy Goes to Med School" (2006)

Dresden Dolls, The, "Delilah" (2006)

Guns 'n' Roses, "Prostitute" (2008)

Hall and Oates, "I'm Watching You (A Mutant Romance)" (1974)

Ian, Janis, "Pro-Girl" (1967)

Iron Maiden, "22 Acacia Avenue" (1982)

John, Elton, "Island Girl" (1975)

John, Elton, "Sweet Painted Lady" (1973)

Ke$ha, "C U Next Tuesday" (2010)

Khia, "My Neck, My Back (Lick It)" (2002)

Kid Rock, "Abortion" (2000)

Kid Rock, "Desperate-Rado" (1993)

Korn, "Thoughtless" (2002)

Lady Gaga, "LoveGame" (2008)

Lauper, Cyndi, "Sally's Pigeons" (1993)

Ludacris, "Ho" (2000)

Ludacris, "Runaway Love" (2007)

McFerrin, Bobby, "Don't Worry Be Happy" (1988)

Minaj, Nicky "Autobiography" (2008)

Mitchell, Joni, "The Beat of Black Wings" (1988)

Motörhead, "Don't Let Daddy Kiss Me" (1993)

Mudhoney, "F.D.K. (Fearless Doctor Killers)" (1995)

Palmer, Amanda, "Oasis" (2008)

Peaches, "Fuck the Pain Away" (2000)

Peaches, "Rock the Shocker" (2006)

Police, "Roxanne" (1978)

Porter, Cole, "Love for Sale" (1930)

Reddy, Helen, "I Am Woman" (1970)

Reed, Lou, "Walk on the Wild Side" (1972)

Salt 'n' Pepa, "None of Your Business" (1993)

Simon and Garfunkel, "The Boxer" (1969)

Smith, Bessie, "Empty Bed Blues" (1928)

Smith, Bessie, "I Want a Little Sugar in My Bowl" (1931)

Snoop Dogg, "Pay for Pussy" (1998)

Steel Panther, "The Shocker" (2009)

Stone Temple Pilots, "Sex Type Thing" (1992)

Summer, Donna, "Bad Girls" (1979)

Summer, Donna, "Hot Stuff" (1979)

Summer, Donna, "Lady of the Night" (1974)

The Offspring, "Kristy, Are You Doing Okay?" (2008)

The Veronicas, "Untouched" (2007)

Time Again, "Streetwalker" (2006)

Travis, Randy, "Three Wooden Crosses" (2002)

Waits, Tom, "Christmas Card from a Hooker in Minneapolis" (1978)

Waits, Tom, "I'm Your Late Night Evening Prostitute" (1991)

West, Kanye, "So Appalled" (2010)

Zappa, Frank, "Teen-Age Prostitute" (1982)

ZZ Top, "Mexican Blackbird" (1987)

ALBUMS

Deicide, *Once Upon the Cross* (1995)

Johnny Cash, *Unchained* (1996)

Serius Jones, *Serius Bizness 2* (2011)

Notes

THE GAY CHAPTER

1. Deborah A. Fisher, Douglas L. Hill, Joel W. Grube, and Enid L. Gruber, "Gay, Lesbian, and Bisexual Content on Television: A Quantitative Analysis across Two Seasons," *Journal of Homosexuality* 52, no. 33/4 (2007): 167–188.

2. Diane Raymond, "Popular Culture and Queer Representation: A Critical Perspective," in *Gender, Race, and Class in Media*, ed. Gail Dines and Jean McMahon Humez (Thousand Oaks, CA: Sage, 2001): 98–110; Elyce Rae Helford, "Feminism, Queer Studies, and the Sexual Politics of *Xena*," in *Fantasy Girls: Gender in the New Universe of Science Fiction and Fantasy Television*, ed. Elyce Rae Helford (Lanham, MD: Rowman and Littlefield, 2000): 135–162; Michael Bronski, *A Queer History of the United States* (Boston, MA: Beacon Press, 2011).

3. This term was first used by television historian David Marc in his book *Comic Visions* [David Marc, *Comic Visions: Television Comedy and American Culture* (London: Unwin Hyman, 1989)].

4. In communications researcher Art Silverblatt's work on genre, he contended: " 'The Flintstones' is, excuse the pun, bedrock family-values fare. Fred is a working-class hero trying to make his way in the world. Wilma is his stay-at-home wife who spends her days shopping, cooking and chatting with a neighbor" [Art Silverblatt, *Genre Studies in Mass Media: A Handbook* (Armonk, NY: ME Sharpe, 2007), 74]. Communications researchers Dylan Pank and John Caro similarly discussed the promotion of family values in both shows: "Spanning the prehistoric to the space age, *The Flintstones* and *The Jetsons* may provide some comfort to the audience with the notion that the North American way of life is enduring and immutable" [Dylan Pank and John Caro, " 'Haven't You Heard? They Look Like Us Now!' Realism and Metaphor in *The New Battlestar Galactica*," in *Channeling the Future: Essays*

on Science Fiction and Fantasy Television, ed. Lincoln Geraghty (Lanham, MD: Scarecrow Press, 2009), 208]. The promotion of the value of capitalism was also discussed by communications theorist Megan Mullen: "*The Flintstones* thus uses the production and narrative conventions of children's cartoon programming to teach the values of consumerism in an innocuous way to viewers of all ages" [Megan Mullen, "The Simpsons and Hanna-Barbera's Animation Legacy," in *Leaving Springfield: The Simpsons and the Possibility of Oppositional Culture*, ed. John Alberti (Detroit, MI: Wayne State University Press, 2004), 70].

5. As media columnist Ray Richmond argued, shows such as *The Flintstones* "tossed in sophisticated little rewards for parents who paid attention" [Ray Richmond, "Toons Tune to Adult Auds," *Variety*, October 7–13, 1996, 37].

6. According to research discussed by communications theorists Wendy Hilton-Morrow and David T. McMahan, viewers older than age 18 years constituted nearly 60 percent of the audience of *The Simpsons* [Wendy Hilton-Morrow and David T. McMahan, "The *Flintstones* to *Futurama*: Networks and Prime Time Animation," in *Prime Time Animation: Television Animation and American Culture*, ed. Carol A. Stabile and Mark Harrison (London: Routledge, 2003)].

7. In Jason Mittell, *Genre and Television: From Cop Shows to Cartoons in American Culture* (New York: Routledge, 2004), 67.

8. Jason Mittell, *Genre and Television: From Cop Shows to Cartoons in American Culture* (New York: Routledge, 2004), 67.

9. In his book *Television: Critical Methods and Applications*, communications theorist Jeremy Butler wrote: "Theatrical cartoons, by virtue of their marginal existence and the distancing factor of drawings (compared to live action), were often permitted to violate social taboos against violence, sexuality, and general chaos. Contemporary Saturday morning cartoons are the enforcers of those taboos. They speak the language of the dominant discourse" [Jeremy G. Butler, *Television: Critical Methods and Applications* (Mahwah, NJ: Lawrence Erlbaum Associates, 2002), 312].

10. Rhonda Wilcox, "Unreal TV," in *Thinking Outside the Box: A Contemporary Television Genre Reader*, ed. Gary R. Edgerton and Brian G. Rose (Lexington, KY: University Press of Kentucky, 2005), 205.

11. James Roman, *From Daytime to Primetime: The History of American Television Programs* (Westport, CT: Greenwood Press, 2005), xxiii.

12. In communication theorist Rebecca Feasey's discussion of television, she wrote: "while children would tune in for the simplistic humour to be found in the silly images and lurid colours, adults were kept entertained by the more sophisticated verbal jokes that were said to dominate such texts" [Rebecca Feasey, *Masculinity and Popular Television* (Edinburgh: Edinburgh University Press, 2008), 33].

13. Jo Johnson, "'We'll Have a Gay Old Time!' Queer Representations in American Prime-Time Animation from the Cartoon Short to the Family Sitcom," in *Queers in American Popular Culture*, ed. Jim Elledge (Santa Barbara, CA: Praeger, 2010), 247.

14. Karma Waltonen and Denise Du Vernay, *The Simpsons in the Classroom: Embiggening the Learning Experience with the Wisdom of Springfield* (Jefferson, NC: McFarland and Company, 2010), 230.

15. In his discussion of *South Park*, James Keller contended that the series has done "much to advance the interests of gays and lesbians simply by addressing their issues, by refusing to erase their presence, and occasionally by taking a meaningful stand against homophobia" [James Keller, "Recuperating and Reviling *South Park*'s Queer Politics," in *Queers in American Popular Culture*, ed. Jim Elledge (Santa Barbara, CA: Praeger, 2010), 299].

16. Carol Queen and Lawrence Schimel, *Pomosexuals: Challenging Assumptions about Gender and Sexuality* (San Francisco, CA: Cleis Press, 1997).

17. Matthew Henry, "Looking for Amanda Hugginkiss: Gay Life on The Simpsons," in *Leaving Springfield: The Simpsons and the Possibility of Oppositional Culture*, ed. John Alberti (Detroit, MI: Wayne State University Press, 2004), 239.

18. This same idea was explored in an episode of sitcom *Community* (2009–) when the notoriously homophobic character Pierce (Chevy Chase) saw an opportunity to expand his business by targeting homosexual consumers.

19. Research, for example, indicates that the trend has been in the direction of increased tolerance of homosexuality over time [Michael Sullivan and John S. Wodardski, "Social Alienation in Gay Youth," *Journal of Human Behavior in the Social Environment* 5, no. 1 (2002): 1–17].

20. Gary Needham, "Scheduling Normativity: Television, the Family, and Queer Temporality," in *Queer TV*, ed. Glyn Davis and Gary Needham (New York: Routledge, 2009), 147.

21. In Brandon Voss, "Big Gay Following: Seth MacFarlane," *The Advocate*, February 27, 2008: 22–23.

22. Michael Musto, "Stewie Griffin," *Out* (May 2005), 64.

23. Jeremy Wisnewski, *Family Guy and Philosophy: A Cure for the Petarded* (Malden, MA: Blackwell, 2007), 146.

24. John Kunder-Gibbs and Kristin Kundert-Gibbs, *Action! Acting Lessons for CG Animators* (Indianapolis, IN: Wiley, 2009), 101.

25. Ted Gournelos, "Puppets, Slaves, and Sex Changes: Mr. Garrison and South Park's Performative Sexuality," *Television and New Media* 10, no. 3 (May 2009), 270.

26. Ted Gournelos, "Puppets, Slaves, and Sex Changes: Mr. Garrison and South Park's Performative Sexuality," *Television and New Media* 10, no. 3 (May 2009), 272.

27. Ted Gournelos, "Puppets, Slaves, and Sex Changes: Mr. Garrison and South Park's Performative Sexuality," *Television and New Media* 10, no. 3 (May 2009), 275.

28. Pabitra Benjamin, "An interview with a High School Activist," in *Restoried Selves: Autobiographies of Queer Asian/Pacific American Activists*, ed. Kevin Kumashiro (Binghamton, NY: Harrington Park Press, 2004), 4.

29. Eric Rofes, "Making Our Schools Safe for Sissies," in *The Gay Teen: Educational Practice and Theory for Lesbian, Gay and Bisexual Adolescents*, ed. Gerald Unks (New York: Routledge, 1995), 81.

30. Lauren Rosewarne, "Is He or Isn't He? The Tawdry Pastime of Sexuality Speculation," *The Conversation*, December 7, 2011. https://theconversation.edu.au/is-he-or-isnt-he-the-tawdry-pastime-of-sexuality-speculation-4607 (accessed January 21, 2012).

31. Jack Williams Brehm, *A Theory of Psychological Reactance* (New York: Academic Press, 1966).

32. Roy F. Baumeister and Brad J. Bushman, *Social Psychology and Human Nature* (Belmont, CA: Wadsworth, 2011), 102.

33. Brad J. Bushman and Joanne Cantor, "Media Ratings for Violence and Sex: Implications for Policy Makers and Parents," *American Psychologist* 58 (2003): 130–141.

34. James M. Olson and Victoria M. Esses, "The Social Psychology of Censorship," in *Interpreting Censorship in Canada*, ed. Allan C. Hutchinson and Klaus Petersen (Toronto: University of Toronto Press, 1999), 283.

35. Diana Kendall, *Framing Class: Media Representations of Wealth and Poverty in America* (Lanham, MD: Rowman and Littlefield, 2011), 91.

36. Ed Christman, "Roadrunner Promo Stumbles with Trumped-up Controversy," *Billboard*, May 13, 1995, 72.

37. In Herbert N. Foerstel, *Banned in the USA: A Reference Guide to Book Censorship in Schools and Public Libraries* (Westport, CT: Greenwood Press, 2002), 160.

38. Lauren Rosewarne, *Part-Time Perverts: Sex, Pop Culture, and Kink Management* (Santa Barbara, CA: Praeger, 2011), 111.

39. Rebecca Arnold, *Fashion, Desire and Anxiety: Image and Morality in the 20th Century* (New York: IB Tauris, 2001), 16.

40. This idea of a positional good—of something only being valuable because other people don't have it—is addressed in an episode of sitcom *The Big Bang Theory* (2007-) as related to having a girlfriend.

41. Mark Bego, *Madonna: Blonde Ambition* (New York: Harmony Books, 1992), 282.

42. Lauren Rosewarne, *Part-Time Perverts: Sex, Pop Culture, and Kink Management* (Santa Barbara, CA: Praeger, 2011).

43. In Peter B. Orlik, *Electronic Media Criticism: Applied Perspectives* (New York: Routledge, 2009), 202.

44. Peter B. Orlik, *Electronic Media Criticism: Applied Perspectives* (New York: Routledge, 2009), 202.

45. See, for example, Melinda Tankard Reist, *Getting Real: Challenging the Sexualisation of Girls* (North Melbourne, Victoria: Spinifex Press, 2009); M. Gigi Durham, *The Lolita Effect* (New York: Overlook Press, 2008); Diane E. Levin and Jean Kilbourne, *So Sexy So Soon: The New Sexualized* Childhood (New York:

Ballantine Books, 2008); Patrice A. Oppliger, *Girls Gone Skank: The Sexualization of Girls in American Culture* (Jefferson, NC: McFarland & Company, 2008); Sharon Lamb and Lyn Mikel Brown, *Packaging Girlhood: Rescuing Our Daughters from Marketers' Schemes* (New York: St. Martin's Griffin, 2006).

46. A spokesperson from the National Society for the Prevention of Cruelty to Children in the United Kingdom, for example, contended that such cartoon porn "is an easy way for paedophiles to persuade kids this type of behaviour is OK. It's posing a danger to children. We need to raise awareness so that something can done about it" ["Kids at Risk from Porn Cartoons," *Sunday Mirror*, October 30, 2011, 29].

47. While in these examples the pornographic animation available online is unauthorized, there are examples of children's entertainment actually being marketed as sexy in order to appeal to an adult audience. In *Part-Time Perverts*, for example, I discussed the marketing of the film *Shrek Forever After* (2010): "a *Vman* men's magazine spread included images taken by Ellen von Unwerth, a photographer known for her erotic images. The photographs showed fashion models posing sexily with Shrek characters, notably a lingerie-clad model leaning against Donkey, two shirtless men fight over Fiona and a male model feeding grapes to Puss In Boots; each offering allusions to human/animal sex" [Lauren Rosewarne, *Part-Time Perverts: Sex, Pop Culture, and Kink Management* (Santa Barbara, CA: Praeger, 2011), 58].

48. Jason Mittell, *Genre and Television: From Cop Shows to Cartoons in American Culture* (New York: Routledge, 2004), 182.

49. Harold Dwight Lasswell, *Propaganda Technique in the World War* (New York: Knopf, 1927).

50. Lauren Rosewarne, *Sex in Public: Women, Outdoor Advertising and Public Policy* (Newcastle: Cambridge Scholar's Press, 2007), 189.

51. Matt Sienkiewicz and Nick Marx, "Beyond a Cutout World: Ethnic Humor and Discursive Integration in *South Park*," *Journal of Film and Video* 61, no. 2 (Summer 2009), 5.

52. Simon Weaver, *The Rhetoric of Racist Humour: US, UK and Global Race Joking* (Burlington, VT: Ashgate, 2011), 1.

THE ORAL SEX CHAPTER

1. Hadley Freeman, "How Best to Win an Oscar: Try Female Oral Sex," *The Guardian* (January 12, 2011). Retrieved March 13, 2012, from http://www.guardian.co.uk/commentisfree/2011/jan/12/to-get-oscar-oral-sex.

2. Cable television, of course, has portrayed the act with much more frequency, including in the series *Sex and the City* (1998–2004), *Six Feet Under* (2001–2005), *Californication* (2007–), and *True Blood* (2008–).

3. Laina Y. Bay-Cheng and Nicole M. Fava, "Young Women's Experiences and Perceptions of Cunnilingus during Adolescence," *Journal of Sex Research* 48, no. 6 (2011): 531–542.

4. Edward O. Laumann, John H. Gagnon, Robert T. Michael, and Stuart Michaels, *The Social Organization of Sexuality: Sexual Practices in the United States* (Chicago, IL: University of Chicago Press, 1994), 101.

5. John H. Gagnon and William Simon, "The Scripting of Oral Genital Sexual Conduct," *Archives of Sexual Behavior* 16 (1987): 1–25, 24.

6. Leslie Kurke, *Coins, Bodies, Games, and Gold: The Politics of Meaning in Archaic Greece* (Princeton, NJ: Princeton University Press, 1999), 203.

7. Ray Laurence, *Roman Passions: A History of Pleasure in Imperial Rome* (London: Continuum, 2009), 78.

8. Virginia Reynolds, *A Lover's Guide to the Kama Sutra* (White Plains, NY: Peter Pauper Press, 2002); Susan Crain Bakos, *The New Tantra Simple and Sexy: Longer, Better Lovemaking for Everyone* (Beverly, MA: Quiver, 2008).

9. In Todd C. Penner and Caroline Vander Stichele, *Mapping Gender in Ancient Religious Discourses* (Danvers, MA: Brill, 2007), 41.

10. See Holt N. Parker, "The Teratogenic Grid," in *Roman Sexualities*, ed. Judith P. Hallett and Marilyn B. Skinner (Princeton, NJ: Princeton University Press, 1997): 47–65.

11. See Robert Parker, "Sacrifice and Battle," in *War and Violence in Ancient Greece*, ed. Hans van Wees (Oakville, CT: David Brown Book Co, 2000): 299–314.

12. Richard Michael, *The ABZ of Pornography* (London: Panther, 1972), 44.

13. Jonathan Light, *The Art of Porn: An Aesthetics for the Performing Art of Pornography* (New York: Light Publishing, 2002), 74.

14. Joseph W. Slade, *Pornography and Sexual Representation: A Reference Guide*, Volume II (Westport, CT: Greenwood Press, 2001), 654.

15. Alan McKee, Kath Albury, and Catharine Lumby, *The Porn Report* (Carlton: Melbourne University Press, 2008), 43.

16. Rebecca Traister, "More Than Lip Service," *The Guardian* (October 27, 2003). Retrieved March 13, 2012, from http://www.guardian.co.uk/world/2003/oct/27/gender.uk.

17. See Lauren Rosewarne, *Part-Time Perverts: Sex, Pop Culture, and Kink Management* (Santa Barbara, CA: Praeger, 2011), for a review on the appearance of images of non-vanilla sexual practice in mainstream film and television.

18. Joseph W. Slade, *Pornography and Sexual Representation: A Reference Guide*, Volume II (Westport, CT: Greenwood Press, 2001), 654.

19. As noted by Robert Jensen and Gail Dines in their research on pornography: "cunnilingus scenes almost always were set up in such a way as to maximize visibility of the woman's vagina" [Robert Jensen and Gail Dines, "The Content of Mass-Marketed Pornography," in *Pornography: The Production and Consumption of Inequality*, ed. Gail Dines, Robert Jensen, and Ann Russo (London: Routledge, 1998), 77].

20. Dave Thompson, *Black and White and Blue: Adult Cinema from the Victoria Age to the VCR* (Toronto: ECW Press, 2003), 113.

21. Robert Jensen and Gail Dines, "The Content of Mass-Marketed Pornography," in *Pornography: The Production and Consumption of Inequality*, ed. Gail Dines, Robert Jensen, and Ann Russo (London: Routledge, 1998), 77.

22. Lauren Rosewarne, "Oral Sex and the Quid Pro Quo," *The Conversation* (August 16, 2012). Retrieved November 1, 2012, from http://theconversation.edu.au/oral-sex-and-the-quid-pro-quo-8863.

23. Laura Backstrom, Elizabeth A. Armstrong, and Jennifer Puentes, "Women's Negotiation of Cunnilingus in College Hookups and Relationships," *Journal of Sex Research* 49, no. 1 (2012): 1–12.

24. Shere Hite, *The Hite Report* (New York: Seven Stores Press, 1981), 286.

25. Shere Hite, *The Shere Hite Reader* (New York: Seven Stories Press, 2003), 188.

26. Lauren Rosewarne, *Part-Time Perverts: Sex, Pop Culture, and Kink Management* (Santa Barbara, CA: ABC-CLIO, 2011), 106.

27. Raewyn Connell, *Masculinities* (Berkeley: University of California Press, 1995).

28. Susan Crain Bakos, *The Orgasm Bible* (Beverly, MA: Quiver, 2008), 10.

29. Edward O. Laumann, John H. Gagnon, Robert T. Michael, and Stuart Michaels, *The Social Organization of Sexuality: Sexual Practices in the United States* (Chicago: University of Chicago Press, 1994).

30. Adam Knee, "Female Power and Male Hysteria," in *Screening the Male: Exploring Masculinities in Hollywood Cinema*, ed. Steven Cohan and Ina Rae Hark (London: Routledge, 1993), 96.

31. In Peter Biskind, "The Vietnam Oscars," *Vanity Fair* (March 2008): 266–280, 275.

32. Linda Williams, *Screening Sex* (Durham, NC: Duke University Press, 2008), 176.

33. Lauren Rosewarne, *Periods in Pop Culture: Menstruation in Film and Television* (Lanham, MD: Lexington Books, 2012).

34. It should, of course, not be inferred that these ideas are mutually exclusive. In an episode of *Dexter* (2006-), the routinely sexually frank—and sometimes sexually *grotesque*—Mazuka (C. S. Lee) made a barb while at a crime scene about having had his tongue in places that smelt better. This scene illustrates that sometimes men might be evolved enough to perform cunnilingus but still deem the task egregious.

35. Mark Allinson, *A Spanish Labyrinth: The Films of Pedro Almodóvar* (New York: IB Tauris, 2006) 88.

36. Laina Y. Bay-Cheng, Adjoa D. Robinson, and Alyssa N. Zucker, "Behavioral and Relational Contexts of Adolescent Female Desire, Wanting, and Pleasure: Undergraduate Women's Retrospective Accounts," *Journal of Sex Research* 46 (2009): 511–524; Juliet Richters, Richard de Visser, Chris Rissel and Anthony M. Smith, "Sexual Practices at Last Heterosexual Encounter and Occurrence of Orgasm in a National Study," *Journal of Sex Research* 43 (2006): 217–226.

37. John H. Gagnon and William Simon, "The Scripting of Oral Genital Sexual Conduct," *Archives of Sexual Behavior* 16 (1987): 1–25, 24.

38. In Patrick Suraci, *Male Sexual Armor: Erotic Fantasies and Sexual Realities of the Cop on the Beat and the Man in the Street* (Falls Village, CT: Invington Publishers, 1992), 237.

39. In Patrick Suraci, *Male Sexual Armor: Erotic Fantasies and Sexual Realities of the Cop on the Beat and the Man in the Street* (Falls Village, CT: Invington Publishers, 1992), 238.

40. Jody Pennington, *The History of Sex in American Film* (Westport, CT: Praeger, 2007), 158.

41. Laura Backstrom, Elizabeth A. Armstrong, and Jennifer Puentes, "Women's Negotiation of Cunnilingus in College Hookups and Relationships," *Journal of Sex Research* 49, no. 1 (2012): 1–12.

42. Laina Y. Bay-Cheng and Nicole M. Fava, "Young Women's Experiences and Perceptions of Cunnilingus during Adolescence," *Journal of Sex Research* 48, no. 6 (2011): 531–542, 532.

43. Shere Hite, *The Shere Hite Reader* (New York: Seven Stories Press, 2003), 188.

44. Laura Backstrom, Elizabeth A. Armstrong, and Jennifer Puentes, "Women's Negotiation of Cunnilingus in College Hookups and Relationships," *Journal of Sex Research* 49, no. 1 (2012): 1–12.

45. In Jim Burns, *Teaching Your Children Healthy Sexuality* (Bloomington, MN: Bethany House Publishers, 2008), 91.

46. Susan Crain Bakos, *Orgasm Loop: The No Fail Technique for Reaching Orgasm during Sex* (Beverly, MA: Quiver, 2008), 79.

47. In Shere Hite, *The Shere Hite Reader* (New York: Seven Stories Press, 2003), 65.

48. Jonathan Light, *The Art of Porn: An Aesthetics for the Performing Art of Pornography* (New York: Light Publishing, 2002), 74.

49. In Patrick Suraci, *Male Sexual Armor: Erotic Fantasies and Sexual Realities of the Cop on the Beat and the Man in the Street* (Falls Village, CT: Invington Publishers, 1992), 239.

50. Laina Y. Bay-Cheng and Nicole M. Fava, "Young Women's Experiences and Perceptions of Cunnilingus during Adolescence," *Journal of Sex Research* 48, no. 6 (2011): 531–542, 532.

51. In Shere Hite, *The Shere Hite Reader* (New York: Seven Stories Press, 2003), 65.

52. Sarah Alexander Chase, *Perfectly Prep: Gender Extremes at a New England Prep School* (New York: Oxford University Press, 2008), 155.

53. Susan Crain Bakos, *The Sex Bible* (Beverly, MA: Quiver, 2006), 80.

54. John H. Gagnon and William Simon, "The Scripting of Oral Genital Sexual Conduct," *Archives of Sexual Behavior* 16 (1987): 1–25, 24.

55. Karin L. Brewster and Kathryn H. Tillman, "Who's Doing It? Patterns and Predictors of Youths' Oral Sexual Experiences," *Journal of Adolescent Health* 42 (2005): 73–80; Edward O. Laumann, John H. Gagnon, Robert T. Michael, and Stuart Michaels, *The Social Organization of Sexuality: Sexual Practices in the United States* (Chicago: University of Chicago Press, 1994).

56. Sarah Alexander Chase, *Perfectly Prep: Gender Extremes at a New England Prep School* (New York: Oxford University Press, 2008), 155.

57. In Shere Hite, *The Hite Report* (New York: Seven Stores Press, 1981), 287.

58. In Shere Hite, *The Hite Report on Male Sexuality* (New York: Knopf, 1981), 719.

59. In Shere Hite, *The Shere Hite Reader* (New York: Seven Stories Press, 2003), 190.

60. Lauren Rosewarne, *Periods in Pop Culture: Menstruation in Film and Television* (Lanham, MD: Lexington Books, 2012).

61. Sarah Alexander Chase, *Perfectly Prep: Gender Extremes at a New England Prep School* (New York: Oxford University Press, 2008), 155.

62. Shere Hite, *The Shere Hite Reader* (New York: Seven Stories Press, 2003).

63. Edward O. Laumann, John H. Gagnon, Robert T. Michael, and Stuart Michaels, *The Social Organization of Sexuality: Sexual Practices in the United States* (Chicago: University of Chicago Press, 1994), 101.

64. Sarah Alexander Chase, *Perfectly Prep: Gender Extremes at a New England Prep School* (New York: Oxford University Press, 2008), 155.

65. John H. Gagnon and William Simon, "The Scripting of Oral Genital Sexual Conduct," *Archives of Sexual Behavior*, 16 (1987): 1–25, 24.

66. Shere Hite, *The Hite Report* (New York: Seven Stores Press, 1981), 295.

67. Lauren Rosewarne, *Periods in Pop Culture: Menstruation in Film and Television* (Lanham, MD: Lexington Books, 2012).

68. Ian Kerner, *She Comes First: The Thinking Man's Guide to Pleasuring a Woman* (New York: HarperCollins Publishers, 2010), 68.

69. Examples of this do however, exist. *Somewhere*, *Hall Pass*, and *Greenberg*, for example, each included cunnilingus scenes between relative strangers.

70. Lauren Rosewarne, "Oral Sex and the Quid Pro Quo," *The Conversation* (August 16, 2012). Retrieved November 1, 2012, from http://theconversation.edu.au/oral-sex-and-the-quid-pro-quo-8863.

THE FLATULENCE CHAPTER

1. Jim Dawson, *Who Cut the Cheese? A Cultural History of the Fart* (Berkeley, CA: Ten Speed Press, 1999), 3.

2. Stephen Bryant, *Art of the Fart* (London: PRC Publishing, 2004), inner flap.

3. Jim Dawson, *Who Cut the Cheese? A Cultural History of the Fart* (Berkeley, CA: Ten Speed Press, 1999), 1.

4. Jim Dawson, *Who Cut the Cheese? A Cultural History of the Fart* (Berkeley, CA: Ten Speed Press, 1999), 2. [My emphasis.]

5. Valerie Allen, *On Farting: Language and Laughter in the Middle Ages* (New York: Palgrave Macmillan, 2007), 14. [My emphasis.]

6. Katla McGlynn, "Kevin Smith Talks Judd Apatow, Weed, and His Post-'Zack and Miri' Depression," *Huffington Post* (October 5, 2009). Retrieved June 29, 2012, from http://www.huffingtonpost.com/katla-mcglynn/kevin-smith-talks-angry-y_b_309496.html.

7. Robert Kolker, *A Cinema of Loneliness* (New York: Oxford University Press, 2011), x.

8. I. M. Stoned, *Weed: 420 Things You Didn't Know (or Remember) about Cannabis* (Avon, MA: Adams Media, 2009), 93.

9. For example, it was described as a "sophomoric mainstream comedy" in Nancy Griffin and Kim Masters' biography *Hit and Run* [Nancy Griffin and Kim Masters, *Hit and Run: How Jon Peters and Peter Guber Took Sony for a Ride in Hollywood* (New York: Simon and Schuster, 1996), 58].

10. Stephen G. Bloom, *Inside the Writer's Mind: Writing Narrative Journalism* (Ames, IA: Iowa State Press), 41.

11. Timothy Jay, *Cursing in America* (Philadelphia, PA: John Benjamins Publishing, 1992), 28.

12. Gale Largey and Rod Watson, "The Sociology of Odors," *The Smell Culture Reader*, ed. Jim Drobnick (New York: Berg, 2006), 31.

13. Don D. Nibbelink, *Fearsome Folklore of Farting* (Berkeley, CA: Frog Books, 2008), 21.

14. Rudolph Altrocchi, *The Playful Spirit: Italian Humor* (Bloomington, IN: iUniverse), 43.

15. Annette M. Holba, "Understanding *Schadenfreude* to Seek an Ethical Response," in *Philosophies of Communication: Implications for Everyday Experience*, ed. Melissa A. Cook and Annette Holba (New York: Peter Lang, 2008), 4.

16. Lauren Rosewarne, "Subversion, Schadenfreude and Drama Addiction in 'Private Games,' " *The Conversation* (August 9, 2012). Retrieved November 1, 2012, from http://theconversation.edu.au/subversion-schadenfreude-and-drama-addiction-in-private-games-8749.

17. Lauren Rosewarne, *Part-Time Perverts: Sex, Pop Culture, and Kink Management* (Santa Barbara, CA: Praeger, 2009), 62.

18. Geoffrey Hughes, *An Encyclopedia of Swearing* (Armonk, NY: M. E. Sharpe, 2006), 160.

19. George Bach and Herb Goldberg, *Creative Aggression: The Art of Assertive Living* (Los Angeles, CA: Wellness Institute, 1974)

20. Leo Charney, "American Film," in *Comedy: A Geographic and Historical Guide*, Volume 1, ed. Maurice Charney (Westport, CT: Praeger, 2005), 85.

21. Simone de Beauvoir, *The Second Sex* (New York: Vintage, 1989), 649.

22. Lauren Rosewarne, *Cheating on the Sisterhood: Infidelity and Feminism* (Santa Barbara, CA: Praeger, 2009), 43.

23. In *This is 40*, Pete farts deliberately to get a rise out of his wife. This idea is taken substantially further in the film *Love Stinks* (1999): Seth (French Stewart) wanted his newly ex girlfriend Chelsea (Bridgette Wilson) to move out: he used farting as an attempt to make her life miserable, aware of how loathsome women generally find such behavior.

24. Lauren Rosewarne, *Periods in Pop Culture: Menstruation in Film and Television* (Lanham, MD: Lexington Books, 2012), 134.

25. Richard Ellmann, ed., *Selected Letters of James Joyce* (New York: Viking, 1976), 185.

26. Susanna Paasonen, "Repetition and Hyperbole: The Gendered Choreographies of Heteroporn," in *Everyday Pornography*, ed. Karen Boyle (New York: Routledge, 2010), 75.

27. Retrieved June 30, 2012, from http://www.youtube.com/playlist?list=PL7B47093D573FC232.

28. Lauren Rosewarne, *Part-Time Perverts: Sex, Pop Culture, and Kink Management* (Santa Barbara, CA: Praeger, 2009), 119.

29. This can similarly be likened to pornographic scenes involving used menstrual products. In *Periods in Pop Culture*, I contended, "in porn it is even more likely that menstrual products are presented as taboo, private objects which get fetishized because of their rarely seen—if not 'gross out'—qualities" [Lauren Rosewarne, *Periods in Pop Culture: Menstruation in Film and Television* (Lanham, MD: Lexington Books, 2012), 145].

THE RUDE GESTURES CHAPTER

1. Nancy Armstrong and Melissa Wagner, *Field Guide to Gestures* (San Francisco, CA: Quirk Productions, 2003), 117.

2. Craig A. Williams, *Epigrams: Martial* (New York: Oxford University Press, 2004), 110.

3. Angus Trumble, *The Finger: A Handbook* (New York: Farrar, Straus and Giroux, 2010), 197.

4. Simon J. Bronner, *Explaining Traditions: Folk Behavior in Modern Culture* (Lexington, KY: University Press of Kentucky, 2011), 239.

5. Alan Dundes and Carl R. Pagter, *When You're up to Your Ass in Alligators: More Urban Folklore from the Paperwork Empire* (Detroit, MI: Wayne State University Press, 1987), 186.

6. Alan Dundes, *Interpreting Folklore* (Bloomington, IN: Indiana University Press, 1980), 57.

7. Catherine Orenstein, *Little Red Riding Hood Uncloaked: Sex, Morality, and the Evolution of a Fairytale* (New York: Basic Books, 2002), 174.

8. Stuart Jeffries, "The Shock Index: Is Giving The Finger Still Offensive?" *The Guardian* (February 22, 2012). Retrieved July 24, 2012, from www.guardian.co.uk/society/2012/feb/22/shock-index-finger-adele-mia.

9. Sarah Sawyer, *Avril Lavigne* (New York: Rosen Publishing Group, 2009), 26.

10. In Stuart Jeffries, "The Shock Index: Is Giving The Finger Still Offensive?" *The Guardian* (February 22, 2012). Retrieved July 24, 2012, from www.guardian.co.uk/society/2012/feb/22/shock-index-finger-adele-mia.

11. Russell Frank, *Contemporary Folklore on the Internet* (Jackson, MS: University Press of Mississippi, 2011), 69.

12. Dave Urbanski, *The Man Comes Around: The Spiritual Journey of Johnny Cash* (Lake Mary, FL: Relevant Books, 2003), 151–152.

13. Nancy Armstrong and Melissa Wagner, *Field Guide to Gestures* (San Francisco, CA: Quirk Productions, 2003), 117–118.

14. In Ethan Sacks, "Madonna Blasts M.I.A. On-Air Middle Finger Salute," *New York Daily News* (February 10, 2012). Retrieved July 18, 2012, from articles.nydailynews.com/2012-02-10/news/31048210_1_material-girl-mia-finger.

15. Stuart Jeffries, "The Shock Index: Is Giving The Finger Still Offensive?" *The Guardian* (February 22, 2012). Retrieved July 24, 2012, from www.guardian.co.uk/society/2012/feb/22/shock-index-finger-adele-mia.

16. In Ethan Sacks, "Madonna Blasts M.I.A. On-Air Middle Finger Salute," *New York Daily News* (February 10, 2012). Retrieved July 18, 2012, from articles.nydailynews.com/2012-02-10/news/31048210_1_material-girl-mia-finger.

17. R.D. Reynolds and Randy Baer, *WrestleCrap: The Very Worst of Pro Wrestling* (Toronto: ECW Press, 2003), 210.

18. Nancy Armstrong and Melissa Wagner, *Field Guide to Gestures* (San Francisco, CA: Quirk Productions, 2003), 117–118.

19. Stuart Jeffries, "The Shock Index: Is Giving The Finger Still Offensive?" *The Guardian* (February 22, 2012). Retrieved July 24, 2012, from www.guardian.co.uk/society/2012/feb/22/shock-index-finger-adele-mia.

20. Nancy Armstrong and Melissa Wagner, *Field Guide to Gestures* (San Francisco, CA: Quirk Productions, 2003), 117.

21. In Bob Tourtellotte, "Golden Globes: Raised Finger Gets Thumbs Down," *Reuters* (January 13, 2009). Retrieved July 18, 2012, from blogs.reuters.com/fanfare/2009/01/13/golden-globes-raised-finger-gets-thumbs-down/.

22. Natalie Angier, "G#%!y Golly: Almost Before We Spoke, We Swore," *New York Times* (September 20, 2005), F1.

23. Lauren Rosewarne, *Part-Time Perverts: Sex, Pop Culture, and Kink Management* (Santa Barbara, CA: Praeger, 2011), 84.

24. "Ryan Gosling Frustrated by Censorship," *The Independent* (January 24, 2011). Retrieved October 15, 2012, from http://www.independent.co.uk/news/people/news/ryan-gosling-frustrated-by-censorship-2192751.html.

25. See for example Danielle Henderson, *Feminist Ryan Gosling: Feminist Theory as Imagined from Your Favorite Sensitive Movie Dude* (Philadelphia, PA: Running Press, 2012).

26. Charles Shaar Murray, *Crosstown Traffic: Jimi Hendrix and the Post-war Rock 'n' Roll Revolution* (New York: St. Martin's Press, 1989).

27. Dorian Solot and Marshall Miller, *I (Heart) Female Orgasm* (New York: Marlowe & Co, 2007), 246.

28. Lauren Rosewarne, "Jarryd Blair's Shocker and a Hurdy Gurdy of Double Standards," *ABC The Drum* (March 18, 2011). Retrieved November 1, 2012, from http://www.abc.net.au/unleashed/45252.html.

29. Lauren Rosewarne, *Part-Time Perverts: Sex, Pop Culture, and Kink Management* (Santa Barbara, CA: Praeger, 2011).

THE EUPHEMISMS CHAPTER

1. Timothy Jay, *Why We Curse: A Neuro-psycho-social Theory of Speech* (Philadelphia, PA: John Benjamins Publishing, 2000), 128.

2. Keith Allan and Kate Burridge, *Forbidden Words: Taboo and the Censoring of Language* (New York: Cambridge University Press, 2006), 243.

3. Kate Burridge, "The Art of Telling It Like It Isn't," *Sydney Morning Herald* (May 27, 2012). Retrieved June 12, 2012, from http://m.smh.com.au/opinion/society-and-culture/the-art-of-telling-it-like-it-isnt-20120526-1zbir.html

4. "The Euphemism: Telling It Like it Isn't," *Time* (September 19, 1969), 28.

5. Andrew Adam Newman, "Rebelling against the Commonly Evasive Feminine Care Ad," *New York Times* (March 15, 2010). Retrieved June 20, 2012, from http://www.nytimes.com/2010/03/16/business/media/16adco.html?_r=1&ref=business

6. Lauren Rosewarne, *Periods in Pop Culture: Menstruation in Film and Television* (Baltimore, MD: Lexington Books, 2012).

7. The See You Next Tuesday euphemism is apparent in the Ke$ha song titled "C U Next Tuesday" (2010). In an episode of *Weeds* (2005–2012), the routinely brazen Celia (Elizabeth Perkins) exited a scene also saying, "See you next Tuesday." In journalist Joe Hildebrand's Tuesday news segment on Australia's *The Morning Show* (2007-), he similarly signs off with the tongue-in-cheek "see you next Tuesday."

8. Nancy L. McCallum and Matthew S. McGlone, "Death Be Not Profane: Mortality Salience and Euphemism Use," *Western Journal of Communication* 75, no. 5 (2011): 565–584, 570.

9. Shonna L. Trinch, "Managing Euphemism and Transcending Taboos: Negotiating the Meaning of Sexual Assault in Latinas' Narratives of Domestic Violence," *Interdisciplinary Journal for the Study of Discourse* 21, no. 4 (2001): 567–610.

10. Judith A. Parker and Deborah Mahlstedt, "Language, Power, and Sexual Assault: Women's Voices on Rape and Social Change," in *Language in the Real*

World: An Introduction to Linguistics, ed. Susan J. Behrens and Judith A. Parker (New York: Routledge, 2010), 144.

11. Research discussed by Robin Warshaw, for example, noted that only 27 percent of raped women thought of themselves as rape victims [Robin Warshaw, *I Never Called it Rape* (New York: Harper & Row, 1988), xxi].

12. In Patricia Easteal and Louise McOrmond-Plummer, *Real Rape, Real Pain* (Ormond, Victoria: Hybrid, 2006), 348.

13. In Nicola Gavey, *Just Sex? The Cultural Scaffolding of Rape* (New York: Routledge, 2005), 158.

14. Judith A. Parker and Deborah Mahlstedt, "Language, Power, and Sexual Assault: Women's Voices on Rape and Social Change," in *Language in the Real World: An Introduction to Linguistics*, ed. Susan J. Behrens and Judith A. Parker (New York: Routledge, 2010), 144.

15. In Jim Wood, *The Rape of Inez Garcia* (New York: Putnam, 1976), 103.

16. In Sylvia Levine and Joseph Koenig, *Why Men Rape: Interviews with Convicted Rapists* (London: WH Allen, 1982), 75.

17. In André Kip and Göran Slutier, *Annotated Leading Cases of International Criminal Tribunals*, Volume VII (Cambridge: Intersentia, 1999), 606.

18. Judith A. Parker and Deborah Mahlstedt, "Language, Power, and Sexual Assault: Women's Voices on Rape and Social Change," in *Language in the Real World: An Introduction to Linguistics*, ed. Susan J. Behrens and Judith A. Parker (New York: Routledge, 2010), 144.

19. As lyricist Pamela Phillips wrote in her book on writing love songs: "being inventive with your language will engage your reader far more than using trite, overused phrases ... To a songwriter ... a euphemism is a way of saying something about love, lust, and sexuality in a brand new way, with a spin on words that perhaps nobody has ever said before" [Pamela Phillips, *The Art of Writing Love Songs* (New York: Allworth Press, 2003), 47].

20. "The Euphemism: Telling it Like it Isn't," *Time* (September 19, 1969), 28.

21. John H. Elliott, "Deuteronomy—Shameful Encroachment on Shameful Parts: Deuteronomy 25:11–12 and Biblical Euphemism," in *Ancient Israel: The Old Testament in Its Social Context*, ed. Philip Francis Esler (Minneapolis: Fortress Press, 2006), 166.

22. Keith Allan and Kate Burridge, *Forbidden Words: Taboo and the Censoring of Language* (New York: Cambridge University Press, 2006), 243.

23. Paul Baker, *Polari: The Lost Language of Gay Men* (New York: Routledge, 2002), 91.

24. John H. Elliott, "Deuteronomy—Shameful Encroachment on Shameful Parts: Deuteronomy 25:11–12 and Biblical Euphemism," in *Ancient Israel: The Old Testament in Its Social Context*, ed. Philip Francis Esler (Minneapolis: Fortress Press, 2006), 166.

25. According to sexuality theorist Giovanni Dall'Orto, traditionally homosexuality constituted "the realm of the unsaid, of whispers, of euphemism, of

circumlocution, of hidden faces" [In Derek Duncan, *Reading and Writing Italian Homosexuality: A Case of Possible Difference* (Burlington, VT: Ashgate, 2006), 44]. See also Ralph Keyes, *Unmentionables: From Family Jewels to Friendly Fire* (London: John Murray, 2010).

26. Jackie Stacey, *Teratologies: A Cultural Study of Cancer* (New York: Routledge, 1997).

27. Lauren Rosewarne, *Part-Time Perverts: Sex, Pop Culture, and Kink Management* (Santa Barbara, CA: ABC-CLIO, 2011).

28. Lauren Rosewarne, *Part-Time Perverts: Sex, Pop Culture, and Kink Management* (Santa Barbara, CA: ABC-CLIO, 2011), 113.

29. Lauren Rosewarne, *Part-Time Perverts: Sex, Pop Culture, and Kink Management* (Santa Barbara, CA: ABC-CLIO, 2011), 6.

30. Tracy Quan, "The Name of the Pose: A Sex Worker by Any Other Name?" in *Prostitution and Pornography: Philosophical Debate about the Sex Industry*, ed. Jessica Spector (Stanford, CA: Stanford University Press, 2006), 344.

31. Timothy Jay, *Why We Curse: A Neuro-psycho-social Theory of Speech* (Philadelphia, PA: John Benjamins Publishing, 2000), 133.

32. Lauren Rosewarne, *Part-Time Perverts: Sex, Pop Culture, and Kink Management* (Santa Barbara, CA: ABC-CLIO, 2011), 114.

33. Robert Hughes, *A Culture of Complaint: The Fraying of America* (New York: Oxford University Press, 1993), 18–19.

34. Sarah Gamble, *The Routledge Companion to Feminism And Postfeminism* (New York: Routledge, 2001), 275.

35. Natasha Walter, *The New Feminism* (London: Little, Brown and Company, 1998).

36. Deborah Cameron, "Words, Words, Words: The Power of Language," in *The War of the Words: The Political Correctness Debate*, ed. Sarah Dunant (London: Virago 1994), 33.

37. Tracy Quan, "The Name of the Pose: A Sex Worker by Any Other Name?" in *Prostitution and Pornography: Philosophical Debate about the Sex Industry*, ed. Jessica Spector (Stanford, CA: Stanford University Press, 2006), 341.

38. Roger Matthews, *Prostitution, Politics and Policy* (New York: Routledge, 2008), 41.

39. Tracy Quan, "The Name of the Pose: A Sex Worker by Any Other Name?" in *Prostitution and Pornography: Philosophical Debate about the Sex Industry*, ed. Jessica Spector (Stanford, CA: Stanford University Press, 2006), 344.

40. Roger Matthews, *Prostitution, Politics and Policy* (New York: Routledge, 2008), 41.

41. Tracy Quan, "The Name of the Pose: A Sex Worker by Any Other Name?" in *Prostitution and Pornography: Philosophical Debate about the Sex Industry*, ed. Jessica Spector (Stanford, CA: Stanford University Press, 2006), 344.

42. Barry J. Blake, *Secret Language: Codes, Tricks, Spies, Thieves, and Symbols* (New York: Oxford University Press, 2010), 256.

43. TVTropes, "Hurricane of Euphemisms." Retrieved June 21, 2012, from http://tvtropes.org/pmwiki/pmwiki.php/Main/HurricaneOfEuphemisms.

44. George Orwell, *Nineteen Eighty-Four* (Fairfield, IA: 1st World Library, 2004), 64.

45. Judith A. Parker and Deborah Mahlstedt, "Language, Power, and Sexual Assault: Women's Voices on Rape and Social Change," in *Language in the Real World: An Introduction to Linguistics*, ed. Susan J. Behrens and Judith A. Parker (New York: Routledge, 2010), 143.

46. Anthony W. Neal, *Unburdened by Conscience: A Black People's Collective Account of America's Ante-bellum South and the Aftermath* (Lanham, MD: University Press of America, 2009), 51.

47. Carolyn Logan, *Counterbalance: Gendered Perspectives for Writing and Language* (Peterborough, Ontario: Broadview Press, 1997), 50.

48. Timothy Jay, *Why We Curse: A Neuro-psycho-social Theory of Speech* (Philadelphia, PA: John Benjamins Publishing, 2000), 128.

THE VEGETARIAN CHAPTER

1. Karen Iacobbo and Michael Iacobbo, *Vegetarians and Vegans in America Today* (Westport, CT: Praeger, 2006), 128.

2. In Karen Iacobbo and Michael Iacobbo, *Vegetarians and Vegans in America Today* (Westport, CT: Praeger, 2006), 128.

3. In Karen Iacobbo and Michael Iacobbo, *Vegetarians and Vegans in America Today* (Westport, CT: Praeger, 2006), 130.

4. Margaret Puskar-Pasewicz, *Cultural Encyclopedia of Vegetarianism* (Santa Barbara, CA: ABC-CLIO, 2010), xv.

5. Stephen B. Oates, *Portrait of America: From Reconstruction to the Present* (Boston, MA: Houghton Mifflin, 1973), 509.

6. In Karen Iacobbo and Michael Iacobbo, *Vegetarians and Vegans in America Today* (Westport, CT: Praeger, 2006), 122.

7. Donna Maurer, *Vegetarianism: Movement or Moment?* (Philadelphia, PA: Temple University Press, 2002), 16.

8. Robin Asbell, *New Vegetarian* (San Francisco: Chronicle Books, 2009), 12.

9. Donna Maurer, *Vegetarianism: Movement or Moment?* (Philadelphia, PA: Temple University Press, 2002), 3.

10. Lauren Rosewarne, *Cheating on the Sisterhood: Infidelity and Feminism* (Santa Barbara, CA: Praeger, 2009), 103.

11. Margaret Puskar-Pasewicz, *Cultural Encyclopedia of Vegetarianism* (Santa Barbara, CA: ABC-CLIO, 2010), 225.

12. Kristina Nelson, *Narcissism in High Fidelity* (Lincoln, NE: iUniverse, 2004), 29.

13. Chris Barsanti, *Filmology* (Avon, MA: Adams Media, 2011), 107.

14. Literature theorist Ruth Bienstock Anolik, for example, discussed how in the 19th century vegetarianism was used as a means to control sexuality [Ruth Bienstock

Anolik, *Horrifying Sex: Essays on Sexual Difference in Gothic Literature* (Jefferson, NC: McFarland and Company, 2007)].

15. Carol J. Adams, *The Sexual Politics of Meat: A Feminist-Vegetarian Critical Theory* (New York: Continuum, 1990), 13.

16. Karen Iacobbo and Michael Iacobbo, *Vegetarians and Vegans in America Today* (Westport, CT: Praeger, 2006).

17. Margaret Puskar-Pasewicz, *Cultural Encyclopedia of Vegetarianism* (Santa Barbara, CA: ABC-CLIO, 2010).

18. Herbert George Wells, *The Time Machine: An Invention* (Orchard Park, NY: 2001), 264.

19. The myth of Hitler's vegetarianism is addressed thoroughly in Carol J. Adams, *The Sexual Politics of Meat: A Feminist-Vegetarian Critical Theory* (New York: Continuum, 1990).

20. Karen Iacobbo and Michael Iacobbo, *Vegetarians and Vegans in America Today* (Westport, CT: Praeger, 2006), 131.

21. Tara Austen Weaver, *The Butcher and the Vegetarian* (New York: Rodale, 2010), 78.

22. Bob Torres and Jenna Torres, *Vegan Freak: Being Vegan in a Non-vegan World* (Colton, NY: Tofu Hound Press, 2005), 145.

23. Lucy Moll made this point in her book on vegetarian food: "Just a decade or two ago, words like hippies, sprouts and Birkenstock sandals were linked to vegetarians, and vegetarianism was seen as cultish to mainstream America" [Lucy Moll, *Vegetarian Times Complete Cookbook* (New York: Macmillan, 1995), 8]. Joanne Stepaniak, in her book about veganism, similarly discussed this issue, noting, "The spurious link [between vegetarianism, veganism and anorexia] has generated a slew of myths about veganism that have made it seem bizarre, cultish, or dangerous" [Joanne Stepaniak, *Being Vegan* (Lincolnwood, IL: Lowell House, 2000), 18].

24. Lauren Rosewarne, *Part-Time Perverts: Sex, Pop Culture, and Kink Management* (Santa Barbara, CA: Praeger, 2011), 103.

25. Margaret Puskar-Pasewicz, *Cultural Encyclopedia of Vegetarianism* (Santa Barbara, CA: ABC-CLIO, 2010), 223.

26. Carol J. Adams, *The Sexual Politics of Meat: A Feminist-Vegetarian Critical Theory* (New York: Continuum, 1990), 16.

27. Carol J. Adams, *The Sexual Politics of Meat: A Feminist-Vegetarian Critical Theory* (New York: Continuum, 1990), 56.

28. Carol J. Adams, *The Sexual Politics of Meat: A Feminist-Vegetarian Critical Theory* (New York: Continuum, 1990), 63.

29. Clare Whatling, *Screen Dreams: Fantasising Lesbians in Film* (Manchester: Manchester University Press, 1997).

30. In Karen Iacobbo and Michael Iacobbo, *Vegetarians and Vegans in America Today* (Westport, CT: Praeger, 2006), 35–36.

31. Amy O'Connor, "Don't Eat a Cow Man," *Vegetarian Times* (September 1995): 16.

THE ALCOHOL CHAPTER

1. In James DeSena, *Overcoming Your Alcohol, Drug and Recovery Habits* (Tucson, AZ: See Sharp Press, 2003), 20.

2. Norman K. Denzin, *Hollywood Shot by Shot: Alcoholism in American Cinema* (New Brunswick, NJ: Transaction Publishers, 2004), 21.

3. Norman K. Denzin, *Hollywood Shot by Shot: Alcoholism in American Cinema* (New Brunswick, NJ: Transaction Publishers, 2004), 21–22.

4. Mike Lewington, "An Overview," in *Images of Alcoholism*, ed. Jim Cook and Mike Lewington (London: British Film Institute, 1979), 22.

5. Mike Lewington, "An Overview," in *Images of Alcoholism*, ed. Jim Cook and Mike Lewington (London: British Film Institute, 1979), 22.

6. Earl Rubington, "The Changing Skid Row Scene," in *The Substance of Sociology: Codes, Conduct and Consequences*, ed. Ephraim H. Mizruchi (New York: Meredith Corporation, 1973), 439.

7. Earl Rubington, "The Changing Skid Row Scene," in *The Substance of Sociology: Codes, Conduct and Consequences*, ed. Ephraim H. Mizruchi (New York: Meredith Corporation, 1973), 439.

8. Mike Lewington, "An Overview," in *Images of Alcoholism*, ed. Jim Cook and Mike Lewington (London: British Film Institute, 1979), 27.

9. In Joseph Helmreich and Paul Marcus, *Warring Parents, Wounded Children, and the Wretched World of Child Custody* (Westport, CT: Praeger, 2008), ix.

10. Mike Lewington, "An Overview," in *Images of Alcoholism*, ed. Jim Cook and Mike Lewington (London: British Film Institute, 1979), 26.

11. William H. Kroes, Bruce Margolis, and Joseph J Hurrell, "Job Stress in Policemen," *Journal of Police Science and Administration* 2 (1974): 145–155; William H. Kroes, *Society's Victim: The Police* (Springfield: IL: Charles C. Thomas, 1986).

12. James Hibberd, "Police Psychology," *On Patrol* (Fall 1996): 26.

13. R. C. Van Raalte, "Alcohol as a Problem among Police Officers," *Police Chief* 44 (1979): 38–40.

14. Chad L. Cross and Larry Ashley, "Police Trauma and Addiction: Coping with the Dangers of the Job," *FBI Law Enforcement Bulletin* (October 2004): 24–32.

15. Lawrence E. Mintz, "Humor and Ethnic Stereotypes in Vaudeville and Burlesque," *Melus* 21, no. 4 (1996): 19–28.

16. Helen O'Hara, "The Worst Irish Stereotypes in Film," *Empire*. Retrieved August 20, 2012, from http://www.empireonline.com/features/irish-stereotypes-in-film/.

17. Helen O'Hara, "The Worst Irish Stereotypes in Film," *Empire*. Retrieved August 20, 2012, from http://www.empireonline.com/features/irish-stereotypes-in-film/.

18. Roger Blaney, "Alcoholism in Ireland: Medical and Social Aspects," *Journal of the Statistical and Social Inquiry Society of Ireland* (1974). Retrieved August 25,

2012, from http://www.tara.tcd.ie/bitstream/2262/7823/1/jssisiVolXXIIIPartI_108 124.pdf.

19. Robert Abelman and David J. Atkin, *The Televiewing Audience: The Art and Science of Watching TV* (New York: Peter Lang, 2011), 119.

20. Tara Ariano and Sarah Bunting, *Television without Pity: 752 Things We Love to Hate (and Hate to Love) about TV* (San Francisco, CA: Chronicle Books, 2006), 285–286.

21. Judith Harwin and Shirley Otto, "Women, Alcohol and the Screen," in *Images of Alcoholism*, ed. Jim Cook and Mike Lewington (London: British Film Institute, 1979), 37.

22. Elizabeth M. Ettore, *Women & Alcohol: A Private Pleasure or a Public Problem?* (London: Women's Press, 1997), 91.

23. Judith Harwin and Shirley Otto, "Women, Alcohol and the Screen," *Images of Alcoholism*, ed. Jim Cook and Mike Lewington (London: British Film Institute, 1979), 38.

24. Mike Lewington, "An Overview," in *Images of Alcoholism*, ed. Jim Cook and Mike Lewington (London: British Film Institute, 1979), 26.

25. Mike Lewington, "An Overview," in *Images of Alcoholism*, ed. Jim Cook and Mike Lewington (London: British Film Institute, 1979), 27.

26. Melinda Kanner, "That's Why the Lady is a Drunk: Women, Alcoholism, and Popular Culture," in *Sexual Politics and Popular Culture*, ed. Diane Raymond (Bowling Green, OH: Bowling Green State University Popular Press, 1990), 191.

27. This issue is discussed more in *Periods in Pop Culture*, where I explored the connection of discipline and self-control to women's self-esteem [Lauren Rosewarne, *Part-Time Perverts: Sex, Pop Culture, and Kink Management* (Santa Barbara, CA: ABC-CLIO, 2011)].

28. Susan E. Chase and Mary F. Rogers, *Mothers and Children: Feminist Analyses and Personal Narratives* (New Brunswick, NH: Rutgers University Press, 2001), 30.

29. Robyn Longhurst, *Maternities, Gender, Bodies and Spaces* (New York: Routledge, 2008), 118.

30. Robyn Longhurst, *Maternities, Gender, Bodies and Spaces* (New York: Routledge, 2008), 128.

31. Lauren Rosewarne, *Part-Time Perverts: Sex, Pop Culture, and Kink Management* (Santa Barbara, CA: ABC-CLIO, 2011), 50–51.

32. In *Cheating on the Sisterhood*, I summarized the literature describing the "good woman," identifying that she must be "stable, emotionally secure, kind, forbearing, supportive, contented, giving, feminine, beautiful, pure, chaste, noble, self-sacrificing, self-abnegating, self-restraining, and self-denying" [Lauren Rosewarne, *Cheating on the Sisterhood: Infidelity and Feminism* (Santa Barbara, CA: Praeger, 2009), 43].

33. Worth noting, a sitcom that subverts the drunk "bad mom" stereotype was *Grace Under Fire* (1993–1998): in it, protagonist Grace (Brett Butler) was a

recovering alcoholic who stayed sober and was dedicated to being a good parent to her three children.

34. Marcus Grant, "The Alcoholic as Hero," *Images of Alcoholism*, ed. Jim Cook and Mike Lewington (London: British Film Institute, 1979), 30.

35. Rob Palkovitz, *Involved Fathering and Men's Adult Development: Provisional Balances* (Mahwah, NJ: Lawrence Erlbaum Associates, 2002), 58.

THE DRUGS CHAPTER

1. Michael D. Lyman, *Drugs in Society: Causes, Concepts and Control* (Burlington, MA: Elsevier, 2011).

2. William N. Kelly, *Pharmacy: What It Is and How It Works* (Boca Raton, FL: CRC Press, 2012), 81.

3. Jane M. Durgin and Zachary I. Hanan, *Durgin & Hanan's Pharmacy Practice for Technicians* (Clifton Park, NY: Delmar, 2009); Robert W. Plant and Peter Panzarella, "Residential Treatment of Adolescents with Substance Use Disorders: Evidence-Based Approaches and Best Practice Recommendations," in *Adolescent Substance Abuse*, ed. Carl G. Leukefeld, Thomas P. Gullotta, and Michelle Staton-Tindall (New York: Springer, 2009): 135–154.

4. In 2001, for example, it was estimated that $150 million was spent on prescription medication in the United States [Jaeun Shin and Sangho Moon, "Direct-to-Consumer Prescription Drug Advertising: Concerns and Evidence of Consumers' Benefit," *Journal of Consumer Marketing* 22, no. 7 (2005): 397–403]. By 2006, this figure had risen to $216.7 billion [James W. Henderson, *Health Economics & Policy* (Mason, OH: South-West Cengage, 2009), 65].

5. Thomas Butler, *Consumer Health: Making Informed Decisions* (Burlington, MA: Jones & Bartlett Learning, 2012), 191.

6. Joy V. Fuqua, *Prescription TV: Therapeutic Discourse in the Hospital and at Home* (Durham, NC: Duke University Press, 2012), 99.

7. Philip Kotler, Joel Shalowitz, and Robert J. Stevens, *Strategic Marketing for Health Care Organizations* (San Francisco: Jossey-Bass, 2008).

8. Government Accountability Office, "Improvements Needed in FDA's Oversight of Direct-to-Consumer Advertising," 2006. Retrieved December 8, 2012, from http://www.gao.gov/products/GAO-07-54.

9. Nortin M. Hadler, *Worried Sick: A Prescription for Health in an Overtreated America* (Chapel Hill, NC: University of North Carolina Press, 2008).

10. Lauren Rosewarne, *Sex in Public: Women, Outdoor Advertising and Public Policy* (Newcastle: Cambridge Scholars Publishing, 2007).

11. See, for example, Walter Lippmann, *Public Opinion* (New York: Macmillan, 1922); Harold Dwight Lasswell, *Propaganda Technique in the World War* (New York: Knopf, 1927); Elizabeth M. Perse, *Media Effects and Society* (Mahwah, NJ: Lawrence Erlbaum Associates, 2002); and Jennings Bryant and Dolf Zillmann,

Media Effects: Advances in Theory and Research (Mahwah, NJ: Lawrence Erlbaum Associates, 2002).

12. While doctors are the people who actually write the prescriptions, studies indicate that doctors are becoming increasingly willing to prescribe whatever a patient requests, or at least feel under patient pressure to do so [Rebecca J. Welch Cline and Henry N. Young, "Direct Marketing Directs Health Care Relationships?" in *Health Communication in Practice: A Case Study Approach*, ed. Eileen Berlin Ray (Mahwah, NJ: Lawrence Erlbaum Associates, 2005): 53–66; Stan Finkelstein and Peter Temin, *Reasonable Rx: Solving the Drug Price Crisis* (Upper Saddle River, NJ: Pearson Education, 2008)].

13. Nortin M. Hadler, *Worried Sick: A Prescription for Health in an Overtreated America* (Chapel Hill, NC: University of North Carolina Press, 2008), 143.

14. Charles W. Lamb, Joseph F. Hair, and Carl McDaniel, *Essentials of Marketing* (Mason, OH: South-Western Cengage Learning, 2012), 494.

15. Martin Lindstrom, *Brandwashed: Tricks Companies Use to Manipulate Our Minds and Persuade Us to Buy* (London: Kogan Page, 2012), 43.

16. Greg Critser, *Generation Rx: How Prescription Drugs Are Altering American Lives, Minds and Bodies* (New York: Houghton Mifflin, 2005), 95.

17. Bill Gifford, "Take Two and Cross Your Fingers," *Men's Health* (September 2006): 144–147.

18. Donna K. Hanmaker, *Health Care Management and the Law: Principles and Applications* (Clifton Park, NY: Delmar, 2011).

19. See Michael Castleman, "Wonderful Wellbutrin?" *Salon* (September 27, 2000). Retrieved September 11, 2012, from www.salon.com/2000/09/26/wellbutrin/.

20. Mary Ebeling, "Marketing Chimeras: The Biovalue of Branded Medical Devices," in *Blowing up the Brand: Critical Perspectives on Promotional Culture*, ed. Melissa Aronczyk and Devon Powers (New York: Peter Lang Publishing, 2010): 241–529.

21. Aharon W. Zorea, *Birth Control* (Santa Barbara, CA: ABC-CLIO, 2012), 106.

22. Linda Seidel, "Dr. Jarvik and Other Baby Boomers: (Still) Performing the Able Body," in *The Body in Medical Culture*, ed. Elizabeth Klaver (Albany, NY: SUNY Press, 2009), 230.

23. Richard Cleland et al. discussed the *you are not alone* appeal in the context of weight-loss advertising [Richard L. Cleland, Walter C. Gross, Laura D. Koss, Matthew Daynard, and Karen M. Muoio, *Weight-Loss Advertising: An Analysis of Current Trends* (Washington DC: Federal Trade Commission, 2002)].

24. Linda Seidel, "Dr. Jarvik and Other Baby Boomers: (Still) Performing the Able Body," in *The Body in Medical Culture*, ed. Elizabeth Klaver (Albany, NY: SUNY Press, 2009), 230.

25. Robin Andersen and Jonathan Gray, *Battleground: The Media* (Westport, CT: Greenwood Press, 2008), 336.

26. Gordon Edlin and Eric Golanty, *Health & Wellness* (Sudbury MA: Jones and Bartlett Publishers, 2010), 369.

27. Thomas Picone, "Pharmaceutical Licensing during the Revolution," in *Licensing Best Practices: The LESI Guide to Strategic Issues and Contemporary Realities*, ed. Robert Goldscheider (New York: John Wiley, 2002), 217.

28. Gayle Greene, *Insomniac* (Berkeley: University of California Press, 2008), 214.

29. Patricia Peppin, "The Power of Illusion and the Illusion of Power: Direct-to-Consumer Advertising and Canadian Health Care," in *Just Medicare: What's In, What's Out, How We Decide*, ed. Colleen M. Flood (Toronto: University of Toronto Press, 2006), 360.

30. Chris Wienke, "Sex the Natural Way: The Marketing of Cialis and Levitra," in *Medicalized Masculinities*, ed. Dana Rosenfeld and Christopher A. Faircloth (Philadelphia, PA: Temple University Press, 2006), 60.

31. Bernardo J. Carducci, *The Psychology of Personality* (Malden, MA: John Wiley and Sons, 2009), 569.

32. John R. Rossiter and Larry Percy, "The a-b-e Model of Benefit Focus in Advertising," in *Understanding Consumer Decision Making*, ed. Thomas J. Reynolds and Jerry C. Olson (Mahwah, NJ: Lawrence Erlbaum Associates, 2001), 209.

33. In Samuel Rosenman, *The Public Papers of Franklin D. Roosevelt* (New York: Random House, 1938), 11.

34. Richard B. Rosse, *The Love Trauma Syndrome: Free Yourself from the Pain of a Broken Heart* (Cambridge, MA: Perseus, 1999), 114.

35. Terence A. Shimp, *Advertising, Promotion, and Other Aspects of Integrated Marketing Communications* (Mason, OH: South-Western Cengage Learning, 2010), 262.

36. Linda Seidel, "Dr. Jarvik and Other Baby Boomers: (Still) Performing the Able Body," in *The Body in Medical Culture*, ed. Elizabeth Klaver (Albany, NY: SUNY Press, 2009), 232.

37. Petr Král, "Nostalgic Branding in Central Europe," in *Diversity in European Marketing: Text and Cases*, ed. Thomas Rudolph, Bodo B. Schlegelmilch, Josep Franch, András Bauer, and Jan Niklas Meise (Wiesbaden: Springer Gabler, 2012), 114.

38. Susan Bordo, *Twilight Zones: The Hidden Life of Cultural Images from Plato to O. J.* (Los Angeles, CA: University of California Press, 1997), 32.

39. In my book *Periods in Pop Culture*, I discussed the importance of young girls feeling as though they had advanced knowledge of menstruation; this was essential in them feeling included in their peer group. I quoted writer Erica Jong, who reflected on the kind of ostracism born from not having such advanced knowledge: "If you were not born knowing about tampons and menstruation, you are considered a retard" [in Lauren Rosewarne, *Periods in Pop Culture: Menstruation in Film and Television* (Lanham, MD: Lexington Books, 2012), 45]. A similar ploy is used in the advertising

of contraception, which contends that it is essential for social acceptance that young girls are appropriately educated.

40. Anne E. Becker, "Nurturing and Negligence: Working on Others' Bodies in Fiji," in *Embodiment and Experience: The Existential Ground of Culture and Self*, ed. Thomas J. Csordas (Cambridge, UK: Cambridge University Press, 1994), 101.

41. Sandra Lee Bartky, "Foucault, Femininity and the Modernization of Patriarchal Power," in *Feminism and Foucault: Reflections on Resistance*, ed. Irene Diamond and Lee Quimby (Boston, MA: Northeastern University Press, 1988): 61–86.

42. William Leiss, Stephen Kline, and Sut Jhally, *Social Communication in Advertising: Persons, Products & Images of Well-being* (New York: Routledge, 1997), 259.

43. Sean Brierley, *The Advertising Handbook* (New York: Routledge, 2005), 32.

44. Matthew Healey, *What Is Branding?* (Hove: RotoVision SA, 2008), 80.

45. In *Periods in Pop Culture*, I extensively discussed this issue of the routine presentation of menstruation as an inconvenience and a hassle [Lauren Rosewarne, *Periods in Pop Culture: Menstruation in Film and Television* (Lanham, MD: Lexington Books, 2012)].

THE ABORTION CHAPTER

1. Lauren Rosewarne, *Periods in Pop Culture: Menstruation in Film and Television* (Lanham, MD: Lexington Books, 2012).

2. Al-Yasha Ilhaam, "Reading Citizen Ruth Her Rights: Satire and Moral Realism in the Abortion Debate," in *Bioethics at the Movies*, ed. Sandra Shapshay (Baltimore, MD: Johns Hopkins University Press, 2009), 32.

3. Steven C. Dubin, *Arresting Images: Impolitic Art and Uncivil Actions* (New York: Routledge, 1992), 133.

4. Hadley Freeman, "A Choice That Films Ignore," *The Guardian* (January 28, 2008). Retrieved September 21, 2012, from www.guardian.co.uk/commentisfree/2008/jan/28/healthandwellbeing.film.

5. Kelly Oliver, *Knock Me Up, Knock Me Down: Images of Pregnancy in Hollywood Films* (New York: Columbia University Press, 2012), 11.

6. Eve Kushner, "Go Forth and Multiply: Abortion in Hollywood Movies of the '90s," *Bright Lights Film Journal* (July 2000): 29. Retrieved September 21, 2012, from http://www.brightlightsfilm.com/29/abortion1.html.

7. Lauren Rosewarne, *Periods in Pop Culture: Menstruation in Film and Television* (Lanham, MD: Lexington Books, 2012).

8. Lauren Rosewarne, *Periods in Pop Culture: Menstruation in Film and Television* (Lanham, MD: Lexington Books, 2012), 182.

9. Kelly Oliver, *Knock Me Up, Knock Me Down: Images of Pregnancy in Hollywood Films* (New York: Columbia University Press, 2012), 87.

10. Worth noting, the Dresden Dolls' song "Mandy Goes to Med School" (2006) is a satirical song about back alley abortionists.

11. Jessica B. Russell and Isabel C. Green, "Perioperative Care and Complications of Gynecologic Surgery," in *The Johns Hopkins Manual of Gynecology and Obstetrics*, ed. K. Joseph Hurt, Matthew W. Guile, Jessica Bienstock, Harold E. Fox, and Edward E. Wallach (Philadelphia, PA: Lippincott Williams and Wilkins, 2011), 392.

12. Dr. Jack Glatt, Medical Director of London's Infertility Advisory Centre, quoted in Susan Faludi, *Backlash: The Undeclared War against Women* (New York: Crown, 1991), 49.

13. Kelly Oliver, *Knock Me Up, Knock Me Down: Images of Pregnancy in Hollywood Films* (New York: Columbia University Press, 2012), 88.

14. Tadeusz Grygier, *Oppression: A Social Theory and Methodology* (New York: Routledge, 1954), 228.

15. Marc Moskowitz, *The Haunting Fetus: Abortion, Sexuality, and the Spirit World in Taiwan* (Honolulu: University of Hawai'i Press, 2001).

16. Kelly Oliver, *Knock Me Up, Knock Me Down: Images of Pregnancy in Hollywood Films* (New York: Columbia University Press, 2012), 142.

17. Andi Zeisler, *Feminism and Pop Culture* (Berkeley, CA: Seal Press, 2008), 143.

18. Theresa Karminski Burke and David C. Reardon, *Forbidden Grief: The Unspoken Pain of Abortion* (Springfield, IL: Acorn Books, 2002); Melinda Tankard Reist, *Giving Sorrow Words: Women's Stories of Grief after Abortion* (Potts Point, NSW: Duffy & Snellgrove, 2000).

19. Lauren Rosewarne, "Feminism aborted in Bachelorette" *The Conversation* (November 4, 2012). Retrieved November 1, 2012, from https://theconversation.com/feminism-aborted-in-bachelorette-9605.

20. Audry Fisch, "Abortion at the Movies," *Salon* (May 16, 2000). Retrieved September 22, 2012, from www.salon.com/2000/05/15/abortion_13/.

21. Dina Smith, "Movies and the Art of Living Dangerously," in *American Cinema of the 2000s: Themes and Variations*, ed. Timothy Corrigan (Piscataway, NJ: Rutgers University Press, 2012), 178.

22. John Gray Geer, *Public Opinion and Polling around the World: A Historical Encyclopedia*, Volume 2 (Santa Barbara, CA: ABC-CLIO, 2004), 141.

THE PENIS CHAPTER

1. In Douglas Keesey, *The Films of Peter Greenaway: Sex, Death and Provocation* (Jefferson, NC: McFarland and Company, 2006), 54.

2. James Wolcott, "The Hung and the Restless," *Vanity Fair* (March 2012). Retrieved October 2, 2012, from http://www.vanityfair.com/hollywood/2012/03/wolcott-201203.

3. Santiago Fouz-Hernández and Alfredo Martinez-Expósito, *Live Flesh: The Male Body in Contemporary Spanish Cinema* (London: IB Tauris and Company, 2007), 197.

4. Lauren Rosewarne, "Where Are the Willies? The Missing Penis in 'Magic Mike,'" *The Conversation* (August 13, 2012). Retrieved October 29, 2012, from http://theconversation.edu.au/where-are-the-willies-the-missing-penis-in-magic-mike-8792.

5. Olly Richards, "*Magic Mike*, and a Brief History of Men Getting Their Kit off on Film," *The Guardian* (July 7, 2012). Retrieved October 2, 2012, from http://www.guardian.co.uk/film/2012/jul/07/magic-mike-male-nudity-on-film.

6. Suzanna Andrews, "She's Bare. He's Covered. Is There a Problem?" *New York Times* (November 1, 1992): 13–14.

7. Susan Bordo, "Does Size Matter?" in *Revealing Male Bodies*, ed. Nancy Tuana (Bloomington, IN: Indiana University Press, 2002), 28.

8. Susan Bordo, "Does Size Matter?" in *Revealing Male Bodies*, ed. Nancy Tuana (Bloomington, IN: Indiana University Press, 2002), 28.

9. Peter Lehman, *Running Scared: Masculinity and the Representation of the Male Body* (Detroit, MI: Wayne State University, 2007), 263, n. 3

10. The issue of whether nudity is an inherently sexual display is a topic routinely discussed in art history research; see, for example, Lynda Nead, *The Female Nude: Art, Obscenity, and Sexuality* (New York: Routledge, 1992); Kelly Dennis, *Art/Porn: A History of Seeing and Touching* (New York: Berg, 2009); Sarah R. Phillips, *Modeling Life: Art Models Speak about Nudity, Sexuality, and the Creative Process* (Albany, NY: State University of New York Press, 2006).

11. See, for example, Paul Tassi, "The Top Ten Most Paused Movie Scenes," *Unreality Magazine* (March 3, 2011). Retrieved October 9, 2012, from http://unrealitymag.com/index.php/2011/03/03/the-top-ten-most-paused-movie-scenes/.

12. Vance Packard, *The Hidden Persuaders* (London: David Mackay, 1957); Brian Wilson Key, *Subliminal Seduction* (Englewood Cliffs, NJ: Prentice Hall, 1972); Brian Wilson Key, *The Clam-Plate Orgy* (Englewood Cliffs, NJ: Prentice Hall, 1980).

13. Gael Chandler, *Film Editing: Great Cuts Every Filmmaker and Movie Lover Must Know* (Studio City, CA: Michael Wiese Productions, 2009), 128.

14. In Dave White, "Wanted: 2,000 Men," *The Advocate* (October 28, 2003): 66.

15. Peter Lehman, "'They Look So Uncomplicated once They're Dissected': The Act of Seeing the Dead Penis with One's Own Eyes," in *The Trouble with Men: Masculinities in European and Hollywood Cinema*, ed. Phil Powrie, Ann Davies, and Bruce Babington (London: Wallflower Press, 2004), 202.

16. James Wolcott, "The Hung and the Restless," *Vanity Fair* (March 2012). Retrieved October 2, 2012, from http://www.vanityfair.com/hollywood/2012/03/wolcott-201203.

17. See Peter Lehman, "Penis-Size Jokes and Their Relation to Hollywood's Unconscious," in *Comedy/Cinema/Theory*, ed. Andrew S. Horton (Berkeley, CA: University of California Press, 1991): 43–59.

18. James Wolcott, "The Hung and the Restless," *Vanity Fair* (March 2012). Retrieved October 2, 2012, from http://www.vanityfair.com/hollywood/2012/03/wolcott-201203.

19. Olly Richards, "*Magic Mike*, and a Brief History of Men Getting Their Kit off on Film." *The Guardian* (July 7, 2012). Retrieved October 2, 2012. from http://www.guardian.co.uk/film/2012/jul/07/magic-mike-male-nudity-on-film.

20. Travis S. K. Kong," Queering Masculinity in Hong Kong Movies," in *Masculinities and Hong Kong Cinema*, ed. Laikwan Pang and Day Wong (Aberdeen, Hong Kong: Hong Kong University Press, 2005): 57–80.

21. Susan Bordo, *The Male Body: A New Look at Men in Public and Private* (New York: Farrar, Straus and Giroux, 1999), 44.

22. James Wolcott, "The Hung and the Restless," *Vanity Fair* (March 2012). Retrieved October 2, 2012, from http://www.vanityfair.com/hollywood/2012/03/wolcott-201203.

23. Brian L. Ott and Robert L. Mack, *Critical Media Studies: An Introduction* (Malden, MA: John Wiley and Sons, 2010), 158.

24. Josephine Metcalf, *The Culture and Politics of Contemporary Street Gang Memoirs* (Jackson, MS: Mississippi University Press, 2012), 79.

25. Susan Bordo, *The Male Body: A New Look at Men in Public and Private* (New York: Farrar, Straus and Giroux, 1999), 45.

26. James Wolcott, "The Hung and the Restless," *Vanity Fair* (March 2012). Retrieved October 2, 2012, from http://www.vanityfair.com/hollywood/2012/03/wolcott-201203.

27. Douglas Rowe, "Full-Frontal Blokes Still Get the Flick," *Sydney Morning Herald* (February 19, 2004). Retrieved October 2, 2012, from http://www.smh.com.au/articles/2004/02/18/1077072699615.html.

28. Peter Lehman, *Running Scared: Masculinity and the Representation of the Male Body* (Philadelphia, PA: Temple University Press, 1993; Santiago Fouz-Hernández and Alfredo Martinez-Expósito, *Live Flesh: The Male Body in Contemporary Spanish Cinema* (London: IB Tauris and Co, 2007.

29. Laura Mulvey, "Visual Pleasure and Narrative Cinema," in *Movies and Methods*, ed. Bill Nichols (Berkeley, CA: University of California, 1985): 303–314.

30. In Douglas Rowe, "Full-Frontal Blokes Still Get the Flick," *Sydney Morning Herald* (February 19, 2004). Retrieved October 2, 2012, from http://www.smh.com.au/articles/2004/02/18/1077072699615.html.

31. Susan Bordo, *The Male Body: A New Look at Men in Public and Private* (New York: Farrar, Straus and Giroux, 1999), 175.

32. Olly Richards, "*Magic Mike*, and a Brief History of Men Getting Their Kit off on Film," *The Guardian* (July 7, 2012). Retrieved October 2, 2012, from http://www.guardian.co.uk/film/2012/jul/07/magic-mike-male-nudity-on-film.

33. In Karen Regelman, "Will Tokyo Tame *The Crying Game*?" *Variety* 22, no. 3 (1993): 68.

34. Olly Richards, "*Magic Mike*, and a Brief History of Men Getting Their Kit off on Film," *The Guardian* (July 7, 2012). Retrieved October 2, 2012, from http://www.guardian.co.uk/film/2012/jul/07/magic-mike-male-nudity-on-film.

35. Jonathon Green and Nicholas J. Karolides, *Encyclopedia of Censorship* (New York: Facts on File, 2005); Kevin S. Sandler, *The Naked Truth: Why Hollywood Doesn't Make X-Rated Movies* (New Brunswick, NJ: Rutgers University Press, 2007); John E. Semonche, *Censoring Sex: A Historical Journey through American Media* (Lanham, MD: Rowman and Littlefield, 2007).

36. William Romanowski, *Reforming Hollywood: American Protestants and the Movies* (New York: Oxford University, 2012).

37. Stephen Vaughn, *Freedom and Entertainment: Rating the Movies in an Age of New Media* (New York: Cambridge University Press, 2006), 52.

38. John E. Semonche, *Censoring Sex: A Historical Journey through American Media* (Lanham, MD: Rowman and Littlefield, 2007), 126.

39. Udo Helms, "Obscenity and Homosexual Depiction in Japan," in *Queer Asian Cinema: Shadows in the Shade*, ed. Andrew Grossman (Binghamton, NY: Harrington Park Press, 2000), 138.

40. In Robert Ebert, *Questions for the Movie Answer Man* (Kansas City, MO: Andrews McMeel Publishing, 1997), 72.

41. Lauren Rosewarne, *Periods in Pop Culture: Menstruation in Film and Television* (Lanham, MD: Lexington Books, 2012), 210.

42. Robert Ebert, *Questions for the Movie Answer Man* (Kansas City, MO: Andrews McMeel Publishing, 1997), 164.

43. John Stoltenberg, *Refusing to Be a Man: Essays on Social Justice* (London: Breitenbush Books, 1989), 96.

44. In Santiago Fouz-Hernández, "Phallic Matters?: Ewan McGregor and the Representation of the Male Body in Peter Greenaway's *The Pillow Book* (1996)," *Men and Masculinities* 8 (2005): 133–147, 137.

45. Santiago Fouz-Hernández and Alfredo Martinez-Expósito, *Live Flesh: The Male Body in Contemporary Spanish Cinema* (London: IB Tauris and Co, 2007), 191.

46. Gwendolyn Audrey Foster, *Captive Bodies: Postcolonial Subjectivity in Cinema* (Albany, NY: State University of New York Press, 1999), 109.

47. Lauren Rosewarne, *Periods in Pop Culture: Menstruation in Film and Television* (Lanham, MD: Lexington Books, 2012), 218.

48. James Wolcott, "The Hung and the Restless," *Vanity Fair* (March 2012). Retrieved October 2, 2012, from http://www.vanityfair.com/hollywood/2012/03/wolcott-201203.

49. Richard Dyer, *Only Entertainment* (London: Routledge, 1992), 137.

50. Lauren Rosewarne, *Periods in Pop Culture: Menstruation in Film and Television* (Lanham, MD: Lexington Books, 2012), 206.

51. Peter Lehman, *Running Scared: Masculinity and the Representation of the Male Body* (Philadelphia, PA: Temple University Press, 1993; Douglas Keesey, *The*

Films of Peter Greenaway: Sex, Death and Provocation (Jefferson, NC: McFarland and Company, 2006).

52. John Walsh, "A Shock to the System," *Independent* (September 11, 1993): 18–22.

53. In Douglas Rowe, "Full-Frontal Blokes Still Get the Flick," *Sydney Morning Herald* (February 19, 2004). Retrieved October 2, 2012, from http://www.smh.com.au/articles/2004/02/18/1077072699615.html.

54. Michael Ferguson, *Idol Worship: A Shameless Celebration of Male Beauty in the Movies* (Sarasota, FL: STARbooks, 2005), 207.

55. Joseph T. McCann, Kelley L. Shindler, and Tammy R. Hammond, "The Science and Pseudoscience of Expert Testimony," in *Science and Pseudoscience in Clinical Psychology*, ed. Scott Lilienfeld and Steven Jay Lynn (New York: Guilford Press, 2003), 96.

56. Peter Lehman, "Melodramatic Penis: Melodrama and Male Nudity in Films of the 90s," in *Masculinity: Bodies, Movies, Culture*, ed. Peter Lehman (New York: Routledge, 2001), 27.

57. In Douglas Rowe, "Full-Frontal Blokes Still Get the Flick," *Sydney Morning Herald* (February 19, 2004). Retrieved October 2, 2012, from http://www.smh.com.au/articles/2004/02/18/1077072699615.html.

58. Peter Lehman, "Melodramatic Penis: Melodrama and Male Nudity in Films of the 90s," in *Masculinity: Bodies, Movies, Culture*, ed. Peter Lehman (New York: Routledge, 2001), 27.

59. In Gene Adair, *Alfred Hitchcock: Filming Our Fears* (New York: Oxford University Press, 2002), 57.

60. In Dave Nemetz, "Jennifer Love Hewitt Bares (Almost) All for Lifetime's 'The Client List,'" *Yahoo!TV* (April 6, 2012). Retrieved October 6, 2012, from http://tv.yahoo.com/news/jennifer-love-hewitt-bares—almost—all-for-lifetime-s—the-client-list-.html.

61. Gwendolyn Audrey Foster, *Captive Bodies: Postcolonial Subjectivity in Cinema* (Albany, NY: State University of New York Press, 1999), 109.

62. Santiago Fouz-Hernández and Alfredo Martinez-Expósito, *Live Flesh: The Male Body in Contemporary Spanish Cinema* (London: IB Tauris and Co, 2007), 205.

63. Peter Lehman, "Penis-Size Jokes and Their Relation to Hollywood's Unconscious," in *Comedy/Cinema/Theory*, ed. Andrew S. Horton (Berkeley, CA: University of California Press, 1991), 46.

THE CIRCUMCISION CHAPTER

1. David Gollaher, *Circumcision: A History of The World's Most Controversial Surgery* (New York: Basic Books, 2000.

2. Hugh Young, "'That Thing': Portrayal of the Foreskin and Circumcision in Popular Media," in *Circumcision and Human Rights*, ed. George Denniston, Frederick Hodges, and Marilyn Fayre Milos (London: Springer, 2009): 239–250.

3. David Gollaher, *Circumcision: A History of The World's Most Controversial Surgery* (New York: Basic Books, 2000), 108.

4. Morris L. Sorrells, "The History of Circumcision in the United States: A Physician's Perspective," in *Circumcision and Human Rights*, ed. George Denniston, Frederick Hodges, and Marilyn Fayre Milos (London: Springer, 2009): 331–338.

5. Michael Kimmell and Amy Aronson, *Men & Masculinities: A Social, Cultural, and Historical Encyclopedia* (Santa Barbara, CA: ABC-CLIO, 2004).

6. Hugh Young, "'That Thing': Portrayal of the Foreskin and Circumcision in Popular Media," in *Circumcision and Human Rights*, ed. George Denniston, Frederick Hodges, and Marilyn Fayre Milos (London: Springer, 2009): 239–250.

7. Jay Geller, *On Freud's Jewish Body: Mitigating Circumcisions* (New York: Fordham University Press, 2007)

8. The idea of accidental circumcision was humorously referenced in an episode of the sitcom *King of Queens* (1998–2007) when Arthur (Jerry Stiller) was a patient at the Forest Hills Jewish Hospital. Arthur begged his daughter Carrie (Leah Remini) to make sure they didn't circumcise him, as though this was something all Jews did to *everybody*.

9. Felix Bryk, *Circumcision in Man and Woman: Its History, Psychology and Ethnology* (Hawaii: University Press of the Pacific, 2001).

10. While female circumcision—more commonly referred to as female genital mutilation—is seldom presented on screen, some examples do exist: *Moolaadé* (2004) and *Desert Flower* (2009) are cinema examples, and the issue was also presented in episodes of *Nip/Tuck* and *Law and Order*.

11. This chapter doesn't focus much on circumcision presented as inextricably linked to religion. That said, this is a narrative theme identifiable in numerous examples. In 2006, for example, comedian Jon Stewart hosted the Academy Awards and at one point remarked, "Congratulations to the winners, and congratulations to Ben Stiller and his amazing green unitard. It's good to have proof that he's Jewish." In an episode of the sitcom *King of Queens* (1998–2007), Arthur (Jerry Stiller) was a patient at the Forest Hills Jewish Hospital and felt obliged to beg his daughter Carrie (Leah Remini) to make sure they didn't circumcise him, as though Jews had a compulsion to do so. In the comedy *Horrible Bosses* (2011), the sexually harassing dentist Dr. Harris (Jennifer Aniston) inspected the crotch of her colleague Dale (Charlie Day) and lasciviously remarked, "I think I can make out our little friend right there. *Shabat shalom*, somebody's circumcised!" In an episode of the sitcom *Curb Your Enthusiasm* (2000–), Palestinian woman Shara (Anne Bedian) was talking dirty to Larry (Larry David) during sex and at one point screamed, "Fuck me like Israel fucks my people! Show me the promised land ... You circumcised fuck!" While in these examples the link was to Judaism, in *East Is East* (1999), the pressing need for Sajid's (Jordan Routledge) circumcision was to comply with the family's Muslim faith.

12. Marvel L. Williamson and Paul S. Williamson, "Women's Preference for Penile Circumcision in Sexual Partners," *Journal of Sex Education and Therapy* 14 (Fall/Winter 1988): 8–12.

13. Hugh Young, "Circumcision as a Memeplex," in *Bodily Integrity and the Politics of Circumcision*, ed. George C. Denniston, Pia Grassivaro Gallo, Frederick M. Hodges, Marilyn Fayre Milos, and Franco Viviani (New York: Springer, 2006): 1–16.

14. The foreskin/zip joke was referenced in an episode of the sitcom *My Name Is Earl* (2005–2009) when Randy (Ethan Suplee) claimed he had gotten his "foreskin jammed in my zipper." A more serious presentation transpired in an episode of the British hospital drama *Casualty* (1986–), when a boy was admitted to hospital to be circumcised after his penis got caught in his zipper.

15. Hugh Young, " 'That Thing': Portrayal of the Foreskin and Circumcision in Popular Media," in *Circumcision and Human Rights*, ed. George Denniston, Frederick Hodges, and Marilyn Fayre Milos (London: Springer, 2009): 239–250.

16. This idea of the cynical rabbi was also presented in an episode of *Weeds* (2005–2015), when the rabbi (Ken Lerner) claimed that performing circumcisions "paid for my summer house."

17. A good example of this transpires in an episode of *Dexter* (2006–), when Debra (Jennifer Carpenter) and colleague Vince (C. S. Lee) are in a tattoo parlor and Debra mocks him by saying, "If she's into needles, why not show her your dick?"

18. Mark S. Blumberg, *Freaks of Nature: What Anomalies Tell Us about Development and Evolution* (New York: Oxford University Press, 2009), 202.

19. Lauren Rosewarne, *Part-Time Perverts: Sex, Pop Culture, and Kink Management* (Santa Barbara, CA: Praeger, 2009), 109.

20. While presented comically, do-it-yourself foreskin reconstruction actually occurred in an episode of the sitcom *Friends* (1994–2004) when Joey (Matt LeBlanc) got a role in a play that required him to be intact.

THE VIBRATOR CHAPTER

1. Suzi Godson, "10 Things You Need to Know Before You ... Buy a Vibrator," *The Times* (October 25, 2008). Retrieved September 29, 2009, from Lexis Nexis.

2. Whitney Strub, *Perversion for Profit: The Politics of Pornography and the Rise of the New Right* (New York: Columbia University Press, 2010), 289.

3. A seemingly accidental side effect of the continued euphemistic talk about vibrators is the coupling of orgasm and women's sexual health. While the health benefits proposed in Victorian times were spurious, more modern research has documented a variety of health benefits from orgasm, which potentially works to legitimize if not normalize masturbation and vibrator use.

4. Lauren Rosewarne, *Part-Time Perverts: Sex, Pop Culture, and Kink Management* (Santa Barbara, CA: Praeger, 2009), 93.

5. Albert Moran and Errol Vieth, *The A to Z of Australian and New Zealand Cinema* (Lanham, MD: Scarecrow Press, 2005), 94.

6. While less humorous, something similar occurs in *The Oh in Ohio* (2006): having become an orgasm addict, Priscilla (Parker Posey) kept her vibrating cell

phone between her legs during a meeting. The phone kept ringing and Priscilla orgasmed.

7. Gayle Rubin, "Thinking Sex: Notes for a Radical Theory of the Politics of Sexuality," in *The Lesbian and Gay Studies Reader*, ed. Henry Abelove (New York: Routledge, 1993), 16.

8. Paula Bennett and Vernon A. Rosario II, *Solitary Pleasures: The Historical, Literary and Artistic Discourses of Autoeroticism* (New York: Routledge, 1995); Thomas Walter Laqueur, *Solitary Sex: A Cultural History of Masturbation* (New York: Zone Books, 2003); Jean Stengers and Anne Van Neck, *Masturbation: The History of a Great Terror* (New York: Palgrave, 2001).

9. Laura Mulvey, "Visual Pleasure and Narrative Cinema," in *Movies and Methods*, ed. Bill Nichols (Berkeley, CA: University of California, 1985): 303–314.

10. "The Agony Principle," BeautifulAgony.com. Retrieved October 18, 2012, from http://www.beautifulagony.com/public/main.php?page=about.

11. Lauren Rosewarne, *Periods in Pop Culture: Menstruation in Film and Television* (Lanham, MD: Lexington Books, 2012), 125.

12. Lauren Rosewarne, *Part-Time Perverts: Sex, Pop Culture, and Kink Management* (Santa Barbara, CA: Praeger, 2009).

CONCLUSION

1. Laura Mulvey, "Visual Pleasure and Narrative Cinema," in *Movies and Methods*, ed. Bill Nichols (Berkeley, CA: University of California, 1985): 303–314.

Bibliography

Abelman, Robert, and David J. Atkin. *The Televiewing Audience: The Art and Science of Watching TV*. New York: Peter Lang, 2011.
Adair, Gene. *Alfred Hitchcock: Filming Our Fears*. New York: Oxford University Press, 2002.
Adams, Carol J. *Living Among Meat Eaters: The Vegetarian's Survival Handbook*. New York: Three Rivers, 2001.
Adams, Carol J. *The Sexual Politics of Meat: A Feminist-Vegetarian Critical Theory*. New York: Continuum, 1990.
"The Agony Principle." BeautifulAgony.com. Retrieved October 18, 2012, from http://www.beautifulagony.com/public/main.php?page=about.
Allan, Keith, and Kate Burridge. *Forbidden Words: Taboo and the Censoring of Language*. New York: Cambridge University Press, 2006.
Allen, Valerie. *On Farting: Language and Laughter in the Middle Ages*. New York: Palgrave Macmillan, 2007.
Allinson, Mark. *A Spanish Labyrinth: The Films of Pedro Almodóvar*. New York: IB Tauris, 2006.
Altrocchi, Rudolph. *The Playful Spirit: Italian Humor*. Bloomington, IN: iUniverse.
Andersen, Robin, and Jonathan Gray. *Battleground: The Media*. Westport, CT: Greenwood Press, 2008.
Andrews, Suzanna. "She's Bare. He's Covered. Is There a Problem?" *New York Times*, November 1, 1992, 13–14.
Angier, Natalie. "G#%!y Golly: Almost Before We Spoke, We Swore." *New York Times*, September 20, 2005, F1.
Anolik, Bienstock. *Horrifying Sex: Essays on Sexual Difference in Gothic Literature*. Jefferson, NC: McFarland, 2007.

Ariano, Tara, and Sarah Bunting. *Television without Pity: 752 Things We Love to Hate (and Hate to Love) about TV*. San Francisco, CA: Chronicle Books, 2006.

Armstrong, Nancy, and Melissa Wagner. *Field Guide to Gestures*. San Francisco, CA: Quirk Productions, 2003.

Arnold, Rebecca. *Fashion, Desire and Anxiety: Image and Morality in the 20th Century*. New York: IB Tauris, 2001.

Asbell, Robin. *New Vegetarian*. San Francisco: Chronicle Books, 2009.

Bach, George, and Goldberg, Herb. *Creative Aggression: The Art of Assertive Living*. Los Angeles, CA: Wellness Institute, 1974.

Backstrom, Laura, Elizabeth A. Armstrong, and Jennifer Puentes. "Women's Negotiation of Cunnilingus in College Hookups and Relationships." *Journal of Sex Research* 49, no. 1 (2012): 1–12.

Baker, Paul. *Polari: The Lost Language of Gay Men*. New York: Routledge, 2002.

Bakos, Susan Crain. *The New Tantra Simple and Sexy: Longer, Better Lovemaking for Everyone*. Beverly, MA: Quiver, 2008.

Bakos, Susan Crain. *The Orgasm Bible*. Beverly, MA: Quiver, 2008.

Bakos, Susan Crain. *Orgasm Loop: The No Fail Technique for Reaching Orgasm during Sex*. Beverly, MA: Quiver, 2008.

Bakos, Susan Crain. *The Sex Bible*. Beverly, MA: Quiver, 2006.

Barsanti, Chris. *Filmology*. Avon, MA: Adams Media, 2011.

Bartky, Sandra Lee. "Foucault, Femininity and the Modernization of Patriarchal Power." In *Feminism and Foucault: Reflections on Resistance*, edited by Irene Diamond and Lee Quimby. Boston, MA: Northeastern University Press, 1988: 61–86.

Baumeister, Roy F., and Brad J. Bushman. *Social Psychology and Human Nature*. Belmont, CA: Wadsworth, 2011.

Bay-Cheng, Laina Y., and Nicole M. Fava. "Young Women's Experiences and Perceptions of Cunnilingus during Adolescence." *Journal of Sex Research* 48, no. 6 (2011): 531–542.

Bay-Cheng, Laina Y., Adjoa D. Robinson, and Alyssa N. Zucker. "Behavioral and Relational Contexts of Adolescent Female Desire, Wanting, and Pleasure: Undergraduate Women's Retrospective Accounts." *Journal of Sex Research* 46 (2009): 511–524.

Becker, Anne E. "Nurturing and Negligence: Working on Others' Bodies in Fiji." In *Embodiment and Experience: The Existential Ground of Culture and Self*, edited by Thomas J. Csordas. Cambridge, UK: Cambridge University Press, 1994: 100–115.

Bego, Mark. *Madonna: Blonde Ambition*. New York: Harmony Books, 1992.

Bennett, Paula, and Vernon A. Rosario II. *Solitary Pleasures: The Historical, Literary and Artistic Discourses of Autoeroticism*. New York: Routledge, 1995.

Biskind, Peter. "The Vietnam Oscars." *Vanity Fair* (March 2008): 266–280.

Blake, Barry J. *Secret Language: Codes, Tricks, Spies, Thieves, and Symbols*. New York: Oxford University Press, 2010.

Blaney, Roger. "Alcoholism in Ireland: Medical and Social Aspects." *Journal of the Statistical and Social Inquiry Society of Ireland* (1974). Retrieved August 25, 2012, from http://www.tara.tcd.ie/bitstream/2262/7823/1/jssisiVolXXIIIPartI_108124.pdf.

Bloom, Stephen G. *Inside the Writer's Mind: Writing Narrative Journalism*. Ames, IA: Iowa State Press.

Blumberg, Mark S. *Freaks of Nature: What Anomalies Tell Us about Development and Evolution*. New York: Oxford University Press, 2009.

Bordo, Susan. "Does Size Matter?" In *Revealing Male Bodies*, edited by Nancy Tuana. Bloomington, IN: Indiana University Press, 2002: 19–37.

Bordo, Susan. *The Male Body: A New Look at Men in Public and Private*. New York: Farrar, Straus and Giroux, 1999.

Bordo, Susan. *Twilight Zones: The Hidden Life of Cultural Images from Plato to O. J.* Los Angeles, CA: University of California Press, 1997.

Brehm, Jack Williams. *A Theory of Psychological Reactance*. New York: Academic Press, 1966.

Brewster, Karin L., and Kathryn H. Tillman. "Who's Doing It? Patterns and Predictors of Youths' Oral Sexual Experiences." *Journal of Adolescent Health* 42 (2005): 73–80.

Brierley, Sean. *The Advertising Handbook*. New York: Routledge, 2005.

Bronner, Simon J. *Explaining Traditions: Folk Behavior in Modern Culture*. Lexington, KY: University Press of Kentucky, 2011.

Bronski, Michael. *A Queer History of the United States*. Boston, MA: Beacon Press, 2011.

Bryant, Jennings, and Dolf Zillmann. *Media Effects: Advances in Theory and Research*. Mahwah, NJ: Lawrence Erlbaum Associates, 2002.

Bryant, Stephen. *Art of the Fart*. London: PRC Publishing, 2004.

Bryk, Felix. *Circumcision in Man and Woman: Its History, Psychology and Ethnology*. Hawaii: University Press of the Pacific, 2001.

Burns, Jim. *Teaching Your Children Healthy Sexuality*. Bloomington, MN: Bethany House Publishers, 2008.

Burridge, Kate. "The Art of Telling It Like It Isn't." *Sydney Morning Herald* (May 27, 2012). Retrieved June 12, 2012, from http://m.smh.com.au/opinion/society-and-culture/the-art-of-telling-it-like-it-isnt-20120526-1zbir.html.

Bushman, Brad J., and Joanne Cantor. "Media Ratings for Violence and Sex: Implications for Policy Makers and Parents." *American Psychologist* 58 (2003): 130–141.

Butler, Jeremy G. *Television: Critical Methods and Applications*. Mahwah, NJ: Lawrence Erlbaum Associates, 2002.

Butler, Thomas. *Consumer Health: Making Informed Decisions*. Burlington, MA: Jones & Bartlett, 2012.

Cameron, Deborah. "Words, Words, Words: The Power of Language." In *The War of the Words: The Political Correctness Debate*, edited by Sarah Dunant. London: Virago 1994: 15–34.

Carducci, Bernardo J. *The Psychology of Personality*. Malden, MA: John Wiley and Sons, 2009.

Castleman, Michael. "Wonderful Wellbutrin?" *Salon* (September 27, 2000). Retrieved September 11, 2012, from www.salon.com/2000/09/26/wellbutrin/.

Chandler, Gael. *Film Editing: Great Cuts Every Filmmaker and Movie Lover Must Know*. Studio City, CA: Michael Wiese Productions, 2009.

Charney, Leo. "American Film." In *Comedy: A Geographic and Historical Guide*, edited by Maurice Charney. Westport, CT: Praeger, 2005: 586–600.

Chase, Sarah Alexander. *Perfectly Prep: Gender Extremes at a New England Prep School*. New York: Oxford University Press, 2008.

Chase, Susan E., and Mary F. Rogers. *Mothers and Children: Feminist Analyses and Personal Narratives*. New Brunswick, NH: Rutgers University Press, 2001.

Christman, Ed. "Roadrunner Promo Stumbles with Trumped-up Controversy." *Billboard* (May 13, 1995): 72.

Cleland, Richard L., Walter C. Gross, Laura D. Koss, Matthew Daynard, and Karen M. Muoio. *Weight-Loss Advertising: An Analysis of Current Trends*. Washington DC: Federal Trade Commission, 2002.

Cline, Rebecca J. Welch, and Henry N. Young. "Direct Marketing Directs Health Care Relationships?" In *Health Communication in Practice: A Case Study Approach*, edited by Eileen Berlin Ray. Mahwah, NJ: Lawrence Erlbaum Associates, 2005: 53–66.

Connell, Raewyn. *Masculinities*. Berkeley: University of California Press, 1995.

Critser, Greg. *Generation Rx: How Prescription Drugs Are Altering American Lives, Minds and Bodies*. New York: Houghton Mifflin, 2005.

Cross, Chad L., and Larry Ashley. "Police Trauma and Addiction: Coping with the Dangers of the Job." *FBI Law Enforcement Bulletin* (October 2004): 24–32.

Dawson, Jim. *Who Cut the Cheese? A Cultural History of the Fart*. Berkeley, CA: Ten Speed Press, 1999.

De Beauvoir, Simone. *The Second Sex*. New York: Vintage, 1989.

Dennis, Kelly. *Art/Porn: A History of Seeing and Touching*. New York: Berg, 2009.

Denzin, Norman K. *Hollywood Shot by Shot: Alcoholism in American Cinema*. New Brunswick, NJ: Transaction Publishers, 2004.

DeSena, James. *Overcoming Your Alcohol, Drug and Recovery Habits*. Tucson, AZ: See Sharp Press, 2003.

Dubin, Steven C. *Arresting Images: Impolitic Art and Uncivil Actions*. New York: Routledge, 1992.

Duncan, Derek. *Reading and Writing Italian Homosexuality: A Case of Possible Difference*. Burlington, VT: Ashgate, 2006.

Dundes, Alan. *Interpreting Folklore*. Bloomington, IN: Indiana University Press, 1980.

Dundes, Alan, and Carl R. Pagter. *When You're up to Your Ass in Alligators: More Urban Folklore from the Paperwork Empire*. Detroit, MI: Wayne State University Press, 1987.

Durgin, Jane M., and Zachary I. Hanan. *Durgin & Hanan's Pharmacy Practice for Technicians*. Clifton Park, NY: Delmar, 2009.

Durham, M. Gigi. *The Lolita Effect*. New York: Overlook Press, 2008.

Dyer, Richard. *Only Entertainment*. London: Routledge, 1992.

Easteal, Patricia, and Louise McOrmond-Plummer. *Real Rape, Real Pain*. Ormond, Victoria: Hybrid, 2006.

Ebeling, Mary. "Marketing Chimeras: The Biovalue of Branded Medical Devices." In *Blowing Up the Brand: Critical Perspectives on Promotional Culture*, edited by Melissa Aronczyk and Devon Powers. New York: Peter Lang Publishing, 2010: 241–529.

Ebert, Robert. *Questions for the Movie Answer Man*. Kansas City, MO: Andrews McMeel Publishing, 1997.

Edlin, Gordon, and Eric Golanty. *Health & Wellness*. Sudbury MA: Jones and Bartlett Publishers, 2010.

Elliott, John H. "Deuteronomy: Shameful Encroachment on Shameful Parts: Deuteronomy 25:11–12 and Biblical Euphemism." In *Ancient Israel: The Old Testament in Its Social Context*, edited by Philip Francis Esler. Minneapolis, MN: Fortress Press, 2006: 161–176.

Ellmann, Richard. *Selected Letters of James Joyce*. New York: Viking, 1976.

Ettore, Elizabeth M. *Women & Alcohol: A Private Pleasure or a Public Problem?* London: Women's Press, 1997.

"The Euphemism: Telling it Like it Isn't." *Time* (September 19, 1969): 28.

Faludi, Susan. *Backlash: The Undeclared War against Women*. New York: Crown, 1991.

Feasey, Rebecca. *Masculinity and Popular Television*. Edinburgh: Edinburgh University Press, 2008.

Ferguson, Michael. *Idol Worship: A Shameless Celebration of Male Beauty in the Movies*. Sarasota, FL: STARbooks, 2005.

Finkelstein, Stan, and Peter Temin. *Reasonable Rx: Solving the Drug Price Crisis*. Upper Saddle River, NJ: Pearson Education, 2008.

Fisch, Audry. "Abortion at the Movies." *Salon* (May 16, 2000). Retrieved September 22, 2012, from www.salon.com/2000/05/15/abortion_13/.

Fisher, Deborah A., Douglas L. Hill, Joel W. Grube, and Enid L. Gruber. "Gay, Lesbian, and Bisexual Content on Television: A Quantitative Analysis across Two Seasons." *Journal of Homosexuality* 52, no. 33/34 (2007): 167–188.

Foerstel, Herbert N. *Banned in the USA: A Reference Guide to Book Censorship in Schools and Public Libraries*. Westport, CT: Greenwood Press, 2002.

Foster, Gwendolyn Audrey. *Captive Bodies: Postcolonial Subjectivity in Cinema*. Albany, NY: State University of New York Press, 1999.

Fouz-Hernández, Santiago. "Phallic Matters?: Ewan McGregor and the Representation of the Male Body in Peter Greenaway's *The Pillow Book* (1996)." *Men and Masculinities* 8 (2005): 133–147.

Fouz-Hernández, Santiago, and Alfredo Martinez-Expósito. *Live Flesh: The Male Body in Contemporary Spanish Cinema*. London: IB Tauris and Company, 2007.
Frank, Russell. *Contemporary Folklore on the Internet*. Jackson, MS: University Press of Mississippi, 2011.
Freeman, Hadley. "A Choice That Films Ignore." *The Guardian* (January 28, 2008). Retrieved September 21, 2012, from www.guardian.co.uk/commentisfree/2008/jan/28/healthandwellbeing.film.
Freeman, Hadley. "How Best to Win an Oscar: Try Female Oral Sex." *The Guardian* (January 12, 2011). Retrieved March 13, 2012, from http://www.guardian.co.uk/commentisfree/2011/jan/12/to-get-oscar-oral-sex.
Fuqua, Joy V. *Prescription TV: Therapeutic Discourse in the Hospital and at Home*. Durham, NC: Duke University Press, 2012.
Gagnon, John H., and William Simon. "The Scripting of Oral Genital Sexual Conduct." *Archives of Sexual Behavior* 16 (1987): 1–25.
Gamble, Sarah. *The Routledge Companion to Feminism and Postfeminism*. New York: Routledge, 2001.
Gavey, Nicola. *Just Sex? The Cultural Scaffolding of Rape*. New York: Routledge, 2005.
Geer, John Gray. *Public Opinion and Polling around the World: A Historical Encyclopedia*, Volume 2. Santa Barbara, CA: ABC-CLIO, 2004.
Geller, Jay. *On Freud's Jewish Body: Mitigating Circumcisions*. New York: Fordham University Press, 2007.
Gifford, Bill. "Take Two and Cross Your Fingers." *Men's Health* (September 2006): 144–147.
Godson, Suzi. "10 Things You Need to Know Before You ... Buy a Vibrator." *The Times* (October 25, 2008). Retrieved September 29, 2009, from Lexis Nexis.
Gollaher, David. *Circumcision: A History of the World's Most Controversial Surgery*. New York: Basic Books, 2000.
Gournelos, Ted. "Puppets, Slaves, and Sex Changes: Mr. Garrison and *South Park*'s Performative Sexuality." *Television and New Media* 10, no. 3 (May 2009): 270.
Government Accountability Office. "Improvements Needed in FDA's Oversight of Direct-to-Consumer Advertising." 2006. Retrieved December 8, 2012, from http://www.gao.gov/products/GAO-07-54.
Grant, Marcus. "The Alcoholic as Hero." In *Images of Alcoholism*, edited by Jim Cook and Mike Lewington. London: British Film Institute, 1979: 30–36.
Green, Jonathon, and Nicholas J. Karolides. *Encyclopedia of Censorship*. New York: Facts on File, 2005.
Greene, Gayle. *Insomniac*. Berkeley, CA: University of California Press, 2008.
Griffin, Kathy. *Official Book Club Selection: A Memoir According to Kathy Griffin*. New York: Ballantine Books, 2009.

Griffin, Nancy, and Kim Masters. *Hit and Run: How Jon Peters and Peter Guber Took Sony for a Ride in Hollywood*. New York: Simon and Schuster, 1996.

Grygier, Tadeusz. *Oppression: A Social Theory and Methodology*. New York: Routledge, 1954.

Guterson, David. *Snow Falling on Cedars*. New York: Vintage Books, 1995.

Hadler, Nortin M. *Worried Sick: A Prescription for Health in an Overtreated America*. Chapel Hill, NC: University of North Carolina Press, 2008.

Hanmaker, Donna K. *Health Care Management and the Law: Principles and Applications*. Clifton Park, NY: Delmar, 2011.

Harwin, Judith, and Shirley Otto. "Women, Alcohol and the Screen." In *Images of Alcoholism*, edited by Jim Cook and Mike Lewington. London: British Film Institute, 1979: 37–50.

Healey, Matthew. *What Is Branding?* Hove: RotoVision SA, 2008.

Helford, Elyce Rae. "Feminism, Queer Studies, and the Sexual Politics of *Xena*." In *Fantasy Girls: Gender in the New Universe of Science Fiction and Fantasy Television*, edited by Elyce Rae Helford. Lanham, MD: Rowman and Littlefield, 2000: 135–162.

Helmreich, Joseph, and Paul Marcus. *Warring Parents, Wounded Children, and the Wretched World of Child Custody*. Westport, CT: Praeger, 2008.

Helms, Udo. "Obscenity and Homosexual Depiction in Japan." In *Queer Asian Cinema: Shadows in the Shade*, edited by Andrew Grossman. Binghamton, NY: Harrington Park Press, 2000: 127–148.

Danielle Henderson, *Feminist Ryan Gosling: Feminist Theory as Imagined from your Favorite Sensitive Movie Dude* (Philadelphia, PA: Running Press, 2012).

Henderson, James W. *Health Economics & Policy*. Mason, OH: South-West Cengage, 2009.

Henry, Matthew. "Looking for Amanda Hugginkiss: Gay Life on *The Simpsons*." In *Leaving Springfield: The Simpsons and the Possibility of Oppositional Culture*, edited by John Alberti. Detroit, MI: Wayne State University Press, 2004: 225–243.

Hibberd, James. "Police Psychology." *On Patrol* (Fall 1996): 26.

Hilton-Morrow, Wendy, and David T. McMahan. "*The Flintstones* to *Futurama*: Networks and Prime Time Animation." In *Prime Time Animation: Television Animation and American Culture*, edited by Carol A. Stabile and Mark Harrison. London: Routledge, 2003: 74–88.

Hite, Shere. *The Hite Report*. New York: Seven Stores Press, 1981.

Hite, Shere. *The Hite Report on Male Sexuality*. New York: Knopf, 1981.

Hite, Shere. *The Shere Hite Reader*. New York: Seven Stories Press, 2003.

Holba, Annette M. "Understanding *Schadenfreude* to Seek an Ethical Response." In *Philosophies of Communication: Implications for Everyday Experience*, edited by Melissa A. Cook and Annette Holba. New York: Peter Lang, 2008: 1–18.

Hughes, Geoffrey. *An Encyclopedia of Swearing*. Armonk, NY: M. E. Sharpe, 2006.

Hughes, Robert. *A Culture of Complaint: The Fraying of America*. New York: Oxford University Press, 1993.

Iacobbo, Karen, and Michael Iacobbo. *Vegetarians and Vegans in America Today*. Westport, CT: Praeger, 2006.

Ilhaam, Al-Yasha. "Reading Citizen Ruth Her Rights: Satire and Moral Realism in the Abortion Debate." In *Bioethics at the Movies*, edited by Sandra Shapshay. Baltimore, MD: Johns Hopkins University Press, 2009: 32–43.

I. M. Stoned. *Weed: 420 Things You Didn't Know (or Remember) about Cannabis*. Avon, MA: Adams Media, 2009.

Jay, Timothy. *Cursing in America*. Philadelphia, PA: John Benjamins Publishing, 1992.

Jay, Timothy. *Why We Curse: A Neuro-psycho-social Theory of Speech*. Philadelphia, PA: John Benjamins Publishing, 2000.

Jeffries, Stuart. "The Shock Index: Is Giving The Finger Still Offensive?" *The Guardian* (February 22, 2012). Retrieved July 24, 2012, from www.guardian.co.uk/society/2012/feb/22/shock-index-finger-adele-mia.

Jensen, Robert, and Gail Dines. "The Content of Mass-Marketed Pornography." In *Pornography: The Production and Consumption of Inequality*, edited by Gail Dines, Robert Jensen, and Ann Russo. London: Routledge, 1998: 65–100.

Johnson, Jo. " 'We'll Have a Gay Old Time!' Queer Representations in American Prime-Time Animation from the Cartoon Short to the Family Sitcom." In *Queers in American Popular Culture*, edited by Jim Elledge. Santa Barbara, CA: Praeger, 2010: 247–272.

Jong, Erica. *Parachutes and Kisses*. New York: Penguin, 1984.

Kanner, Melinda. "That's Why the Lady is a Drunk: Women, Alcoholism, and Popular Culture." In *Sexual Politics and Popular Culture*, edited by Diane Raymond. Bowling Green, OH: Bowling Green State University Popular Press, 1990: 183–199.

Karminski Burke, Theresa, and David C. Reardon. *Forbidden Grief: The Unspoken Pain of Abortion*. Springfield, IL: Acorn Books, 2002.

Keesey, Douglas. *The Films of Peter Greenaway: Sex, Death and Provocation*. Jefferson, NC: McFarland and Company, 2006.

Keller, James. "Recuperating and Reviling *South Park*'s Queer Politics." In *Queers in American Popular Culture*, edited by Jim Elledge. Santa Barbara, CA: Praeger, 2010: 273–302.

Kelly, William N. *Pharmacy: What It Is and How It Works*. Boca Raton, FL: CRC Press, 2012.

Kendall, Diana. *Framing Class: Media Representations of Wealth and Poverty in America*. Lanham, MD: Rowman and Littlefield, 2011.

Kerner, Ian. *She Comes First: The Thinking Man's Guide to Pleasuring a Woman*. New York: HarperCollins Publishers, 2010.

Key, Brian Wilson. *The Clam-Plate Orgy*. Englewood Cliffs, NJ: Prentice Hall, 1980.
Key, Brian Wilson. *Subliminal Seduction*. Englewood Cliffs, NJ: Prentice Hall, 1972.
Keyes, Ralph. *Unmentionables: From Family Jewels to Friendly Fire*. London: John Murray, 2010.
"Kids at Risk from Porn Cartoons." *Sunday Mirror* (October 30, 2011): 29.
Kimmell, Michael, and Amy Aronson. *Men & Masculinities: A Social, Cultural, and Historical Encyclopedia*. Santa Barbara, CA: ABC-CLIO, 2004.
Klip, André, and Göran Slutier. *Annotated Leading Cases of International Criminal Tribunals*, Volume VII. Cambridge: Intersentia, 1999.
Knee, Adam. "Female Power and Male Hysteria." In *Screening the Male: Exploring Masculinities in Hollywood Cinema*, edited by Steven Cohan and Ina Rae Hark. London: Routledge, 1993: 87–102.
Kolker, Robert. *A Cinema of Loneliness*. New York: Oxford University Press, 2011.
Kong, Travis S. K. "Queering Masculinity in Hong Kong Movies." In *Masculinities and Hong Kong Cinema*, edited by Laikwan Pang and Day Wong. Aberdeen, Hong Kong: Hong Kong University Press, 2005: 57–80.
Kotler, Philip, Joel Shalowitz, and Robert J. Stevens. *Strategic Marketing for Health Care Organizations*. San Francisco: Jossey-Bass, 2008.
Král, Petr. "Nostalgic Branding in Central Europe." In *Diversity in European Marketing: Text and Cases*, edited by Thomas Rudolph, Bodo B. Schlegelmilch, Josep Franch, András Bauer, and Jan Niklas Meise. Wiesbaden: Springer Gabler, 2012: 113–130.
Kroes, William H. *Society's Victim: The Police*. Springfield: IL: Charles C. Thomas, 1986.
Kroes, William H., Bruce Margolis, and Joseph J. Hurrell. "Job Stress in Policemen." *Journal of Police Science and Administration* 2 (1974): 145–155.
Kundert-Gibbs, John, and Kristin Kundert-Gibbs. *Action! Acting Lessons for CG Animators*. Indianapolis, IN : Wiley, 2009.
Kurke, Leslie. *Coins, Bodies, Games, and Gold: The Politics of Meaning in Archaic Greece*. Princeton, NJ: Princeton University Press, 1999.
Kushner, Eve. "Go Forth and Multiply: Abortion in Hollywood Movies of the '90s." *Bright Lights Film Journal* (July 2000): 29. Retrieved September 21, 2012, from http://www.brightlightsfilm.com/29/abortion1.html.
Lamb, Charles W., Joseph F. Hair, and Carl McDaniel. *Essentials of Marketing*. Mason, OH: South-Western Cengage Learning, 2012.
Lamb, Sharon, and Lyn Mikel Brown. *Packaging Girlhood: Rescuing Our Daughters from Marketers' Schemes*. New York: St. Martin's Griffin, 2006.
Laqueur, Thomas Walter. *Solitary Sex: A Cultural History of Masturbation*. New York: Zone Books, 2003.
Largey, Gale, and Rod Watson. "The Sociology of Odors." In *The Smell Culture Reader*, edited by Jim Drobnick. New York: Berg, 2006: 29–40.
Lasswell, Harold Dwight. *Propaganda Technique in the World War*. New York: Knopf, 1927.

Laumann, Edward O., John H. Gagnon, Robert T. Michael, and Stuart Michaels. *The Social Organization of Sexuality: Sexual Practices in the United States*. Chicago: University of Chicago Press, 1994.

Laurence, Ray. *Roman Passions: A History of Pleasure in Imperial Rome*. London: Continuum, 2009.

Lehman, Peter. "Melodramatic Penis: Melodrama and Male Nudity in Films of the 90s." In *Masculinity: Bodies, Movies, Culture*, edited by Peter Lehman. New York: Routledge, 2001: 25–42.

Lehman, Peter. "Penis-Size Jokes and Their Relation to Hollywood's Unconscious." In *Comedy/Cinema/Theory*, edited by Andrew S. Horton. Berkeley, CA: University of California Press, 1991: 43–59.

Lehman, Peter. *Running Scared: Masculinity and the Representation of the Male Body*. Detroit, MI: Wayne State University, 2007.

Lehman, Peter. "'They Look So Uncomplicated once They're Dissected': The Act of Seeing the Dead Penis with One's Own Eyes." In *The Trouble with Men: Masculinities in European and Hollywood Cinema*, edited by Phil Powrie, Ann Davies, and Bruce Babington. London: Wallflower Press, 2004: 196–206.

Leiss, William, Stephen Kline, and Sut Jhally. *Social Communication in Advertising: Persons, Products & Images of Well-being*. New York: Routledge, 1997.

Levin, Diane E., and Jean Kilbourne. *So Sexy So Soon: The New Sexualized Childhood*. New York: Ballantine Books, 2008.

Levine, Sylvia, and Joseph Koenig. *Why Men Rape: Interviews with Convicted Rapists* London: WH Allen, 1982.

Lewington, Mike. "An Overview." In *Images of Alcoholism*, edited by Jim Cook and Mike Lewington. London: British Film Institute, 1979: 22–29.

Light, Jonathan. *The Art of Porn: An Aesthetics for the Performing Art of Pornography*. New York: Light Publishing, 2002.

Lindstrom, Martin. *Brandwashed: Tricks Companies Use to Manipulate Our Minds and Persuade Us to Buy*. London: Kogan Page, 2012.

Lippmann, Walter. *Public Opinion*. New York: Macmillan, 1922.

Logan, Carolyn. *Counterbalance: Gendered Perspectives for Writing and Language*. Peterborough, Ontario: Broadview Press, 1997.

Longhurst, Robyn. *Maternities, Gender, Bodies and Spaces*. New York: Routledge, 2008.

Lyman, Michael D. *Drugs in Society: Causes, Concepts and Control*. Burlington, MA: Elsevier, 2011.

Marc, David. *Comic Visions: Television Comedy and American Culture*. London: Unwin Hyman, 1989.

Matthews, Roger. *Prostitution, Politics and Policy*. New York: Routledge, 2008.

Maurer, Donna. *Vegetarianism: Movement or Moment?* Philadelphia, PA: Temple University Press, 2002.

McCallum, Nancy L., and Matthew S. McGlone. "Death Be Not Profane: Mortality Salience and Euphemism Use." *Western Journal of Communication* 75, no. 5 (2011): 565–584.

McCann, Joseph T., Kelley L. Shindler, and Tammy R. Hammond. "The Science and Pseudoscience of Expert Testimony." In *Science and Pseudoscience in Clinical Psychology*, edited by Scott Lilienfeld and Steven Jay Lynn. New York: Guilford Press, 2003: 77–108.

McGlynn, Katla. "Kevin Smith Talks Judd Apatow, Weed, and His Post-'Zack and Miri' Depression." *Huffington Post* (October 5, 2009). Retrieved June 29, 2012, from http://www.huffingtonpost.com/katla-mcglynn/kevin-smith-talks-angry-y_b_309496.html.

McKee, Alan, Kath Albury, and Catharine Lumby. *The Porn Report*. Carlton: Melbourne University Press, 2008.

Metcalf, Josephine. *The Culture and Politics of Contemporary Street Gang Memoirs*. Jackson, MS: Mississippi University Press, 2012.

Michael, Richard. *The ABZ of Pornography*. London: Panther, 1972.

Mintz, Lawrence E. "Humor and Ethnic Stereotypes in Vaudeville and Burlesque." *Melus* 21, no. 4 (1996): 19–28.

Mittell, Jason. *Genre and Television: From Cop Shows to Cartoons in American Culture*. Routledge: New York, 2004.

Moll, Lucy. *Vegetarian Times Complete Cookbook*. New York: Macmillan, 1995.

Moran, Albert, and Errol Vieth. *The A to Z of Australian and New Zealand Cinema*. Lanham, MD: Scarecrow Press, 2005.

Moskowitz, Marc. *The Haunting Fetus: Abortion, Sexuality, and the Spirit World in Taiwan*. Honolulu: University of Hawai'i Press, 2001.

Mullen, Megan. "*The Simpsons* and Hanna-Barbera's Animation Legacy." In *Leaving Springfield: The Simpsons and the Possibility of Oppositional Culture*, edited by John Alberti. Detroit, MI: Wayne State University Press, 2004: 63–84.

Mulvey, Laura. "Visual Pleasure and Narrative Cinema." In *Movies and Methods*, edited by Bill Nichols. Berkeley, CA: University of California, 1985: 303–314.

Murray, Charles Shaar. *Crosstown Traffic: Jimi Hendrix and the Post-war Rock 'n' Roll Revolution*. New York: St. Martin's Press, 1989.

Musto, Michael. "Stewie Griffin." *Out* (May 2005): 64.

Nead, Lynda. *The Female Nude: Art, Obscenity, and Sexuality*. New York: Routledge, 1992.

Neal, Anthony W. *Unburdened by Conscience: A Black People's Collective Account of America's Ante-Bellum South and the Aftermath*. Lanham, MD: University Press of America, 2009.

Needham, Gary. "Scheduling Normativity: Television, the Family, and Queer Temporality." In *Queer TV*, edited by Glyn Davis and Gary Needham. New York: Routledge, 2009: 143–158.

Nelson, Kristina. *Narcissism in High Fidelity*. Lincoln, NE: iUniverse, 2004.
Nemetz, Dave. "Jennifer Love Hewitt Bares (Almost) All for Lifetime's 'The Client List.'" *Yahoo!TV* (April 6, 2012). Retrieved October 6, 2012, from http://tv.yahoo.com/news/jennifer-love-hewitt-bares—almost—all-for-lifetime-s—the-client-list-.html.
Newman, Andrew Adam. "Rebelling against the Commonly Evasive Feminine Care Ad." *New York Times* (March 15, 2010). Retrieved June 20, 2012, from http://www.nytimes.com/2010/03/16/business/media/16adco.html?_r=1&ref=business.
Nibbelink, Don D. *Fearsome Folklore of Farting*. Berkeley, CA: Frog Books, 2008.
Oates, Stephen B. *Portrait of America: From Reconstruction to the Present*. Boston, MA: Houghton Mifflin, 1973.
O'Connor, Amy. "Don't Eat a Cow Man." *Vegetarian Times* (September 1995): 16.
O'Hara, Helen. "The Worst Irish Stereotypes in Film." *Empire*. Retrieved August 20, 2012, from http://www.empireonline.com/features/irish-stereotypes-in-film/.
Oliver, Kelly. *Knock Me Up, Knock Me Down: Images of Pregnancy in Hollywood Films*. New York: Columbia University Press, 2012.
Olson, James M., and Victoria M. Esses. "The Social Psychology of Censorship." In *Interpreting Censorship in Canada*, edited by Allan C. Hutchinson and Klaus Petersen. Toronto: University of Toronto Press, 1999: 268–289.
Oppliger, Patrice A. *Girls Gone Skank: The Sexualization of Girls in American Culture*. Jefferson, NC: McFarland & Company, 2008.
Orenstein, Catherine. *Little Red Riding Hood Uncloaked: Sex, Morality, and the Evolution of a Fairytale*. New York: Basic Books, 2002.
Orlik, Peter B. *Electronic Media Criticism: Applied Perspectives*. New York: Routledge, 2009.
Orwell, George. *Nineteen Eighty-Four*. Fairfield, IA: 1st World Library, 2004.
Ott, Brian L., and Robert L. Mack. *Critical Media Studies: An Introduction*. Malden, MA: John Wiley and Sons, 2010.
Paasonen, Susanna. "Repetition and Hyperbole: The Gendered Choreographies of Heteroporn." In *Everyday Pornography*, edited by Karen Boyle. New York: Routledge, 2010: 63–76.
Pabitra, Benjamin. "An Interview with a High School Activist." In *Restoried Selves: Autobiographies of Queer Asian/Pacific American Activists*, edited by Kevin Kumashiro. Binghamton, NY: Harrington Park Press, 2004: 1–6.
Packard, Vance. *The Hidden Persuaders*. London: David Mackay, 1957.
Palkovitz, Rob. *Involved Fathering and Men's Adult Development: Provisional Balances*. Mahwah, NJ: Lawrence Erlbaum Associates, 2002.
Pank, Dylan, and John Caro. "'Haven't You Heard? They Look Like Us Now!' Realism and Metaphor in *The New Battlestar Galactica*." In *Channeling the Future: Essays on Science Fiction and Fantasy Television*, edited by Lincoln Geraghty. Lanham, MD: Scarecrow Press, 2009: 199–216.

Parker, Holt N. "The Teratogenic Grid." In *Roman Sexualities*, edited by Judith P. Hallett and Marilyn B. Skinner. Princeton, NJ: Princeton University Press, 1997: 47–65.

Parker, Judith A., and Deborah Mahlstedt. "Language, Power, and Sexual Assault: Women's Voices on Rape and Social Change." In *Language in the Real World: An Introduction to Linguistics*, edited by Susan J. Behrens and Judith A. Parker. New York: Routledge, 2010: 139–163.

Parker, Robert. "Sacrifice and Battle." In *War and Violence in Ancient Greece*, edited by Hans van Wees. Oakville, CT: David Brown Book Company, 2000: 299–314.

Penner, Todd C., and Caroline Vander Stichele. *Mapping Gender in Ancient Religious Discourses*. Danvers, MA: Brill, 2007.

Pennington, Jody. *The History of Sex in American Film*. Westport, CT: Praeger, 2007.

Perse, Elizabeth M. *Media Effects and Society*. Mahwah, NJ: Lawrence Erlbaum Associates, 2002.

Peppin, Patricia. "The Power of Illusion and the Illusion of Power: Direct-to-Consumer Advertising and Canadian Health Care." In *Just Medicare: What's In, What's Out, How We Decide*, edited by Colleen M. Flood. Toronto: University of Toronto Press, 2006: 355–378.

Phillips, Pamela. *The Art of Writing Love Songs*. New York: Allworth Press, 2003.

Phillips, Sarah R. *Modeling Life: Art Models Speak about Nudity, Sexuality, and the Creative Process*. Albany, NY: State University of New York Press, 2006.

Picone, Thomas. "Pharmaceutical Licensing during the Revolution." In *Licensing Best Practices: The LESI Guide to Strategic Issues and Contemporary Realities*, edited by Robert Goldscheider. New York: John Wiley, 2002: 215–223.

Plant, Robert W., and Peter Panzarella. "Residential Treatment of Adolescents with Substance Use Disorders: Evidence-Based Approaches and Best Practice Recommendations." In *Adolescent Substance Abuse*, edited by Carl G. Leukefeld, Thomas P. Gullotta, and Michelle Staton-Tindall. New York: Springer, 2009: 135–154.

Puskar-Pasewicz, Margaret. *Cultural Encyclopedia of Vegetarianism*. Santa Barbara, CA: ABC-CLIO, 2010.

Quan, Tracy. "The Name of the Pose: A Sex Worker by Any Other Name?" In *Prostitution and Pornography: Philosophical Debate about the Sex Industry*, edited by Jessica Spector. Stanford, CA: Stanford University Press, 2006: 135–154.

Queen, Carol, and Lawrence Schimel. *Pomosexuals: Challenging Assumptions about Gender and Sexuality*. San Francisco, CA: Cleis Press, 1997.

Raymond, Diane. "Popular Culture and Queer Representation: A Critical Perspective." In *Gender, Race, and Class in Media*, edited by Gail Dines and Jean McMahon Humez. Thousand Oaks, CA: Sage, 2001: 98–110.

Regelman, Karen. "Will Tokyo Tame *The Crying Game*?" *Variety* 22, no. 3 (1993): 68.
Reist, Melinda Tankard. *Getting Real: Challenging the Sexualisation of Girls*. North Melbourne, Victoria: Spinifex Press, 2009.
Reist, Melinda Tankard. *Giving Sorrow Words: Women's Stories of Grief after Abortion*. Potts Point, NSW: Duffy & Snellgrove, 2000.
Reynolds, R. D., and Randy Baer. *WrestleCrap: The Very Worst of Pro Wrestling*. Toronto: ECW Press, 2003.
Reynolds, Virginia. *A Lover's Guide to the Kama Sutra*. White Plains, NY: Peter Pauper Press, 2002.
Richards, Olly. "*Magic Mike*, and a Brief History of Men Getting Their Kit off on Film." *The Guardian* (July 7, 2012). Retrieved October 2, 2012, from http://www.guardian.co.uk/film/2012/jul/07/magic-mike-male-nudity-on-film.
Richmond, Ray. "Toons Tune to Adult Auds." *Variety* (October 7–13, 1996): 37.
Richters, Juliet, Richard de Visser, Chris Rissel, and Anthony M. Smith. "Sexual Practices at Last Heterosexual Encounter and Occurrence of Orgasm in a National Study." *Journal of Sex Research* 43 (2006): 217–226.
Rofes, Eric. "Making Our Schools Safe for Sissies." In *The Gay Teen: Educational Practice and Theory for Lesbian, Gay and Bisexual Adolescents*, edited by Gerald Unks. New York: Routledge, 1995: 79–84.
Roman, James. *From Daytime to Primetime: The History of American Television Programs*. Westport, CT: Greenwood Press, 2005.
Romanowski, William. *Reforming Hollywood: American Protestants and the Movies*. New York: Oxford University, 2012.
Rosenman, Samuel. *The Public Papers of Franklin D. Roosevelt*. New York: Random House, 1938.
Rosewarne, Lauren. *Cheating on the Sisterhood: Infidelity and Feminism*. Santa Barbara, CA: Praeger, 2009.
Rosewarne, Lauren. "Is He or Isn't He? The Tawdry Pastime of Sexuality Speculation." *The Conversation* (December 7, 2011), Retrieved January 21, 2012, from https://theconversation.edu.au/is-he-or-isnt-he-the-tawdry-pastime-of-sexuality-speculation-4607.
Rosewarne, Lauren. "Feminism aborted in Bachelorette." *The Conversation* (November 4, 2012), Retrieved November 1, 2012, from https://theconversation.com/feminism-aborted-in-bachelorette-9605.
Rosewarne, Lauren. "Jarryd Blair's Shocker and a Hurdy Gurdy of Double Standards." *ABC The Drum* (March 18, 2011). Retrieved November 1, 2012, from http://www.abc.net.au/unleashed/45252.html.
Rosewarne, Lauren. "Oral Sex and the Quid Pro Quo." *The Conversation* (August 16, 2012). Retrieved November 1, 2012, from http://theconversation.edu.au/oral-sex-and-the-quid-pro-quo-8863.
Rosewarne, Lauren. *Part-Time Perverts: Sex, Pop Culture, and Kink Management*. Santa Barbara, CA: Praeger, 2009.

Rosewarne, Lauren. *Periods in Pop Culture: Menstruation in Film and Television*. Lanham, MD: Lexington Books, 2012.

Rosewarne, Lauren. *Sex in Public: Women, Outdoor Advertising and Public Policy*. Newcastle: Cambridge Scholars Publishing, 2007.

Rosewarne, Lauren. "Subversion, Schadenfreude and Drama Addiction in 'Private Games.'" *The Conversation* (August 9, 2012). Retrieved November 1, 2012, from http://theconversation.edu.au/subversion-schadenfreude-and-drama-addiction-in-private-games-8749.

Rosewarne, Lauren. "Where Are the Willies? The Missing Penis in 'Magic Mike.'" *The Conversation* (August 13, 2012). Retrieved October 29, 2012, from http://theconversation.edu.au/where-are-the-willies-the-missing-penis-in-magic-mike-8792.

Rosse, Richard B. *The Love Trauma Syndrome: Free Yourself from the Pain of a Broken Heart*. Cambridge, MA: Perseus, 1999.

Rossiter, John R., and Larry Percy. "The a-b-e Model of Benefit Focus in Advertising." In *Understanding Consumer Decision Making*, edited by Thomas J. Reynolds and Jerry C. Olson. Mahwah, NJ: Lawrence Erlbaum Associates, 2001: 185–216.

Roth, Philip. *The Dying Animal*. New York: Houghton Mifflin, 2001.

Rowe, Douglas. "Full-Frontal Blokes Still Get the Flick." *Sydney Morning Herald* (February 19, 2004). Retrieved October 2, 2012, from http://www.smh.com.au/articles/2004/02/18/1077072699615.html.

Rubin, Gayle. "Thinking Sex: Notes for a Radical Theory of the Politics of Sexuality." In *The Lesbian and Gay Studies Reader*, edited by Henry Abelove. New York: Routledge, 1993: 3–44.

Rubington, Earl. "The Changing Skid Row Scene." In *The Substance of Sociology: Codes, Conduct and Consequences*, edited by Ephraim H. Mizruchi. New York: Meredith Corporation, 1973: 123–135.

Russell, Jessica B., and Isabel C. Green. "Perioperative Care and Complications of Gynecologic Surgery." In *The Johns Hopkins Manual of Gynecology and Obstetrics*, edited by K. Joseph Hurt, Matthew W. Guile, Jessica Bienstock, Harold E. Fox, and Edward E. Wallach. Philadelphia, PA: Lippincott Williams and Wilkins, 2011: 306–321.

"Ryan Gosling Frustrated by Censorship." *The Independent* (January 24, 2011). Retrieved October 15, 2012, from http://www.independent.co.uk/news/people/news/ryan-gosling-frustrated-by-censorship-2192751.html.

Sacks, Ethan. "Madonna Blasts M.I.A. On-Air Middle Finger Salute." *New York Daily News* (February 10, 2012). Retrieved July 18, 2012, from articles.nydailynews.com/2012-02-10/news/31048210_1_material-girl-mia-finger.

Sandler, Kevin S. *The Naked Truth: Why Hollywood Doesn't Make X-Rated Movies*. New Brunswick, NJ: Rutgers University Press, 2007.

Sawyer, Sarah. *Avril Lavigne*. New York: Rosen Publishing Group, 2009.

Seidel, Linda. "Dr. Jarvik and Other Baby Boomers: (Still) Performing the Able Body." In *The Body in Medical Culture*, edited by Elizabeth Klaver. Albany, NY: SUNY Press, 2009: 229–241.

Semonche, John E. *Censoring Sex: A Historical Journey through American Media*. Lanham, MD: Rowman and Littlefield, 2007.

Shimp, Terence A. *Advertising, Promotion, and Other Aspects of Integrated Marketing Communications*. Mason, OH: South-Western Cengage Learning, 2010.

Shin, Jaeun, and Sangho Moon. "Direct-to-Consumer Prescription Drug Advertising: Concerns and Evidence of Consumers' Benefit." *Journal of Consumer Marketing* 22, no. 7 (2005): 397–403.

Sienkiewicz, Matt, and Nick Marx. "Beyond a Cutout World: Ethnic Humor and Discursive Integration in *South Park*." *Journal of Film and Video* 61, no. 2 (Summer 2009): 5–18.

Silverblatt, Art. *Genre Studies in Mass Media: A Handbook*. Armonk, NY: M. E. Sharpe, 2007.

Slade, Joseph W. *Pornography and Sexual Representation: A Reference Guide*. Westport, CT: Greenwood Press, 2001.

Smith, Dina. "Movies and the Art of Living Dangerously." In *American Cinema of the 2000s: Themes and Variations*, edited by Timothy Corrigan. Piscataway, NJ: Rutgers University Press, 2012.

Solot, Dorian, and Marshall Miller. *I (Heart) Female Orgasm*. New York: Marlowe & Company, 2007.

Sorrells, Morris L. "The History of Circumcision in the United States: A Physician's Perspective." In *Circumcision and Human Rights*, edited by George Denniston, Frederick Hodges, and Marilyn Fayre Milos. London: Springer, 2009.

Spencer, Scott. *Endless Love*. New York: Knopf, 1979.

Stacey, Jackie. *Teratologies: A Cultural Study of Cancer*. New York: Routledge, 1997.

Stengers, Jean, and Anne Van Neck. *Masturbation: The History of a Great Terror*. New York: Palgrave, 2001.

Stepaniak, Joanne. *Being Vegan*. Lincolnwood, IL: Lowell House, 2000.

Stoltenberg, John. *Refusing to Be a Man: Essays on Social Justice*. London: Breitenbush Books, 1989.

Strub, Whitney. *Perversion for Profit: The Politics of Pornography and the Rise of the New Right*. New York: Columbia University Press, 2010.

Sullivan, Michael, and John S. Wodardski. "Social Alienation in Gay Youth." *Journal of Human Behavior in the Social Environment* 5, no. 1 (2002): 1–17.

Suraci, Patrick. *Male Sexual Armor: Erotic Fantasies and Sexual Realities of the Cop on the Beat and the Man in the Street*. Falls Village, CT: Invington Publishers, 1992.

Tassi, Paul. "The Top Ten Most Paused Movie Scenes." *Unreality Magazine* (March 3, 2011). Retrieved October 9, 2012, from http://unrealitymag.com/index.php/2011/03/03/the-top-ten-most-paused-movie-scenes/.

Thompson, Dave. *Black and White and Blue: Adult Cinema from the Victoria Age to the VCR*. Toronto: ECW Press, 2003.

Torres, Bob, and Jenna Torres. *Vegan Freak: Being Vegan in a Non-vegan World*. Colton, NY: Tofu Hound Press, 2005.

Tourtellotte, Bob. "Golden Globes: Raised Finger Gets Thumbs Down." *Reuters* (January 13, 2009). Retrieved July 18, 2012, from blogs.reuters.com/fanfare/2009/01/13/golden-globes-raised-finger-gets-thumbs-down/.

Traister, Rebecca. "More Than Lip Service." *The Guardian* (October 27, 2003). Retrieved March 13, 2012, from http://www.guardian.co.uk/world/2003/oct/27/gender.uk.

Trinch, Shonna L. "Managing Euphemism and Transcending Taboos: Negotiating the Meaning of Sexual Assault in Latinas' Narratives of Domestic Violence." *Interdisciplinary Journal for the Study of Discourse* 21, no. 4 (2001): 567–610.

Trumble, Angus. *The Finger: A Handbook*. New York: Farrar, Straus and Giroux, 2010.

TVTropes. "Hurricane of Euphemisms." Retrieved June 21, 2012, from http://tvtropes.org/pmwiki/pmwiki.php/Main/HurricaneOfEuphemisms.

Urbanski, Dave. *The Man Comes Around: The Spiritual Journey of Johnny Cash*. Lake Mary, FL: Relevant Books, 2003.

Van Raalte, R.C. "Alcohol as a Problem among Police Officers." *Police Chief* 44 (1979): 38–40.

Vaughn, Stephen. *Freedom and Entertainment: Rating the Movies in an Age of New Media*. New York: Cambridge University Press, 2006.

Voss, Brandon. "Big Gay Following: Seth MacFarlane." *The Advocate* (February 27, 2008): 22–23.

Walsh, John. "A Shock to the System." *Independent* (September 11, 1993): 18–22.

Walter, Natasha. *The New Feminism*. London: Little, Brown and Company, 1998.

Waltonen, Karma, and Denise Du Vernay. The Simpsons *in the Classroom: Embiggening the Learning Experience with the Wisdom of Springfield*. Jefferson, NC: McFarland and Company, 2010.

Warshaw, Robin. *I Never Called It Rape*. New York: Harper & Row, 1988.

Weaver, Simon. *The Rhetoric of Racist Humour: US, UK and Global Race Joking*. Burlington, VT: Ashgate, 2011.

Weaver, Tara Austen. *The Butcher and the Vegetarian*. New York: Rodale, 2010.

Wells, Herbert George. *The Time Machine: An Invention*. Orchard Park, NY: 2001.

Whatling, Clare. *Screen Dreams: Fantasising Lesbians in Film*. Manchester: Manchester University Press, 1997.

White, Dave. "Wanted: 2,000 Men." *The Advocate* (October 28, 2003): 66.

Wienke, Chris. "Sex the Natural Way: The Marketing of Cialis and Levitra." In *Medicalized Masculinities*, edited by Dana Rosenfeld and Christopher A. Faircloth. Philadelphia, PA: Temple University Press, 2006: 45–64.

Wilcox, Rhonda. "Unreal TV." In *Thinking outside the Box: A Contemporary Television Genre Reader*, edited by Gary R. Edgerton and Brian G. Rose. Lexington, KY: University Press of Kentucky, 2005: 201–225.

Williams, Craig A. *Epigrams: Martial*. New York: Oxford University Press, 2004.

Williams, Linda. *Screening Sex*. Durham, NC: Duke University Press, 2008.

Williamson, Marvel L., and Paul S. Williamson. "Women's Preference for Penile Circumcision in Sexual Partners." *Journal of Sex Education and Therapy* 14 (Fall/Winter 1988): 8–12.

Wisnewski, Jeremy. Family Guy *and Philosophy: A Cure for the Petarded*. Malden, MA: Blackwell, 2007.

Wolcott, James. "The Hung and the Restless." *Vanity Fair* (March 2012). Retrieved October 2, 2012, from http://www.vanityfair.com/hollywood/2012/03/wolcott-201203.

Wood, Jim. *The Rape of Inez Garcia*. New York: Putnam, 1976.

Wurtzel, Elizabeth. *Bitch: In Praise of Difficult Women*. New York: Doubleday, 1998.

Young, Hugh. "Circumcision as a Memeplex." In *Bodily Integrity and the Politics of Circumcision*, edited by George C. Denniston, Pia Grassivaro Gallo, Frederick M. Hodges, Marilyn Fayre Milos, and Franco Viviani. New York: Springer, 2006: 1–16.

Young, Hugh. " 'That Thing': Portrayal of the Foreskin and Circumcision in Popular Media." In *Circumcision and Human Rights*, edited by George Denniston, Frederick Hodges, and Marilyn Fayre Milos. London: Springer, 2009: 239–250.

Zeisler, Andi. *Feminism and Pop Culture*. Berkeley, CA: Seal Press, 2008.

Zorea, Aharon W. *Birth Control*. Santa Barbara, CA: ABC-CLIO, 2012.

Index

Abelman, Robert, 123
Abortion, viii, ix, x, 153–73, 237
Abortion grief, 165–66
About a Boy, 102–3, 113
About Last Night, 177
Absent referent, 100
Absolutely Fabulous, 126, 127, 128
Absolute Strangers, 171
Acropolis Now, 102
Activism, 7, 8, 90, 93, 94, 103, 106, 107, 114, 162–63, 168, 171
Adams, Carol J., 93, 100, 111
Adams, Ryan, 80
Addiction, 115–16, 117, 120, 124, 126, 145, 149, 169, 186
Adele, 55, 57
Adolescence, 8, 59–60, 72, 107, 123–24, 127, 223
Adventures of Priscilla, Queen of the Desert, The, 215
Advertising, ix, 15, 57, 60, 68, 69, 90, 111, 131–52, 154, 178, 217, 218, 234, 238
Aesthetics, 29, 96, 97, 150, 181, 187, 188, 195, 199, 200–202, 204–5, 213, 214, 216

Ageing, 150
Aggression, 38, 41–42, 51–52, 53–54, 55, 64, 65, 75, 105, 124, 125, 175, 188
Alexandra's Project, 235
Alfie, 155, 159, 160
Alive or Dead, 223
Allan, Keith, 68, 74
Allen, Valerie, 36
Allen, Woody, 197–98
Allinson, Mark, 23
All My Children, 169
All the Right Moves, 177
Altered States, 177
Altrocchi, Rudolph, 41
American Dad!, 2, 98, 112
American Flyers, 177
American History X, 182
American Horror Story, 159, 160, 164, 229
American Pie, 28, 29, 223
American Psycho, 180, 184–85, 186
Amok, 160
Amos, Tori, 72
Anal sex, 64

Anatomie de l'enfer (Anatomy of Hell), 175
Anchorman, 177
Andersen, Robin, 139
Anderson, Pamela, 114
Andrews, Suzanna, 177
Angier, Natalie, 62
Animal House, 117, 122
Ann Vickers, 153
Anomie, 155
Another World, 161
Anthropology, 29, 52, 71
Anthropomorphism, 6
Antiestablishmentism, 51, 58, 59, 64, 97, 196
Apatow, Judd, 37–38
Archer, 2, 121, 224
Archie Bunker's Place, 115
Arctic Monkeys, 80
Are You Being Served?, 81
Ariano, Tara, 123
Armed for Action, 177
Arme Riddere (Jackpot), 221
Armstrong, Nancy, 51, 58, 61, 62
Arnold, Rebecca, 11
Aronofsky, Darren, 62
Arrested Development, 128, 208, 213–14
Arthur, 116
Arthur 2: On the Rocks, 116
As the World Turns, 169
Asbell, Robin, 92
At Play in the Fields of the Lord, 177
Austin, "Stone Cold" Steve, 60
Austin Powers: International Man of Mystery, 47
Autumn, Emilie, 73
Avatar: The Last Airbender, 99, 110

Bach, George, 42
Bachelorette, 77–78, 165
Backstrom, Laura, 25, 27

Bad Biology, 186
Bad Lieutenant, 119, 184
Bad Santa, 116
Baer, Randy, 60
Baker, Paul, 74–75
Bakos, Susan Crain, 22, 27
Banishment, The, 166
Barfly, 119
Barnyard, 91
Barsanti, Chris, 97
Bartky, Sandra Lee, 150
Basic Instinct, 183
Baumeister, Roy F., 9
Bay-Cheng, Laina Y., 26, 29
BeautifulAgony.com, 230
Beavis and Butt-Head, 3
Becker, Anne E., 150
Bego, Mark, 12
Being Erica, 206, 211
Belle and Sebastian, 71
Bells, The, 164
Ben 10: Ultimate Alien, 111
Ben Folds Five, 165
Bergerac, 119
Bestiality, 7, 12
Better Than Chocolate, 21
Beverly Hills, 90210, 123
Big Bang Theory, The, 90, 130, 206
Big Love, 33, 41, 158, 180
Bill Bailey: Live at the Apollo—Part Troll, 90
Billboard, 11, 57, 60
Billy Madison, 116
Biology, 30, 44, 103, 105, 127, 134, 179
Bisexuality, 98, 112, 126
Black Books, 124, 126
Black Donnellys, The, 121
Black Swan, 17
Blair, Jarryd, 64
Blake, Barry J., 81
Blaney, Roger, 122
Blazing Saddles, 35, 36, 42–43
Bloom, Stephen G., 38

Blossom, 108, 123
Blue Valentine, 17, 18, 19, 63, 156
Blue Velvet, 177
Blumberg, Mark S., 213
Bonaduce, Danny, 60
Bones, 99–100
Boogie Nights, 178, 179
Borat, 181
Bordo, Susan, 147–48, 177, 182, 185, 187
Bored to Death, 90, 98, 102, 113
Boys Don't Cry, 30
Braceface, 100
Breakfast Club, The, 56–57
Breakfast on Pluto, 156
Breasts, 45
Brehm, Jack Williams, 9
Brierley, Sean, 151
Bring It On, 54
Bronner, Simon J., 52
Brooklyn's Finest, 120
Brown Bunny, The, 179
Brown Sugar, 219, 223–24, 233
Bruce Almighty, 61
Bryant, Jennings, 35
Buffy the Vampire Slayer, 99, 101, 113
Bunning, Jim, 58
Bunting, Sarah, 123
Burlesque, 4, 120
Burns, Jim, 27
Burridge, Kate, 68, 74
Bushman, Brad J., 9, 10
Butch Jamie, 112

Cabaret, 169
Cable television, vii, x, 3, 13
Caddyshack, 38
Cage the Elephant, 81
Caligula, 175
Californication, 23, 27, 53, 118, 119, 129, 177, 212
Callahan, John, 59

Cannonball Run 2, 56
Cantor, Joanne, 10
Captain America: The First Avenger, 107
Carducci, Bernardo J., 141
Carne trémula (Live Flesh), 23, 30
Carpool, 44
Cash, Johnny, 57, 58, 60
Cassidy, David, 60
Castration, 206, 208
Censorship, viii, ix, x, 10, 11, 73, 183, 188–89
Chandler, Gael, 178
Changeling, The, 195
Change-Up, The, 224
Charney, Maurice, 42–43
Chase, Sarah Alexander, 29, 31, 32
Chase, Susan E., 127
Chasing Amy, 37
Cheers, 115, 122, 211
Cherrybomb, 129
Chicago Hope, 212, 213
Child abuse, 100, 129, 198, 208, 210–11. *See also* Pedophilia
Children, 1–3, 7, 13, 14, 38, 68–69, 70, 127–28, 129–30, 144, 145, 164, 223
Children's Hospital, 216
China Beach, 154
Cholesterol, 139, 142–43, 145, 146, 148
Christman, Ed, 11
Cider House Rules, The, 159, 160, 171
Circumcision, vii, ix, 195–216, 237
Citizen Ruth, 154, 157–58, 171
Civility, 122, 195–200
Class, 36, 51, 74, 79, 91, 196, 199, 202, 204
Cleanliness, 102, 199–200, 202, 214. *See also* Hygiene
Click, 42
Client List, The, 193
Clinton, Bill, 27
Clinton, Hillary, 59

Closer, The, 120
Clueless, 76, 82
Coach Carter, viii, 169
Cocktail, 115
Cold Case, 128, 129, 161
Cold Chisel, 165
Color of Night, 177, 179
Comedy, x–xi, 1, 2, 6, 16, 36, 37, 39, 41, 42, 43, 82, 83, 102, 116, 120, 127, 130, 173, 180, 181, 212, 221, 222, 223, 224
Come Fill the Cup, 118
Come What May, 153
Coming Home, 17, 20, 22–23, 24, 25, 30
Community, 61, 104
Connell, Raewyn, 22
Consent, 65
Consumer behavior, viii, 9–13, 87, 132, 133, 134, 138, 140, 147, 149
Contender, The, 113
Contraception, 137, 149, 151–52
Cook, the Thief, His Wife & Her Lover, The, 179
Cooler, The, 19
Cosmetic surgery, 148
Count Duckula, 98
Coyote Ugly, 115
Crash, 189
Crazy Heart, 118
Crazy. Stupid. Love., 192
Crimen ferpecto (*Ferpect Crime*), 164
Criminality, 7–8, 39, 72–73, 84–85, 116, 120, 164, 167, 227
Criminal Minds, 167
Critser, Greg, 136
Crowe, Sheryl, 158
Cruise, Tom, 8, 63
Crusader Rabbit, 2
Crying Game, The, 178, 179, 185, 188

CSI, 99, 227
Cultural studies, ix, 1
Cunnilingus, vii, ix, xi, 17–34, 63–64, 67, 87, 237
Curb Your Enthusiasm, 28, 31–32, 177

Dallas, 128
Damage, 177
Dances with Wolves, 40, 43
Danny Phantom, 103, 105
Darby O'Gill and the Little People, 122
Dawson, Jim, 35, 36
Dawson's Creek, 113, 208, 211
Days of Our Lives, 161
Days of Wine and Roses, 125
Dead Europe, 184
De Beauvoir, Simone, 46
Deconstructing Harry, 197–98
Dedication, 224, 227
Deer Hunter, The, 184
Degrassi: The Next Generation, 222, 224, 226
Deicide, 11
Delinquents, The, 172
Delta Spirit, 80
Demolition Man, 89, 109–10
Demonization, x–xi, 1, 4, 5, 9, 74, 77, 87, 89, 101, 104, 114, 116, 122, 126, 131, 157, 170, 171, 195, 197, 216, 225–26, 228, 233
Denzin, Norman K., 116
Departed, The, 122
Depression, 102–3, 135, 136, 138, 140, 142, 145, 146–47, 165, 186, 235
Der Untergang (*Downfall*), 101, 102
Desirability, ix, 40, 53–54, 131, 143–44
Desperate Housewives, 196, 199, 201, 203, 206, 207, 210, 211
Detective Story, 167
Dexter, 199, 200
Dharma & Greg, 91, 92, 95, 96, 97, 106, 204, 215
Diabetes, 138, 139, 140

Dictator, The, 96
Did You Hear about the Morgans?, 105
DiFranco, Ani, 74, 162–63
Dines, Gail, 20
Dirt, 223, 229
Dirty Dancing, 161
Dirty Sexy Money, 128
Dirty talk, 62, 77–78
Disability, 17, 30, 127, 137–38, 169
Disgust, 19, 31, 35, 36–37, 41–42, 48–49, 59, 72, 154, 181, 199, 200, 201
Disney, 13, 188
Dissociation, 68, 71–73, 100
Doctor Who, 111
Dogma, 161
Dogtooth, 17
Domestic violence, 71
Don't Look Now, 17, 22–23
Don't Tell Mom the Babysitter's Dead, 54
Donnie Darko, 42
Dostoyevsky, Fyodor, 42
Dr. T and the Women, 24
Drawn Together, 2
Dread, 100
Dreamers, The, 187, 191
Dresden Dolls, The, 73.
Drew Carey Show, The, 130
Drowning by Numbers, 205
Dubin, Steven C., 154
Dundes, Alan, 52
Du Vernay, Denise, 5
Dyer, Richard, 190

Easteal, Patricia, 71
Eastenders, 201, 204
Eastern Promises, 180, 182
East Is East, 199, 203
Easy A, 234–35
Ebeling, Mary, 136
Ebert, Robert, 189
Eccentricity, 124, 125, 126, 127

Edlin, Gordon, 139
8 Mile, 62
8 Million Ways to Die, 119
Ego, 28, 29, 58, 170, 175, 197, 198, 232, 234. *See also* Self-esteem
El crimen del padre Amaro (The Crime of Father Amaro),162
Elliott, John H., 74, 75
El Topo, 179
Emasculation, 23, 25, 32–34, 52–53, 212, 232, 234
End of Days, 120
Eproctophilia, 48
ER, 205
Erectile dysfunction, 69, 131, 140, 141, 143–45, 234. *See also* Impotency
Erection, 52, 69, 83, 136, 176–77, 186. *See also* Penis
Escape from LA, 89, 109–10
Escapism, 123, 237
Esses, Victoria M., 10
Euphemism, x, xi, 10, 33, 67–85, 100, 218–19, 220–21
Euthanasia, 173
Everything Is Illuminated, 94–95, 109, 112–13
Exhibitionism, 175, 179, 184
Expecting Mary, 172
Extreme Movie, 45, 220, 221, 223

Facebook, 63, 64
Factotum, 119
Fame, 169
Family Guy, 2, 4, 6–9, 10, 12, 14, 15, 16, 46, 122, 130, 156–57
Family Matters, 123
Fargo, 180, 182, 200
Fassbender, Michael, 179, 190
Fast Show, The, 91
Fast Times at Ridgemont High, viii, 168, 169

Fatness, 36, 37, 49, 56, 136, 143. *See also* Obesity
Fava, Nicole M., 26, 29
Feces, 35
Felicity, 156
Fellatio, ix, 18, 19–20, 26, 67
Femininity, 44–46, 53, 54, 99, 110, 111–12, 129, 170
Ferguson, Michael, 191
Fertility, 153, 161–62
Fetish, 48–49, 63, 78, 215, 226
Fibromyalgia, 134, 148
Field, Sally, 139
Fight Club, 178
Find Me Guilty, 42
Fisch, Audry, 168
Fisher King, The, 184
Flight of the Conchords, 56
Flintstones, The, 2, 3, 4
Flirting with Disaster, 197
Folklore, 52, 119
Fools Rush In, 155
Forbearance, 46–47
Foreplay, 20, 21, 26–28
Forgetting Sarah Marshall, 181, 183, 185
Forrest Gump, 129
40 Days and 40 Nights, 186
40-Year-Old Virgin, The, 220
Foster, Gwendolyn Audrey, 190, 193
4 luni, 3 saptamâni si 2 zile (4 Months, 3 Weeks, 2 Days), 160, 161
Four Rooms, 82
Fouz-Hernández, Santiago, 176, 190, 193–94
Frank, Russell, 56
Freeman, Hadley, 17, 19, 154
Friends, 91–92, 94, 95, 96, 97, 109, 112, 116–17
Friends with Money, 235
Frontline, 169
Full House, 69
Full Monty, The, 176, 185

Funny People, 37
Futurama, 98, 101, 106

Gagnon, John H., 18, 24, 28–29, 30, 32
Gallows humor, 206–7, 210
Game of Thrones, 83
Gavey, Nicola, 72
Geer, John Gray, 170
Getaway, The, 20
Ghost and the Darkness, The, 121
Ghost Rider, 57
Ghost World, 40, 221
Girl with the Dragon Tattoo, The, 21
Glee, 109
Glengarry Glen Ross, 57
Go Fish, 21
Godfather II, The, 169, 170
Golanty, Eric, 139
Goldberg, Herb, 42
Gollaher, David, 195, 196, 199
Gone with the Wind, 200
Good Guys, The, 88
Good life, 151, 152
Good Luck Chuck, 48
Good Wife, The, 17, 26
Gordon's Great Escape, 98
Gosford Park, 113
Gosling, Ryan, 18, 63, 192
Gournelos, Ted, 7, 8
Governess, The, 177
Graduate, The, 128
Grant, Marcus, 129
Gray, Jonathan, 139
Grease, 72
Greenaway, Peter, 175, 179, 191
Greenberg, 20, 169–70
Greene, Gayle, 140
Grey's Anatomy, 69, 158
Grief, 123, 165–66
Griffin, Kathy, 60
Growing Pains, 123
Grygier, Tadeusz, 164

Index   315

Guilt, viii, 73, 101, 103, 104, 106, 131, 144–45, 150, 152, 164–65, 167–68, 199
Guns 'n' Roses, 79
Guterson, David, 11
Gwai wik (Re-cycle), 165
Gynecology, 24, 68, 161

Hadler, Nortin M., 134
Hae anseon (The Coast Guard), 172
Hairspray, 184
Hall and Oates, 80
Halloween II, 88
Halloween: Resurrection, 101, 102
Hall Pass, 30, 192
Hangover, The, 54
Hanna-Barbera, 2–3, 16
Happy Days, 107
Happy Endings, 130
Harold and Kumar Escape from Guantanamo Bay, 214
Harold and Kumar Go to White Castle, 45
Harsh Times, 172
Harvey, 116
Harwin, Judith, 124, 125
Hawn, Goldie, 126
Hays code, vii, x
Hazell, 119
Healey, Matthew, 151
Heartbreak Kid, The, 45
He liu (The River), 219
Helms, Udo, 189
Hendrix, Jimi, 64
Henry Fool, 119
Henry, Matthew, 5–6
Heterosexuality, 4, 5, 24, 54, 63, 64, 77, 97, 112, 191, 192
Hey Arnold, 40
Hey, Happy! 178
Hidden Secrets, 167–68
High Fidelity, 61, 97, 109, 167, 168
Hippies, 87, 90, 91, 95–100, 103, 104, 106, 109, 112, 113, 196

Hitchcock, Alfred, 193
Hite, Shere, 21, 26, 27, 29, 31, 32, 33
Hitler, Adolf, 101
Hoffa, James ("Jimmy"), 59
Hold Me, Thrill Me, Kiss Me, 227
Homoeroticism, 191
Homophobia, 8, 15–16, 113, 192
Homosexuality, vii, x, xi, 1–16, 32, 52, 67, 75, 76–77, 82, 106, 123, 181, 191–93, 198, 206, 226, 227, 235
Homosexual panic, 191–93
Hope Springs, 186
Hostel, 88, 202
House, 41, 68, 83, 128, 205
Howdy-Doody, 3
How I Met Your Mother, 81, 100–101, 104, 218, 234
How the Garcia Girls Spent Their Summer, 223, 229
How to Lose a Guy in 10 Days, 96, 99, 109
Hughes, Geoffrey, 42
Hughes, Robert, 78–79
Humiliation, 33, 41, 44, 49, 181, 224
Hurlyburly, 228
Hush-a-Bye Baby, 171
Hygiene, 69, 118, 163, 199, 204, 207, 214. *See also* Cleanliness
Hysteria, 217, 219

Iacobbo, Karen, 87, 100, 102
Iacobbo, Michael, 87, 100, 102
Ian, Janis, 80
Identity, 22, 44, 47, 55, 71, 73–74, 75, 91, 94, 112–13, 126, 149–50, 186, 197
Identity Thief, 220
If These Walls Could Talk, viii, 162, 166
I Give It a Year, 181
I Had an Abortion, 168
Ilhaam, Al-Yasha, 154

I'll Cry Tomorrow, 125
Immaturity, 38, 39, 43, 59, 211
Impotency, 56, 140, 143. *See also* Erectile dysfunction
In a Lonely Place, 119
Incest, 12, 14
Individualism, 147, 149–50, 152
In Living Color, 39–40
Insanity, 185, 186. *See also* Madness
Intercourse, 17, 20, 21, 22, 26, 27, 28, 30, 55, 68, 223, 233
Internalization, 24–25, 31, 204
Internet, 10, 48
In the Cut, 19
In the Realm of the Senses, 183
Intimacy, 18, 33–34, 35, 48, 49, 62, 65, 77, 144
Iron Maiden, 80
Ironweed, 118–19, 129
It's Always Sunny in Philadelphia, 115

Jack and Bobby, 166
Jackson, Janet, 59
Jagger, Mick, 126
James, Mickie, 63
Jamie Foxx Show, The, 108
Jay, Timothy, 38, 67, 68, 78, 85
Jay and Silent Bob Strike Back, 37, 42
Jeffries, Stuart, 54–55, 59, 61
Jennifer's Body, 214
Jensen, Robert, 20
Jetsons, The, 2, 3
Joey, 88
John, Elton, 80
John Tucker Must Die, 98
Johnson, Jo, 4–5
Jones, Serius, 60
Joyce, James, 48
Judging Amy, 206, 208, 211
Jui kuen (Drunken Master), 130
Juno, 154, 155, 156
Just Married, 234
Just Shoot Me, 121, 125, 126, 127, 128

Kama Sutra, 18
Kama Sutra: A Tale of Love, 88
Kanner, Melinda, 125–26
Kendall, Diana, 10
Ken Park, 28, 29
Kerner, Ian, 34
Khia, 75–76, 77
Kid Rock, 80, 166
Kids Are Alright, The, 17, 225, 226, 233
Killing, The, 92, 112
King, Billie Jean, 55
King of Queens, 220
King of the Hill, 105, 107
Knee, Adam, 23
Knocked Up, 37, 154, 155
Koenig, Joseph, 72
Kolker, Robert, 38
Kong, Travis S. K., 181
Korn, 71
Král, Petr, 146
Kroes, William H., 120
Kundert-Gibbs, John, 7
Kundert-Gibbs, Kristin, 7
Kung Fu, 110
Kurke, Leslie, 18
Kushner, Eve, 155, 156

Lady Gaga, 82
Lamb, Charles W., 134
Largey, Gale, 39
Last Chance Harvey, 165, 168
Late Late Show with Craig Ferguson, The, 195
Late Show with David Letterman, 58
Laumann, Edward O., 18, 32
Lauper, Cyndi, 158
Laurel Canyon, 28, 34
Laurence, Ray, 18
Lavigne, Avril, 54, 55
Law and Order, 119, 129, 162
Law and Order: Special Victims Unit, 119, 123, 162, 184, 212, 213
Law and Order: UK, 120

League, The, 208
Leap Year, 122
Leaving Las Vegas, 119
Legally Blonde, 106
Lehman, Peter, 178, 179, 183, 192, 193, 194
Leiss, William, 151
Leonard Part 6, 105
Lesbianism, 1, 6, 21, 63, 95, 98, 112, 127, 163, 167, 171, 198, 208, 224, 226. *See also* Homosexuality
Letterman, David, 58, 61, 62
Leverage, 122
Levine, Sylvia, 72
Lewington, Mike, 117, 118, 119, 120, 125
Lewinsky, Monica, 27
Liar Liar, 83
Lie with Me, 21
Life before Her Eyes, The, 165
Life on Mars, 76, 82
Light, Jonathan, 19, 27
Lindstrom, Martin, 135
Linguistics, 67, 68, 71, 74–75, 78–79, 81, 83
Lirkod (The Belly Dancer), 180, 182
Living Single, 105
Logan, Carolyn, 84
Logan's Run, 110
Loneliness, 116, 142, 217, 233–34
Longhurst, Robyn, 127
Lost Weekend, 119
Love, Courtney, 54, 55, 75
Love Bites, 232
Love with the Proper Stranger, 159, 161
Ludacris, 73, 80
L-Word, The, 163, 167, 224

M*A*S*H, 219, 234
MacFarlane, Seth, 7
MacGruber, 172
Mack, Robert L., 185
Mad, 60

Mad Men, 156, 218, 220
Madness, 101, 175, 184–85. *See also* Insanity
Madonna, 12, 58, 59, 60
Magic Mike, 176, 185
Maher, Bill, 58, 62
Mahlstedt, Deborah, 71, 72, 73, 84
Male gaze, 190
Malkovich, John, 195
Margaret, 20, 168, 169
Marketing. *See* Advertising
Marriage, 6, 7, 45, 118, 158, 166, 167, 169, 170, 226, 232
Married with Children, 88, 108–9, 199, 202–3
Martial, 18, 32, 52
Martinez-Expósito, Alfredo, 176, 190, 193–94
Marx, Nick, 15
Masculinity, 22, 23, 25, 32–34, 44, 47, 52, 110–12, 140, 183, 185, 199
Masochism, 103
Master, The, 43
Masturbation, vii, ix, xi, 49, 67, 68, 83, 229–31. *See also* Vibrators
Match Point, 167
Matrix, The, 57
Matthews, Roger, 79
Maude, 169
Maurer, Donna, 91, 92, 93, 114
McCain, John, 59
McCallum, Nancy L., 70
McCartney, Linda, 94, 114
McCartney, Paul, 94, 114
McFerrin, Bobby, 146
McGlone, Matthew S., 70
McGregor, Ewan, 100, 179, 190
McKee, Alan, 19
McOrmond-Plummer, Louise, 71
Meaning of Life, The, 82
Media effects, 15, 133
Media literacy, 9
Meet the Fockers, 212

Men in Black, 59
Men with Brooms, 231
Menstruation, 23, 31, 33, 48, 67, 137, 151, 154, 155, 189, 190, 191, 230, 235
Mental illness, 17, 183, 184. *See also* Insanity; Madness
Mentalist, The, 129
Metcalf, Josephine, 185
M.I.A., 53–55, 59–60, 61
Miami Vice, 105, 112
Michael, Richard, 19
Miller, Marshall, 64
Minaj, Nicky, 165–66
Mintz, Lawrence E., 120, 122
Mitchell, Joni, 166
Mittell, Jason, 3
Monkees, The, 108–9, 110
Monster's Ball, 20–21
Monty Python and the Holy Grail, 42
Moonlighting, 157, 158
Morality, 53, 101, 117, 119, 125, 157, 159, 190
Morning After, The, 125
Moskowitz, Marc, 164
Motherhood, 13, 69–70, 124, 126–29, 145, 166–67, 170, 172, 206, 207, 208, 211
Motörhead, 72
Mrs. Brown's Boys, 225
Mrs. Parker and the Vicious Circle, 119
Mudhoney, 162
Mulvey, Laura, 187, 230, 238
Munich, 183
Murray, Charles Shaar, 64
My Big Fat Greek Wedding, 94, 109
My Little Pony: Friendship Is Magic, 98–99
My Science Project, 52, 56
My So-Called Life, 225
Mystery Men, 42
Mythbusters, 39

Naked, 167
Naked Gun, 56
Naked Gun 2½: The Smell of Fear, The, 221
National Lampoon's Christmas Vacation, 56
Navratilova, Martina, 126
NCIS, 92
Neal, Anthony W., 84
Ned's Declassified School Survival Guide, 40, 41
Nelson, Kristina, 97
New Tricks, 120
Nibbelink, Don D., 39, 46
Nicklaus, Jack, 139
Night Fall, 182
9 Songs, 21, 229, 232
Nip/Tuck, 200–201, 203, 204, 205
No Cure for Cancer, 87–88, 111
No Impact Man: The Documentary, 90
Normalization, x, 4, 6, 137–41, 168
Nostalgia, 38, 131, 145, 146–47, 150
Not Another Teen Movie, 45, 112, 223, 229
Notting Hill, 99
Nutty Professor, The, 36
NYPD Blue, 120

Oates, Stephen B., 90
Obama, Barack, 59
Obesity, 36, 181. *See also* Fatness
Objectification, 15, 53
October Baby, 153
Office, The, 102, 108, 113, 126, 127, 205
Office Space, 55
Off-label drugs, 135–37
Offspring, The, 73
O'Grady, 102
O'Hara, Helen, 121, 122
Oh in Ohio, The, 220, 221, 231, 232
Old School, 130
Oliver, Kelly, 155, 159, 162, 164

Olson, James M., 10
Opening Night, 126
Oral sex. *See* Cunnilingus; Fellatio
Orange County, 128
Orenstein, Catherine, 53
Orgasm, ix, 20, 21, 22, 23, 24, 25, 26, 28, 29, 30, 31, 33, 34, 219, 220, 223, 229, 230, 231, 232
Orlik, Peter B., 13
Orwell, George, 67, 84
Othering, 1, 77, 87
Ott, Brian L., 185
Otto, Shirley, 124, 125
Over Her Body, 47
Oz, 183

Paasonen, Susanna, 48
Pabitra, Benjamin, 8
Pacifism, 96, 98, 99, 107, 110
Pagter, Carl R., 52
Palindromes, 161, 162, 172
Palkovitz, Rob, 129
Palmer, Amanda, 71
Paparazzi, 52, 54, 56, 58
Parenthood, 224, 233
Parents Television Council, 62
Parker, Judith A., 71, 72, 73, 84
Partridge Family, The, 60
Party Animal, The, 221
Party of Five, 118, 122, 123, 157, 158
Pathology, 62, 117, 135, 216
Patriotism, 87
Peaches, 64, 75–76, 77
Pedophilia, 7, 8, 12. *See also* Child abuse
Peeping Tom. *See* Voyeurism
Peeping Tom, 184
Penis, viii, ix, 18, 24, 27, 29, 30, 33, 51–52, 68, 69, 77, 81, 82, 175–216, 218, 232, 238
Penner, Todd C., 18
Pennington, Jody, 25
Peppin, Patricia, 140
Percy, Larry, 141

Perry, Luke, 8, 123
Phallocentrism, 185. *See also* Penis
Phallus. *See* Penis
Philadelphia, 76, 82
Piano, The, 179
Picone, Thomas, 140
Pie in the Sky, 119
Pillow Book, The, 179
Pink, 54, 55, 75
Place in the Sun, A, 158
Play Misty for Me, 17, 22, 23
Playboy, 13, 14
Police, The, 80
Political correctness, 10, 58, 79, 80, 81
Polygamy, 33
Pop, Iggy, 57, 58
Pornography, 13, 14, 19, 20, 21, 23, 27, 48, 49, 126, 175, 177, 190, 194, 217, 226, 229, 230, 231
Porter, Cole, 80
Postcards from the Edge, 121
Postfeminism, 79
Postmodernism, 5
Potency. *See* Virility
Powerpuff Girls, The, 113
Pregnancy, viii, 87, 91, 92, 137, 154, 155, 156, 157, 158, 159, 160, 162, 166, 167, 168, 169, 170, 172
Prime Suspect IV, 169
Princess and the Cobbler, The, 101
Privacy, 6, 35, 43, 49, 138, 154, 222, 224, 225, 229, 235
Private Matter, A, 171
Private Practice, 172
Promiscuity, 54, 73, 74, 75, 98, 120, 124, 125–26, 128, 166, 226
Proposal, The, 187
Prospero's Books, 179
Prostitution, 78, 79, 80, 81, 116, 124, 180, 186, 200. *See also* Sex work
Psychiatry, 15, 143, 150
Psychoanalysis, 183

Psychology, ix, 9, 10, 24, 38, 42, 67, 70–75, 120, 125, 141, 164, 166, 213
Psychosis, 205
Pubic hair, 28, 189
Pulp Fiction, 107
Punishment, viii, 103, 124, 158, 162, 163, 166, 167, 168, 222, 237
Punk, 55, 57, 58, 76, 96, 105
Pushing Daisies, 124, 126
Puskar-Pasewicz, Margaret, 89–90, 96, 100, 109, 114

Quality of life, 143, 151, 152
Quan, Tracy, 78, 79
Queer as Folk [United Kingdom], 76, 77, 82
Queer as Folk [United States], 198, 207, 208
Queer theory, ix, 1, 225
Quiet Man, The, 122
Quinceañera, 215

Racism, 7, 15–16, 120, 122
Raising Hope, 130
Rape, 52, 71–73, 80, 84–85, 170, 182
Rapping, Elayne, 187, 193
Reactance theory, 9–11, 12
Ready or Not, 94
Reagan, Ronald, 58
Real Time with Bill Maher, 58
Rebus, 119–20
Reddy, Helen, 111
Red Green Show, The, 101
Reed, Lou, 80
Religion, vii, 2, 79
Remember the Daze, 67
Ren and Stimpy Show, The, 3, 12
Rescue Me, 232, 233
Revelation, 88
Revolutionary Road, viii, 166
Reynolds, R. D., 60,
Rice, Stephanie, 63
Richards, Olly, 176

River City, 98, 112
Road House, 115
Road to Ruin, The, 154
Road to Wellville, The, 219
Road Trip, 176
Rock of Ages, 63
Rockefeller, Norman, 58
Roe vs. Wade, 154, 171
Rofes, Eric, 8
Rogers, Mary F., 27
Roman, James, 3
Romance and Cigarettes, 203, 204
Roosevelt, Franklin D., 141
Roseanne, 40, 41, 90, 92, 93, 100, 105, 108, 167
Rosse, Richard B., 143
Rossiter, John R., 141
Roth, Philip, 48
Rourke, Mickey, 62, 119
Rowe, Douglas, 187, 191
Rubin, Gayle, 225, 229
Rubington, Earl, 118
Rugrats: All Grown Up, 44
Rush, 88
Ryan, Rex, 60

Sabotage, 193
Sabrina, the Teenage Witch, 93
Sajtóvadászat (Press Hunting), 111
Salo—120 Days of Sodom, 175
Salt 'n' Pepa, 81
Sarah's Choice, 153
Satire, x, 3, 9, 13, 15
Saved by the Bell, 123
Saw, 105
Sawyer, Sarah, 55
Scary Movie 3, 38
Schadenfreude, 40–41, 224
Scott Pilgrim vs. the World, 59, 103
Scrubs, 102, 165, 167, 197, 207, 208, 216
Se7en, 183
SeaQuest DSV, 88, 109
Second-wave feminism, 22, 24

Index 321

Secret Life of the American Teenager, The, 156
Secret Life of Us, The, 165, 169
Segel, Jason, 37, 181, 190
Seidel, Linda, 137–38, 140, 144
Seinfeld, 171, 172, 199, 201, 203, 207, 209–10, 211–12
Self-diagnosis, 134–35
Self-esteem, 71, 203, 204. *See also* Ego
Self-prescription, 134
Self-surveillance, 150
Semonche, John E., 188–89
Series 7: The Contenders, 167
Seven Pounds, 106
Seven Psychopaths, 119, 122
Sex and the City, 29–30, 44–45, 70, 146, 167, 196, 200, 203, 204, 214, 217, 218, 227, 231
Sex toys. *See* Vibrators
Sexual liberation, 22, 24, 74, 97, 98, 228, 229, 233, 235
Sex work, 78, 79. *See also* Prostitution
Seymour, Jane, 139
Shakespeare, William, 36, 164
Shallow Grave, 183
Shame, 8, 138, 139, 168, 217, 223
Shame, 179, 183, 186
She's the One, 226, 228, 232, 233
Shimp, Terence A., 144
Shocker, The, 51, 62, 64–65
Shock value, 58, 59–61
Shortbus, 97
Show—don't tell, 89, 186, 221
Sideways, 78, 119
Sienkiewicz, Matt, 15
Simon, William, 18
Simon and Garfunkel, 80
Simple Life, The, 201
Simpsons, The, 1, 2, 3, 4–6, 7, 9, 10, 12, 14, 16, 42, 88, 94, 95, 99, 103, 105, 109, 114, 116, 121, 124, 126, 171, 173
Simpsons Movie, The, 176

Sitter, The, 26, 29, 34
Six Feet Under, 164, 169, 170, 183
16 Blocks, 120
Skins, 169
Slackers, 227
Slade, Joseph W., 19, 20
Sliver, 231
Smith, Bessie, 74, 75
Smith, Bob, 3
Smith, Dina, 169
Smith, Kevin, 37, 38
Snakes on a Plane, 183
Snoop Dogg, 81
Social engineering, 9
Sociology, ix, 10, 18, 22, 25, 39, 91, 95, 109, 118, 119, 120, 124, 127, 136, 140, 154, 179, 181
Solot, Dorian, 64
Something to Talk About, 182
Somewhere, 28
Sons of Anarchy, 89
Sopranos, The, 21, 32, 225, 226, 233
Sorrells, Morris L., 196
South of Nowhere, 158
South Park, 1, 2, 3, 4, 6–9, 10, 12, 13, 15, 16, 99, 100, 111
Spader, James, 189
Spanking the Monkey, 128
Speedy, 61
Spencer, Scott, 48
Spooks, 162
Squeeze, The, 119
Stalker, 90
Starting out in the Evening, 172
Star Trek, 109
State and Main, 202, 203
Steel Panther, 63, 64
St. Elsewhere, 216
Step Brothers, 43
Stepford Wives, The, 225
Stigma, x, xi, 20, 71, 77, 79, 133, 138–39, 157, 158, 219, 234
Stiller, Ben, 20, 45, 181, 212

Stoltenberg, John, 190
Stone Temple Pilots, 71, 72
Strictly Sexual, 229
Strub, Whitney, 219
Subliminal images, 178
Suckling, The, 165
Summer, Donna, 75, 80
Sunset Boulevard, 125
Superbad, 31
Suraci, Patrick, 24, 29, 31
Sweetest Thing, The, 25, 30

Teenagers. *See* Adolescence
Teen Witch, 82
Teeth, 183
10, 46, 55
Terminator 2: Judgment Day, 177
That '70s Show, 109, 127, 128, 218, 219
There's Something about Mary, 181, 183, 185, 212, 231
Things You Can Tell Just by Looking at Her, 165
3rd Rock from the Sun, 48, 99, 100, 107
30 Rock, 39, 196, 233
This Is 40, 47, 48
This World, Then the Fireworks, 183
Thompson, Dave, 20
Thunderpants, 38
'Til Death, 199, 200, 201, 203, 204, 207
'Til Death Do Us Part, 210
Time Again, 80
Titanic, 54
Tomcats, 177
Too Much, Too Soon, 125
Top Chef, 41
Torres, Bob, 89, 104
Torres, Jenna, 89, 104
Total Request Live, 93
Trainspotting, 100
Traister, Rebecca, 19
Transamerica, 104
Transvestism, 5
Travis, Randy, 80

Travolta, John, 8, 72
Trinch, Shonna L., 71
Tropic Thunder, 36
True Blood, 104
True Romance, 55
Trumble, Angus, 52
TVTropes, 82
28 Days, 118, 216
21 Grams, 161
Two and a Half Men, 43, 214, 228
2 Broke Girls, 227–28
2 Days in Paris, 181, 184
Two Girls and a Guy, 34
2Pac, 71

Ugly Truth, The, 222, 230
Unborn, The, 164
Undressed, 204, 213
Unhappily Ever After, 91, 107
United States of Tara, The, 107
Un prophète (A Prophet), 164
Unusuals, The, 217
Urbanski, Dave, 57
Urine, 35, 41, 45, 68, 138

Vagina, 27, 31, 64, 68, 69, 70, 82, 111, 183, 220, 221, 224, 230
Vagina dentata, 183
Valentine's Day, 220, 233
Values, 2, 55, 74, 75, 84, 87, 89, 96, 97, 98, 99, 106, 112, 151, 190, 196, 208
Vander Stichele, Caroline, 18
Vanilla sex, 12, 19, 64, 222, 227, 228, 234
Varsity Blues, 83
Vaughn, Stephen, 188, 189
Veganism, 87, 89, 90, 92, 94, 96, 97, 98, 101, 102, 103, 104, 105, 109, 112, 114
Velvet Goldmine, 190
Venture Bros., The, 2
Venus, 172
Vera Drake, 159, 160
Veronica Mars, 109, 128
Veronicas, The, 74, 75

Index

Veronica's Closet, 36
Very Harold & Kumar Christmas, A, 216
Very Peculiar Practice, A, 95, 109
Very Special Episodes, 123
Vibrators, vii, viii, ix, x, xi, 81, 217–35
Violence, 14, 18, 42, 71, 94, 96, 98–99, 100, 121, 127, 133, 193, 211. *See also* Domestic violence
V.I.P., 114
Virginity, 27, 210, 220
Virility, 52
V-lick, 51, 62–64
Voice from the Grave, 164
Voyeurism, ix, 20, 24, 49, 73, 223, 230, 235
Vulnerability, 125, 180, 182–83, 184, 187, 227

Wagner, Melissa, 51, 58, 61, 62
Waitress, 154, 155, 156
Waits, Tom, 79, 80
Waking Ned Devine, 122
Walking Dead, The, 231
Walsh, David, 27
Walsh, John, 191
Waltonen, Karma, 5
War Horse, 122
Warner Bros., 16
Wassup Rockers, 213, 214
Wasted, 220
Watson, Rod, 39
Weaver, Simon, 16
Weaver, Tara Austen, 104
Weeds, 123, 203, 210–11
Wells, Herbert George, 101
West, Kanye, 52, 58
West Wing, The, 167
Wet Hot American Summer, 39
What about Mimi?, 92, 106
What Happens in Vegas, 182
What I Like about You, 108
What Price Hollywood? 118

What to Expect When You're Expecting, 195, 196, 207, 208, 216
When a Man Loves a Woman, 128
Where Are My Children?, 153
Whipped, 222
White Chicks, 43–44, 45
Wienke, Chris, 140
Wild at Heart, 163
Wild Things, 54, 177, 179
Will & Grace, 113, 126, 127, 220
Williams, Craig A., 51–52
Williams, Linda, 23
Wire, The, 120, 122
Wisnewski, Jeremy, 7
Wolcott, James, 176, 177, 179, 180, 182, 186, 190
Women in Love, 182
Wonder Boys, 119
Wood, Jim, 72
Wrestler, The, 62
Wrestling, 60, 63, 181, 182
Wurtzel, Elizabeth, 53, 55, 60

XXL, 176

Year of the Carnivore, 229
Year One, 47, 209, 210
Yellow Handkerchief, The, 161
Young, Hugh, 195, 197, 202, 205, 207
Young Adam, 179
Young Ones, The, 96, 103
Y tu mamá también (And Your Mother Too!), 196, 201, 214, 215

Zack and Miri Make a Porno, 231
Zappa, Frank, 79
Zeisler, Andi, 164
Zeitgeist, 22, 23, 170
Zoom, 42
Zorea, Aharon W., 137
ZZ Top, 80

About the Author

Lauren Rosewarne, PhD, is a senior lecturer in the School of Social and Political Sciences at the University of Melbourne, Australia. She is an expert in sex, gender, and popular culture and is the author of four other books: *Sex in Public: Women, Outdoor Advertising, and Public Policy* (2007); *Cheating on the Sisterhood: Infidelity and Feminism* (2009); *Part-Time Perverts: Sex, Pop Culture, and Kink Management* (2011); and *Periods in Pop Culture: Menstruation in Film and Television* (2012). Dr. Rosewarne has also written numerous book chapters, opinion pieces and short stories, and has appeared extensively in the media.